Happi

Lots of love from,

Amanda

x x
x

THE CENTURIONS

THE CENTURIONS

FROM GRACE TO RAMPRAKASH

Patrick Murphy

FAIRFIELD BOOKS

Fairfield Books
17 George's Road, Fairfield Park, Bath BA1 6EY
Tel 01225-335813

The first edition of this book, with 20 subjects, was published in 1983
A paperback edition, adding Dennis Amiss, was published in 1986
These editions were published by J.M. Dent & Sons Ltd
This edition, first published in 2009, adds four further chapters,
contains revisions and significant additions to several of the other
chapters, has a new introduction and uses many different photographs
and some fresh statistical tables

ISBN 978 0 9560702 4 1

Cover design by Rob Taylor

Printed and bound in Great Britain by
Midway Colour Print, Holt, Wiltshire

Contents

Statistical pages

The 25 centurions
and the hundreds they scored

J.B. Hobbs	197
E.H. Hendren	170
W.R. Hammond	167
C.P. Mead	153
G. Boycott	151
H. Sutcliffe	149
F.E. Woolley	145
G.A. Hick	136
L. Hutton	129
G.A. Gooch	128
W.G. Grace	126
D.C.S. Compton	123
T.W. Graveney	122
D.G. Bradman	117
I.V.A. Richards	114
Zaheer Abbas	108
M.C. Cowdrey	107
A. Sandham	107
T.W. Hayward	104
J.H. Edrich	103
M.R. Ramprakash	103
G.M. Turner	103
L.E.G. Ames	102
D.L. Amiss	102
G.E. Tyldesley	102

Acknowledgements

So many have co-operated in the three versions of this book, over the past 25 years. Of course, it was essential to interview the survivors among the batsmen themselves, and to that end I managed to get to 14 of the 25, plus Sir Donald Bradman who replied by return post from Adelaide to a detailed series of questions I put to him. I still have that air-mail letter, occupying pride of place at home. Yet flesh on the bone was needed from players who had witnessed at first hand the deeds of these illustrious batsmen. Eye-witness accounts are always preferable to a scissors-and-paste job, based on the culling of newspaper cuttings in the library. So many were touchingly kind, especially those not in the best of health. I recall Percy Fender, blind and frail, receiving me warmly in his Horsham home. Len Hopwood, that fine Lancashire all-rounder, was just trying to come to terms with the loss of his son in his prime, yet he found the time to give me his memories of Ernest Tyldesley, till then a slightly shadowy figure for me. Roley Jenkins, as ebullient as ever, was generosity itself at his Worcester home, and up at Leeds Bill Bowes radiated genial wisdom in his late seventies. Marvellous men of cricket like Alec Bedser, Alan Knott, Alf Gover and Ray Illingworth took time out from their active lives to answer my questions with courtesy and interest.

Others from the world of cricket were invaluable with introductions, suggestions and background information. My thanks to A.C. Smith, Bob Willis, Gladstone Small, Leslie Deakins, Jim Cumbes, Cyril Goodway, Bert Avery, Ken Turner, Alec Stewart, Jack Simmons and Don Oslear. From the media, special thanks to Don Mosey, Jack Bannister, Ken Kelly, Peter West, Alan Lee, Brian Scovell, David Frith, Alan Hughes, Richard Maddock, Gerald Howat, John Arlott, David Foot, Peter Baxter, Angus Fraser, Frank Keating and Adam Mountford.

My publisher, Stephen Chalke, has been a constant source of encouragement and wise counsel, believing in the project straight away. Mercifully there are still some sports publishers left who are not in thrall to the cult of the celebrity, obsessed with the bottom line. Stephen cares more about the spirit and contents of a book than whether he can cut a deal with a major bookseller, and long may he prosper with that noble ideal.

As I write these words, it occurs to me that so many of these kind folk have passed away since I first started work on this project in the autumn of 1982. I dedicate this book to them, with immense respect for the spirit of friendship and decency that is still associated with the game of cricket.

Patrick Murphy
March 2009

Introduction

On Saturday August 2nd 2008 a total of 1,124 spectators witnessed cricket history at the Headingley stadium in Leeds. The vast majority of them (968) were Yorkshire CCC members, and those few who forked out to defy the stereotype about Yorkshire folk and their brass saw something that will never be achieved again: a batsman completing his 100th first-class century.

Surrey's Mark Ramprakash made 103 not out, in the process becoming the 25th batsman in the history of first-class cricket to reach that landmark. When W.G. Grace became the first in 1895, he was 47 years old and, in the eyes of his adoring contemporaries, a phenomenon. With bowlers having held sway for most of Grace's wonderful career, the nearest challenger among batsmen at the time was Arthur Shrewsbury, who had scored fewer than half of Grace's hundred centuries. Grace's achievement was duly lionised in the pages of *Wisden* the following year and, amid the eulogies, the former England captain A.G. Steel ventured to suggest that the feat of scoring a hundred hundreds would never be emulated. Perhaps Mr Steel's statement can be seen in the context of typically Victorian self-confidence and in the genuine belief that W.G. Grace was a genius. Indeed he was, the marvel of his age – the most famous Victorian gentleman after W.E. Gladstone.

From Grace to Ramprakash. The line stretches 113 years, and it will go no further. That assessment is not based on any sort of quasi-Victorian bombast, that the cricketers of this age will remain superior to their successors. Quite simply, there will not be enough first-class cricket played in the future for anyone to score a hundred centuries. That is why, after initially celebrating the 20 batsmen on that exclusive list in 1983 and updating this book in 1987 to recognise the arrival of Dennis Amiss, I can now sign it off with finality: 25 and out. Justin Langer, the Australian captain of Somerset, is the nearest – on 84 – but he only plays first-class cricket now during an English summer and, at the age of 38, at his present rate of progress, he would have to play another five years to get there.

Research into the number of first-class innings played in a season by members of the hundred hundreds club reveals how impossible it will be for further batsmen to join. In Mark Ramprakash's first full season with Middlesex, the county played 24 first-class games, 22 of them in the championship. In the 2008 season each county played only 16 matches, and Ramprakash managed just 23 first-class innings. The highest number of first-class innings played was 30. No batsman scored more than six hundreds. England regulars Kevin Pietersen and Ian Bell managed 12 and 17 innings respectively. A trawl through the careers of the other members of the exclusive club from Grace to Ramprakash reveals the massive gap between past eras and that of today:

W.G. Grace – 59 innings in the 1888 season.
Jack Hobbs – 63 in 1907.

Les Ames – 60 in 1928.
Frank Woolley – 52 in 1938, at the age of 51!
Tom Graveney – 57 in 1953.
Geoffrey Boycott – 50 in 1966.
Glenn Turner – 43 in 1973.

The status of past first-class cricket matches seems highly dubious in some cases, which led to a distortion of batting records. In 1868 Grace scored a hundred in each innings for the South of Thames against the North of Thames, and he scored a couple of double centuries in the same fixture in the 1870s. In 1932 Herbert Sutcliffe made more than 3,000 runs, including 14 hundreds. One of them was for H.D.G. Leveson Gower's X1 against All India. Consider Smokers v. Non-Smokers, Army and Navy v Oxford and Cambridge Universities, I Zingari v the Gentlemen of England – the list of matches that spuriously attained the rank of first-class is a diverting read through the dusty pages of *Wisden*. This is not to belittle any of the outstanding batsmen of the past. You must play the opposition that is set out before you at any given time. But there are no such relaxed opportunities available today to a batsman; even the counties' occasional games against universities have now lost their first-class status.

The astonishing rise and rise of Twenty20 cricket since 2003 means that the amount of first-class cricket will continue to be reduced. The Twenty20 cash cow has galvanised cricket's bean counters all over the world and the biggest challenge is to shoe-horn even more of these tournaments into an overcrowded calendar. International players are now dipping out of Test series because they prefer the extra riches available for less work and less time away from home. The first series of the Indian Premier League was watched on television in that country by 101 million people, and the first World Twenty20 Final in 2007 by 48 million.

The charms of county cricket do not reflect this materialistic, consumer-friendly age, where bitesize portions of the game suit hectic lifestyles. Satellite television, never knowingly underselling its product, will continue to crank up the hyperbolic coverage of Twenty20, and players will become more and more unconcerned about the depth and variety offered by four-day cricket. It is human nature to accept more money for doing less work.

So let us celebrate a rare achievement, managed just 25 times, rather than bemoan cricket's rapidly changing landscape. These batsmen have varied styles, abilities and temperaments. Masterful players such as Hobbs, Hammond, Hutton, Gooch, Cowdrey and Graveney. Solid, resolute performers like Mead, Sutcliffe, Boycott, Edrich and Hayward. Batsmen of genius in Bradman, Woolley, Compton and Richards. Some were superior players on bad wickets, some were unobtrusive, some gloried in offside play. Some, like Hick and Ramprakash, infuriated and at times delighted their followers when playing for England; both of them left a sense of wistfulness that they did not do themselves justice. Yet the peerless style of Ramprakash and his dazzling footwork surely would spark memories of another favourite of The Oval, the great Jack Hobbs – if by some miracle of science an observer had been ageless enough to have seen both players at their best.

To score a hundred hundreds, you needed to have played at least fifteen years, preferably in county cricket, unless you were a genius like Bradman who posted a century every three innings. Writing that figure down still necessitates a shake of the head and an admiring, low whistle. Consistency and stamina are vital ingredients, and luck. You need the mental strength to come to terms with cricketing middle age, slowing reactions and an awareness of the 'business shots', the ones that can be played with the minimum of risk and the maximum of effectiveness on all wickets. The 98 hundreds Jack Hobbs scored after he passed forty years of age is a testament to his ageless skills. It is essential to be able to adapt, to cope with bowling trends. Colin Cowdrey, one of the elite, told me, 'Cricket is evolutionary, and it's up to the batsman to build on what he's got and prepare for the future when things might not work out. The proudest thing for me in my career is that I kept surviving.' That applies especially to 12 of these 25 batsmen who had their careers interrupted by a World War. Picking up the threads after a gap of four or six years must have been severely taxing.

Colin Cowdrey adapted impressively during the last few years of his career and to the end he played fast bowling as well as anyone, even at the age of 42 in Tests against Lillee and Thomson. Jack Hobbs was the same forty years earlier. At the age of 51 he played the fiery Learie Constantine better than anyone else in the land. For nearly thirty years he had taken on and mastered a formidable array of bowling talent and was never cowed. W.G. Grace blocked the shooters as a young man on treacherous wickets, took on the lob bowlers in later years, then mastered the fast bowlers with illegal actions in the 1880s. Don Bradman had to deal with the threat of Bodyline in 1932/33, Walter Hammond learned to accumulate on the legside after his majestic cover-driving was starved by niggardly, accurate bowlers. Denis Compton's chronic knee problems did not stop his effervescent flow of runs until his late thirties. Glenn Turner could hardly get the ball past the inner ring of fielders during his formative years in English county cricket, yet the demands of the limited-overs game plus the desire to enjoy life at the crease led to a consistent stream of thrilling assaults in the later years of his career. Graham Gooch started his Test career with two noughts on a wet pitch against Lillee and Thomson, battled nobly against a formidable array of West Indian fast bowlers, triumphed against the devastating reverse swing practised by the Pakistanis Waqar Younis and Wasim Akram and did not succumb cheaply too often to the leg-spinning wiles of Warne, Kumble and Abdul Qadir. Gooch survived. Just like all the other redoubtable batsmen in cricket history. The challenge remains the same, if not the bowlers' methods.

In his early period as the game's dominant batsman, W.G. Grace had to combat the superiority of the bowlers. Pitches were often prepared by turning sheep out on them to graze, and fast bowlers could be frighteningly erratic on the dangerous wickets. The staggering mastery of Grace was vociferously acknowledged one day in 1868, when he blocked four shooters in a row in the first over. The crowd that day at Lord's rose as one and cheered him loudly. By the 1890s, however, the pendulum had swung the other way. The wickets had become truer and faster and, with the motor still in its infancy, the heavy roller (whether hand or horse-drawn) moved slowly up and down the square, compressing the substance and binding it together. In the 1900 edition of *Wisden*, Lord Harris bemoaned the new age of batting prosperity: 'I am afraid that not only lengthy scores but the want of liveliness on these artificial wickets will tend to make the game dull and reduce its popularity.' Not for the first or last time the autocratic nobleman proved less than sagacious in his assessment – by common consent, the period 1890-1914 was the Golden Age of Cricket, under the positive influence of thrilling amateur batsmen, great variety of bowling and excellent wickets. Spinners often opened the bowling alongside fast bowlers, the over rate was high, and the line of attack was usually of a full length at, or just outside, the off-stump, encouraging flowing off-drives. In the Edwardian age most top-class batsmen were too proud to use their pads when a bat could do the necessary defending – C.B. Fry said sniffily that it would be demeaning to a batsman's craft. The brilliant Victor Trumper batted 89 times for Australia between 1899 and 1912, and he was lbw just five times. His English equivalent, the lordly Old Harrovian A.C. MacLaren, was given out lbw only three times in 61 Test innings between 1894 and 1909.

The supremacy of bat over ball lasted until the 1930s when the lbw law was altered to prevent batsmen padding away deliveries that pitched outside the off-stump, even though the ball might have broken in to hit the wicket. So the in-swing bowler and the off-spinner grew in influence. The use of the new ball also restored the balance towards the bowlers. Not until 1907 was a second new ball an option at all, and then only after 200 runs had been scored. In 1948, though, Don Bradman's Australian side had the benefit of a new ball after every 55 overs, and Lindwall, Miller and Johnston were so dominant that even the great Len Hutton was dropped once in the series. Over the next sixty years the new ball has been available between 65 and 100 overs, and wickets and outfields have become greener, keeping the ball shiny, so that spinners were marginalised until the 1980s when Abdul Qadir demonstrated that a sharply turning leg-break can undo the very best batsman. But the fascinating craft of spin bowling, perfected by Shane Warne and embellished by Muttiah Muralitheran, still had to jostle for attention alongside the proliferation of short-pitched, intimidatory fast bowling and reverse swing. Batsmen have to keep adapting, especially in the modern age where the multiplicity of competitions necessitates a change of approach almost daily.

One area where the modern batsman misses out on his education is the chance to play on uncovered wickets, on grounds up and down the country where the differing soils mean the pitches vary. The growing commercialisation of the game, and the need to mollify sponsors and the television paymasters, mean that the game must start as soon as possible once the rain stops, so the wickets must be covered. So we shall never return to the days when a player, using a light bat and blessed with soft hands and nimble footwork, could win a match with a finely crafted fifty. Graham Gooch treasures the experience of batting against Derek Underwood on a damp pitch in the mid-seventies; it developed his craft of batsmanship. The swift footwork of Ramprakash, allied to his ease around the crease and soft hands, would surely be of benefit to him if he were transported back a century and had to combat the flight and turn of Wilfred Rhodes or the varied brilliance of S.F. Barnes. That would be a fascinating contest.

Ramprakash would adapt to the challenges, because that is what batsmen do. Watching him play so adroitly in recent years, all grace and timing, is to understand that the principles of batting have remained the same since the twilight of Grace's glorious career at the dawn of the twentieth century. The ball is propelled from predictable areas of the crease, its speed is now depressingly uniform, and over rates are pathetically low – yet class batting remains orthodox in its principles. Ramprakash continues to demonstrate elegantly that batting is a 'sideways-on' art, even though modern cricketing iconoclasts prefer the audacious slogging of limited-overs matches.

Is Ramprakash a great player? Judged by certain criteria, no. A personal view is that great batsmen are consistent over a long period, they are adaptable against all types of bowling, dominant, a major influence regularly on the course of a match, making vital runs in all conditions when needed, and they have succeeded markedly at the highest level, Test cricket. An admiring old sweat of a county bowler once said of Grace: 'I puts the ball where I likes, and 'e puts it where 'e likes.' That air of dominance is preferable in a great batsman, but not essential. An opener can be a great player by a cussed refusal to be intimidated or overwhelmed when conditions and/or bowling excellence are forensically examining his technique and bravery. An air of permanence and imperturbability can frustrate the best bowling attacks. If that opener survives, and builds impressive foundations early in the match, he has set up the chance of victory for his side.

Given this personal list of criteria, I can only nominate ten of the 25 as great batsmen: Grace, Hobbs, Sutcliffe, Hammond, Bradman, Hutton, Compton, Boycott, Richards and Gooch. The other 15 have been outstanding players, but they lack at least one of the necessary ingredients. Sutcliffe makes it because of his remarkable Test record, averaging nine runs per innings more for England than in first-class cricket, and Boycott's staunch performances in his 40th year against the ruthless West Indians should never be minimised. Both resolute Yorkshiremen were ideally suited to the role of an opening batsman, and they delivered consistently. In their own way, they dominated. They had to be prised out.

I can hear the sound of E.W. Swanton and Neville Cardus spinning apoplectically in their graves at the exclusion of Frank Woolley from the list of ten. A wonderful entertainer, Cardus' favourite batsman, yet his Test record was modest. I think Woolley was a great cricketer – due to his all-round skills as fielder and spin bowler and his thrilling batting – but not a great batsman. Les Ames belongs in the same category. The only wicket-keeper to score a hundred centuries, he was almost as dazzling a batsman in the Kent team as Woolley, and his tally of 418 stumpings is astonishing, an indication of the influence of the leg-spinners 'Tich' Freeman and Doug Wright in the Kent attack for so many years. A great all-rounder, Ames, but not a great batsman.

Those who cavil at my attenuated list of great batsmen from the club of 25 may wish to dwell on the fondness of this age for dubbing anyone 'great' who has played sport exceptionally well for a couple of years. The media contribute to this hyperbolic tendency. *Sky Sports* labours under the impression that professional football began in 1992, the year they annexed the sport with their booty. On that basis Bobby Moore, Jimmy Greaves, George Best, Stanley Matthews, Duncan Edwards and John Charles are mere footnotes in English football history. The same applies to cricket. I do not believe that England have had a great player since Graham Gooch, from 1990 to 1993, but you would not think so from the way successful players are elevated beyond their proper status by a reverential media, desperate for new heroes. Kevin Pietersen is capable of greatness as a batsman, and it may be that an influential role in a successful tilt at the Ashes in the summer of 2009 will qualify him in that select group inhabited by only Ricky Ponting and Sachin Tendulkar among contemporary batsmen. Yet judgement must be deferred on Pietersen. Too often it is not in modern sport.

Qualification for the Hundred Hundreds Club does not automatically confer greatness. There are immortal players in the group of those who have scored more than 80 hundreds but fell short of the century. Garry Sobers, Rohan Kanhai, J.T. Tyldesley, Peter May, Sunil Gavaskar, Javed Miandad and Barry Richards were great batsmen, in this observer's opinion. So were Brian Lara and Graeme Pollock, who both finished on 64 hundreds. Perhaps undue attention is given to the scoring of a hundred; many matches have become stultified because the captain wants one of his players to reach three figures. By contrast, the history of cricket is littered with wonderful innings of less than a hundred that, in the circumstances, could truly be said to have won a match.

The modern first-class cricketer often cites one-day cricket as the reason why great batsmen such as Grace, Hobbs and Hammond would not prosper today – a Pavlovian response to a few frames of grainy newsreels and the certainty that ground fielding is superior today. Yet Bradman would surely shine in one-day cricket, given his amazing footwork, speed between the wickets and his superb eye. Patsy Hendren and Andy Sandham, who played the hook shot as well as anyone else in history, would have relished the proliferation of short-pitched bowling, and their running between the wickets was as impressive as Bradman's. For thirty years Jack Hobbs was a great player on all pitches against all types of bowling; limited-overs cricket would not faze The Master. Frank Woolley, one of the longest straight hitters, would just stand and deliver, like Graeme Pollock did in the 1960s and 70s. Minimal footwork matters little when you have a magnificent eye, a glorious follow-through and wonderful timing. The major challenge for those earlier members of the 25 club is that they would score their runs at a slower rate. The modern captain regards twenty overs an hour as naïve and tactically suicidal, unless there is a hefty fine to circumvent and he puts on the joke bowlers. Boredom waiting for the umpires to adjudicate on the latest complaint about the ball's shape would be Bradman's biggest concern.

The story of these 25 batsmen is in itself the story of modern cricket. The year 1864 is one of those dates etched in the cranium of any cricket anorak. It was the year when bowlers were at last allowed to deliver from over the arm, the year when *Wisden Cricketers' Almanack* was first published and when W.G. Grace made his debut in important cricket. The flame of batting eminence has passed on down the decades from the crafty old doctor whose health Queen Victoria often enquired about to a twinkle-toed boy from Bushey whose erotic version of the tango gave the sixty-something Arlene Phillips a fit of the vapours every Saturday evening in front of millions of TV viewers.

'You look like a mesmerising matinee idol,' gushed la Phillips; she could easily have been describing Walter Hammond or Denis Compton from another era.

From Grace to Ramprakash. From lob bowling to helmets. From the days when the county ground that staged a Test also picked the England side, to the time when Dennis Lillee could kick Pakistan's captain up the backside and get away with it. From three-day Tests to one lasting ten days in 1939, finally aborted so that England's party could get the steamer home from Durban. From distinguished amateurs refusing to tour Australia for business reasons to night cricket and coloured clothing, following Kerry Packer's successful challenge to the Establishment. From Jim Laker laconically hitching up his trousers and accepting warm handshakes as he strolled off at Old Trafford, having taken 19 Australian wickets for 90, to Monty Panesar's demonic celebrations after one of his long hops has been caught by cover point. *Autres moeurs, autres temps.* But the past informs the present, and an awareness of cricket history allows rational perspective on what is going on now in the game. That is why Mark Ramprakash's hundred at Headingley last August was so welcome, giving the opportunity to take a step back from the frenetic cricket calendar in 2008 and re-assess the significant signposts in the game's history.

Patrick Murphy
March 2009

1

W.G. Grace

'I hate defensive strokes, you can only get three off 'em'

William Gilbert Grace

Born

Downend, Bristol

18 July 1848

Died

Mottingham, Kent

23 October 1915

First hundred

224*   England v Surrey, The Oval, 1866

Age: 18 years 12 days

100th hundred

288   Gloucestershire v Somerset, Bristol, 1895

Age: 46 years 303 days

Last hundred

166   London County v Marylebone Cricket Club, Crystal Palace, 1904

Age: 56 years 1 day

Career record

M	Inn	NO	HS	Runs	Average	100s	50s
879	1,493	105	344	54,896	39.55	126	254

Test record

M	Inn	NO	HS	Runs	Average	100s	50s
22	36	2	170	1,098	32.29	2	5

W.G. Grace was surely the greatest player the game has ever known, or ever will know. The reason is simple – he created modern cricket by his own example and force of personality. For almost forty years he played first-class cricket and he was the dominant force in thirty of them. Ten batsmen have surpassed his total of 126 first-class centuries, but none of them – not Hobbs, nor Hammond, nor Bradman, nor Richards – has been so pre-eminent in his time as Doctor William Gilbert Grace.

When he entered first-class cricket in 1865, it was still a slightly shady pursuit with the best players intent on getting as much money as possible out of it. Cricket was a provincial game – the first tour to Australia had just taken place, but only because a proposed lecture tour by Charles Dickens had fallen through and the sponsors had to think of something to appease the Australians. By the time W.G. Grace played his last first-class game in 1908, it was the national sport – enlarged from a pleasant rural pastime into something binding counties together and spreading deep into the affections of normal unsentimental Englishmen. The Royal Family regularly asked about the doctor's health, and his appearance at cricket matches sparked off waves of hysteria totally out of character with the undemonstrative times in which he lived. After Gladstone, he was the best-known Victorian Englishman and – *pace* the MP for Newark – surely the best-loved.

The breadth of his playing career ensured that he made runs against bowlers of all types on varying surfaces. His first-class career spanned a record 43 years. At the age of 48 years and 17 days, he remains the oldest player to score a triple century. In his early days, wickets were dangerous – one batsman was killed at Lord's in 1870 – yet Grace faced them with equanimity, turning in seasonal figures that are astonishing in their consistency and supremacy. In the same year that the Lord's wicket claimed the life of a batsman, Grace amazed hard-bitten professional bowlers by his bravery on a deadly Lord's pitch. For the Gentlemen against the Players, he scored 66 against Tom Emmett and George Freeman, two Yorkshiremen who enjoyed legendary duels against him over the years. Freeman later recalled Grace's bravery: 'That day it was a marvel the Doctor was not maimed or killed outright. I often think of his pluck when I watch a modern batsman scared if a medium-paced ball hits him in the hand; he should have seen our expresses flying about W.G.'s ribs, shoulders and head in 1870.' Just a few figures underline his dominance. In the decade 1871 to 1880, he averaged 49 in first-class cricket with his nearest challenger on 26, having scored almost a third of Grace's runs. He also took a little matter of 1,174 wickets, more than anyone but Alfred Shaw. For eleven of the fourteen seasons between 1866 and 1879, he topped the batting averages. When he scored 2,739 runs at an average of 78.25 in 1871, the runner-up totalled 1,068 at 24.12.

From his early days he met and mastered wild, tearaway fast bowlers like 'Foghorn' Jackson and 'Tear 'Em' Tarrant; through the 1880s he dealt with men like Spofforth, Peate and Shaw, and a decade later with Richardson, Lockwood, Lohmann, Peel and Giffen, immortal bowlers on wickets that were still sporting. By 1900 Grace had scored 121 of his 126 centuries and only then were the wickets playing easier and truer. By now, at the age of 52, he was coming to terms with Rhodes, Hirst, Braund, Ernest Jones, Noble and the cunning googly bowler, Bosanquet. He was still good enough to score 74 on a fast wicket for the Gentlemen against the Players in 1906 at the age of 58 – this, in a season when there were no Test matches, was automatically the most important game of the year and not a place for the temperamentally unstable. Not that Grace ever showed such weakness, even if his beard was eventually streaked with grey and his back creaked as the ball was cut fiercely past him at point.

His cricketing longevity was remarkable and so was his influence on batting. Never before had one player embodied the principles of batsmanship that we now take for granted. He lacked the magical qualities of a Ranjitsinhji, the controlled violence of a Jessop, the beauty of a Trumper or a Spooner. Grace had backbone – solid, sensible orthodoxy. From his early days, his mother and uncle had taught him the virtues of a straight bat – indeed his redoubtable mother had often been heard to scold him after rash shots in his formative years in county cricket – and he never forgot the basics. He simply played the right strokes to the right ball in a manner no other batsman had consistently achieved. His stance was upright, his backlift high and he brought the bat down on shooters astonishingly quickly; as James Shaw, the Nottinghamshire bowler once remarked, 'Oh yes, he blocks the shooters, but he blocks 'em to the boundary.' The faster the bowling, the happier he was – he had no time for subtle leg glances or pushes to the onside for singles, he loved to smack the ball through the covers and straight drive it back past the bowler. 'Games aren't won by leaving the ball alone,' he would say in that curiously high-pitched voice of his. 'I hate defensive strokes, you can only get three off 'em.' He hit powerfully, an extension of a personality that was full of gusto and confidence. Pictures of him batting in the nets underline that fact that his left elbow remained high, despite advancing years and thickening waistline. For a heavy man, he was very nimble on his feet and he possessed the knack of all great batsmen to place the ball where there was no fielder. Perhaps this stemmed from his early days, when it was commonplace to bat against teams comprising eighteen or twenty-two players. When you have learned to slip the ball through such a cordon of fielders, the demands of first-class cricket must seem comparatively untaxing.

Like the man himself, his attitude to batting was simple and unvarnished. He was once asked, 'How do you stop a shooter?' He replied, 'Why, you put your bat to the ball.' He played with his left leg very close to the bat, and when playing back in defence, his right foot moved near to the line of the ball. When going forward, the left shoulder pointed to the bowler – the lessons in the back garden of his home had been assimilated. His basic attitude was to play each ball on its merits – as James Shaw despaired, 'I put the ball where I likes and 'e puts it where 'e likes.'

C.B. Fry was not the kind of man or cricketer to be overawed by the achievement of others but he was dogmatic about the influence of W.G. Grace. Fry wrote of him, 'He revolutionised batting. He turned it from an accomplishment into a science. He turned the old one-stringed instrument into a many-chorded lyre. Where a great man has led, many can go afterwards, but the honour is his who found and cut the path. The theory of modern batting is, in all essentials, the result of W.G.'s thinking and working on the game.'

Contemporary pictures and rare film footage do not do him justice. Physically, he soon filled out from the young stripling to a massive, bearded man and that image remained in the public consciousness for the remaining years of his life. The beard satisfied the Victorian craving for authority and his innate self-confidence was tolerantly viewed as the characteristic of a born leader. In photographs of his batting, he looks a faintly comical figure to later generations accustomed to sleek, lissom sporting heroes: the bat looks too small in those massive hands, the great, grizzled beard gives him a homely, avuncular air and surely those enormous feet encased in brown boots could not carry the attack to the bowler? Yet he was no figure of fun to his admiring colleagues or suffering bowlers. As the legendary Yorkshireman, Tom Emmett, graphically put it, 'He should be made to play with a smaller bat.' It was Tom who bewailed loudly after yet another hammering by W.G. that 'it's Grace before meat, Grace after meat and Grace all the time.'

Grace's stamina was remarkable. Apart from his forty years in first-class cricket, he played countless other games in a season – it has been reliably estimated that his record in minor cricket totalled 25,000 runs (including 90 centuries) and more than 4,000 wickets. With joyous enthusiasm he would dash off to grounds up and down the country to play cricket; he knew his railway timetables more intimately than his medical books. In 1876 he demonstrated both his stamina and batting mastery in one unforgettable August week. On the Saturday he scored 344 for the MCC against Kent at Canterbury, and the following day was spent in a cross-country train en route to Bristol. On the Monday he made 177 not out against Nottinghamshire, then later in the week took 318 not out off the Yorkshire bowlers. A little matter of 839 runs, average 419.5, in an age when travel owed nothing to motorways and much to patience and good humour. Before August was over – he totalled 1,249 runs from ten first-class innings – he travelled from Bristol to Grimsby to score 400 against a team of twenty-two. The outfield was not closely mown, and every run was physically completed by the inexhaustible Grace and his weary batting partners.

When he completed his hundredth century in 1895, the feat was embellished by two further examples of the legendary Grace stamina. It was a bitterly cold May day at Bristol, and Gloucestershire was entertaining Somerset. The prospect of Grace's century proved more riveting to the public than the General Election which was taking place and, as the snow-flakes whirled around W.G.'s beard, he hammered away a slow donkey-drop from Sammy Woods to the legside boundary. The crowd predictably roared itself hoarse, Grace raised his cap with as much false modesty as he felt he should display and Sammy Woods said to himself, 'Now we'll get the old devil out.' Not a bit of it – he scored 288 and both Woods and the wicket-keeper (A.P. Wickham, who later became a clergyman) always subsequently maintained that Grace allowed just five balls to pass his bat the entire innings. He did all this at the age of forty-eight, on a bitingly cold day, with the inevitable emotional pressure and the social responsibility of making a lunchtime speech amid the champagne that he willingly quaffed halfway through his innings.

When he was ninth out, caught at slip, he was still to have the last laugh of the day on Sammy Woods, a wholesome, ebullient character who loved the doctor like a brother. Over a celebratory dinner that night Sam tried to forget that he had Grace plumb lbw when he had made three and that he hammered a wicked shooter to the boundary when he entered the nineties. He was proud to have been involved in a day of cricket history and genuinely pleased for his old adversary. Yet Sam vowed to get his own back in a characteristic way – he would drink the old man under the table that night. It was not to be – Grace drank everything on offer and, at midnight, he cajoled the woozy Woods into a game of whist till two o'clock in the morning.

One further example of his remarkable physical powers occurred when Grace was over forty and had been fielding at Old Trafford for the best part of a day while Lancashire piled up more than 400 runs. A Gloucestershire fielder's throat was split open on a boundary fence after he had chased the ball and failed to stop in time. Grace took charge and held the open wound steady for fully thirty minutes until qualified medical help and equipment arrived. The lucky fielder was A.C.M. Croome, who later became cricket correspondent of *The Times*. Years later he wrote, 'If his hand had slipped just once, I would not be here to tell the tale.'

His colossal strength not only enabled him to shine in other sports – he was a fine hurdler when young – but also propelled him into being the greatest all-rounder the game had known at that time. In 1876 he became the first to score 2,000 runs and take 100 wickets in a season. He performed 'the double' seven times. He just had to be in the action – whether diddling out 2,879 batsmen with his cunning slow-medium deliveries that cut into leg, or grabbing 871 catches in his massive hands. His stamina was not only productive in terms of performance but also in earning money. I doubt if any other cricketer has, pro rata, earned more than W.G. Grace; early on he realised how hard a bargain he could drive. He and his brother, E.M., were the backbone of the Gentlemen side in their prestigious tussles with the Players – when he threatened to pull out of the games along with his brother unless they were paid, W.G. soon had financial satisfaction. He was just too important to overlook and he knew it. Once he had qualified as a doctor, he made it clear to Gloucestershire that he would retire unless they could find him a locum to take over the practice during the summer. We can safely assume that W.G. had no intention of spurning the game he loved to distraction, but the Gloucestershire committee could not better him on brinkmanship. They found him a locum and in later years two filled the breach – both paid for by the committee. The generous expenses he picked up from his county and anyone else willing to hire his services were a mockery of his amateur status, yet at the same time, an acknowledgement of his unique place in cricket and public affection. In 1891, on his second visit to Australia, all his expenses were paid – including a locum for his practice – plus an extra £3,000.

During his great season of 1895, no less than three testimonials were opened for him. They were run by the MCC, Gloucestershire CCC and the *Morning Telegraph* newspaper, and they raised a total of £9,073 8s. 3d. Five years later, when Grace started the London County team, he was paid £600 a year, with munificent expenses. He always drove a hard financial bargain, and it remains a mystery what this man of simple tastes did with his money. When he died in 1915, he left £7,278 10s 1d in his will, a tidy sum certainly but surprisingly low considering the vast amount he had earned for so many decades.

In defence of Grace it must be said that he was not always acquisitive in his business dealings. He offered his services in innumerable benefit matches for the professional bowlers he had scourged up and down the land, and he looked after the poor in his practice with devoted altruism. He knew how valuable he was to the game of cricket and so did the administrators. Legend has it that it was often possible to read the following notice outside a cricket ground: 'Admission threepence; if Dr W.G. Grace plays, admission sixpence.' Grace knew that people not remotely interested in cricket were interested in him. If someone had told him he was a 'superstar', he would have blinked at a phrase he did not understand – but he was assuredly the precursor of a public relations juggernaut that rolled in more sophisticated times and disrupted the private lives of cricketers such as Compton, Hobbs, Bradman, Warne, Tendulkar and Botham.

Grace enjoyed being a celebrity, but then it was more enjoyable to be one in his period. The devotion of the public, the respect of his Queen and the companionship of his playing colleagues touched his simple soul deeply. The homage the press paid him made his dealings with reporters that much easier; they contented themselves with recording faithfully his scores and eschewing more weighty considerations such as whether he was a cheat. The modern trend of erecting sporting heroes on a plinth of adjectival excess only to dash them to the ground within a year would have perplexed and angered the simple country doctor. As a personality he would have satisfied the hunger of the most demanding of sports editors, but he would not have enjoyed the slow-motion replays and the scrutiny of his playing assets and behavioural defects on the field.

Opinion is divided on whether Grace cheated: his supporters tend to be those who played with him a long time, who grew to love his little idiosyncrasies and sense of fun. On the other hand men of similar independence of mind were convinced that Grace bent the rules to suit himself. S.F. Barnes was a great bowler and a man who did not respect institutions unless they deserved that respect. He wrote, 'I once appealed for a catch at the wicket, being certain that he had played it, but the umpire said no. When Grace got to my end he said, "I played it, Barnes." I replied, "I know you did and so does everyone else but this chap," meaning the umpire, and that was the nearest I ever got to getting his wicket.' E.J. Smith – known to everyone as 'Tiger' – also had firm views about Grace's flexible attitude to the rules. 'Tiger' Smith began his career at about the same time that Grace was easing out of first-class cricket, but he played innumerable minor matches with him. Seventy years later, he would often tell me about the doctor's sharp practice: 'I kept out of his way because he could be a proper autocrat and I was just starting out and didn't want to upset him. But I often saw him stand his ground and refuse to go when given out. The umpires needed the money, they wanted to stay on the list and they knew that W.G. could get them struck off.'

H.D.G. Leveson Gower, England captain and at one time chairman of the selectors, had a massive affection for the old man, but he did concede that he occasionally bent the rules to suit his own powerful ego. Once Leveson Gower organised a match at Limpsfield and, with many fine cricketers present, Grace captained his side. On this occasion Grace won the toss and walked in to bat with Bobby Abel, that splendid little player who gave such great service to Surrey and, occasionally, England. They faced up to a young man who eventually played for his country and who, for a short period, was extremely fast – Neville Knox. Grace snicked a fast delivery from Knox to the wicket-keeper and, as the fielding side joyously celebrated, Grace stood his ground. As he rubbed his arm, he shouted: 'I didn't come here for nothing, nor did all these spectators! Play on!' After a batting exhibition that delighted the crowd, he was out and returned to sit beside Leveson Gower in the pavilion. On being asked if he had touched the ball from Knox, he said: 'Of course – but I wasn't going. They didn't get my ashes that time, did they?'

Perhaps his gamesmanship was harmless enough, but there was no doubt that he liked his own way. His reaction to a controversial decision one day at The Oval epitomised his autocratic outbursts; one of the Gloucestershire batsmen was run out in less than sporting circumstances and W.G., who had watched the incident from the pavilion, bellowed out to the umpires: 'I can't have it, and I won't have it and I shan't have it!' The nearest Surrey fielder, who was leaning on the boundary fence, looked up at him and shouted: 'You've got to have it!' and indeed this was one argument that Grace lost, much to his chagrin.

Yet the bulk of his contemporaries put it down to a simple desire to be the artful dodger, without malice and with a twinkle in his eye. As one old sweat put it, 'I never knew the old 'un get up to sharp doings. No, he kept the ring of the law all right. But goodness me, the rum things he did do inside it!' Most of the umpires were old playing cronies, and they knew what to expect from him; they would smile indulgently as he appealed from point for lbw or rubbed his forearm solicitously after the ball had kissed his gloves on the way to the wicket-keeper. He loved to outwit someone who had pretensions to matching him in cunning. It happened one day to A.N. Hornby, that truculent captain of Lancashire and England. Hornby was fed up with W.G.'s habit of changing the field behind the batsman's back and telegraphing the kind of delivery the bowler should send down to gull the unsuspecting batsman. Hornby tried to get his own back: he told Johnny Briggs where to deliver the ball and, as Grace stood there, waiting for it, Hornby signalled for first slip to tip-toe over to leg-slip. Briggs was halfway through his run-up when Grace cackled: 'I can see what you're doin', I can see what you're doin'.' He loved a game within a game, and his pleasure at such a success was harmless and childlike – reflecting a sense of fun that belonged to 'apple pie' beds and booby traps, rather than subtlety.

So many stories have attached themselves to him that some at least have the kernel of truth. The sheer multiplicity of Grace anecdotes is testimony to the fact that he was larger than life, that he was a character. As the most famous medical practitioner in England, it was inevitable that all the hoary old jokes about doctors should be visited on his broad back. There was the time when he allegedly reacted to a troublesome birth by remarking, 'The baby's dead, the mother's in a bad way, but I do believe I can save the father.' Or the advice given by him to a mother of twins, who thought they had measles: 'Put 'em in bed together and don't bother me unless they get up to 208 for two at lunch.' Whether or not he uttered such gems is irrelevant. He was such a character that he could have said them.

Grace may have lacked intellectual fibre, it may have taken him a long time to get his medical diploma, but I suspect he was a very good country doctor. He cared for his patients – hence the insistence on a locum – and he dealt out generous measures of jovial, hearty good sense as he did his rounds. In a working-class parish where money was scarce, W.G. Grace was more of a social worker than a harassed, money-conscious general practitioner. The landed gentry who craved his glittering services on the cricket field may have found him a hard man to barter with, but not so his patients. Invariably he gave his services free to the poor.

His relentless hold on the affection of the public can be gauged by the fact that only Bradman has ever had more column inches written about him. One bibliography of cricket lists forty-five publications associated with him, yet there are only two under his own name. He was lucky that a journalist, Arthur Porritt, was on hand to assemble his random reminiscences into coherent form – Grace was never a forensic thinker about the game, he was instinctive and forgetful about his towering performances. Porritt wrote that Grace was 'singularly inarticulate' about his cricketing deeds but he loved him dearly: 'About Dr W.G. Grace there was something indefinable – like the simple faith of a child – which arrested and fascinated me. He was a big grown-up boy, just what a man who only lived when he was in the open air might be expected to be. A wonderful kindliness ran through his nature, mingling strangely with the arbitrary temper of a man who had been accustomed to be dominant over other men.'

Grace remained a schoolboy at heart, even in his last years. He loved boisterous, practical jokes, hated reading and, when he transferred his attentions to bowls, displayed the same keenness as on the cricket field – he became the first President of the English Bowls Association. Like other childlike adults he could be petty, but he quickly recovered. As A.A. Thomson felicitously wrote, 'He never lets the sun go down upon his wrath, though there were some colourful sunsets while it lasted.' He could be easily hurt. At Trent Bridge in 1899 he played his last Test after the crowd barracked him for failing to bend quickly enough at point to stop the fierce cutting of Noble and Hill. His batting skills were still relatively undimmed but this admission that 'it's the ground – it's too far away' was poignant. His break with Gloucestershire in 1900 hit him hard; he felt the committee was interfering in selection policy and, in turn, his autocratic ways had picked up a few enemies at the club over the years. As he left to join London County, his resignation letter was a typical blend of sentiment and defiance: 'I have the greatest affection for the county of my birth, but for the committee as a whole the greatest contempt.'

He played good quality cricket for the next five seasons with London County, enjoying the comradeship and, with one eye on himself as a tourist attraction, the money that reflected his deserved fame. His glorious 74 in the Gentlemen v Players match at the age of 58 showed the younger generation a glimpse of his mettle and, although he announced he would never play again, he continued in club cricket almost till the end of his life. His last game was one week after his 66th birthday – he scored 69 not out – the asterisk still meant a lot to him.

The Great War troubled him. He hated the idea of his fellow-cricketers being slaughtered in the mud of France, even though his patriotism had forced him to write a famous letter to the *Sportsman* magazine in 1914, which exhorted county cricketers to stop playing the game and to join the armed forces as quickly as possible. H.D.G. Leveson Gower visited him at his Surrey home just before he died and found him in a melancholy mood; the loss of his cricketing friends saddened him, and the Zeppelin raids over London rattled him. On being reminded that a man who tamed the fastest and fiercest of bowlers should not be concerned by a few Zeppelins, he said wearily, 'I could see those beggars. I can't see these.' In October 1915 he died after a heart attack in his garden, as he was tending his roses with the same delicacy that he would deliver healthy-lunged children into his Gloucestershire parish long, long ago. When he was buried, the cemetery chapel was packed with cricketers, mourning the loss of a man who had seemed immortal and ageless.

After the war the administrators at Lord's wished to symbolise the national affection for him. The Grace Gates were duly erected and, fittingly, the simple inscription was the idea of F.S. Jackson, a man who had played for England alongside W.G. The words were, like the subject itself, simple and direct:

To the Memory of
William Gilbert Grace
THE GREAT CRICKETER

He was more than a great cricketer, he was an innovator, the right man in the right place at the right time. From his example other batsmen learned how to play fast bowling, how to play forward correctly. Because he revolutionised the art of batting, he automatically did the same for bowling: to attempt to curb his mastery, bowlers had to devise new methods of attack, to vary flight and speed, and captains had to conceive new fielding positions. Grace acknowledged the influence of his elder brother, E.M., especially in the way he attacked fast bowling. He also believed his brother, G.F., would have been an even greater player if he had lived through his fever in 1880. Despite the links of heredity, he stood on his own and neither his brothers, nor anyone else, could match his output, influence or popularity. One single entry in *Wisden* confirms his remarkable effect on cricket. In the Births and Deaths section, only one woman was included, decade after decade: W.G.'s mother, the woman who reared five sons, three of whom played for England.

Statisticians examine his record minutely in these more cynical times and state that he played a long time to get his runs, that he only averaged 39 in first-class cricket. Any professional cricketer a century later who has heard of W.G. Grace will state automatically that a man of that size and age, a batsman who stood with his left toe cocked off the ground, a player with such a high backlift, could not possibly adapt to the modern game and its physical demands. A cricketer – like any other sportsman – can only be judged by his performance at that time, on how he reacted to the contemporary tactical challenges. Grace showed his adaptability after the age of forty as his physical size began to resemble his national stature. He found he could not thrust out his left foot to the offside in the manner of his pristine youth, so he learned to pull the ball to the onside. His eye was still remarkable, his powers of hitting unimpaired and his confidence to play the shot as bullish as ever. He mastered the pull shot and, in the process, set up the great seasons of his middle age. Seventy years after he first bowled at Grace, the great Wilfred Rhodes would still acknowledge what an effective hitter he was: 'He would take a good length ball from outside his off-stump and bang it over mid-on's head like a cannon ball.' Grace was fifty years of age when he first encountered the subtleties of Rhodes, so we can assume that his ability to adapt took a heavy toll of bowlers for many years. When modern county cricketers sneer at Grace from the lofty heights of a few hundred wickets at a mediocre cost, I prefer to believe the testimony of a shrewd Yorkshireman who was proved right 4,187 times at the bowling crease.

2

Tom Hayward

'He used to make my arm ache' (C.J. Kortright)

Thomas Walter Hayward

Born

Cambridge

29 March 1871

Died

Cambridge

19 July 1939

First hundred

112   Surrey v Kent, The Oval, 1893

Age: 22 years 129 days

100th hundred

139   Surrey v Lancashire, The Oval, 1913

Age: 42 years 90 days

Last hundred

116   Surrey v Yorkshire, Lord's, 1914

Age: 43 years 137 days

Career record

M	Inn	NO	HS	Runs	Average	100s	50s
712	1,138	96	315*	43,551	41.79	104	218

Test record

M	Inn	NO	HS	Runs	Average	100s	50s
35	60	2	137	1,999	34.46	3	12

Eighteen years after Sammy Woods tried to drink the old doctor under the table, the feat of a hundred hundreds was repeated by a man who was, in many ways, similar to the Great Cricketer. Like Grace, Tom Hayward had been a model of consistency over a long period of seasons, he based his success on an orthodox, unhurried style, he came from a cricketing family and, temperamentally, he could be as bloody-minded as W.G. when the mood suited him.

Hayward had cricket in his blood; the Hayward production line was almost as impressive as the one that rumbled out of Bristol in the 1840s. Tom was the son of Daniel Hayward, by common consent the best professional batsman in the country in the 1860s. Tom's father and his uncle Thomas had played for Surrey and, by the time young Tom was born in 1871, the family had moved to Cambridge, with significant results. Hayward senior became groundsman at Parker's Piece, that famous area of ground in Cambridge that saw the dawning of the genius of Hobbs and Ranjitsinhji and the imperturbable majesty of young Tom Hayward. Within a couple of years Tom had shown that the family genes had issued forth another cricketer of class, and he set out to mould his technique on the excellent wickets at Parker's Piece.

He first played for Surrey in 1893. He was bowled first ball by Joe Cresswell, the Warwickshire fast bowler. In the following match he scored the first of 104 centuries. He made an immediate impression with his sound, graceful method and clean driving, and *Wisden* demurely remarked: 'We do not wish to seem over-sanguine, but we shall be greatly disappointed if he does not in the immediate future obtain a very high position.' So it proved. By 1896 he was playing for England – he did so 35 times – and for 20 years in succession he made 1,000 runs in a season. On two occasions he made over 3,000 runs, and his total of 3,518 in 1906 remained a record until Compton and Edrich broke it in 1947 against vastly inferior bowling. In that 1906 season he performed the unique feat of four centuries in successive matches in one week.

Like W.G. Grace, Tom Hayward was a wonderfully phlegmatic player of fast bowling. He was a typical product of the nineteenth-century school of batsmanship: upright, patient, a front-foot player who stroked the ball formidably hard once his eye was in. He would calmly take stock of the bowling and conditions when he arrived at the wicket and then gradually unfurl his shots. He could play all round the wicket, but his specialities were the cut and the off-drive. On the plumb Oval wickets at the turn of the century Hayward's off-driving was full of grandeur and power. Great slow bowlers like Blythe and Rhodes would wheel away for hours, pitching on or outside the off-stump, imprecating Hayward to loft an off-drive; yet all those hours of net practice under the tutelage of his father had taught him the value of a still head, a straight bat and a powerful follow-through. As he warmed to his task, Hayward's chocolate-brown Surrey cap would be pushed further back on his head – a sure sign to the bowlers that all was well with him and that he expected to be there for some time. On 58 occasions at The Oval, that equanimity was reflected in a Hayward century.

It would be wrong to assume that the bulk of Hayward's 43,000 runs were accumulated with an inevitability that stemmed from perfect batting conditions. His innings for the Players against the Gentlemen in 1906 has rightly earned him a place in cricket history. He made just 54, but it came in an all-out total of 199 on a fiery wicket that had recently been watered and left to dry under a hot sun. Earlier in the day Arthur Fielder had taken all ten wickets to hustle out the Gentlemen for 167, and the amateur fast bowlers, Walter Brearley and Neville Knox, were determined to inflict the same punishment. Hayward was badly hit in the first over but carried on batting valiantly against the bounce of Knox and Brearley. The other professional batsmen – Bowley, J.T. Tyldesley, Rhodes, Denton, John Gunn, Hayes and Lilley – cut a sorry figure as they backed away from the fast bowling onslaught that claimed all but one of the wickets. Only Hayward stood four-square, taking innumerable blows on the chest and fingers, all the while getting in line with the ball. It was a classic innings from a classic batsman and cogent proof that the best innings do not always encompass three figures. No wonder C.J. Kortright, the fastest bowler of that period, said of Hayward: 'He used to make my arm ache.' W.G. Grace, of course, was the acknowledged master of fast bowling over a longer period of time than Hayward (and on more dangerous wickets) but, in his day, no professional batsman was more at ease against them.

Yet Hayward was not just a masterful performer against the quick bowlers – and a conversation with P.G.H. Fender confirmed this in my view. A little matter of 68 years had elapsed between an innings of Hayward's and my talk with Fender, but the memory of it was still fresh in his mind. The occasion was the match in August 1914 between Surrey and Kent, Jack Hobbs' benefit game. On a rain-affected wicket Hayward scored 91 out of 234 all out. Colin Blythe, that most beautiful of slow left-arm bowlers, took nine for 97 and Fender, who batted for a time with Hayward, said it was the best bad-wicket innings he ever saw. From a man who saw Jack Hobbs display his greatness regularly on difficult wickets, this is high praise indeed. Fender scored 48 in characteristic style in that Surrey innings and recalls, 'Mine was just biff-bang stuff, but Hayward met everything in the middle of the bat. It was a masterpiece' – a masterpiece at the age of 43, with his career just two weeks to run, against Blythe, Woolley and Fielder, not to mention a certain A.P. Freeman who was to cause some problems after the war.

For the last ten years of his time at Surrey, Hayward's name was overshadowed by that of Jack Hobbs. That must nevertheless have given him great pleasure, because Tom Hayward was largely instrumental in bringing Hobbs to the first-class game. Like Hayward, Hobbs came from Cambridge and on one occasion at short notice he stepped into a local side scheduled to meet a Tom Hayward XI in Cambridge. Hayward bowled at the youngster, was immediately impressed and arranged a trial for him at The Oval. The rest can be told in a subsequent chapter, but it is clear that Jack Hobbs would have been lost to the game without Hayward's quiet encouragement. When Hobbs' father died in 1902 – three years before his son ever played for Surrey – Hayward arranged a charity match for the widow and her family. A year later Hobbs was offered a contract by Surrey – and, as soon as he could, Hayward went to see the Surrey secretary, C.W. Alcock, and arranged a £10 bonus for young Hobbs in view of his family's financial worries. Hobbs did not know about this for years afterwards, but it is a measure of the awe in which he held Hayward that, for several seasons, he could not bring himself to call his fellow-professional by his first name, even when he was capped by Surrey. He could not even invite him to his wedding; he was too shy in the presence of such a dominating person.

Eventually the relationship between Hobbs and Hayward blossomed and so did their opening partnerships. Hobbs always acknowledged the good fortune of being able to watch the best professional batsman in the country at the other end, to see how he coped with awkward wickets and testing bowlers. By the time their partnership had been severed by war in 1914, they had set a new record for century opening stands of 40. In 1907 they achieved something that has never been beaten: in the space of one week they added more than 100 for the first wicket no less than four times, 106 and 125 against Cambridge University and 147 and 105 against Middlesex. They were a handsome pair of openers, both defensively sound but with a rich array of strokes and a reluctance to be tied down. It would have given them infinite pleasure to succeed together in Tests, but they opened only once, at Lord's in 1909 against Australia. They put on just 23 and 16 and Hayward, who played against the advice of his doctor, was dropped for good at the age of 38.

It is easy to see why the shy Hobbs would look up to Hayward in those days of the early twentieth century. Hayward was a typical product of the Victorian age, a provincial figure but proudly so, a man who belonged to a community and looked forward to returning there to bask in the glory of his worldwide deeds for his country. If he did not tour with England in the winter, he would come to Cambridge and enjoy the respectful welcome; his self-confidence ensured that Surrey County Cricket Club paid him enough to live comfortably. He was a proud professional and, in his own way, did much to raise the status of the breed. In previous decades some professional cricketers had been notorious for their inability to hold their liquor or keep track of their money. Public-spirited captains like Yorkshire's Lord Hawke would try to invest their cash for them before it disappeared down their throats. A man of Tom Hayward's stature had no need for such paternalism, he knew the value of self-discipline and, as senior professional at The Oval for the last decade before the war, he expected a similar code of conduct from the other pros. At away matches every professional knew what time he must appear in the dining room and how he should dress, and Hayward cracked down very hard on any midnight skylarking in the hotels. It did not really matter who was the Surrey captain at any given time – Tom Hayward was the boss. With his tall, commanding bearing, rugged good looks and bushy moustache, he looked like an irascible yet kindly regimental sergeant-major.

Like W.G. Grace, Tom Hayward knew his own mind and his commercial worth and, if the offer was not satisfactory to him, he would withhold his services. In 1896 he withdrew from the Oval Test against Australia because he wanted £20 appearance money, twice the going rate. The rubber depended on the Oval Test but Hayward would not budge, because he felt the amateurs were getting too much money when they were allegedly of independent means. Note the date – 1896. He was just 25, in his first season as a Test player and only beginning to establish himself in the Surrey team. Hayward was no blind respecter of institutions, even if he became one himself by his batting eminence. A decade after his first brush with authority he again ruled himself out of a contest with Australia, refusing to go on the 1907/08 tour because the terms were not right. He could be equally single-minded with his employers at The Oval: in 1898 both Hayward and J.T. Brown scored triple centuries in the same week and, when Hayward heard that Yorkshire had given Brown a cash reward, he told the Surrey committee he would make do with single centuries in future. Furthermore they could forget about him bowling the medium-pace off-breaks that had picked up 114 wickets in the previous season. Thereafter he bowled reluctantly, sparingly, and with a highly developed sense of grievance.

He was a proud man who set himself high professional standards. After his wonderful season of 1906 he was unprepared for the dazzling quartet of googly bowlers (Vogler, Faulkner, Schwarz and White) that came over from South Africa in the following year. He was dogged by knee trouble and a thickening waistline, and his difficulties against the googly bowlers were magnified by the success of his junior partner, Jack Hobbs. One day Hobbs was bowled round his pads after a simple miscalculation against the ball that turned into him. Hayward, watching from the pavilion, laughed loudly: 'Ah, there's the master of the googly showing us how to play it.' Judging by the respect Hobbs had for Hayward, we can charitably assume that remark stemmed from frustration at his own performances, rather than from envy of Hobbs' mastery.

If he could never pick the googly, Hayward still had many more days in the sun ahead of him, days when the chocolate cap was pushed back with relish from the broad, sweating brow. Recurring knee trouble slowed his progress in the field and – mercifully – gave him a good excuse not to bowl, but he could still roll out the centuries. He scored more than 2,000 runs in 1911, and all the while he was advancing with measured tread towards the day when he could at least sit on the same statistical pedestal as W.G. Grace. It came on Friday 27 June 1913 against Lancashire at his beloved Oval. With his colleagues failing, he batted nearly five hours for 139 to achieve his hundredth hundred in first-class cricket. It was not one of his most fluent knocks; he was cut over the eye when his score was 16 and hit several times. As he acknowledged the cheers of the 5,000 spectators with his usual dignity, he did not know that in years to come, Jack Hobbs would always envy him for getting the appropriate hundred in front of his own supporters.

By 1913 mammoth scores were becoming commonplace, and Hayward's feat was therefore received with more decorum than that of Grace in 1895. Nevertheless, the tributes were warm and deserved. A.C. MacLaren, a man who knew more than enough about the technique of batting, wrote: 'I doubt if any professional has been more careful in his living or more painstaking in his methods to attain success for the captains for whom and the sides for which he has played. Let me beg all young players today to note the use of the left shoulder, and how the left leg is brought across for Hayward's off-drive. Note, too, that he never gets back onto his wicket and then plays forward, as some have got into the way of doing.'

One satisfying season remained for Hayward before the Golden Age of Cricket was blown away for ever by the Great War. In 1914 Surrey won a truncated championship, and Hayward captained the side in the last few matches in the absence of C.T.A. Wilkinson; he did so shrewdly and capably, which came as no surprise. Woe betide any of the players stepping out of line when the gleam was in his eye! In a fortnight in August – with war already declared and a sense of unreality hanging over cricket grounds – Hayward demonstrated his ageless mastery for the last time: 122 against Kent, 91 in the return match and 116 against Yorkshire, adding 290 with Hobbs for the first wicket against Drake, Booth, Hirst, Rhodes and Kilner. His last match was against Gloucestershire at The Oval: he scored just a single but had the satisfaction of catching the last man off Percy Fender's bowling as Surrey won by an innings. So Surrey's pre-war history was ended by the hands of one of its most illustrious players.

When cricket resumed in 1919, Hayward was 48 and clearly too old and unfit to play again. He spent several happy years at Oxford, coaching the undergraduates, taking their banter in genial fashion and doing his best to avoid breaking into a sweat in the nets. He would bowl his off-breaks and steadfastly refuse to bat, despite the entreaties of his young pupils. Just once he relented, playing a couple of majestic off-drives and then walking out of the net. He would rarely talk about his batting deeds but loved to sit watching the undergraduates learning their trade against the county sides. He would happily sit all day in the pavilion, still wearing his Surrey cap, his walrus moustache giving him a melancholy air that was belied by his pleasure at suddenly meeting an old friend.

His brother Dan was in charge of the rival pavilion at Cambridge and, after his retirement from the Parks, he lived contentedly enough in his home town. It was there that he died in July 1939, at the age of 68, his life ending on the brink of the Second World War, just as his great playing career had been extinguished by the Great War of 1914. It was somehow appropriate that he died in his home town, in the place where he felt at ease throughout his life. It was even more fitting that he should live to see the whole of Jack Hobbs' wonderful career, to experience the glow of satisfaction that a jewel picked out by him from Parker's Piece in 1901 should dazzle the world for the next 33 years. It is no mean effort to score a hundred hundreds and to usher onto the cricketing stage an even more impressive player. That must have been worth a tug or two on the chocolate cap.

3

Sir Jack Hobbs

'By his behaviour and ability, he earned
respect for himself and his profession'
(G.O. Allen)

John Berry Hobbs

Born

Cambridge

16 December 1882

Died

Hove, Sussex

21 December 1963

First hundred

155   Surrey v Essex, The Oval, 1905
Age: 22 years 140 days

100th hundred

116   Surrey v Somerset, Bath, 1923
Age: 40 years 143 days

Last hundred

116   Surrey v Lancashire, Old Trafford 1934
Age: 51 years 163 days

Career record

M	Inn	NO	HS	Runs	Average	100s	50s
826	1,315	106	316*	61,237	50.65	197	270

Test record

M	Inn	NO	HS	Runs	Average	100s	50s
61	102	7	211	5,410	56.94	15	28

No one scored more hundreds or runs than Jack Hobbs, yet to profile him within such a context is dismissive. He certainly was no run machine; he often said the papers would do cricket a favour if they refrained from publishing the first-class averages, that he cared little for hundreds but that his friends would be disappointed if he missed out. He made a habit of giving his wicket away as soon as he reached three figures (unless, of course, the circumstances of the game demanded extra commitment from him) and, of his 197 centuries, no fewer than 51 of them were scores of between 100 and 110.

What was the secret of Jack Hobbs, that quality which turned grizzled old cricketers misty-eyed at the very mention of his name? He was not a character of the Hendren or Compton mould, while others like Phil Mead were more impressively prolific, and he lacked the intimidating presence of W.G. Grace, the power of strokeplay of Hammond or Woolley and Bradman's rapacity. From the distance he looked ordinary enough on the field: medium of height, slim, wiry, thoughtful. No gestures, no flamboyance. Yet the public adored him, probably more for his sheer ordinariness than his wonderful batting achievements. He came from a poor home, and he never forgot it; the experience moulded a quiet determination which was masked by his graceful behaviour. The small boys, the lad from the corner shop enjoying a free half-day, the office clerk spending a Saturday at that most unlovely ground, The Oval, they all could warm to Jack Hobbs, identify with him, wish him well and declare with passionate intensity that the day's light was dimmed whenever he was out. He was an ordinary, decent man of wonderful skills, yet on the same level as his worshippers.

Jack Hobbs brought batting to a level of perfection that has never been matched. Grace was a more creative batsman in that he moulded batting technique to the emerging game of first-class cricket, but it was Hobbs who refined the art. He was as sound as Hutton, as daring as Bradman and his temperament was the equal of Sutcliffe. He simply understood how to bat, he instinctively knew what to do with the bowled ball. He never had an hour's coaching in his life; he just watched, listened and put into practice the advice given by his father before he was ten: 'Don't draw away.' Bill Bowes summed up the effortless mastery of the man thus: 'When he stood at the wicket before playing the shot, he looked a great player. All was ease, grace and confidence.'

During a thirty-year period in first-class cricket, he met and mastered every type of bowling – swervers, fast bowlers, cutters, seamers, top-spinner, leg-spinners, off-breaks and googlies. When he was over fifty, he was occasionally ruffled by short-pitched intimidatory bowling, but that was a human frailty in a man whose batting seemed god-like for so many blissful years. His mastery of the basics enabled him to pass through three distinct phases of batting – before the 1914 War, he was a glorious dasher, revelling in the knowledge that he had all the shots, then for a decade afterwards he was simply 'the Master', a mature artist, while for the last few years of his career his beautiful technique enabled him to come to terms with physical stresses. One of the most revealing statistics about Hobbs is that he scored no less than 98 hundreds after his 40th birthday in 1922. He scored 26,441 runs (average 58.63) after his 40th birthday, a record that will surely never be beaten. When he reached his century of centuries in May 1923 he had only batted once with Herbert Sutcliffe, a partnership that was to prove legendary – so he had done enough for any mortal before embarking on his most famous collaboration. Just one more fact to consider, and it confirms what an attacking player Hobbs must have been: no one has bettered his total of 20 hundreds before lunch, 13 of them on the first day. Gilbert Jessop, a name synonymous with fast scoring, is next in line with 13.

It is one of the human touches of Hobbs' career that luck was on his side on several crucial occasions. Tyros like Grace and Bradman made their own luck by sheer willpower, battering down the door of opportunity, but Jack Hobbs could easily have been lost to the game before he was twenty. He was the first of twelve children living in a Cambridge back street; his father, a pro cricketer *manqué*, had to make do with groundsman's and net bowler's duties and, when he died in 1902, the sensitive, eldest son felt his responsibilities keenly. At the age of 20 he had to make a start on some sort of career. Enter Tom Hayward, as we have already seen. Without his kindness, encouragement and ability to put the right word into the right ears at certain times, Jack Hobbs' batting genius would have been smothered by the deadening hand of poverty. He was turned down by Essex – the club never answered a letter of recommendation from an old friend of his father – and Hayward's influence at The Oval remained his only hope. He was as good as his word and, after satisfactory trials, he was taken on the staff. It seems incredible from a distance of a century ago, but Hobbs had to qualify by residence for two years before making his first-class debut for Surrey; he could not even return home to Cambridge in the winter, although he characteristically ensured his mother received a generous portion of his wage.

He was 22 years and five months old upon entering first-class cricket. At that age Bradman had scored 334 in a Test, Hutton had improved on that with 364 and Compton had scored two hundreds for England. Hobbs had been content to bide his time, watching, taking stock and drinking everything in at The Oval. Perhaps he realised how lucky he was, how he managed to be in the right place when a vacancy occurred. In his first organised cricket match he made up the team when it was one short. Later he impressed Tom Hayward in a charity game but only played because the local side had ten men. On his debut for Surrey at Lord's, while qualifying, he scored a splendid half-century against the Cross Arrows, yet would not have played but for Tom Richardson's injury. He fitted snugly into the Surrey first team as an opener by dint of ability but also because Bobby Abel's long tenure as

Hayward's partner had come to an end. Then in 1907 his first England tour to Australia was secured because batsmen of the calibre of Fry, MacLaren, R.E. Foster, Warner, J.T. Tyldesley and Hayward could not, or would not, go.

Even on his first-class debut – on Easter Monday 1905 – the fates were kind. None of the four contenders for the place of Hayward's partner was available for a variety of reasons – in some cases, because it was early in the season and bitterly cold – and by another stroke of fortune, the Surrey captain, Lord Dalmeny, was absent. Tom Hayward was the stand-in skipper, and he decided to take Hobbs in with him. A considerate action: he must have known how nervous his young protégé was.

The opposition on that day was the Gentlemen of England, captained by W.G. Grace, and by a happy coincidence the first three men to score a hundred hundreds took the field at the same time. At the end of Hobbs' career, the pattern repeated itself when, in 1934, he played with and against Walter Hammond and Don Bradman, the two men who dominated the world's bowlers for the next decade.

As W.G. loomed at point, Hobbs made 18 and a polished 88, impressing both sets of players and showing he could not be rattled by Grace's little ways. In the second innings he thought of a quick single to W.G.'s bowling, but the old man was too mentally sharp: 'Thank you, youngster, just tip it back here and save my old legs.' He did so – but tapped other deliveries a little harder and scored his 88 in two hours. The following week he scored 155 against Essex, the county that had rejected him. Did an anonymous clerk in the Essex office blush at the event?

After the Essex match Hobbs was presented with his county cap by an admiring Lord Dalmeny. I wonder if a cap has ever been presented so early to a player? One can assume that the kindly Hayward was instrumental in accelerating that award; he knew his family needed the extra money and also that Surrey had unearthed a jewel of a batsman.

The story of the next ten years is familiar: a worrying loss of form for most of his first season, nearly 2,000 runs the following year, a splendid, mature England debut in Australia and fascinating battles with the South African googly bowlers in 1907 and on the 1909 tour. He began the second of his four great opening partnerships – with Wilfred Rhodes – in South Africa, and their contrasting styles served England magnificently in Australia in 1911/12 and again in South Africa in 1913/14. Hobbs always said that Rhodes was the best runner of all his illustrious partners; just a nod was sufficient, and they were home before the fielders could take stock. They were the first opening partners not to call, relying on intuition and trust, and in their happy collaboration only two run-outs occurred – on the admission of Rhodes, both his fault.

The performance of Hobbs on the difficult matting wickets in South Africa against the wonderful googly bowlers established his credentials as the world's best batsman, just five years since his debut before the quizzical eyes of W.G. Grace. Googly bowling was in its infancy – it had been discovered by B.J.T. Bosanquet at the turn of the century – but it had already won Test matches for Bosanquet and for the South African quartet of Vogler, Faulkner, Schwarz and White. Many famous batsmen of the time were perplexed by the new form of attack; they would play the off-drive from the front foot and, to their horror, watch the ball dip in to the leg from basically a leg-break action. Tom Hayward never fathomed its intricacies, and R.E. Foster – classical batsman of the public-school style – wrote sniffily in *Wisden* that the googly would mean the demise of offside play.

The matting wickets in South Africa made the googly even more formidable because of the extra bounce. Only Hobbs, with his deft footwork, swift reactions and instinctive awareness of the bad ball, prospered. He used the classic methods: pushing forward if he thought the ball could be smothered, and going back as far as possible to play off the pitch. His ability to spot the point of pitch was uncanny, and somehow he could sense which ball was the googly. The South African quartet was never the same again and Hobbs, demonstrating how a great player can adapt to changing bowling methods, returned home with his captain, H.D.G. Leveson Gower, paying him due homage: 'I have never seen better batting either in England or anywhere else.'

Challenge always brought out the best in Jack Hobbs. Gathering runs for the sake of it was never his forte, at any stage of his career. Mastering the South African spinners was a matter of unaffected pride to him, and an innings of 69 not out at Edgbaston in 1909 against Australia also pleased him immensely. On a pitch badly affected by rain Hobbs was lbw first ball. In England's second innings the target was 105 on a difficult wicket. Fry and Hobbs – two men on a 'king pair' – knocked off the runs in even time, a wonderful effort in the circumstances. Now C.B. Fry was no blushing violet and he was entitled to be pleased with his 35 not out, yet even this engaging egotist was moved to write of his young partner: 'I have to say that this was as great an innings as I ever saw played by any batsman in any Test match, or any other match. His quickness with his bat and his skill in forcing the direction of his strokes made me feel like a fledgling.' In later years, Hobbs would diffidently acknowledge: 'I played really well – you know when you play well.'

The year 1914 was the peak of Hobbs' career. After 1919 he was more certain, more masterful, the complete player – but before the Great War he was a dazzling improviser. During the 1914 season A.C. MacLaren, the former England captain, recognised the genius of Hobbs by commissioning a film on his technique. MacLaren selected 98 shots illustrating ten strokes and, when they were reproduced in book form, MacLaren's eulogistic words were in contrast to his usually stern pronouncements: 'He has never departed from sound methods, but has kept his natural free game pure throughout his career. I never recollect him being sent back to the pavilion, having played the wrong game for the occasion.'

One can only hazard a guess at the kind of entertainment Jack Hobbs would have given had not more important matters distracted mankind from 1914 to 1918. He always said he was twice the player before the war – afterwards, he had to play more off the back foot. He was rising 37 when first-class cricket resumed, approaching middle age in playing terms, and, if he had to adapt to the ravages of time, he did so with typical grace, economy of movement and with little depreciation in aesthetic appeal. His post-war phase was even more glorious, his place in the public's heart more affectionately fixed than ever before. He entered a prodigious period of consistency – 35,017 runs in 15 years, 131 of his 197 hundreds and only once (in 1923) was his average less than 50. Before Bradman, he was the most consistent run-getter of all time, yet no one worried less about the sheer slog of carving out big scores. He was, quite simply, the Master, and the runs came automatically, the product of a wonderful technique, a keen, tactical intelligence and a serene temperament.

Hobbs often pointed out to his friends that the post-war bowlers were not quite as good as their predecessors, that the wickets were better and that he was fortunate enough to play all his career under the old lbw rule, which had enabled him to play off-spinners on a turning wicket with his pads. Yet surely Hobbs, the man who dominated every type of bowling on all wickets over thirty years, would have solved the technical problems caused by the new lbw law? He batted according to the laws of his time, but he was so skilful at playing the ball coming into him, so strong on the legside, that just a little tinkering with that smooth engine would have sufficed.

His technique was solidly and elegantly based: relaxed, perfectly balanced, so that he could go back or forward in an instant. His footwork was so fast – even in his forties – that he could dictate the length of the ball. He gripped the bat firmly with his bottom hand, which helped him play all the shots. He manipulated the ball with consummate ease, almost checking the shot, so that it travelled slowly to the fielder, while he stole a single. Only Leonard Hutton, among the great batsmen, has approached this touch on the ball. Hobbs delighted in placing the ball into a space, then watching the fielding captain plug the gap, only to plunder the position where the fielder had been. His running between the wickets was sage, assured, graceful – and totally demoralising.

Hobbs liked to get off the mark as soon as he took strike; it was common knowledge around the county circuit and many plans were laid to try to run him out in the first over. Jack Mercer, splendid bowler for Glamorgan and Sussex and a close friend of Hobbs, devised a scheme with the aid of his Glamorgan captain, Maurice Turnbull. 'We were due to play Surrey in a week and so we practised and practised, running out batsmen in the middle. Come the day, I bowled the first ball, expecting Jack to stroke it slowly to cover point – he hit it like a bullet past square leg to the boundary. He grinned down the wicket at me, almost as if he knew what we'd been planning.'

F.R. Brown told me that the ambition of Hobbs early in his innings lay far beyond getting one off the mark: 'In my early days at Surrey, Jack was nudging fifty years of age, but he used to tell me that the time for easy runs was at the start of an innings, despite the new ball. He said the bowlers weren't loosened up at the start, and he would try to pick up as many fours as he could to disconcert them and knock them off their length. I can vouch for his effectiveness.' So can Bill Bowes: 'The first time I bowled at him, he went down on one knee and hit me past the left hand of square-leg. The ball had pitched seven or eight inches outside off-stump. My jaw dropped, and George Macaulay at mid-on shouted reassuringly: "It's no good you peepin' – he'll do that three times an over when his eye's in." And he did. I had to think harder bowling at Jack Hobbs than against any other player.'

When necessary he could launch blistering assaults on certain bowlers. This was usually in the interests of the side; perhaps the wicket was a difficult one and Hobbs would worry about the influence of the opposition's star bowler. His treatment of Charlie Parker was legendary among the old Gloucestershire players. With his left-arm spin Parker was a destroyer on the helpful Cheltenham wickets, and Hobbs would usually knock him out of the attack by driving him several times over cover. Parker, who always knew Hobbs had the mastery over him, would slouch away to third man and refuse to bowl until Hobbs was out. Reg Sinfield – Parker's team-mate in the 1930s – recalled a game at Cheltenham, when Hobbs was dropped at slip early on off Sinfield's bowling. 'He said, "Bad luck, Reg, I'll give you my wicket when I get a hundred." Charlie Parker heard that and moaned, "Oh God, that means he will get one." It was a devil of a wicket, an old-fashioned sticky one, and Jack smashed Charlie out of sight. I was bowling at him just after he got his hundred and he said, "Look out, Reg!" and put up a simple caught and bowled to me. It was an amazing innings – Bradman wouldn't have made ten on that wicket.'

That parting shot from Sinfield was echoed by every contemporary of Hobbs I have interviewed. Les Ames confirmed the magnificence of the Hobbs/ Sutcliffe partnership at Melbourne on the 1928/29 tour of Australia. England needed 332 to win, and a thunderstorm soaked the wicket. The hot sun came out, and Hobbs and Sutcliffe had to face a typical Melbourne sticky wicket, the worst of its type in Australia. Hobbs had his cap knocked off, and he and his great partner were beaten and bruised many times. They somehow survived, adding 105 before Hobbs was lbw for 49, and Sutcliffe steered England to a great three-wicket victory. Les Ames watched that stand and recalls: 'It was an absolute pig of a wicket, we should have been out for less than a hundred. I have never seen such an exhibition of bad-wicket batting.'

Hobbs was aged 46 at the time. On that tour he became the oldest to make a Test century, at the age of 46 years 82 days. Effortlessly he adjusted his technique to suit the tactical situation, his physical powers and the needs of his side. Two years before the classic Melbourne performance, he and Sutcliffe had wrested back the Ashes with a historic stand of 172 on an Oval wicket soaked by overnight rain and rendered spiteful by warm sunshine. Clearly Arthur Richardson's off-breaks from round the wicket to a six-man legtrap should have been more productive; Arthur Mailey and Clarrie Grimmett also did not do themselves justice. Yet the conditions were foul – Sutcliffe was hit in the face by one ball that popped – and England had a bare 22 runs lead on the first innings, with the Ashes depending on the result. Jim Laker would have posed a much sterner test, and Hobbs later agreed that someone like Parkin, Astill or Macaulay would have been unplayable. Having made such allowances, it was nevertheless a *tour de force*; both men made famous hundreds, the wicket dried out and England won by 289 runs.

For Hobbs the joy of batting was never far from the surface, despite the occasional crisis that he would steel himself to surmount. His wry remark to Sutcliffe on the morning of their classic Oval partnership ('I think the rain has done us') typified a humour that was always gentle, occasionally ingenuous. He was no show-off, but he loved to see the expression on the face of his old friends as he played some dazzling shot or other. Once Arthur Mailey managed to get Hobbs on a dry, dusty wicket that was ideal for his expansive leg-spin. Mailey bowled him a leg-break that pitched on middle and leg and turned a long way towards the off. Hobbs stroked him in front of square leg for four and smiled at Mailey: 'Poor old Arthur, they always put you on when it won't turn!' Alf Gover remembered his playful genius – and again the victim was the misanthropic Charlie Parker in masterly style. With the bowlers distractedly trying to get at Gover, the *coup de grace* arrived. Gover recalled: 'Charlie bowled at Jack with four men very close in on the offside. He was bowling away from the bat on a turning wicket, and he wanted to keep Jack down that end. Off the last ball of the over Jack leaned back and calmly placed the ball past slip for a precious single. Jack chuckled, "What about that, Charlie?" and Charlie, snatching his cap, could only sniff – "Bloody marvellous!" From a man like Parker that was quite a compliment.'

Gover loved to talk about another stroke by Hobbs that lingered in his memory sixty years later when we talked. Hobbs captained an all-professional Surrey side against Northants and, with Sandham ill, he took Gover in first with him. Gover – a career batting average of nine – asked Hobbs to look after the dangerous Austin Matthews, a lively fast-medium bowler who later played for England. Hobbs did so, and one particular delivery from Matthews convinced the young Gover of his partner's genius: 'Jack thought it was an in-swinger and leaned into it; but it moved away off the seam. Matthews had one hand up in the air, thinking he had got through his defence, but Jack rocked back and cut it wide of cover for four.'

The amateurs of his time regarded Hobbs with a mixture of affection and respect. R.E.S. Wyatt, who led him in his last Test in 1930, recalled how helpful and charming he was to the nervous young captain. Percy Fender, Hobbs' captain at Surrey for many years, said he was a marvellous bridge between the skipper and the other professionals: 'He would talk to them and make sure we were all on the same wavelength in the team.' G.O. Allen first met him in 1921 when he was at Oxford; Hobbs asked him if he was nervous before a game and, when Allen confirmed that he was, Hobbs replied: 'So am I, and I wouldn't have it any other way.' Allen told me: 'He was so charming to me, who was just a young student. He did so much for the professional players over the years. By his behaviour and ability he earned respect for himself and his profession.'

That was important to Hobbs. He was happy to leave the duties of captaincy to Herbert Strudwick if the amateur captain was unavailable, but he always insisted on the highest standards from his fellow professionals. Alf Gover received early notice of this when he first came into the Surrey side; he had had some bad luck with his bowling and was loudly bemoaning this state of affairs in the dressing-room, interspersed with a few colourful adjectives. Hobbs said quietly, 'Alfred, come over here,' and proceeded to lecture him about his responsibilities as a Surrey cricketer on and off the field. Thereafter Gover never swore in the dressing-room and for several years could not bring himself to call Jack anything other than 'Sir'.

His standing in the eyes of the public was Olympian during the 1920s. When he passed Grace's total of centuries at Taunton in 1925, he was bewildered by the battery of cameras and reporters. He found it hard to come to terms with being a public figure, yet accepted it with his usual shy grace. Much of the ballyhoo distressed him, but some of it was a great source of amusement. For instance, when he equalled Grace's total of 126 centuries, Percy Fender brought him out some ginger ale in a champagne glass. By gratefully taking the toast Hobbs unwittingly stirred up a hornet's nest among the temperance bodies. Indignant letters to *The Times* spluttered that a national hero had let them down and thereby encouraged the working classes to quaff even more alcohol. It was a farcical claim, especially against such an abstemious man, but it made Hobbs chuckle in his retirement.

In the last few seasons of his wonderful career his powers inevitably declined, but not to a demeaning extent. He was rattled by some short-pitched bowling by 'Hopper' Read of Essex – F.R. Brown remembered him saying to Read, 'If you bowl properly, I'll play properly' – and more seriously, by Bill Bowes of Yorkshire. Bowes is frank about his intentions: 'I knew I couldn't bowl him, so I wanted to get him hitting in the air.' Hobbs protested in an uncharacteristically public way: after the first bouncer, he walked down the pitch to the bowler's end and patted a spot. At the goading of George Macaulay, Bowes bowled another bouncer – 'I saw Jack coming up to my end again and I said "Not there, Jack" and, pointing to a place in my run-up, I said "Up there." Jack said "Sorry, Bill" and proceeded to walk past the wicket and pat a spot. He was rattled but, although he was fifty years of age, he was still a great player.' Hobbs did not resume his innings after lunch; he was said to have sunstroke.

If his feathers were ruffled by that assault, he showed his greatness against fast bowling in the following summer of 1933. Learie Constantine and Manny Martindale were in England with the touring West Indian team, determined to show that anything Larwood and Voce could do under Jardine, they could return with interest. When the West Indies came to The Oval to play Surrey, W.H. Ferguson, the tourists' scorer, told Hobbs he would not get many runs, because Martindale had pronounced he was finished. Hobbs smiled at the barb, looked out of the dressing-room and surprisingly forecast, 'I think I'll get a hundred today, that looks a good wicket.' He made 221 in six-and-a-half hours and, afterwards, Martindale came into the Surrey dressing-room and said, 'Mistah Hobbs, yous a great player.' It was Hobbs' first game of the season, and he was stiff for a week. He was, after all, 51.

One season remained, and an innings against Maurice Tate accelerated his retirement. He made 79 against Sussex in cool, unhurried fashion, but it took him more than four hours and, in frustration, he ran himself out for the second time that season. When he returned to the dressing-room, he said: 'That's it, I'm finished – I just can't move my feet any more.' His last innings in first-class cricket was neatly appropriate: he scored 18, the same score that opened his account in 1905.

His prestige at his retirement was deservedly massive, and nothing in the remaining thirty years of his life altered his reputation one jot. In 1953 the Master's Club was formed at the instigation of John Arlott, and they would meet annually on Hobbs' birthday – old cricketing and business friends, supplemented by a few of the young breed. They were happy, mellow meetings illuminated by the man's modest pride in the company about him.

He was proud to be the first professional games player to be honoured with a knighthood in 1953, although initially he tried to refuse it, in case his friends would think he had changed. His knighthood marked the full circle of the social revolution that turned the professional cricketer from little more than a serf into a man to be respected. He always wanted to remain a professional cricketer, and the sports shop he founded in 1920 gave him precious financial independence and clarity of mind. In his quiet way Jack Hobbs moulded events to his satisfaction; in 1924 he at first refused to accompany England to Australia because he wished to have his wife with him. At first the MCC refused permission – only amateurs had previously been accorded such a privilege – and there was a worrying impasse for a month. Hobbs began to make plans for a private tour with his wife to South Africa, but finally Lord's relented. Mr and Mrs Hobbs went to Australia, and the partnership of Hobbs and Sutcliffe prospered – but the great man had shown the principled side to his nature.

His fellow-professionals revered him. Jack Mercer told me in all sincerity that he had tried to model his life on the way that Hobbs lived. He admired his human touches: 'Whenever he went in the nets before the game, he would encourage youngsters to bowl at him. He always made sure at least one of them clean-bowled him, he knew what it would mean.' When I visited John Langridge he showed me the prize possession from his career – a signed photograph of Langridge catching Hobbs at slip from the 1933 season. Alf Gover chuckled at Hobbs' impish sense of humour: the 'apple pie' beds, the times he'd shout 'he's out' and the next batsman would be on his way to the middle before he realised it was Jack's little joke. F.R. Brown remembered Jack setting up the dour Jardine to demonstrate some textbook cover drives in the dressing-room, only to see the light bulb come crashing down on his distinguished Harlequin cap.

He set new standards of sportsmanship and decency. There is an evocative photograph from the 1920s showing Hobbs just after being dismissed by a googly from G.T.S. Stevens for 87. In later years Stevens would say, 'Jack waved and shouted, "Well bowled, Mr Stevens, I never picked that one."' This to an amateur eighteen years his junior. Stevens felt as if he had been knighted and that night proudly worked out his average against Hobbs: it was 1 for 257.

John Arlott said Hobbs never grumbled about umpires. 'In all his career, Jack reckoned he had the wrong end of a decision just once. When I pressed him for details, he said: "No, he was a damned good umpire," and he wouldn't discuss it further.'

The statistical roll-call from his career is awesome. He shared in a stand of a hundred for the first wicket on no less than 166 occasions (15 of them in Tests) – with Sandham 66 times, with Hayward 40, and 26 with Sutcliffe. He never 'bagged a pair' – much to his pleasure. He missed six seasons through war and illness and would have amassed thousands more runs if he had so wished. Cricket can only be grateful his genius lasted so long and flowered so luxuriantly.

4

Philip Mead

'Hard enough for four is hard enough'

Charles Philip Mead

Born

Battersea, London

9 March 1887

Died

Boscombe, Bournemouth

26 March 1958

First hundred

109   Hampshire v Yorkshire, Southampton, 1906
Age: 19 years 64 days

100th hundred

100*   Hampshire v Northamptonshire, Kettering, 1927
Age: 40 years 132 days

Last hundred

104   Hampshire v Essex, Southend, 1936
Age: 49 years 161 days

Career record

M	Inn	NO	HS	Runs	Average	100s	50s
814	1,340	185	280*	55,061	47.67	153	258

Test record

M	Inn	NO	HS	Runs	Average	100s	50s
17	26	2	182*	1,185	49.37	4	3

In the spring of 1903 two optimistic young cricketers presented themselves at The Oval, eager to impress the authorities of Surrey County Cricket Club. One was Jack Hobbs, the other a 16-year-old slow left-arm bowler from Battersea, a few miles from The Oval. Within the space of twenty-four hours Hobbs had been clean bowled twice in trial matches by the sturdy teenager – for 37 and 13. It was a minor hiccup in the serene progress of Hobbs towards greatness, but for Charles Philip Mead it was the only highlight of his time at The Oval. Despite scoring a hundred in a London schools match at the age of ten, the Surrey club saw his future in slow bowling – mediocre slow bowling as it turned out, and at the end of the 1903 season he was not retained at The Oval.

Imagine the slaughter over the next thirty years if Mead had stayed at The Oval! Think of him coming in after Hobbs and Hayward, or Hobbs and Sandham of later vintage! Instead, Philip Mead joined Hampshire in 1904 and launched a career that established him as one of the most prolific batsmen of all time. He was the first left-hander to score a century of hundreds. Only Hobbs, Hendren and Hammond have bettered his total of 153 centuries, and just three batsmen – Hobbs, Woolley and Hendren – have surpassed his 55,061 runs. He holds one record that will surely never be approached; his totals of 48,892 runs and 138 centuries are, in both cases, more than any man has ever scored for one team. He scored 1,000 runs in a season on 27 occasions – only Grace and Woolley with 28 have done better – nine times he made 2,000 runs in a season and twice 3,000 runs. No wonder an admiring Herbert Sutcliffe wrote, 'I wonder if there has been another player in the game who understood more of the science of batsmanship than Mead?'

He certainly had the respect of his opponents, but Mead never really struck a responsive chord with the spectators – partly because he was a dour, solemn character, partly because of his pragmatic batting methods. He was tallish, with shoulders sloping like a bottle; with wide hips, a pear-shaped body and strong bowed legs, he rolled out to bat with the intention of staying there all day. On his arrival at the crease, he went through the same ritual before every ball: he would look towards the square leg umpire, tug the peak of his cap four times in his direction, then ground his bat in the blockhole and tap away four times. After that, he would take four shuffling steps into position. Only then was he ready to face the bowler. He did that before every delivery in thirty-one years of first-class cricket, during his 1,340 innings. He wore out countless peaks on his caps and, no matter how often the bowler tried to hustle him out of his routine, Mead would never allow him to deliver until he was ready.

The 'Mead Shuffle' would be copied by generations of Hampshire schoolboys in back gardens and parks, but otherwise he never caught their imagination. He was 'the unbowlable', lacking the romantic hitting prowess of Woolley, the courtly mastery of Hobbs, the impishness of Hendren. Mead's left-hand batting was chockful of commonsense; he would nudge, tickle, glide and accumulate. Occasionally he would lean forward and punch an off-drive – he seemed to have longer arms than normal – and rarely would he loft the ball. He would often aver, 'Hard enough for four is hard enough.'

Mead may have looked sluggish on his feet but, in fact, he got into position remarkably quickly. When he moved he was well balanced and he was in position to play the ball with time to spare. Les Ames stood behind the stumps for Kent on many occasions when Mead's footwork and positional skills were too much for 'Tich' Freeman's leg-spin. Ames recalled, 'No one played "Tich" better. Players like Hammond and Hendren might murder "Tich" on occasions, but he would also get them out. Not so with Phil. He seemed to play everything round to leg and he always spotted the googly. He got into position smartly and often played him a yard down the wicket, invariably in the middle of the bat.'

He played straight and after a time, in the words of R.E.S. Wyatt, 'his bat seemed twice the normal size.' Indeed, the waggish Cecil Parkin once suggested that Mead's bat should be taken to a carpenter for a close shave. With his imperturbable calm he was a superb player of fast bowling, a point confirmed by G.O. Allen, one of the fastest bowlers of the 1920s: 'He was dogged, extremely correct and a very good, proficient player. He was never hurried out of his rhythm, kept his head still and watched the line of the ball. He may not have caught the eye, but the players in the middle knew just how good he was.'

Bill Bowes was fascinating on Mead's positional skills. Maurice Leyland had told him what a good 'leaver' Mead was and, when Bill first met him, he asked if he would demonstrate it during the forthcoming match. 'After he'd scored thirty-odd, he started on me – I was throwing up my arms as the ball missed his off-stump by a couple of inches. I couldn't believe it; I wish I'd never said a word.' In fact, Mead had a very fine record against the excellent Yorkshire attacks over the years, and Bill Bowes offered this technical assessment of him:

> He was never out of position for the shot. If you beat his bat, his pad was always there as a second line of defence – remember this was before the change in the LBW law. He didn't hit the ball strongly off the front foot, and I would try to get him playing forward. Having said that, he could quickly recognise a half volley and lean into it just a little harder. He didn't hook, but liked to nudge it square and backward. Phil would always hit the bad ball for four and push singles off good deliveries so easily that you would be amazed that he had reached fifty or a hundred so comparatively quickly. He had this knack of playing the ball slowly enough to a fielder to steal a single, then as the field was brought in to stop the ones, he'd chip over their heads for two.

Alf Gover confirmed that Mead hit the ball harder than many realised: 'The first time I played against him, I was in my usual position at short leg. Phil said, "I wouldn't stand too close if I were you, young fellow," but I stood my ground. Soon the ball went like a rocket past my ear off a short-pitched delivery, and he grinned wickedly at me.'

Yet his reputation as a slow scorer never left him. His physical bulk gave the impression of solidity, and he never thought of playing to the crowd to gain affection. When Mead was chosen to tour Australia ahead of Woolley in 1928, Gerry Weighall, the former Kent player, described the Hampshire man as a 'leaden-footed carthorse'. On close examination of Mead's career the description was grossly unfair, even though admittedly he lacked the charm of Woolley's batting. Most of Mead's hundreds were scored at a rate of 40 to 45 runs an hour in the days when captains did not deliberately slow down the play. Assessed on the modern method of runs per balls faced, Mead would appear positively skittish. G.O. Allen recalled a double hundred by Mead that appeared in impressively fast time and was compiled with certainty of strokeplay – it was in 1929, for the MCC team that had toured Australia, and he scored 233 in five hours against Lord Hawke's XI, a side containing bowlers of the calibre of Allen, Jupp, Haig and Rhodes. With Hendren as partner, Mead added 272 in 150 minutes.

In 1911, the year he came second in the national averages with 2,562 runs, Mead scored 401 runs in two days in a total of six hours and ten minutes. Against Warwickshire he made 207 not out and the next day, against Sussex, he made 194. The total runs included 66 boundaries, and his rate of scoring was more than 65 runs an hour. Yes, Mead was a stodgy performer! No less an authority than R.W.V. Robins believed this to be so. Once when Mead's dourness had driven the mercurial leg-spinner to distraction, he moaned: 'Mead, you've been in since ten past twelve and you've just stonewalled!' In vain did Mead protest that his score was 218 and that he had taken less than five hours in the process.

The England selectors usually preferred the more elegant and dashing Woolley to Mead, and one can hardly quibble at that. Yet it must be observed that Mead's Test average was 49.37 compared with Woolley's 36.07. The England selectors gave him an extended run just once – in his first series, in Australia in 1911/12 – and he failed, scoring just 105 runs at an average of 21. In 1921, when Gregory and MacDonald were frightening many England batsmen, one of the best players of fast bowling had to wait until the last two Tests to shore up the batting. He did not fail – 47 and 182 not out – and both Tests were drawn. He played just once more against Australia, in the first Test at Brisbane in 1928. He scored 8 and 73 – out lbw to Clarrie Grimmett both times – and, when Percy Chapman decided to play an extra bowler for the rest of the series, Mead shuffled away and devoted more time to following horse racing. No doubt Gerry Weighall felt justice had been done. Mead's Test average against Australia was nevertheless 51.87.

His treatment at the hands of the selectors served to deepen his already morose nature. He would carp a little about those lucky enough to play for more favoured counties, and he seems to have had a point. He simply decided to keep churning out the runs, gaining immense pleasure from frustrating bowlers. He did not believe in net practice before a season started, or even during the season, rightly surmising that he got enough match practice. He would say to the other Hampshire batsmen: 'You lead in May, and I shall catch you in June.' He once scored a century in the first county match of the season and roundly declared that he had not timed one shot. When asked the last time he had a bat in his hand, he replied: 'Last Scarborough Festival.'

He lacked a sense of humour and could not see the funny side of a remark addressed to him by an Australian during the 1928/29 tour: 'Ah, Mead, how good to see you, I recall watching your father play in 1911.' He lacked the ability to laugh at himself and he had a strongly developed sense of injustice. Once at Bournemouth he batted most of the morning against Surrey without attempting to play many shots. He played almost as stodgily as his reputation suggested and when he was tackled about it by the Surrey players at lunchtime, he pointed to their captain, P.G.H. Fender, 'That b------ let me down in South Africa last winter. I bowled at him in the nets for three quarters of an hour. When it was my turn to bat, he couldn't be found to bowl at me. Well, he can bowl all day now.'

He was not amused when the ebullient Lionel Tennyson decided to pull his leg about his alleged slow scoring. Now Tennyson deeply respected his batsman's ability and soundness and knew that the jibes pricked him deeply. One day, as Mead proceeded in his usual, unhurried way to the inevitable century, Tennyson arranged to have a telegram sent out to the middle. The captain and the other professionals watched with glee as Mead looked quizzically at the messenger, opened the envelope and read the missive: 'Mead – get on or get out – Tennyson.'

Mead's solemn nature left him bereft of intimate companions in the Hampshire dressing-room. He and Jack Newman were fairly close through their passion for horse racing and they would dolefully share hard-luck stories, but the charges of selfishness were regularly laid at Mead's door. The talent money system used by Hampshire meant that scores of 49 and 99 were not only frustrating but cost him money. The desire for 'another bag of coal for the winter' meant he was an unreliable judge of a run at certain periods of his innings, and invariably he would be the one to survive muddles that originated with him. In his last season in the Hampshire side it was common knowledge that his team-mates were vying with each other to run him out at every opportunity. They failed: he was not run out once in 1936. Philip Mead often had the last word – with colleagues as well as opposition fast bowlers.

Bill Bowes recalled an incident which suggested that all was not well between Mead and his team-mates. Hampshire had been caught on a vile sticky wicket, and Yorkshire's Hedley Verity was running through the side. Mead, a great defensive player on bad wickets, was combating Verity with immense skill and application. Finally he accepted the single that Verity had been offering to get him away from the strike and, as he ran to the other end, he said, 'Don't think I don't know what you're up to, but it's time the youngsters learned how to bat.' Yet it was his job to take Verity and save the game.

Did he have a batting weakness? R.E.S. Wyatt, one of the shrewdest of cricket judges, thought he could be worried by in-swingers to a legside field. Reg Sinfield agreed, remembering bowling the best three consecutive balls of his career to dismiss Mead. 'I always kept a mental note of the way the top batsmen played,' he explained, 'and Phil would get off the mark most of the time by tickling one round the corner. When he came in, I asked for no less than four short-legs, even though my off-spin would be leg-breaks to the left-hander. My captain, Bev Lyon, thought I was mad but I got my own way. First ball, he was plumb lbw and given "not out", the next one was dropped at the wicket and the third time the keeper managed to hang onto the catch! Phil wasn't best pleased.'

He never was, if it meant going back to the pavilion, his cigarettes and the racing page. They could always wait for the interval, when he could reflect on how many bags of coal lay within his compass that day. Percy Fender, his *bête noire*, winkled him out one day with a typically creative piece of captaincy. Mead was making his inexorable progress towards lunch with twenty or so runs against his name. Fender suddenly realised that Mead had never seen Bob Gregory bowl his slow leg-spin that hardly ever turned. 'I put Bob on for the last over before lunch and told him to pitch them up. Mead had no idea what was in store, so I placed three fielders round the corner on the legside with exaggerated care. Mead kept shuffling into his stance and looking around at the leg-trap, and I could see his mind ticking over. For the first three balls, he pushed out suspiciously and each time, after playing the stroke, he would look round at the three legside fielders. The fourth delivery didn't turn at all, it came straight on a little quicker, Mead played for the turn, the ball got an outside edge and slip caught it.' A tactical coup for Fender but at the same time it was a tribute to the respect he had for Mead that he realised something unorthodox was needed to prise him out before he settled in to his post-prandial, prolific groove.

In his last season he predictably scored his 1,000 runs, including two hundreds. Hampshire, recognising his gargantuan feats for them, paid his salary for another year and opened a subscription for him. Just before the Second World War, he played Minor Counties cricket for Suffolk – averaging 76 and 71 – and coached at Framlingham College. Alec Bedser played against him for Surrey Seconds in 1939 and remembers Mead scoring 132 in about three hours. 'He didn't run around much, he seemed to hit the ball hard and with no apparent effort. His eyes were going a little, but he hit everything in the middle of the bat.'

Tragically he went blind after running a sports shop in Southampton and a pub near Bournemouth and often turned up at Dean Park, where he was a shy, modest visitor to the Hampshire dressing-room. John Arlott thought he had mellowed over the years and was an agreeable companion: 'He would never criticise the modern players. He thought he would have had trouble with the in-swingers and negative field placings of the modern game' – perhaps he remembered his occasional problems with Sinfield and being outwitted by Fender. Although completely blind, Mead would sit happily discussing cricket, able to tell whether someone was playing well by the sound of his bat: 'He's not middlin' 'em, is he?' he would chuckle. How appropriate – an innings by Mead had its own distinct sound, one of solidity as the ball met the middle of a staunch, unyielding bat.

He died in 1958, a few days after his 71st birthday. He had faced his blindness as calmly as the thunderbolts of 'Tibby' Cotter when he made his impressive debut – 41 not out – for Hampshire against the Australians in 1905. His death brought a re-assessment of his worth, an acknowledgement that you cannot be a stodgy player and score 55,000 runs (all of them in three-day games), and the fervent wish that more players with his defence and sheer competence would soon appear on the horizon. Hardly any did, and it would have been instructive to step into a time machine, whisk Philip Mead into the 1970s and watch him cope with the aggression and intimidation of Thomson, Lillee, Holding, Roberts, Imran Khan and Croft.

Alec Kennedy, his old team-mate, used to say that only Jack Hobbs rivalled Mead's ability to score a run off every ball, if he so wished. Kennedy paid tribute to Mead's ability on turning wickets: 'He almost seemed to prefer batting when the ball was doing something.' Philip Mead preferred batting full stop; or rather he preferred making runs, not less than 1,609 of them in a six-week period in 1921, or in 1927 a matter of 1,257 in fourteen innings. He was twice top of the national batting averages, second three times and third on four occasions.

Unwittingly Mead's immovability led to the blossoming of one of the greatest medium-pace bowlers of all time. On 26 July 1922 Hampshire was making slow progress against Sussex at Eastbourne. Philip Mead was batting in his detached style, and Maurice Tate was bored and frustrated. His career as an off-spinner was stagnating, and he was making few runs to boot. As he ran up to bowl to the stolid Mead for the umpteenth time, he suddenly decided to bowl the fastest delivery of his life out of sheet frustration. It pitched on his leg-stump and whipped across at great speed to hit the top of the off-stump. Tate, sufficiently encouraged by the dismissal, took to the nets, perfected his style and, within two years, he was a great bowler. Towards the end of his life Mead confessed he had been greatly surprised by the quality and speed of that delivery. When asked if he had said anything to Tate as he passed him en route to the pavilion, Mead chuckled and revealed the attitude of the run machine: 'Say anything? Not me, I never encouraged bowlers!' No, no one could ever suggest that of Philip Mead.

5

Patsy Hendren

'One day he will be given out, smile before wicket'
(Neville Cardus)

Elias Henry Hendren

Born

Turnham Green, London

5 February 1889

Died

Tooting Bec, London

4 October 1962

First hundred

134*   Middlesex v Sussex, Lord's, 1911
Age: 22 years 121 days

100th hundred

100   MCC v Victoria, Melbourne, 1928
Age: 39 years 272 days

Last hundred

103   Middlesex v Surrey, Lord's, 1937
Age: 48 years 206 days

Career record

M	Inn	NO	HS	Runs	Average	100s	50s
833	1,300	166	301*	57,611	50.80	170	275

Test record

M	Inn	NO	HS	Runs	Average	100s	50s
51	83	9	205*	3,525	47.63	7	21

The batting record of Patsy Hendren is a towering monument to his ageless skills, but it tells only part of the story of this most lovable of men. If he had been a mediocre player who passed through first-class cricket for a couple of seasons, he would nevertheless have left warm memories of a man who believed in entertainment, in free expression of personality.

A look at his achievements first. Only Jack Hobbs has beaten his 170 centuries, and just Hobbs and Frank Woolley have passed his total of 57,611 runs. In the list of double centurions, his total of 22 is third to Bradman and Hammond. He was the most prolific scorer of runs in the 1920s – 28,711 – and only Hammond has scored more in any decade. After a traumatic start his Test career blossomed, and in 51 Tests he averaged 47 with seven hundreds. He made more centuries at Lord's – 74 – than anyone.

He was a thrilling batsman, incapable of ever being dull, a compact parcel of energy. With a marvellous eye, supple wrists and dazzling footwork, he whacked the ball rather than steered it. He had all the shots, none more dazzling than the pull and the hook. G.O. Allen, his Middlesex colleague for many years, considered him one of the greatest players of slow bowling in the game's history. A complete craftsman with no real flaw, he may have lacked that intangible spark of genius but, for all that, he was one of the finest batsmen in the period between the two wars.

Patsy would be the last person to cavil, but I have always believed it unfair that his prodigious batting talents have been somewhat obscured by the laudable desire to pay tribute to his charming, spirited nature. On the other hand, it may be said that the batting style mirrors the man's character and, if you think about Bradman, about Hammond, Compton, Hutton, Boycott, or many other high-class players, the point is apposite. It was Patsy's generosity of spirit, his sense of fun and of honourable challenge that beguiled spectators and opponents alike and made him one of the most popular cricketers in the game's history. Those who witnessed his final match for Middlesex in 1937 still talk about the moment when 10,000 emotional spectators sang 'For He's A Jolly Good Fellow' as soon as he had reached his century. Ian Peebles, a team-mate for Middlesex and England, wrote, 'He had a talent for attracting the instant and lasting affection of all sections of society to a greater degree than any other sportsman or games player in my experience.' Joe Hardstaff, that fine Nottinghamshire batsman, told me: 'Happiness exuded from Patsy; he would walk into a room and immediately everyone would feel happier for his presence.'

Note the name 'Patsy'. He was christened Elias after being born in Chiswick of Irish parents, but no name was ever more unlikely for that sturdy india-rubber frame, for the owner of that long upper lip, mobile mouth, jolly round face and twinkling eyes. He looked Irish and so his team-mates called him 'Pat', his intimates 'Murphy'. Jack Hearne, his partner in so many productive stands, dubbed him 'Spud', while to the crowd he was ever 'Patsy'. No one could ever think of him as 'Hendren' in the way they would view Bradman,

Hammond, Sutcliffe with a proper mixture of awe and respect. No sensible person ever held Patsy in awe. As Neville Cardus put it so evocatively, 'His smile says Patsy – one day he will be given out, smile before wicket.' Even *Wisden* relaxed its magisterial guard to pronounce in its obituary of Patsy Hendren that 'no game in which he was engaged could be described as dull.'

No doubt Patsy was responsible for some fairly effervescent games in the back streets of Chiswick when he was a lad at the turn of the century. His origins were as humble as could be imagined: one of six children of Irish parents, both of whom were dead by the time he was fourteen. Lamp posts and trees were the wickets for Patsy, yet he managed to develop a batting potential that ran in the family – his brother, Denis, played for Northamptonshire without ever rivalling Patsy's ability. At the age of fifteen, Patsy was playing for Turnham Green, watched benignly by an old bearded man who knew a little about the game. 'That's right, young 'un,' he would say, 'hit 'em like that and you'll play for England.' The bluff character with the beard was W.G. Grace, now living in the capital and playing occasionally for London County. At about the same time J.T. Hearne, the great Middlesex bowler, brought a side over to play the local team and Patsy made a good impression by batting capably through four overs against Tom Richardson, not the great Richardson of old, it is true, but still a lively proposition on the uncertain Chiswick Park wicket.

Also playing that day was G.W. Beldam, the Middlesex opening bowler and cricket photographer. He managed to arrange an interview at Lord's with the captain, Gregor MacGregor, who told Patsy; 'You must eat more pudding if you want to become a cricketer.' Perhaps the Cambridge graduate, England wicket-keeper, Scottish rugby international and successful businessman did not realise that puddings were fairly scarce in the Hendren home. Patsy did not take it to heart, was greatly encouraged and in 1905 he was on the Lord's staff, selling scorecards and bowling in the nets for hours to wealthy MCC members.

He had enjoyed no formal coaching, a fact that did not escape the attention of Pelham Warner. The England captain was one of those kindly amateurs who believed in picking out young talent, nurturing and encouraging it through a period of years, in the belief that it would eventually flourish. He was often proved correct – the careers of Harry Lee and Jack Hearne bear witness – and, in the case of Patsy Hendren, his support eventually triumphed. It was Patsy's fielding that impressed Warner in those early days at Lord's; almost to the end of his career, Patsy remained a wonderful fielder, either in the outfield or in the slips. Warner felt that anyone who could field so decisively had cricket in his blood. So Patsy made his Middlesex debut in 1907, batting number eight, and for the eight seasons until the war the encouragement of Warner was not rewarded by any consistency. When war broke out, he was nearly 26; he had played 131 championship matches and scored just over 5,000 runs, for an average of nearly 30. Was the legendary Warner talent-spotting on the decline?

The first season after the war marked the start of Patsy's advance towards batting maturity: he scored 1,655 runs at an average of 61, then 2,520 also at 61 the following year, and in 1920/21 he travelled with the England team to Australia. The next phase of his career had begun and, in common with the previous stages, he met with adversity right away. Although he scored three fifties in his first three Tests in Australia, he was never very impressive, even though prolific in the State games. Back home in England, the pattern was more pronounced – he made 2,000 runs in the 1921 season, yet just 17 runs in four innings for England. Gregory and MacDonald were too much for him, and he was still very nervous on the big occasions. At Trent Bridge he was bowled second ball by a vicious break-back, he ran out Donald Knight in the second innings and at Lord's he was bowled third ball. The cynics had a field day about 'Warner's pet', that he only played for England because he was a Middlesex man.

He had to live with the jibes about his Test Match temperament for several seasons as he piled up massive scores for Middlesex in delightful style. He began to assert himself in 1924/25 against Australia, averaging 39, then in 1926 he scored his first Test hundred against them. Another followed on Jardine's tour of 1928/29 and thereafter he was more or less a fixture in a very strong England batting line-up. On the 1929/30 England tour of the West Indies he not only established himself as the number one folk hero, but he broke all records for an overseas season – 1,766 runs, average 126 (including four double hundreds), and in Tests he averaged 115 for 693 runs. His handling of the fast bowlers on that tour was, in the opinion of George Gunn and Wilfred Rhodes, the finest they had seen: he hooked and pulled Constantine with thrilling control. He patented one stroke that was pure Patsy: to a short ball outside his off-stump, he would draw back from the wicket and slash out with his arms fully extended. Half cut, half square drive, the ball would travel at blistering speed between point and cover. On the hard, fast West Indian wickets, it was a productive shot and the crowds, accustomed to expressive batting, adored him. His antics kept them constantly amused. One of his favourite tricks in the West Indies was to creep in close on the legside as the bowler was running in; the spectators would shout 'Watch dat man; watch dat Patsy!', the batsman would be alerted and Patsy would make a great show of feigned petulance that he had been rumbled. For the rest of his days in cricket, Patsy would tell the tale with inspired mimicry.

F.R. Brown confirmed to me the quality of Patsy's mimicry, especially of the West Indian accent – 'He'd say "Hello dere, man" to anyone in the dressing room.' One day Patsy saw the chance to outwit his great West Indian friend Learie Constantine, and he enlisted Freddie Brown's help. 'We were both playing for the MCC and Patsy asked me to bowl a googly on middle and leg for Constantine. He was sure that Learie would try to lap it and, sure enough, he did. Patsy caught him at deep square leg and, as the ball was going towards him in the air, he was chuckling. He caught it and said to Learie: "Dere you are, man, dere you are." Even Learie had to laugh at the quality of the accent.'

He was no less popular in Australia. The Hill at Sydney, never the subtlest or friendliest area, took Patsy to their heart. They enjoyed his dazzling out-fielding, the way he caught the ball in baseball fashion in front of his head, the good-natured reaction to an apple being thrown at him (take a bite and bowl it back at them) and his habit of jumping the fence and swigging a beer at the fall of a wicket. Once a barracker on the Hill called him an 'ugly little b--------' and Patsy, recognising that at least two-thirds of the description was accurate, nevertheless decided to seek revenge. He told the barracker he would be over to see him at the fall of a wicket; eventually he started to climb over the fence in search of the loud-mouthed drunk, and the Hill cheered Patsy to the echo as his taunter fled.

Patsy's humour was good-natured, uncomplicated and, above all, he knew when to stop. Japes would come to him spontaneously, as R.E.S. Wyatt once discovered in a friendly match in South Africa. Patsy was playing for the opposition scratch side, and Ian Peebles was partnering Wyatt, a man who always saw the serious side of cricket, whether or not the game was of first-class status. No one could ever accuse Patsy of that frame of mind and, when Peebles played forward and missed, Patsy, fielding at mid-on, shouted, 'Come on, he's missed it!' Peebles, assuming the wicket-keeper had fumbled the ball for byes, raced up the pitch to find Wyatt still in his ground. It suddenly dawned on both men that mimicry of the Wyatt voice had just been added to the copious Hendren comic repertoire.

R.W.V. Robins fell victim to a similar trick in a championship match one damp afternoon at Derby. Patsy always admired the way Robins played the spinners – he would get down the pitch, trust his luck and play them defensively on the walk if he could not drive. If he missed the 'walking shot', he would carry on to the pavilion, leaving the formality of a stumping. This particular day Tommy Mitchell was plying his leg-spin and Robins, playing the 'walking shot', missed and kept walking. Patsy, his partner, shouted 'Get back, he's missed it!' Robins spun round and did a spectacular crash-dive into his crease. As he collected the vestiges of his dignity, and deplored his muddy shirt, he looked up to see the bails on the ground and the wicket-keeper in idle chatter with his slips. Stumped Hendren, bowled Hendren.

During one match at Trent Bridge Jack Hearne was up till dawn playing cards and drinking. He and Patsy were the not out batsmen overnight, and Hearne was in a dreadful state when play resumed. He implored Patsy to look after him, to keep him away from Larwood until he had sorted himself out. Patsy was typically solicitous, led him onto the pitch and escorted him out to the wicket, all the while enquiring after the health of his colleague, who was too occupied moaning about the bright glare of the sun. Patsy said when they reached the middle, 'I reckon we're a little early, Jack, we're the only ones out here,' and in his befuddled state, Hearne believed him and sat down. It was only when he heard the cries in the distance that it dawned on him – Patsy had edged him forty yards away from the umpires and fielders, and he was sitting on a spot halfway to the boundary.

He would delight in foxing both spectators and players about the true destination of the ball. One of his favourite tricks was to chase after the ball, stop, seem to pick it up and stand there. As the batsmen hesitated over another run, they could not be sure whether the ball was twenty yards past Patsy or in his hand. Once he gulled Surrey's Alan Peach when fielding at long on; he caught Peach's straight drive one-handed, put it straight into his pocket and looked around for the ball. Peach assumed he had hit a six and, as it was the end of the over, Patsy walked towards the middle. When he reached Peach, he said, 'What are you doing here, Alan?' and, when Peach replied that he had hit a six, Patsy produced the ball and said; 'No you didn't, I caught you.' Even the umpires were unsure. Joe Hulme, a Middlesex team-mate, also fell victim to Patsy's spontaneous humour when Errol Holmes swept a ball to long leg at The Oval. Hulme lost it in the background of the gasometers and Patsy shouted, 'There it is, Joe.' Hulme, an athletic man, flung himself full length, only to discover that he had frightened a low-flying blackbird. The ball had already hit the fence before he started to dive.

Alf Gover ran up to bowl at Patsy one day, all fire and brimstone and rumbling effort, only to collapse with laughter, because Patsy was sticking his tongue out at him. Gover is the source of another story that is classic Patsy. In 1928 Gover was a young, enthusiastic quick bowler, anxious to make a name for himself and unworried about how many batsmen he frightened out in the process. He was playing at Lord's for the first time and met Patsy in the dressing-room. Patsy eyed him up and down and said, 'Are you fast?' On receiving the expected affirmation from the cocky young Gover, Patsy said, 'Well, go easy on me, young feller. I'm getting on and you might hit me.' Gover had no qualms about 'going easy' on this rotund little man and, when Patsy came in, he had three balls to face from Gover. He hooked the first one for four, crashed the next to the third man boundary and the next was hooked for six. Gover said, 'I thought he had just been lucky until Jack Hobbs asked me what I was playing at when the over ended. When I told Jack what Patsy had said, he burst out laughing and told me Patsy was the best hooker in the world. For the rest of his career, Patsy would ask me for a short one to get him off the mark!'

Patsy's fondness for the hook brought him injury just once. In 1931 he was badly hit on the head by Harold Larwood, and many on the field thought he was dead. Joe Hardstaff was at cover point and recalled, 'His back legs were twitching as he lay motionless on the ground. He was carried off the field, and we were all terribly upset.' Patsy was taken unconscious to hospital but was back on the field within three weeks. Even then he turned that frightening event into comic advantage two years later when he wore the first protective helmet against the West Indians, Constantine and Martindale. It had three peaks, the brainchild of his wife, and Patsy said he was wearing it because at his age (44) he did not want to be badly injured by the fast bowlers. That season he scored more than 3,000 runs with eleven centuries. As Alf Gover had discovered, the old boy could be a supreme bluffer.

Patsy never experienced that perceptible deterioration in powers that so perturbed Jack Hobbs. In his last season, at the age of 50, he scored over 1,800 runs and he was still perfectly capable of delighting the crowd on a batting as well as a comic level. When he was asked why he had decided to retire, he replied: 'While you can still say why, rather than when.' It had given him immense pleasure to play O'Reilly so capably when he encountered the great Australian leg-spinner for the first time in 1934; although O'Reilly dismissed him four times in the Test series, Patsy scored three hundreds against him, including one for England – at the age of 45.

Near the end of his career, he was delighted to play alongside two youngsters who shared his view that cricket was a game of fun. Bill Edrich and Denis Compton joined the Lord's staff at the same time, and they idolised Patsy; they could not believe that the great man would want to spend so much time in their naïve company, but they were wrong. He never turned them away, quite the reverse. He would often say, 'Now, lads, come and sit over here for a minute and I'll tell you about Joe Small in the West Indies back in '29.' Bill Edrich told me that he learned more about cricket from Patsy in his early days than from anyone since. He recalls the game against Somerset in 1937, when Patsy showed him how to play that splendid left-arm spinner, Jack White. 'Watch my feet,' Patsy told him. 'You need to get far enough down the wicket to play the half volley; don't be afraid to get close to the ball.' Both men got hundreds that day. Denis Compton remembered Patsy's advice one day when he came in to face two fairly quick bowlers: 'I hope you've got your box on today, son?' Above all, Patsy was always there, never too busy to impart a few technical tips to the two youngsters; when rain stopped play, it was a consolation to know that soon Patsy would come over and say, 'Right, lads, let's have a little chat.'

He was even more generous with his time when he retired from first-class cricket. He coached at Harrow, then with Sussex, and from 1952 to 1960 he was the Middlesex scorer. Patsy was no Bill Frindall at that job, he was never particularly good at sums, and he could easily be distracted by the presence of some old playing chums in the scorers' box. Current players from other counties would seek him out, a fact that touched him. He always loved the young – from his blissfully happy marriage there were no children – and they gravitated to a simple, lovable man, a man without conceit about his tremendous record. The players from that Middlesex era in the 1950s speak with unaffected love of him, remarking on his one idiosyncrasy: he was very particular about who drove him to the various county fixtures. Edrich and

Compton, his two pre-war protégés, were on Patsy's blacklist, they were just too fast behind the wheel. He preferred speed over a distance of 22 yards.

Eventually, the duties of scorer became too much for him and he retired in 1960. One night his wife was woken by what seemed like a large sob by her husband. A qualified nurse, she deduced he had suffered a stroke. He died in a London hospital in May 1962, aged 73. Earlier that month his brother Denis also passed away.

At his death Sir Jack Hobbs said that Patsy 'was as good a player as anyone' and, if that was a typically kind remark, it was Hobbs' own way of making the cricket world realise that there was far more to Patsy Hendren than his delightful personality. Les Ames considered him a wonderful player of slow bowling: 'I used to look forward to his duels with "Tich" Freeman. Patsy went further down the wicket to him than anyone I can remember.' F.R. Brown, another fine leg-spinner, said everyone relished the challenge of bowling at Patsy: 'I could never see him coming down the wicket but, as my arm would be coming over, he'd be two yards down the pitch. If you beat him, he'd grin and say "well bowled"; he always had a smile for you, and I consider him one of the most endearing men I've met anywhere.' Bill Bowes remembered a wonderful exhibition by Hendren on a drying pitch against Wilfred Rhodes at Bradford in 1929. 'It was an education to see him get down the pitch to the greatest bowler I've seen and flat-bat him through the covers. Twice he hit Wilfred into the football ground and then we thought we'd got him when he slipped – but, as he fell forward, he managed to kill the ball. Wilfred took his sweater; he'd had enough of this man.' Hendren that day, batting at number four, got 116 not out in a total of 154.

He was a bad starter and, like Denis Compton, an unpredictable runner. (A soccer player of professional status, too, Hendren played for England in a Victory international in 1919; he was very quick on his feet and on the turn, but he sometimes forgot that his partners lacked his dynamism.) He could never learn to open his account in the leisurely manner of a Hobbs, languidly playing the ball to cover and trotting home. Patsy wore his nervous heart on his sleeve and his first run was completed with open delight, hugging the bat in his arms as if someone was going to take it away from him. Perhaps that was part of Patsy's appeal; he was fallible, human, he knew what failure was like and the deprivations stemming from grinding poverty.

He had no idiosyncrasies in batting, other than a backside that jutted out defiantly in his low stance. He had great strength of wrist and arm, which helped him control the blade and give power to the easy circular sweep of his bat. When playing forward, he compensated for his lack of height by getting a great distance to the pitch of the ball, with arms that were thrust out to their full extent. Those powerful wrists would allow him to clip a short-length ball through the covers without lofting it, and for the hook shot he would pick the length of the ball quickly, his excellent footwork would get him into the right position – back and into the wicket – and he would play the shot down with horizontal bat. He could usually play the hook in front of square, the hallmark of a top-class player.

He played against Grace and Trumper, and his career in the game lasted more than fifty years. His mentor, Sir Pelham Warner, survived him for just one year. He lived to see the end of Compton's career and the start of Geoffrey Boycott's. Patsy proved he had the character to supplement his innate skill, and he remained an inspiration to the young. He was not the ideal senior professional, because he lacked the necessary steel to admonish. To Patsy life was about making people laugh, keeping the ball down in the hook shot, wondering which of the youngsters could take a joke and leading a good Christian life. Jim Sims, hardly a po-faced character himself, summed up Patsy's common touch: 'Wherever he went, he was recognised by all manner of people. The cockney would say "Wotcher, Patsy", and the ordinary person would smile at him. At the end of a train journey the engine driver and his mate would lean out of the cab and nod. Patsy would go to them and give them a couple of half crowns, thanking them for getting him back home.'

A devout Roman Catholic, he would never spurn fund-raising activities at his local church. He was methodical and precise in his habits and, in clear, beautifully legible style, would answer every letter he received. Once he had a letter from a French monastery; some Irish trainee priests were asking him for details of cricket gear, the best value, etc. etc. By return post Patsy sent them all the equipment they needed, free of charge.

He never forgot the favours afforded him when he was a pallid little orphan in need of a few puddings. No one ever starved at Patsy Hendren's cricketing table – players, umpires, spectators, they all got second helpings.

6

Frank Woolley

'To see a hundred by Woolley would keep you going for years'
(Bill Bowes)

Frank Edward Woolley

Born

Tonbridge, Kent

27 May 1887

Died

Halifax, Nova Scotia, Canada

18 October 1978

First hundred

116   Kent v Hampshire, Tonbridge, 1906
Age: 19 years 23 days

100th hundred

176   Kent v Middlesex, Lord's, 1929
Age: 42 years 93 days

Last hundred

162   Kent v Sussex, Tunbridge Wells, 1938
Age: 51 years 29 days

Career record

M	Inn	NO	HS	Runs	Average	100s	50s
979	1,532	85	305*	58,969	40.75	145	295

Test record

M	Inn	NO	HS	Runs	Average	100s	50s
64	98	7	154	3,283	36.07	5	23

No batsman has hit the ball harder or further for a longer period of time than Frank Woolley. In the opinion of many good judges, he was the greatest left-hander the game has ever seen, even if Mead was statistically more impressive, Leyland had a better Test record and Sobers proved his greatness in a later period. Woolley batted with a grace, power and individuality that charmed the critics and brought grudging admiration from his opponents. Neville Cardus waxed more lyrically about Woolley than any other player ('When he was out, it seemed as if the sun had set'), but hard-headed Yorkshiremen like Bill Bowes were equally impressed: 'To see a hundred by Woolley would keep you going for years.'

Patsy Hendren, not surprisingly, had *le mot juste* for Woolley: 'Here comes the lion-tamer,' he would say as he made his angular, stiff-legged way to the crease. At six feet three inches, Woolley justified the soubriquet 'Stalky' that his colleagues bestowed upon him but, once he had taken guard, the harsh edges disappeared from his style. It was almost impossible to bowl a good length to a man so tall: he could transform anything into a half volley or long hop without major adjustment of feet or body. He hit like a golfer; a wide swing allowed him to time his shot to the appropriate length and away the ball would soar. He stroked, rather than hit, the ball, playing with an ease that was positively tranquil. The contrast between the sweating, straining fast bowler and the dismissive air with which Woolley would deal with the deliveries was remarkable. Yet he seemed the soul of courtesy as he stroked twenty runs in an over. Somehow the game did not have any harsh or combative overtones when Woolley batted; unassertively, inscrutably, he would annihilate great bowlers with the kind of detachment a butler uses when he passes the sherry.

There were no airs or graces about Frank Woolley, no overt concessions to the crowd. He lacked the common touch of Hendren, indeed he never once dreamed of playing to the gallery. He knew the spectators were happy enough with him as a cricketer – and so were most of his opponents in those more chivalrous, unsophisticated days. At Canterbury in 1930 Woolley toyed with the Australians with his usual languid radiance, quickly reaching his half-century and taking a liking to Alan Fairfax's medium pace in the meantime. Fairfax, perturbed that the ball kept disappearing over the long-on and mid-wicket boundaries, asked his captain, Vic Richardson, if it was all right to keep bowling at Woolley's off-stump. Richardson replied with relish: 'All right, it's bloody marvellous, we're enjoying it!'

His method was simplicity itself. He would stand as upright as possible at the crease with hands high on the long-handled bat and feet slightly apart. He would pick up his bat with a long, easy sweep and it would come firmly down, close to the line of the off-stump. The great South African left-hander Graeme Pollock would be the closest comparison in recent decades. As Bill Bowes remembered with a shudder, 'He was always in a position to hit you off front foot or back.' R.E.S. Wyatt studied his method many times when they batted together: 'He was so perfectly poised. He could assume rapidly another position while retaining his initial balance. Even when bowled, he looked graceful. He played with such ease that I cannot remember seeing him in a defensive position – and there was no point in bowling short at him, he would swat it away, half-pull, half-hook. His straight driving was absolutely devastating: I have never seen anyone hit the ball harder back over the bowler's head.'

Les Ames, who partnered Woolley in so many thrilling assaults for Kent, said Woolley's elegant dominance stemmed from steely determination. 'He simply would not be dictated to. He often used to say to me, "This chap's bowling too well, we've got to get after him," and he led the attack.' Ames, vastly experienced and not the kind of man to live in the past, thought Ian Botham the only man who could latterly be compared to Woolley in attitude and power of strokes, but Ames maintained that Botham could not play the kind of innings he saw at Bradford in 1931 against Yorkshire. 'We had been put in on a wet wicket, and Hedley Verity looked unplayable. I came in and Frank said to me, "I don't know who this new bowler is, but he's good – I'll take him." He did so, and he pulverised Verity.' Woolley made 188 out of 296 for four on a dreadful wicket. It took him 3½ hours and included seven sixes, five off Verity. One of the other two sixes came off the bowling of Bill Bowes, a shot he will never forget. 'It was the last ball before lunch,' Bowes told me, 'and when I saw him coming down the pitch at me, I pitched it short. He hit it on the up, and it sailed over the pavilion at long on. Up and up it went; it was like a pea in the distance, right out of the ground. He hit me further than anyone ever managed, and I was pretty quick in those days, I can tell you . . .'

That Bradford innings was typical of the flavour of Woolley's batting: it had a wonderful, quixotic gallantry about it, especially when he was tilting at the fast bowlers. An innings by Woolley never seemed to last very long – few of the good things in life do – and that ephemeral quality added to the attraction of the man. English spectators, accustomed to mundane feats, would hug themselves with glee when Woolley was at the crease: he played the same way all his life, whatever his score. He was out 35 times in the nineties, and he made nought 89 times. On his retirement he wrote, 'It was never a question of the nervous nineties, I was out many times forcing the game. We were never allowed to play for our averages in the Kent side or take half an hour to get the necessary ten runs.' That unselfish attitude, and the precarious nature of his batting, should be borne in mind when the statistically-minded consider his career record.

Very well, let us examine his statistical achievements. A career average of 40.75 and one of 36.07 in Tests does not look terribly impressive in the context of an age of batting cornucopia. Yet any man who consciously took the risks that he did would be more than happy with a run-tally of 58,969 (second only to Hobbs), a total of 145 centuries (seventh in the list), and a little matter of 1,000 runs in 28 seasons (a shared record with Grace). Let us not forget his other cricketing qualities – the greatest number of catches by a fielder (1,018) and more than 2,000 wickets with slow left-arm bowling that, in the opinion of the Kent wicket-keeper Fred Huish, was superior to that of the brilliant Colin Blythe. He performed the 'double' of 2,000 runs and 100 wickets four times, a record, and did 'the double' of 1,000 runs and 100 wickets eight times. Of course, Woolley played a long time to build up such impressive figures but, by any standards, he was one of the greatest all-round cricketers the game has known. And entertainment, not statistical prowess, was his abiding aim.

Scores of batsmen have more impressive Test records, but I wonder how many of them could have played the type of innings he played at Lord's in June 1921? Twice Woolley led England from parlous starts to some sort of respectability, but it was the manner of his counter-attacks against Gregory and MacDonald that was so thrilling and legendary. On a fiery wicket, against great bowlers backed up by brilliant fielding, Woolley scored 95 and 93 out of 187 and 283; he was stumped in the first innings, going for his shots with the last man in, and his dismissal in the second innings was a freak, Hendry miraculously catching a pull from a long hop. That was the way Woolley played his cricket; runs for the side were more important than the prestige of Test centuries. In his retirement Woolley modestly reasoned that both innings were worthy of 150 in normal circumstances, and cricket history has accorded them a deserved status.

It has always seemed appropriate that Woolley played for Kent. The tents, the bunting, the animated atmosphere of those intimate grounds in the hop county seemed to strike a chord in him. He came into the Kent side when their reputation for dynamic, attractive cricket was deservedly high, and for the next 32 years Woolley did nothing to dim its lustre. Genius has no geographical limitations, and one can only speculate how much encouragement he would have received if he had wandered down to the county ground at Derby, Leicester or Edgbaston in those days. Would he have been able to bowl in the nets with an England cricketer when he was just twelve years of age? That was the happy introduction of Frank Woolley to Kent cricket. Born and reared in Tonbridge he just picked up the game along with his brothers, one of whom later played for Gloucestershire and Northants. One day he happened to be standing at a net on the Angel cricket ground, watching a slow left-armer practising. Asked if he bowled, Woolley confirmed that he was of the same style and was asked to join in. The youngster was sufficiently impressive to be told to keep in touch with officials at the county ground. He needed no second bidding, and he remained deeply grateful to his partner in that first net practice, Colin Blythe.

Blythe's acumen was rewarded by encouraging words from the Kent manager, Tom Pawley, and Woolley developed his bowling and batting under Blythe's benevolent tutelage. In 1906, when he was 19, Woolley made his debut for Kent – ironically Blythe was injured – and his experiences in that game would have been enough to daunt lesser men.

On a hot, sunny June day Woolley walked onto the turf at Old Trafford, unaware that the next six hours' play would stay forever in his memory. Despite his ability as a slip fielder, he was initially posted at third man, to face the dazzling square-cutting of one of the shot's greatest exponents, J.T. Tyldesley. Soon Tyldesley launched into a low, skimming square cut that was nevertheless catchable. It hit Woolley on the breastbone, the batsmen ran three and the crowd laughed. He was moved to mid-on and, a few minutes later, dropped Tyldesley off a skier. It hit Woolley on the back of the neck. He never heard the cry of 'no-ball' so, as far as he was concerned, that was a dropped catch. He was moved to mid-off and two overs later he chased another skier from Tyldesley. He misjudged it, the ball hit his boot and Old Trafford hooted once more with derision at this gangling youth with no co-ordination. When he bowled his left-arm spin, Tyldesley climbed into him – he took one for 103 in 26 overs. At close of play, Lancashire were all out 531, Tyldesley 295. The following day Woolley, batting at number eight, was bowled third ball for nought. Could it possibly get worse? Happily he recovered his nerve and made a blistering 64 in the second innings. Soon he was scoring a hundred against Hampshire in ninety minutes – at Tonbridge, his home town.

His talent was remarkable, and his gaucheness and naivety were also a source of wonder and amusement. When he first played against Surrey, he had only heard of Tom Hayward among the opposition but had no idea where he batted and what he looked like. Midway through the Surrey innings, at the fall of a wicket, he said, 'When does Tom Hayward come in?' and was mortified to be told, 'He was the second man you bowled out.'

Woolley adorned that pre-war Kent side, but he was just one of many magnificent players. Kent won the championship in 1906, 1909, 1910 and 1913, and the influence of the amateur batsman confirmed his initial impression that the only way to bat was by attacking the bowlers. Subsequently Woolley always felt that the quality of cricket before 1914 was much higher than afterwards, that men like Hammond would need to be at the very peak of form to get in the England side. Woolley managed that in 1909 for the first time and he remained in it until 1926, an unbroken run of 52 consecutive Test appearances. His bowling was keeping pace with his thrilling batting – he performed the 'double' three times before he was 27 – and in the 1912 Oval Test against Australia his match analysis was ten for 49.

His most spectacular pre-war innings was in Hobart, Tasmania on the 1911/12 tour of Australia. He scored 303 not out, including two sixes and 47 fours, and owed it all to Sydney Barnes. Woolley had been complaining to Barnes that he never seemed to be batting higher than number seven on the trip and here he was in Hobart, down to bat at number eight. Barnes told him, 'As soon as our innings starts, get your pads on. Phil Mead's due in first wicket down, but I'll take care of that. Walk in to bat as soon as one of the openers is out.' Woolley did as he was told, and the captain, Frank Foster, did not know anything about the switch until he noticed Woolley thrashing the Tasmanian bowlers out of sight. The whereabouts of Mead have never been ascertained: perhaps the racing page had proved even more engrossing than usual.

It seems ironic that a man of Woolley's consummate batting ability should be turned down by the Army during the Great War because of poor eyesight. Cricket lovers can only be grateful to that unknown medical officer, otherwise Woolley might have suffered the same fate as his great friend and mentor, Colin Blythe – killed in France in 1917.

After the war Woolley still had twenty years' first-class cricket left in him, and his example ensured that Kent remained popular visitors on any ground. His attitude to batting never changed as his captain, Lord Cornwallis, once discovered. Woolley was destroying the Nottinghamshire attack with his familiar abandon, and the skipper suggested to him that he should consolidate his innings just a little. He was told in no uncertain terms, 'I can only play one game, Captain Cornwallis.' Woolley proceeded to hit the next four balls to the boundary and was caught off the fifth.

Only one way of playing, indeed – and a thrilling one it was. At Dover in 1937 he showed the Gloucestershire bowlers his way of playing. Kent needed 217 to win in 95 minutes and Woolley, going in first, set the tempo of the attack: he made 44 out of 68 in 25 minutes, and Kent won with 24 minutes to spare.

Jack Mercer told a lovely story that illustrates Woolley's supreme confidence: 'When we played Kent at Cardiff, I got Frank caught with a late in-swinger, which pleased me greatly. In the return game at Maidstone, I tried him again with a slowish in-swinger. He hit it straight back at me, I got a hand to it, yet it still went for six. Frank called to me that he'd been waiting to do that since Cardiff!'

Les Ames maintained that Woolley was the greatest entertainer of his age, apart from Bradman. 'Just look at the crowds he used to draw. The Kent match was invariably the choice of a beneficiary, because of Frank. Wherever we played, we got the best gates, due to his batting and influence on the rest of us. He could score so quickly that our bowlers had extra time to bowl the opposition out.' H.V. Levett – 'Hopper' Levett – was sent in as night-watchman ahead of Woolley for simple economic reasons. 'In those days the gate was vitally important, and Frank was such a great attraction that he would put thousands on the crowd. County treasurers couldn't afford to have him dismissed late in the day.'

Woolley suffered two major disappointments in his post-war career, and they both concerned Australia. In 1928 English batting was at a peak of efficiency, depth and variety that has not been emulated since. Woolley scored 3,352 runs, including twelve hundreds, yet was not selected for the winter tour to Australia. Maurice Leyland – thirteen years his junior – was picked ahead of him, a justified choice as it proved, but the selection of Mead was bitterly criticised. He was the same age as Woolley but lacked his bowling and fielding ability. The furore only served to confirm the affection that Kentish supporters felt for their languid hero, but Woolley kept a dignified silence on the matter.

In 1934 Woolley was unwisely recalled for the Fifth Test at the age of 47. The captain, R.E.S. Wyatt, felt he might demoralise O'Reilly but he made 4 and 0. Worse was to come: Les Ames ricked his back and Woolley had to keep wicket in the second innings. He let through 37 byes, extras was third top scorer in the innings and England lost by 562, a disastrous end to Woolley's Test career. Why a man of his age with no previous experience kept wicket is beyond my comprehension, and it was a sad experience for Woolley, one that he did not deserve.

He did deserve the accolades that came his way on his retirement in 1938. It was fitting that he should captain the Players in their match against the Gentlemen at Lord's. An abstemious, reserved man, he had done much to raise the status of the professional in his time. Woolley was respected by all cricketers, except for one man – Douglas Jardine. Woolley never forgot the autocratic way he was treated by Jardine, when he captained England against New Zealand at Lord's in 1931. It was bad enough to send a great slip fielder down to third man and fine leg without any explanation, but worse was to come. As the bowler ran up, Jardine stopped him imperiously and shouted, 'Go to B, Woolley' – the 'B' referring to the numbered sections of the grandstand. Still Jardine was not satisfied and one ball later halted play again and called out: 'I said B, Woolley, not C!' It was unforgivable behaviour towards a great cricketer, and Woolley felt he had been made to look inferior in front of a large crowd.

Woolley bore life's misfortunes with quiet stoicism – including the loss of his son on active service during the Second World War and when his house at Cliftonville was blown up. And only one thing used to rattle him as a player; he could never work out why he had been dismissed. Many old players have confirmed to me that Woolley would stand at his crease after he had been bowled, waiting in vain for a call of 'no ball'. Bill Bowes told me: 'Whenever he was out, he would keep looking over his shoulder on the way back, in case the umpire had changed his mind.' Les Ames remembered when he hit a ball straight to cover, who took it beautifully, but Woolley patted away at the pitch, getting ready for the next delivery, under the impression that it had been a bump ball. F.R. Brown told me that he once refused to go when he had bowled him out of the rough created by Alf Gover's footholds. Woolley asserted that the wicket-keeper had padded the ball onto the stumps and Frank Chester, that great umpire, had to tell Woolley to leave.'

Perhaps a remark made by Woolley on another occasion to Frank Chester gives some clue to his attitude to being dismissed. It was 1923, and Kent were playing Warwickshire at Dover; the young medium-pacer, R.E.S. Wyatt, had dismissed Woolley lbw in the first innings and then had him caught in the gully in the second. Chester gave him out unhesitatingly and Woolley stared down the wicket incredulously before departing. Afterwards Woolley told the umpire, 'I wasn't disputing your decision, Frank. I just couldn't believe that such an awful bowler could get me out twice!' Perhaps he was so confident of his ability, so sure in his touch that he convinced himself that he alone could get himself out, not any bowler.

Certainly the Australians were aware of Woolley's non-walking reputation. During the great innings of 93 in the 1921 Lord's Test, Nigel Haig walked out to join the valiant Woolley. On arriving at the wicket, he heard the following conversation between Woolley and the rumbustious Australian captain, Warwick Armstrong:

ARMSTRONG: 'Nobody but a bloody Pom would have stood there!'

WOOLLEY: 'Nobody but an Australian would have appealed in the first place.'

Flashpoints in Test matches are not the exclusive preserve of the 'action replay' era!

One more personal criticism of Woolley, and then an end to it: he was spectacularly mean. All of his contemporaries have told me this and, in most cases, they brought the subject up. It was common knowledge along the county grapevine that Woolley would permit himself an occasional drink as long as it was bought for him. No one I interviewed could recall him returning the favour. The scurrilous joke among the professionals during the 1930s was that he did once buy a drink on an Australian tour: a tonic water to share with his wife. The preoccupation with money shines through a revealing interview with David Frith in the *Cricketer* magazine in 1976. Just two years before his death, he was complaining that his abilities were not sufficiently rewarded in talent money, compared with others in the Kent side. He told Kent's president, Lord Harris, that an American had informed him he would earn far more by playing baseball and that he was tempted to give up cricket. Lord Harris promised Woolley a testimonial if he would continue in cricket, vowing, 'You'll get more than W.G. did.' Soon afterwards, Lord Harris died, and the fund for Woolley raised £900. Judging by the tenor of his remarks to David Frith, he felt he should have made immeasurably more money out of his career. That must have preyed on his mind in the 1950s when he was reduced to working at Butlin's Holiday Camp at Clacton, coaching guests and organising nets. At his death in 1978 another fund had been opened among Kent supporters to help pay for his medical fees, but it had about as much success as the one organised forty years previously.

It seemed a pity that money matters preyed on his mind, because he played like a millionaire. Even in the nets he hit the ball with devastating power, as Doug Wright confirmed: 'I would never bowl at him, because I couldn't get my length. I spent all the time dodging a ball that clattered straight back at me. You could tell by the look on his face that he didn't think much of bowlers.' Godfrey Evans, who was on the Kent staff for the last two years of Woolley's career, felt that only Ted Dexter hit the ball with comparable power, and Les Ames pointed out that he was different from the majority of great players because he consistently hit the ball in the air. 'He would back himself to clear the fielders. As I was next man in, I was always expecting to walk out at any time but, my word, he was rich entertainment.'

Ames considered his main weakness was against slow-bowling – he lacked the patience: 'He wouldn't dance down the wicket to them, but play them from the crease.' This view was supported by P.G.H. Fender, who often ensnared him with his leg spin: 'I always made sure my mid-on, Miles Howell, dropped back a little for him. If I dropped one short, he would hit it in the air and I had him caught once or twice by Howell. I remember also getting him with a faster, stiff-arm leg-break which bowled him.'

He was a magnificent player of fast bowling, and Ames said: 'He would have a field day against the modern fast bowlers who pitch it too short.' R.E.S. Wyatt agreed: 'His bat was all middle against the quick bowlers, he had so much time to spare.' Perhaps the need for quick singles would perturb Woolley if he came back today; he was a poor runner between the wickets with an irritating habit of turning after the first run and then stopping dead in his tracks after a couple of yards and watching the ball. Les Ames would always do the calling in their productive stands, to their mutual satisfaction, although when Woolley batted in his usual fashion, quick singles were never really necessary.

Woolley believed that it was a disadvantage to be a left-hander. He felt he had trouble coping with the bowler's rough which affected his cover driving and that he was vulnerable outside his off-stump because most right-arm bowlers could move the ball away from the left-hander's bat. He also thought the pre-1935 lbw law favoured right-handers; they could pad away with impunity to certain deliveries, whereas the left-hander was often more vulnerable.

The very idea of Frank Woolley complaining about having to use his bat is risible. No other great batsman seemed to relish more the impact of bat on ball; to shoulder arms would be an affront to his dignity. Perhaps he felt those dreadful umpires would spoil his fun if he let the ball hit his pads. Frank Woolley may have taken a slightly curmudgeonly view of life, but on the cricket field he spent his talents with the prodigality of a sailor on shore leave.

In his last years Woolley was still a remarkably handsome man: erect, bright-eyed, with an impressive head of full silver hair, he looked like one of those urbane Hollywood actors who played dignified old English gentlemen. He loved to sit quietly with his old colleagues at the Canterbury ground, and Doug Wright recalled his incredulity at the modern field-setting: 'But Doug, they've got no man out straight,' he would say. 'Why aren't they hitting them over the top?' How was Woolley to know that the game had become so esoteric, so competitive? Or was he still judging cricket in the best way – simply, sensibly and without jargon?

7

Herbert Sutcliffe

'Ah, Mr Warner, I love a dog-fight'

Herbert Sutcliffe

Born

Summerbridge, Yorkshire

24 November 1894

Died

Cross Hills, Yorkshire

22 January 1978

First hundred

145   Yorkshire v Northamptonshire, Northampton, 1919

Age: 24 years 241 days

100th hundred

132   Yorkshire v Gloucestershire, Bradford, 1932

Age: 37 years 227 days

Last hundred

107*   Yorkshire v Northamptonshire, Northampton, 1939

Age: 44 years 231 days

Career record

M	Inn	NO	HS	Runs	Average	100s	50s
747	1,088	123	313	50,138	51.95	149	227

Test record

M	Inn	NO	HS	Runs	Average	100s	50s
54	84	9	194	4,555	60.73	16	23

Herbert Sutcliffe's career is a marvellous testimony to the eminence that can be achieved by intelligence, application, soundness and, above all, a good temperament. His strokeplay was far inferior to that of Hobbs, Woolley, Hendren or Hammond, yet for a decade he was as indispensable to the England side as anyone.

He was a natural opener, the kind of man whom Alec Bedser craved during his tenure as chairman of the England selectors in the 1970s. He may have lacked elegance, variety of strokes and flair, but he knew his limitations, his value to the side and he had the confidence to force the pace if his captain demanded. Above all, Sutcliffe possessed the most remarkable self-confidence, to a degree only approached by W.G. Grace. His *sang froid* made Ian Botham look like a tremulous teenager in comparison. On the field Sutcliffe's demeanour graphically revealed his attitude: the bowlers were mere hewers of wood and drawers of water, there for his pleasure, indulgence and interest. If they managed to shave his stumps with a good delivery, that was due to an aberration on his part, not any merit by the bowler.

Once Alf Gover beat Sutcliffe seven times in two overs with classic break-backs and late movement off the seam. At the end of the second over, with Gover convinced the dismissal was only a matter of time, Sutcliffe leaned on his bat, crossed his legs and said, 'Well bowled, Alfred, I shall get a hundred now, I've got it out of my system.' He did, too. Bill Voce experienced the same reaction at Bramall Lane, Sheffield, after beating Sutcliffe five times in one magnificent over. At its end, Voce stood in the middle of the wicket and his frustrated cry was also tinged with admiration: 'Look at that b------, standing there as if he's just hit me for six sixes!'

One day Middlesex played Yorkshire, and G.O. Allen bowled fast and well right from the start. Early on, he bowled a superb out-swinger at Sutcliffe, the ball deviated after a loud snick and the appeal for a wicket-keeper's catch seemed a formality. Frank Chester, the umpire, rushed down to Sutcliffe's end, saw the mark of the new ball on the off-stump and said, 'I thought so, it hit the stump – not out.' But it was the attitude of Sutcliffe that astonished Allen: 'There he stood, leaning on his bat, looking around him, totally unperturbed as the rest of us chattered about my misfortune and Frank Chester's brilliant decision. To Herbert, the next ball was important, he could do nothing about the previous one.'

Sutcliffe demonstrated that unflappable quality to eleven incredulous Australians, two umpires and his batting partner at Sydney in December 1932. The situation was pure Sutcliffe; he had already survived one eight-ball over in which he played at and missed seven deliveries, and he scratched his way to 49 without ever looking comfortable. He then played a delivery from Bill O'Reilly hard onto his stumps without removing a bail. R.E.S. Wyatt, his partner at the other end, takes up the story: 'I've never seen a ball played so hard onto the wicket without dislodging a bail. Everyone gathered round the stumps, some of the Australians were blowing hard at the bails in amusement, some came up from the deep field to observe the phenomenon and Bill O'Reilly stood there, cursing his luck. Herbert stood apart from it all, waiting for the fuss to die down, so he could get back to work.' When the fielders had exhausted their vocabulary, Sutcliffe went on to make 194, his highest Test score.

Sutcliffe's self-confidence was so colossal, his temperament so serene, his batting methods so effective, that he must have been an immense morale-booster to any side as he walked out to bat. Jack Hobbs had four marvellous opening partners during his career, yet Sutcliffe was the only one on whom he sometimes seemed to rely. Just occasionally, the great man would appear fallible and Sutcliffe's tenacious presence would be vastly reassuring. After he retired, Hobbs would tell an affectionate story about the first time they opened against Australia. It was at Sydney in 1924 and Hobbs, in his usual custom, took the first over from Kelleway, a bowler with the ability to move the ball away late. In that over Hobbs gave a masterly demonstration of how to leave a ball swinging late – he was into position early, dropping his wrists at the right instant and, although Hobbs knew exactly what he was doing, he must have looked a little unsafe. At the end of that over, Sutcliffe came down the pitch and said to the Master: 'Best to leave the new ball alone, Jack.' As Hobbs later said affectionately, 'I knew we'd found the right opener for England.' How true – the fledgling Sutcliffe helped add 157 and 110 in that match, scoring a hundred on his debut against Australia.

It seemed that Sutcliffe could never countenance the possibility of being dismissed, an act of positive thinking that must have been of incalculable benefit to him. As Bill O'Reilly wrote, 'He would look down the pitch and sniff at you as if you were the bloke sent out to pick up bones.' At The Oval in 1926, Sutcliffe first shared in that wonderful partnership with Hobbs on a spiteful wicket, then, as the wicket eased, he carried the innings to give England an impregnable position. In the last over of the day, with his score on 161, he was bowled off his pads by Arthur Mailey and strode off, smacking his pads with his bat in disgust. It was not enough that he had played one of the great innings of all time; in his eyes Homer had nodded.

Neville Cardus gleaned a fascinating insight into the diamond-hard mind of Sutcliffe one morning at Leeds. Maurice Tate, one of the greatest of medium -pace bowlers, dismissed Sutcliffe with an unplayable delivery and, later in the pavilion, Cardus commiserated. 'What do you mean, bad luck?' was the Sutcliffe riposte. 'I could have played it, but a man in the pavilion moved.' As Cardus wrote, 'He was more than indignant; he was outraged. I had blotted the Sutcliffe family escutcheon.'

Lest anyone assume that Sutcliffe was a hoarder of runs for their own sake, a collector of not-outs to boost his average, I must come to his defence. None of his contemporaries I interviewed demurred from the statement of Norman Yardley: 'He was a thorough team man, dedicated to his side. If quick runs were needed, Herbert would do his absolute best to get them, even though foreign to his nature. No one could ever accuse Herbert of selfishness.' Both Yardley and Bill Bowes remembered vividly the treatment he handed out to Kenneth Farnes at Scarborough in 1932; Farnes was rash enough to feed Sutcliffe's favourite hook shot and, even with two deep fine legs, he hooked him time after time for six. He advanced from 100 to 194 in forty minutes and that night Farnes broke down and cried in front of Bowes, convinced that Sutcliffe had finished him as a bowler. Fortunately he recovered his self-respect, vowed never to bowl short again at Sutcliffe and played 15 times for England.

That knock at Scarborough was no isolated instance: in that same 1932 season, he hit eight sixes in his 132 against Gloucestershire and the bowling of Parker, Goddard, Sinfield and Hammond. The following year there was another splendid performance – 113 against Northants, including ten sixes, on a treacherous wicket. Northants had been bowled out for 27 before lunch, and Sutcliffe decided to attack the dangerous off-spin of V.W.C. Jupp. He scored his 113 out of 181 in two hours, and eight of his sixes came off Jupp's bowling, five of them in two overs.

R.E.S. Wyatt had fond memories of Sutcliffe's unselfishness. On the 1927/28 tour of South Africa, he opened with Sutcliffe against Eastern Province and in the second innings needed about 170 to win. Wyatt had entered the nineties, while his partner was in the seventies, and Sutcliffe said to Wyatt, 'Look here, you've got a chance to get a hundred, we need about twelve to win. Take the strike.' Wyatt, on his first England tour and anxious to make the Test side, needed no second bidding and gratefully reached his century. 'That was typical of Herbert,' he told me. 'Other great players would have tried to catch me up, to put me in my place. He was never the kind of man to thrust himself to the forefront and, what's more, he never avoided the nasty stuff, like some other big names.'

In his twenty years in first-class cricket, Sutcliffe scored 50,135 runs with 149 centuries. He never knew a period of prolonged failure at any stage and he passed 2,000 runs in a season on fourteen consecutive occasions. Three times he scored 3,000 runs in a season. He took part in 145 stands of more than a hundred for the first wicket, 69 of them with Percy Holmes and 26 with Jack Hobbs. His Test record is unsurpassed by an Englishman and only bettered by Don Bradman, Graeme Pollock and George Headley (the last two by a decimal point) – his average is 60.73 in all Tests and 66.85 against Australia, in his day the ultimate furnace of temperament. With a Test average almost nine runs above his overall first-class average, Sutcliffe was the Test Match batsman *par excellence*.

Despite his wonderful record he was always second best to his famous partners in the affection of the public. Jack Hobbs held a unique position in the cricket world before he ever opened with Sutcliffe, and nothing subsequently dimmed that lustre. Percy Holmes only played seven times for England, yet his brilliant batting regularly overshadowed the calm, measured contributions of Sutcliffe. Both men shared the same birthday, and a friendship that began in a Leeds train as they noticed each other's cricket bags continued for the rest of their lives. Sutcliffe always acknowledged the jaunty contributions of Holmes, his senior by seven years, and would never miss the opportunity to commiserate over his scanty number of England caps. He felt Holmes' positive strokeplay was an ideal complement to his efforts and treasured Holmes' remark as they unpadded following their record stand of 555 at Leyton in 1932: 'By heck, Herbert, if my back hadn't been givin' me trouble, we'd have brayed 'em!'

Even after Holmes' retirement, Sutcliffe was happy to share the spotlight with Leonard Hutton. Sir Leonard confirmed to me that Sutcliffe was the best opener he ever partnered, that his example and advice were unsurpassed and that he never pulled rank on him. For his part Sutcliffe was uncharacteristically lavish in his praise of the young Hutton: 'I am only setting up these records for Hutton to break them,' he once said.

Perhaps underneath the refined arrogance on the field, Sutcliffe knew deep down that he was not a truly great player, that he had achieved statistical greatness by a massive effort of character, tenacity and iron will. If Hobbs was the elegant willow, Sutcliffe was oak through and through; a handsome, strong man, his batting was not handsome or graceful. He had just a handful of shots – the hook, the pull, the off-drive and a back-foot force through gully or point that invariably got him off the mark. All of these strokes were sensibly and ruggedly played; the hook was accomplished with a bent right arm as he swept across the flight of the ball, so that it ended up as a hoick, rather than a hook in the style of a Hendren. He would hook in the air – hence the many sixes – and this often led to his dismissal. Another productive shot was an awkward shovelling flick down to fine leg, and his off-drive was a sturdy 'smack' with the wrists turning on impact. In his stance the bat face would point towards cover; on the pick-up, it would face towards gully, but he brought it down straight. He often looked stiff and awkward, occasionally out of position and unbalanced as the ball deviated suddenly, but he was a late adjuster with the art of playing defensive shots with a loose bottom hand. Thus on a turning wicket he would look vulnerable – but he would battle it out. His relish of a bad-wicket innings was never more evident than in his remark to Sir Pelham Warner after his historic 161 against Australia in 1926: 'Ah, Mr Warner, I love a dog-fight!'

Sutcliffe thought through an innings; he saw it in stages. He admitted his habit of hooking in the air worried him initially, but he would calculate that for every failure with that shot he had ten successes – 'and an average of eighty will do for me.' He would not hook until he had scored 40 if both fine leg and square leg were in position. Only after a couple of hours could he back himself to bisect the two fielders. If there was either a fine leg or square leg, then he would hook right from the start of his innings.

His running between the wickets was superb and helped offset the times when he was becalmed. A push, a glide, a nod to his partner and the scoreboard would keep ticking over. He was a master at pushing the ball into an open space; he seemed to be able to remember exactly where the fielders had been stationed.

Transcending all other qualities was his extraordinary strength of mind. He was more ruthless than Hobbs or Holmes; he would reason that he should cash in if it was his lucky day, because the next time he might have no control over events. Was he a lucky batsman? Perhaps he was, in that he was fortunate enough to be blessed with the gift of mental clarity, the realisation that the previous ball cannot send you back to the pavilion. He grasped this axiom in his second season in first-class cricket, in 1920. He battled through the Yorkshire innings against Essex at Southend, to carry his bat for a century that, in his own admission, was a fortunate affair. That fine new-ball bowler, J.W.H.T. Douglas, made the ball swing and dip prodigiously, but somehow Sutcliffe hung on, being dropped three times, while more experienced colleagues floundered. That night he dined with Douglas and a few friends and, although they talked much about his bad luck, Sutcliffe sensed that the fighting instinct that was never far from the surface of Douglas's cricket had encountered a worthy adversary. Four years later Sutcliffe scored 255 not out against Douglas; he had learned to make his own luck.

A self-made cricketer, he was also a self-made businessman. Sutcliffe soon grasped the value of his cricketing prestige and wasted no time in capitalising on it. He started up a sports shop in Leeds in partnership with the rubicund character, George Macauley, and, when Sutcliffe realised that his partner was not fully involved, he severed the partnership with all the ruthlessness that epitomised his batting. Thereafter Sutcliffe's business career matched his cricketing deeds in efficiency and his time in the dressing-room was always constructively spent, as Norman Yardley recalled: 'If he was not out at lunch, he would have a quick wash, lay out his kit and then produce his briefcase. He would write a few letters, don his pads and be ready to bat again. Mentally, it seemed no problem at all to divorce business from cricket and vice-versa.' Once he gave Alf Gover a tip that served Gover well in his own business career: 'I came across him at The Oval, doing his accounts during a halt for rain. He said to me, "Just doing my accounts, Alfred. If ever you work for yourself, do your own ledgers, because then you'll know where the money is going." When I started at the cricket school in Wandsworth, I remembered his advice.' Gover also recalled an instructive remark when he stayed at Sutcliffe's house one weekend. Sutcliffe showed him around the house with proper pride, pointing out the double garage doors, a cherished memento of a tour here, an antique desk there. He took him out into the garden and reeled off the types of vegetable and fruit on display and then said, 'I might as well make commercial use of the ground, Alfred.'

From the top of his immaculately cut, dark hair to the pure whiteness of his boots, Sutcliffe looked a cricketer. He was of the new breed of cricket professional, a man who knew his commercial worth and was proudly conscious of his standing in his local community and beyond the shires of Yorkshire. He had been commissioned in the Sherwood Foresters in the 1914-18 War and had observed the gentlemanly order of social matters. His accent was a whimsical contrast to the broad, flat vowels of Roy Kilner, Percy Holmes, Emmott Robinson and the other doughty members of that great Yorkshire side. He used eau de cologne in the dressing room after a shower, read the financial pages of the newspapers avidly and wrote every word of his autobiography, in an age when such a chore was invariably handed over to journalistic 'ghosts'. Somehow Sutcliffe seemed *with* the Yorkshire side, not *of* it: on away trips, he would stay in a hotel while the others made do with boarding houses. Yet he was a proud professional and, when Lord Hawke asked him to become Yorkshire's first professional captain in 1927, Sutcliffe refused, while stating that he would serve loyally under whoever was appointed. He was fanatical about raising the status of the cricket professional – he would tell youngsters just coming into the side, 'You may not make the grade, but make sure your manners and bearing are better than those of the amateurs. Try in every way to be better than them, remember you are representing Yorkshire, not just yourself.' Bill Bowes was given a Sutcliffe wigging during his first away match for Yorkshire; he went into the dining room at tea-time and prepared to tuck into the fare with all the eagerness of a young, strong fast bowler who had worked hard in the previous two hours. Sutcliffe leaned over to him and whispered, 'Bill, you don't look right – go and put your blazer on.' Bowes never went to tea again without his uniform.

Hitler's War ended his career when he was 44, just as the Kaiser's War had delayed his entry into first-class cricket until his 25th year. He was still a considerable force, averaging 54 in his final season, still a neat, immaculate figure with his cricketing faculties as sharp as his business antennae. His gloomy forecast that the 1935 revision of the lbw law would reduce his effectiveness was not borne out by his runs in the subsequent four seasons: 1,532 in 1936, then 2,162 the following year, 1,790 in 1938 and 1,416 in his last season. He did not seem to appreciate that the new law was in itself a great compliment to his defensive prowess, his mastery at using the pads as the last line of defence. No batsman did more to force that revision through than Herbert Sutcliffe.

It seems incredible that such a wonderful opener did not accompany G.O. Allen on his gallant tour to Australia in 1936/37, a tour that saw the estimable Hedley Verity open the England innings in one Test. Perhaps it was thought that Sutcliffe's powers of concentration were on the wane, that the new lbw law would affect him. No one who saw him batting calmly and resourcefully for Yorkshire against the 1938 Australians could doubt that this man was still a great 'big match' performer.

He lived a long and happy old age and died in a nursing home at the age of 83, shortly after demonstrating to at least one elderly female inmate that his powers of stamina and decisiveness had not been solely confined to the cricket pitch. His son, Billy, captained Yorkshire in the 1950s – one of his middle names was 'Hobbs' – but the burden of being the son of the great Sutcliffe was too great. Herbert had long been accustomed to the standing ovations he received on every Yorkshire ground where he attended play, and he would acknowledge the tributes with his usual patrician dignity. He remained a stickler for the old virtues, informing John Hampshire in all sincerity that his erratic, attractive batting would improve if he attended church regularly, and telling Barry Wood in 1972 that his England career would flourish if he would only get his hair cut. Wood was not sure whether to be flattered by the letter from the great man or amazed at the advice.

Bill Bowes was terribly fond of Sutcliffe and admired the stoical way he bore the pain of acute arthritis in his last years. 'He was a very great man. I never knew him guilty of a shabby or underhand act.'

In his immaculate suits he looked like a sleek, confident civil servant, the absolute master of his portfolio. At the crease he batted like a canny Yorkshire businessman, declaring a dividend when he was good and ready and eking out his rations in the meantime. At his death, another famous self-made Yorkshireman was ploughing the same furrow. Who said there was no continuity in cricket?

Batsmen with 75 to 99 hundreds

J.W. Hearne	96
C.B. Fry	94
M.W. Gatting	94
C.G. Greenidge	92
A.J. Lamb	89
A.I. Kallicharran	87
W.J. Edrich	86
R.B. Kanhai	86
G.S. Sobers	86
J.T. Tyldesley	86
P.B.H. May	85
R.E.S. Wyatt	85
J.L. Langer	84
J. Hardstaff, junior	83
D.S. Lehmann	82
S.M. Gavaskar	81
M.E. Waugh	81
Javed Miandad	80
M. Leyland	80
B.A. Richards	80
M.L. Hayden	79
S.G. Law	79
C.H. Lloyd	79
S.R. Waugh	79
K.F. Barrington	76
J.G. Langridge	76
C. Washbrook	76
H.T.W. Hardinge	75

8

Ernest Tyldesley

'His batting was like the man himself: modest yet
firm of character, civilised in its call for action'
(Neville Cardus)

George Ernest Tyldesley

Born

Worsley, Lancashire

5 February 1889

Died

Rhos-on-Sea, Denbigh

5 May 1962

First hundred

107   Lancashire v Sussex, Old Trafford, 1912
Age: 23 years 99 days

100th hundred

122   Lancashire v Northamptonshire, Peterborough, 1934
Age: 45 years 152 days

Last hundred

137   Lancashire v Sussex, Old Trafford, 1935
Age: 46 years 191 days

Career record

M	Inn	NO	HS	Runs	Average	100s	50s
648	961	106	256*	38,874	45.46	102	191

Test record

M	Inn	NO	HS	Runs	Average	100s	50s
14	20	2	122	990	55.00	3	6

If you gathered a group of cricket enthusiasts around a table, gave them all a scrap of paper and a pen and asked them to write down the names of the men who scored a hundred centuries, the results would be instructive. They would whip through many of the great names: Grace, Hammond, Boycott, Hutton – they would be no problem. Some would look smug at remembering Mead, Hayward and Sandham and the middle-aged element would probably winkle out Turner, Edrich and Cowdrey from the recesses of their minds. One name, though, would remain elusive to the majority: George Ernest Tyldesley. His name would be greeted by either an irritated 'Oh yes, Tyldesley' or an aggressive 'Who?'

He was the eighth batsman to reach a hundred hundreds, and only W.G. Grace took longer and was older at the time of achievement. He scored more runs and centuries for Lancashire than anyone else in its history – more than Washbrook, Paynter, MacLaren, Hallows and his brother, J.T. Tyldesley. His Test average was ten points better than his first-class average, an unchanging sign of class.

Ernest Tyldesley was one of the finest professional batsmen of the inter-war period and surely one of the unluckiest. Like Andrew Sandham and Percy Holmes, he lived in the wrong period; with such a plethora of batting talent available to the England selectors, Tyldesley had to make do with whatever came his way and retain his sense of proportion when thanked for his pains and bundled back to county cricket.

He was also unlucky to be the brother of a batting genius. J.T. Tyldesley – Johnny Tyldesley – was one of the most brilliant players of the period before 1914, and no one who saw him bat for an hour ever forgot him. Audacious, dynamic and resourceful, he deservedly stands in the pantheon of great English players. At the height of his powers, Johnny told all those who cared to listen that he had a kid brother at home who would turn out to be a better player. At the time only Trumper, and the young Hobbs, could match the genius of J.T.T., never mind a boy sixteen years his junior. His words were dismissed as simple fraternal duty.

When Ernest made his Lancashire debut in 1909, he was 20 and still very much in the shadow of his brother. The pair added 43 in Ernest's first match – against Warwickshire – and, although he made 61, he looked a mundane player with none of his brother's panache. The following year he made just 302 runs in 20 innings, in 1911 a total of 479 with an average of 25.21, and in 1912 a slight improvement to 503 at 29.58. At last – in 1913 – he broke through the mediocrity and made 1,306 runs at 31.85, but even then he was overshadowed by J.T.T. When Ernest scored a fine 110 against Surrey, his brother's magnificent 210 harvested all the newspaper eulogies.

In a perverse way, the Great War helped Ernest's career. When first-class cricket resumed in 1919, he was just 30 years of age, but his brother was 46, with his halcyon days behind him. Army training had toughened up the slight physique, and consequently his offside play developed a new power.

Before the war, he had been almost exclusively an on-side player. Batting now at number three, his brother's old position, he methodically began to silence those snide whispers of nepotism. Len Hopwood, who played with Ernest for many years in the Lancashire side, remembered the criticisms of his technique as he tried to come out of the shadow of his great brother: 'They used to say that Ernest's back swing started in the direction of point, rather than in line with the middle stump. Ernest would reply: "It's not where it starts, it's where it finishes that matters." How right he was – the bat was straight enough at the crucial moment.' Hopwood had a great opportunity to watch Tyldesley's technique during one memorable week in 1934, when the pair added 273 against Glamorgan and then 315 against Gloucestershire. Hopwood scoffed at the suggestion that Tyldesley's technique was faulty: 'During those partnerships I studied him closely and, believe me, no bat ever looked straighter, or broader or more punishing.'

Just as the batting of Frank Woolley epitomised the county where he lived and its way of playing cricket, so did Ernest Tyldesley in the post-war Lancashire team. By the *force majeure* of geography Lancashire had to play on wetter wickets, slower outfields and on more taxing surfaces than Woolley faced for at least half the season. The tactical need for Lancashire was a sensible, solid platform leading to a big enough total to allow brilliant bowlers like MacDonald, Parkin and Dick Tyldesley the chance to get the opposition out twice. It worked; between 1926 and 1934 Lancashire won the county championship five times.

They did so at a cost, being valued more in the north than in the south, where strong amateur influence still dictated tactics at certain stages of the season. If Harry Makepeace's dictum that there should be 'no fours before loonch' was a deliberate exaggeration of Lancashire's attitude to batting, nevertheless they had a workmanlike batting line-up, accustomed to posting 300 for two at close of play and then praying for rain. With the lbw law still favouring batsmen who used their pads, Lancashire's batsmen did not ignore the first principles of their technique: bat and pad close together and if the ball pitched outside the off-stump, get the bat out of the way and shove the pad across. Anyone bowled by an off-spinner would face a severe inquest in the Lancashire dressing-room.

Little wonder that Lancashire batsmen of that era were judged a pretty dour lot. Ernest Tyldesley suffered in the generalisation. It was unfair to an elegant, unruffled player who excelled in the off-drive, the cut, the hook and the flick off his legs. His leg glance was beautiful; leaning forward, perfectly balanced, he would flick the ball round delicately off his pads. He never seemed brutal in his treatment of bowlers, he would answer their technical questions with the practised grace of a classics master in a tutorial. Even when he hooked – that lip-smacking shot, that excursion into the 'macho' world of a Botham – it was with deference to the bowler, an acknowledgement that unfortunately he had been forced into taking drastic measures and 'I sincerely hope I haven't knocked your ball out of shape, sir.' Bill Hitch, Surrey's hale fellow of a fast bowler, felt the draught of Tyldesley's hooking once at The Oval. Lancashire started the day with four wickets in hand, a hundred runs in arrears and a long tail to keep Tyldesley company. Hitch began the morning with four slips and a gully observing his tremendous pace. Within half an hour, three of the slips had been moved to defensive positions on the legside to combat Tyldesley's hooking. He made 236 in five hours, and the game was easily saved.

G.O. Allen had good reason to remember the underrated talent of Ernest Tyldesley. In 1929 Allen bowled fast and straight to take ten for 40 for Middlesex against Lancashire, who were bowled out for 241. Allen bowled eight men – including Tyldesley, but not before he had made 102 against six men who bowled for England at some stage. Allen recalled, 'That was a typically sound, stubborn innings by Ernest. Adversity brought out the best in him, and he made many high-class hundreds without getting the praise he deserved.'

Under-rated, yes. Inconsistent, no. In 1926 he made twelve fifties in thirteen consecutive innings, including a run of ten in ten, a feat only equalled by that master of consistency, Don Bradman. That year he scored 2,826 runs and in 1928 amassed 3,024 runs. It was not enough to force his way into the England side for any length of time when all the household names were available.

Ernest Tyldesley's treatment by the selectors was in keeping with some of the eccentric decisions made during the 1920s by that august body of men. In 1921, a season of lightning-fast wickets and a 'scorched earth' bowling policy by the Australians, Tyldesley was picked for the First Test at Trent Bridge. He was out first ball, chopping a very fast ball from Gregory onto his stumps. In the second innings Gregory bowled him again for seven – he mishooked a short one onto his forehead and it fell on his stumps. Tyldesley was dropped. The selectors tried to persuade C.B. Fry, a mere stripling at 49, to return, but that wise man would have none of it. Instead they brought in men of the calibre of Alf Dipper, a one-paced journeyman with Gloucestershire, Wally Hardinge, a reliable county player and no more than that, and Andy Ducat, an attractive run-getter on the Oval billiard tables whose main cricketing claim to fame would be that he died while batting at Lord's in 1942. Worse was to follow for the professional pride of Tyldesley: among the new caps was one A.J. Evans (Winchester, Oxford University, Hampshire and Kent), who was selected on the strength of an innings of 69 not out for the MCC against the Australians earlier in the tour. Evans contented himself with just eight innings in that season – 217 runs – and never has an England cap been gained so easily in a modern home series.

As the selectors ran out of options, Tyldesley was at last recalled for the Fourth Test on his home ground, Old Trafford. In his only innings, he made 78 not out on a damp pitch; in the opinion of many Australian players, it was easily the best innings against them on the tour and the most dazzling post-war one for England until Hammond's dominance in 1928/29. After that, he had to be retained for the final Test and, although not reproducing the splendour of Old Trafford, he made a solid 39.

His reward was a single Test against South Africa in 1924 and one appearance when the Australians came again in 1926. He made 81 against them – and was immediately dropped. He managed to scrape a place on the boat to Australia for the 1928/29 tour (3,000 runs was a reasonable recommendation, even though not enough for Frank Woolley), yet he managed just one Test, taking the injured Sutcliffe's place and scoring 31 and 21. Thereafter the way was barred by Hammond.

That tour was a frustrating one for Tyldesley; he never really forced his way into contention by weight of runs, a great disappointment to him after an excellent tour to South Africa in the previous winter. On the matting wickets he had mastered Nupen's devastating off-cutters with aplomb. The ball that turned in on him held few terrors, and the extra bounce of the matting meant his slightly crooked pick-up was not punished by balls keeping low. He topped the batting averages in the Tests – 520 runs at 65 – and the South Africans thought him the best player they had seen there since Jack Hobbs nearly twenty years before.

The Test at Melbourne in 1929 ended Tyldesley's Test career. He could not be dismissed as a failure: 990 runs at an average of 55 with three hundreds. In comparison, his brother only averaged 30 in his 31 Tests. Ernest had done his best, but Hammond was a great player; moreover, Tyldesley's fielding (a safe catcher but a slow mover) could never be counted as an asset.

He returned to county cricket and continued to pile up charming centuries, including one of 256 not out that took just six hours at the age of 41. When he reached his hundredth hundred in 1934, it must have come as a surprise to many cricket experts outside Lancashire. The post-war Tyldesley had always been consistent, dedicated, a pretty batsman – but surely not of the elite? He certainly batted like a master in 1934, limbering up early with 239 against Glamorgan in just over six hours. On 7 July he scored 122 in three-and-a-half-hours against Northants to register his century of centuries. The venue seemed somehow appropriate: Peterborough. That cathedral city is hardly noted for its cricketing history and, while Boycott chose a Test Match for his achievement, Hayward The Oval, and Woolley and Compton picked Lord's, Ernest Tyldesley reached his ambition on a fustian ground that is no longer on the first-class list. No matter; he had long been used to counting his blessings. His only regret was that his brother had not lived to see it: he died in 1930.

The innings at Peterborough was just one of many splendid performances in 1934 by Tyldesley, now aged 45. He made eight hundreds, including one against the Australians (off-driving Grimmett and Fleetwood-Smith with controlled precision), and altogether made 2,487 runs at 57.83, to finish third in the national averages. Just to complete a marvellous season, Lancashire won the championship. With Tyldesley playing so fluently, it came as a surprise when he announced his retirement; the persuasive tongues of Lancashire cricket were mobilised, and Tyldesley stood up at the celebration dinner and announced he would play on for as long as he was needed.

He made a couple of appearances in the 1936 season as an amateur before finishing for good. For the rest of his life he kept in close contact with the club, serving on the committee and behaving with the grace and good manners that characterised his batting. G.O. Allen spoke with affection of many happy yarning hours in Ernest's company at Old Trafford; no doubt a certain match at Lord's in 1929 exercised their memories on occasions. Les Ames recalled what a splendid team man he was on the Australian tour, swallowing hard his disappointment at his form, volunteering to bowl in the nets and offering to do twelfth man duties when more selfish team-mates longed for the beach. R.E.S. Wyatt, who toured with him in South Africa, said he was the best senior professional he ever met on an England trip. 'His good fellowship had nothing to do with his excellent form with the bat. Ernest was as sound as a bell from first to last. A thorough gentleman.' Bill Bowes said he was one of the few cricketers who smiled and said 'Hello' during a Roses match: 'A Lancastrian who smiled at us during those three days was an exceptional person.' Len Hopwood remembered Tyldesley's great influence on a Lancashire side that contained more than one stormy petrel: 'He had no time for selfish cricketers and was a great advocate of side before self. He would come down like a ton of bricks on anyone exhibiting such signs. He was kindly and considerate and never one to give a snap judgement. "You've got to wait and see," was his reaction to a rash suggestion.' Hopwood recalled one occasion when Tyldesley strayed from his customary dignified attitude to the game; it came after Gloucestershire had contrived to beat Lancashire for the first time for many seasons. Alf Dipper, the man who played against Australia in 1921, was so overcome at the victory that he threw his cap into the air in jubilation, an act of demonstrativeness of which Tyldesley thoroughly disapproved. The sequel came shortly afterwards at Lord's when Middlesex – or more particularly R.W.V. Robins – annoyed Lancashire with some provocative and questionable tactics. Tyldesley's sense of propriety was so outraged that he announced to his team-mates: 'If we win this match, I'll do a Dipper and throw my blooming cap into the air.' When Lancashire turned probable defeat into a splendid victory, ten pairs of eyes focused on Tyldesley as the last Middlesex wicket fell: he shouted 'hurrah' and threw his cap into the air. Hopwood said, 'We just couldn't believe it – the most unassuming and dignified player in the game giving a performance like that, and at Lord's of all places.'

Among the premier batsmen of his time, he was perhaps a little too diffident. He had long ago cured himself of the cross-bat tendency that caused his brother to wince, but he was always a nervous starter. He seemed dogged by myopia and self-consciousness; he would thrust forward indiscriminately until he had gauged the state of the wicket. Then the strokes would flow, the strokes that he had watched men like MacLaren, Spooner and his brother play while learning his trade. Yet with Ernest, those strokes lacked the 'hauteur' of the Edwardian age: 'toujours la politesse', the 'parfit gentle knight' rather than the D'Artagnan of his brother. That lack of a dominant strain must count against him when assuming his standing in the highest company, but there could be no quibbles about his style. R.C. Robertson-Glasgow bowled against him many times for Oxford and Somerset, and he admired Tyldesley greatly: 'On him were the sure signs of mastery – extreme lateness of stroke and the easy answer to each question of the ball.'

Neville Cardus saw most of Tyldesley's great innings. He wrote, 'His batting was like the man himself: modest yet firm of character, civilised in its call for action. He never exceeded the privileges of class and manners.' If he had played for another county and batted in a less utilitarian environment, he might have been a coruscating batsman. He remained proudly and emphatically a Lancastrian with a quiet, dry wit. Len Hopwood visited him towards the end of his life and was shocked to see him suffering cruelly from rheumatoid arthritis; the two old friends talked fondly about their days together for over an hour and not once did Ernest mention any of his own performances. As Hopwood stood up to leave, Ernest smiled bravely and whispered, 'We had some fun, didn't we, Hoppy?'

Hopwood did not see him again but will never forget his unselfishness, even on his death-bed. George Duckworth was the last of his team-mates to see him before he died in 1962. After he had made the ritual enquiry about his health, Ernest replied: 'Well, Ducky, I've seen the man about me eyes and one of 'em's goin': this chest o' mine is givin' me soom trouble; and ah keep getting' soom pain in me back. Mind you, there's nothin' the matter wi' me!' Ernest Tyldesley never believed in making a fuss about anything.

9

Walter Hammond

'Whenever I saw him bat, I felt sorry for the ball'
(Leonard Hutton)

Walter Reginald Hammond

Born

Dover, Kent

19 June 1903

Died

Kloof, Natal, South Africa

1 July 1965

First hundred

110   Gloucestershire v Surrey, Bristol, 1923
Age: 19 years 324 days

100th hundred

116   Gloucestershire v Somerset, Bristol, 1935
Age: 31 years 359 days

Last hundred

188   MCC v South Australia, Adelaide, 1947
Age: 43 years 220 days

Career record

M	Inn	NO	HS	Runs	Average	100s	50s
634	1,005	104	336*	50,551	56.10	167	185

Test record

M	Inn	NO	HS	Runs	Average	100s	50s
85	140	16	336*	7,249	58.45	22	24

Walter Hammond was a rare first edition in the library of cricketers. The genuine article. His deeds illuminate many pages in *Wisden*, yet Hammond could not be appreciated from the scorebook alone. In the opinion of his contemporaries, he was on a different plane – majestic, assured, poised, a devastating amalgam of the physical and mental attributes that make up a great batsman. He was not a flamboyant batsman, he introduced no novelty of technique; he simply personified the classics of the game to the highest possible degree. The left leg was never far from the bat when he played forward, the footwork was that of a born dancer and he dismissed the ball from his presence. His very name radiated authority. The popular press found it easier to dub him 'Wally' and so did the bulk of his team-mates, but that was tantamount to calling Churchill 'Winnie' or de Gaulle 'Charlie'. Walter Hammond. The emperor of batting.

Len Hutton, who played several Tests with Hammond, summed up his majesty neatly: 'Whenever I saw him bat, I felt sorry for the ball.' When he joined his Gloucestershire team-mates in the nets, the spin bowlers would deliver to him, then rush to the side of the net as the ball crashed past them like howitzers. At Lord's in 1938 he gave the Australians one chance during his prodigious innings of 240; Chipperfield got a hand to a sharp caught-and-bowled chance, yet the ball rebounded yards back into play from the pavilion rails. Chipperfield retired from the match with a broken finger.

Hammond's control was so awesome that bowlers in county cricket measured success by the number of times they passed his bat or caused him to play defensively, rather than in dismissals. Charlie Elliott – Test umpire, England selector – recalled fielding to him in the 1930s when he scored four successive hundreds against Derbyshire: 'If you didn't get him in the first ten minutes, he would just do as he liked.' Doug Wright, magnificent leg-spinner for Kent and a colleague of Hammond in the England side, told me: 'It was a pleasure to bowl at him. If you managed a maiden at him, it made your season and, when he hit me vast distances, I felt like applauding. He was the best cricketer I ever saw.'

Note that – the best cricketer. He was not just a wonderful batsman, he was a high-class medium-pace bowler with an action straight out of the Tate/Bedser gallery. His slip fielding was superb; he never seemed to hurry, yet he would take the sizzling edge with time to spare. F.R. Brown said he never saw Hammond take a catch one-handed or dirty his flannels: those dancing feet always got him into position. Charlie Parker, devastating Gloucestershire slow bowler when the wicket favoured him, owed much to the predatory catching of Hammond at slip. 'Caught Hammond, bowled Parker' became as familiar a sight in the newspapers as 'caught Tunnicliffe, bowled Rhodes' of earlier vintage . . . no less than 229 times, in fact.

His aloofness on and off the field accentuated the feeling of cricketing divinity. Everything he did had the air of a thoroughbred: striding to the wicket, blue handkerchief peeping from his pocket, his entry into the fray was, in the eyes of many, worth the admission price alone. It is remarkable that all his contemporaries I interviewed would eventually say the same thing: 'You should have seen him walk out to bat.' He brought the same detached superiority to his beautiful bowling action, with its curving run-up and thrilling delivery, and to his fielding. His physique was perfect: just over medium height, broad-shouldered, deep-chested, with massive forearms and an ease and grace of movement that marked him out as a natural player. He seemed to excel at every athletic pursuit; in his youth Southampton's manager begged him to take up soccer as a career, and he played three seasons for Bristol Rovers in the early 1920s. The handicap system could never deny him in the games the England cricketers would play on the ships that took them to Australia, West Indies and South Africa.

Although small boys would forget their scorebooks and charts when he batted, his record deserves scrutiny. He made 167 hundreds, scored just over 50,000 runs, took 732 wickets and held 819 catches. It would have been even more impressive but for a combination of bad luck, illness, war and administrative dogmatism, which together robbed him of seven full seasons.

In his early years, only his talent came easy to him. He spent some time in Malta – his father was in the Army – until he was shipped over to Cirencester Grammar School in the Cotswolds. His father was killed in the Great War, and the schooldays were solitary ones for Hammond, who had learned to look after himself in those formative years in Malta. Apart from a natural athletic flair, nothing seemed to interest him. After scoring 365 not out in a house match, his name was noted by the county and he played a couple of games for them as an amateur. Cricket seemed a pleasant enough diversion as a career (he lacked the early commitment of Hobbs, Grace or Bradman), and he was preparing himself for his first year as a professional when the rulebook thwarted him. Lord Harris, that influential martinet at Lord's, was piqued that a boy born in Dover had slipped through the net of his beloved Kent, and he insisted that Hammond serve a two-year residential period in Gloucestershire before being allowed to play county cricket. Although irked, Hammond had little else on the horizon apart from resisting the blandishments of professional soccer (he felt the money was not sufficient) so he settled down to serve his penance. He became assistant coach at Clifton College, under the dictatorial guidance of John Tunnicliffe, 'Long John' of 'caught Tunnicliffe, bowled Rhodes' fame. They did not see eye to eye on attitudes to batting, but there is no doubt that Tunnicliffe's advice and example helped Hammond become one of the greatest slip fielders of all time.

After three years Hammond had played just 16 first-class innings for Gloucestershire and, when he finally entered county cricket in 1923, his rashness revealed how the delay had frustrated him. For the next three seasons his average hovered around the 30 mark and, although his class was obvious, influential judges agreed with Tunnicliffe that the boy was too headstrong, he had too many shots to offer. They agreed his off-driving was superb but criticised the way he hooked in the air. He had never been coached until he joined the Gloucestershire staff and, even then, the only man who occasionally offered some advice was George Dennett, the eminent slow left-arm bowler. It looked as if Tunnicliffe, the sage of Pudsey, might have judged his man astutely; perhaps he would always be just an 'iffish' county batsman.

One innings altered the balance. On 19 August 1925 Hammond scored 250 not out at Old Trafford against the best fast bowler in the world (MacDonald), the outstanding off-spinner (Parkin) and an England leg-spinner of the future (Dick Tyldesley); Gloucestershire were 20 for two when Hammond strode to the wicket, and he stayed another five-and-a-half hours. No longer could there be any doubt over his quality. The England selectors prepared to see him bat at number four in the following summer against the Australians. He looked the ideal man to help wrest back the Ashes.

Alas for fond hopes. Hammond missed the historic 1926 season altogether and nearly died. The reason can now be acknowledged after decades of enigmatic words and glances from so many of Hammond's England and Gloucestershire team-mates, and the investigative palm should be handed to the veteran West Country cricket writer, David Foot.

In his definitive, impeccably researched biography of Hammond (*The Reasons Why*), Foot reveals beyond all doubt that Hammond picked up a sexually-transmitted disease on a tour to the West Indies in 1925/26. I had an inkling of this years ago while writing the autobiography of E.J. 'Tiger' Smith, the Warwickshire and England wicket-keeper/batsman. He told me he had contracted malaria on that tour, which flared up at times for the rest of his long life, but added darkly, 'I wasn't the only one to have caught something on that tour.' No amount of prompting from me could elicit anything more precise from the old man, and out of respect I desisted. But I gleaned as much from several other contemporaries down the years. David Foot finally nailed the truth in the late 1990s.

The received wisdom was that Hammond had been laid low by mosquito bites and blood poisoning on that Caribbean tour and that medical skills out there were not advanced enough to restore him to health. That was indeed so, but Hammond's weakness for women – already evident, to the envy of his Bristol Rovers and Gloucestershire colleagues – had exposed him to an illness that nearly nipped an illustrious career in the bud.

He remained forever grateful to Sir Pelham Warner, that sympathetic, influential encourager of young talent, for meeting him when the boat docked at Bristol. Warner continued to tell Hammond he would one day play for England and, along with his formidable mother – who supervised his recuperation with matriarchal zeal – Hammond eventually recovered physically. But not psychologically.

In 1926 penicillin was not available to treat such a disease and it is David Foot's contention, backed up by solid medical research, that the mercury used to treat Hammond lead to erethism, a condition that causes personality disorders: violent mood swings, remoteness, unaccountable anger and impatience.

Some may cavil at Foot's interest in Hammond's private life, but I support an old friend and respected journalist. Every contemporary interviewed by both Foot and myself eventually offered the view that Hammond was disturbingly moody and that impacted on every dressing-room he occupied after 1926. Those mood swings affected his captaincy of England: his inability to connect with his team-mates, his reluctance to bowl when the team needed him, his sense of social inferiority and his obsession with money and class.

He agonised over turning amateur in 1937 so that he could captain England, thereby improving his social status. He proved sadly lacking as a leader through his personal defects. His liaison with a South African society hostess led to an acrimonious divorce and subsequent re-marriage, and that clearly hampered his ability to make a decent fist of captaining England in Australia during the winter of 1946/47. By common consent he was hopeless at the job and, distracted and patently unfit, not worth his place in the team.

Without that desperate illness and the psychological impact which affected Hammond for the rest of his life, he would surely have been an even greater cricketer. Certainly more popular. He was never the same man after that West Indies tour, and his team-mates at Bristol noticed how much older he looked when he was finally fit enough to resume county duties in the spring of 1927. But he returned as a batsman on the brink of greatness, soon to achieve it.

Something had happened during his convalescence that fused his talents into a whole; no longer did he charge recklessly after the bowling, now he would trust to his delicious footwork, his sportsman's eye and a straight bat. He scored a thousand runs in May, the third batsman to do so. Throughout that 1927 season he made bowlers pay for his illness, for the pettiness of Lord Harris, for the arid years of his youth. One innings that season encapsulated his grandeur – and again it was at Old Trafford. One Friday morning in May the Lancashire team had their eyes on an early finish and a trip to the races. No one would quibble at their optimism: Gloucestershire, with two wickets down, were just 44 ahead and only this young dasher Hammond barring the way. In the first over of the morning – bowled by the great MacDonald – Hammond drove five fours in succession. He then hooked MacDonald with the arrogance that stems from complete mastery. In three hours Hammond made 187 devastating runs and saved the game.

Eighteen months later and he was ready to conquer a bigger stage. Percy Chapman's 1928/29 side to Australia contained a marvellous array of talent, but Hammond, with 905 runs in the series, dwarfed everyone. Bradman's capacity for gargantuan scores had not yet reached a worldwide audience so Hammond was the wonder of the age. His methods were simple: he realised the wickets were good enough to accelerate retirements among the bowling fraternity, so he decided to eliminate risk, occupy the crease for as long as possible, playing 'through the V', that arc between extra cover and midwicket. The hook was dropped from the plentiful repertoire, and so was the glance. He only used the cut in the last Test, after some of the Australian players had ribbed him over dinner that he could not play the shot. Hammond, so determined to prove himself a great batsman, vowed to show the cocky Australians; he was out for 38 and 16 in the last Test, on each occasion caught in the gully off square cuts. Henceforth Hammond would never take any notice of Australian whimsy.

By 1929 Hammond was the greatest batsman in the world, even if he judged the hook shot too risky and the pull a lottery on wickets favouring seam and swing bowlers. He compensated in many other areas, and his disciplined technique allowed him to make stately progress through the pages of cricket history. Yet his superiority lasted just one year: at the end of the 1930 season Don Bradman had surpassed him in quantity and he looked even more infallible. Bradman's dominance throughout the 1930s gnawed away at Hammond; it seemed that whenever he made a hundred, Bradman would reply with a double hundred. When England amassed 903 for seven declared at The Oval in 1938, Hammond would not declare until he had received medical assurances that Bradman's injured ankle would prevent him from batting. Again in 1938 Denis Compton threw his wicket away after making a joyous hundred in his first Test against Australia only to be told by his captain: 'Don't ever do that to me again. Never give the Australians your wicket.' John Tunnicliffe would have approved of such ruthlessness.

Bradman seemed to rattle Hammond, even when he did not wear pads. In the Third Test at Adelaide in 1933 Hammond was established in his cool mastery as the end of play neared. Bradman was brought on to bowl on a captain's whim and Hammond walked down the wicket to his partner, Les Ames, and warned him not to take risks against such innocuous bowling. Hammond was bowled with a high full toss and stalked away in fury. Ames told me, 'I have never seen him so angry. He was outraged at showing weakness against Bradman.'

In the 1934 series Hammond had a miserable time and did not score one fifty; Bradman won the rubber with a double and a triple century. At Sydney in 1936 Hammond's double hundred set up a two-nil lead in the series, but Bradman turned the series with scores of 270, 212 and 169 and Australia won three-two. An incident in the Fourth Test at Adelaide illustrated the difference between the two great batsmen of the age – England started the final day on 148 for three, needing another 244 to win. Hammond was not out and clearly the man Bradman had to dismiss early. He was bowled third ball of the morning by Fleetwood-Smith, and he strode off with that air of unconcern that was so maddening in failure, so coldly impassive on his days of plenty. George Duckworth, who was sitting with the shattered England side, voiced the thoughts of many: 'We wouldn't have got Don out first thing in the morning with the Ashes at stake.' Australia won that Test and the final one.

Hammond knew all about the unflattering comparisons, and they only served to drive him deeper into his shell of introspection. Bradman and Hammond were the rival captains in 1938, and their relationship was cool and wary. After an incident on the first morning of the opening Test in the 1946/47 series, they only spoke to each other when the coin was being tossed. Hammond thought Bradman had been caught by Ikin at slip and felt he should have 'walked'; Bradman went on to score a rehabilitatory 187, and Hammond resigned himself to being bested by the malign finger of fate that had brought two such masters together in opposition at the same time. Why, even on their first appearance on the same field Bradman gained the upper hand: he ran Hammond out with a brilliant pick-up from cover and answered Hammond's double hundred with 87 and 182 not out. From that moment at Sydney in November 1928, Bradman had Hammond in his sights.

If the little Australian had the edge over him throughout the 1930s, no one else did. He could be comparatively passive against Bill O'Reilly's accurate leg-stump attack but, apart from the inexplicable lapses in the 1934 series, O'Reilly did not enjoy much success against him. O'Reilly would have none of the talk about his superiority over Hammond; all his life he spoke of him in the most glowing terms. Hammond went through periods of famine, but he felt that was due to lack of challenge, rather than any deterioration. When he was needed, he showed his mettle, especially on bad wickets. Doug Wright recalled the game at Bristol in 1939 when Hammond scored 153 not out in a total of 284 all out. The wicket was so bad that no Kent player got more than 40 and, with Tom Goddard taking 17 wickets in the match, Gloucestershire won by an innings and 40 runs. Wright took nine for 47, including the hat-trick, yet 'I just couldn't bowl at Wally. It was the most fantastic performance I've ever seen, the work of a genius.'

At Melbourne in 1936 he played an innings of 32 that, on a rain-affected pitch threatening throat and temple, was remarkable. Ten years later Alec Bedser witnessed another miraculous effort at Brisbane; two inches of rain had fallen in the night and the wicket was spiteful. The ball took divots out of the pitch every time it landed. Keith Miller, that chivalrous cricketer, kept the ball well up to the batsman, yet one of his half volleys at medium pace spat off the pitch and knocked Cyril Washbrook's cap off as he played forward. Only Hammond looked comfortable, as Bedser recalls: 'When it was short, he stood aside and let it go. If pitched up, he let fly, playing straight past the bowler to eliminate risk. He hit cleanly and sensibly, and in the circumstances it was the best bad-wicket innings I've seen.' He made 32 in two hours and was not hit once; at the other end Bill Edrich was battered black and blue while making 16.

Adversity saw him at his best. At Lord's in 1938 the fast bowling of Ernie McCormick swept away Hutton, Barnett and Edrich for just 31 runs.

Hammond made 240 of the most perfect runs imaginable, crashing the fast bowlers away off front and back foot like a mixture of Dexter and Cowdrey at their best. It was utterly safe, dignified and breath-taking. 'A throne-room innings,' Cardus called it. Even then, Bradman's shadow stalked Hammond. On a damp pitch the Australian captain saved the match with a brilliant, quick-footed 103 not out.

Hammond was an unemotional cricketer, yet he liked to demonstrate his astonishing virtuosity when the mood was on him. One day at Cheltenham Tom Goddard was quaffing a lunchtime pint after bowling out Leicestershire on a typical Cheltenham turner. Goddard was no blushing violet, and Hammond became restless at his confident assertions. He told Goddard that he was not really much of a bowler and sat back for the expected reaction. When Goddard finished his expostulations, he was invited to go out onto the pitch where he had sent the opposition packing an hour earlier. The other Gloucestershire players followed and took up their fielding positions as Goddard bowled an over at Hammond. 'I'll play you with the edge of my bat, Tom,' he said, and proceeded to play six sharply-turning deliveries with an area of willow not more than an inch and a half wide. He blocked all six deliveries, walked away and, en route to the dressing-room, called out, 'I told you you couldn't bowl, Tom.' My source for this story is Reg Sinfield, one of the fielders that day.

Hammond once indulged himself in similar fashion in the nets at Bristol. He had just returned from an Australian tour and did not know that the club had prepared a practice wicket for the spinners. The idea was to familiarise Goddard, Sinfield and Parker with a turning wicket early in the season so that they could judge their line and length and avoid turning the ball too much. None of the first-team batsmen could last more than four overs on the pitch until Hammond had a knock. Not one ball passed him until he felt sorry for the bowlers, dropped his bat and took up a baseball bat that he had brought back from his tour. He played the three spinners easily enough with that until Charlie Parker, frustrated and humiliated, threw a ball at him. He caught the ball and sent it soaring out of the net with his baseball bat. He laughed, walked off and, when out of earshot, Parker announced, 'You have just seen the greatest exhibition of batting you will ever witness – but don't tell him I said so!'

He was not popular with his team-mates at Bristol. They felt he should have bowled more often; Reg Sinfield thought they would have won two championships if he had done so. He sometimes seemed in a world of his own, occasionally saying nothing to anybody for two days, yet carrying on with the game. When he batted in the nets he would ask the fast bowlers to use a new ball and then he would take a fiendish delight in smashing it straight back at them. When he was captain, he had his own way of dealing with young players, as George Emmett discovered. Emmett, a strokemaker of great ability and charm, was left out for several games and went to see his captain for advice. He received one sentence: 'Well, Emmett, you're not a very good player, are you?'

Emmett never received any explanation why he was occasionally dropped down the order and once asked plaintively, 'What's he got against me?' George Lambert, a whole-hearted, skilful fast bowler, was heard to say, 'When am I going to get a murmur of praise from him?' Jack Crapp, who batted alongside Hammond for many years, only remembered one piece of advice from the great man: 'The Hollies leg-break isn't turning!' Charles Barnett, dashing opening batsman who played for Hammond briefly with England and for a decade at Gloucestershire, had no time for him for a variety of reasons. Barnett appears to be the only one virulently ill-disposed to Hammond, but so many other Gloucestershire contemporaries were more sad than bitter. Hammond was their hero, but he couldn't relate to them.

Like most great batsmen, Hammond wanted to strike when the pickings were easy and would be happy to get away from it at certain strategic times. When he batted with Reg Sinfield, he would say, 'Reg, you take it for the first few overs, you're more used to it than I am' – and after that, Sinfield would just be a runner for him. Joe Hardstaff had a furious row with him in 1937 during that ill-fated Adelaide Test; Hardstaff was nearing his fifty towards the end of play and he wanted to reach it before the close. 'I played O'Reilly off my legs for a comfortable single, possibly even two. Wally stayed rooted at his end and wouldn't come. I was amazed and two balls later, with my concentration upset, he bowled me with a beauty. I was so annoyed at Wally; he wanted to keep clear of O'Reilly.'

Hammond was respected by some team-mates and opponents, but he lacked the intimate touch that makes friends. He knew the loneliness of greatness just as he knew the isolation of youth. He was made captain of his county and country because he was the best cricketer in the land, not through any skills at the job. F.R. Brown reckoned he was the worst captain he had ever played under: 'He did everything by the clock, rotating his bowlers at set stages.' On the 1946/47 tour he was apart from his side except during matches; while the team travelled on sweaty, interminable train journeys, Hammond journeyed by expensive car. Len Hutton recalled a 700-mile car journey in Australia, when the only words he said to him were 'Keep an eye out for a garage; we need some petrol.' And this to a batsman highly rated by the captain! He could never understand that experienced players held him in awe, that they looked to him for guidance. Hammond felt he should captain by inspiration, and when his flow of runs dried up through fibrositis and the weight of personal problems the tour was doomed. He even criticised his players for fraternising with the opposition over a few post-match drinks.

Denis Compton, an individual never averse to such social opportunities but nevertheless a resolute, brave competitor, said Hammond's personal example on that tour was the worst he ever saw: 'The players looked to the captain for guidance, but it was not there. The only time we saw him was at the grounds.'

With his batting crippled by fibrositis, his personal life was also in a mess on that tour. News of his impending divorce broke as the team landed in Australia, and Hammond could not see why his personal affairs should be a matter of public interest. He had fallen in love with a South African beauty queen and, worried about the reaction from the Establishment, had installed her with his mother in a house in Gloucestershire. Throughout that Australian tour, Hammond was taking telephone calls from either woman, each giving their side of their continuing quarrels. It only served to darken a nature that was gloomy enough.

He remarried, left abruptly for South Africa and settled in Durban. After Australia he was lost to first-class cricket, apart from a couple more matches when he turned out to boost Gloucestershire's coffers. His final appearance was in the 1951 August Bank Holiday game at Bristol against Somerset; public interest was huge, and the ovation accorded Hammond would have melted many men. If his waistline was thicker, his chest rather stouter, he still moved with that old liquid grace on his way out to bat. There the good news ends: he scratched around for half an hour to score seven singles before Horace Hazell bowled him and put him out of his misery. Arthur Milton partnered him: 'It was terribly sad to see him struggle. I had been brought up on his exploits and longed to see him do well. Yet there he was, cursing quietly as he mistimed balls he once hammered.' He strained a muscle while batting, did not re-appear for a second knock and fielded immobile at slip. That was the last time Bristol saw him in the uniform that always seemed to fit him better than any mortal man: cricket whites.

Bad luck dogged him in South Africa. He took a partnership in the motor trade, and his partner ran off with all the money. He suffered a fractured skull in a frightening car crash in 1960, when his legs were trapped under the dashboard and he could not escape as a train bore down on him at a level crossing. The doctors said only a man with a marvellous constitution could have survived. He was glad enough to take a job as a coach/ groundsman at Natal University and happy to fly over to Bristol in 1962, to try to boost Gloucestershire's membership drive. Visits by members of successive England touring sides found him cheerful enough. On the 1964/65 tour they had a whip-round to pay for Hammond's journey to Port Elizabeth for the final Test and his stay in a hotel, because he was short of funds. But he was reluctant to discuss his great days and uninterested in modern cricket. He never really recovered from that horrific car smash and died in 1965, at the age of 62. An appeal was launched in Bristol for his widow and dependents, and his redoubtable mother attended a memorial service. A decade later, a poignant reminder of Hammond turned up in a Gloucester antique shop – the silver cigarette case given to him by his team-mates when he remarried.

Nothing in life came easy to him, apart from his glittering athletic prowess, small comfort to him when misery cast its hand on his psyche. Little things used to upset him; he could not see why Hobbs and Sutcliffe were each given £100 by a newspaper after their wonderful bad-wicket performance at Melbourne in 1929, when Hammond received nothing for his double hundred earlier in the match. Slights and insults would arouse him, as J.W.H.T. Douglas discovered once at Chelmsford. Hammond was caught at cover but he stood his ground, convinced it was a 'bump' ball. At the interval, Douglas called him a cheat; Hammond kept his own counsel and scored 244. The following day, as Gloucestershire walked out to field, Hammond announced quietly to his captain, Harry Rowlands, that he would like to bowl. He proceeded to bowl frighteningly fast, knocking the bat out of Douglas's hands.

Les Ames and G.O. Allen thought him the best offside player they ever saw, and both made the point that he was pulverisingly effective off both back and front foot. R.E.S. Wyatt believed him to be the hardest hitter of all the great batsmen he saw. Bill Bowes recalled being told by Hammond that every ball should be hit hard enough for two; he felt his back foot excellence gave him a crucial yard extra to see the ball.

The general view among his contemporaries was that he would have had to adapt more to the modern game than the other great players. G.O. Allen believed that, as Hammond set himself to play on the offside, his body was locked into a certain position; by getting inside the ball, he was slightly off balance for legside shots. Les Ames thought that short-pitched bowling would unnerve him and the alteration of the bowler's line to middle-and-leg would restrict him. Norman Yardley said he loved batting against spinners and that his majestic drives off the back foot would be difficult against fast bowling aimed at the heart. Joe Hardstaff confirmed that Larwood always liked to bowl at Hammond; he felt he was apprehensive. Certainly Learie Constantine rattled him at Old Trafford in 1933; after being hit on the jaw, Hammond gave himself up in the leg-trap soon afterwards and entered the English dressing-room with the words, 'If that's what Test cricket has come to, I'm giving up.' More than once he was troubled by Farnes and Nichols when Essex played Gloucestershire.

If he batted today, perhaps he would simply ride the fast bowlers, duck out of the way of the short-pitched deliveries. Perhaps, protected by a helmet, he would hand out the kind of medicine suffered by MacDonald in 1927. It may be that he would learn how to play the hook, the cut and the glance. A man who could humiliate Parker and Goddard on turning wickets could not be without resource. The spinners and the fast-medium bowlers would be no problem; he always played spin off the pitch, rather than from the hand, and his back-foot driving would relish medium pace. During the England tour to South Africa in 1956/57 he confessed that he would not have been able to score quickly against the nagging bowling of Trevor Goddard, left-arm medium pace over the wicket to a legside field. That is hard to believe – he would surely adapt while using the patience that drove the 1929 Australians to distraction.

Whatever his shortcomings, Hammond was a genius of his time, worshipped by crowds and revered by his colleagues. When Gloucestershire won the toss and batted at Bristol, Tom Goddard would say to the bowlers: 'Right lads, we can go off to the beach at Weston-super-Mare now, Wally will see us all right.' Among all the tributes to a great batsman, one sticks in my mind and it came from Sam Cook, the Gloucestershire slow bowler and later a first-class umpire. In his first season Sam needed a blazer for the team photograph, and Hammond gave him one of his. Now Sam lacked the awesome physique of his captain, yet if he noticed that the shoulders came halfway down his arms he did not care. He posed proudly for the photo, took the blazer home to Tetbury on the bus, and it stayed in his home until his death. He sometimes wore it when pottering in his garden, but usually it hung in his wardrobe, a cherished family heirloom. When Sam showed me that blazer and told me who first wore it, he rolled his Cotswold burr around the two words – 'W.R.' The pride in his voice revealed everything about the greatness of Walter Reginald Hammond.

From 99th to 100th

number of innings taken to score that last 100

G. Boycott	1
D.G. Bradman	1
M.C. Cowdrey	1
T.W. Graveney	1
G.A. Hick	1
I.V.A. Richards	1
Zaheer Abbas	1
E.H. Hendren	2
W.G. Grace	3
G.A. Gooch	4
L. Hutton	5
D.C.S. Compton	6
C.P. Mead	6
L.E.G. Ames	7
H. Sutcliffe	7
G.M. Turner	7
J.B. Hobbs	8
G.E. Tyldesley	9
F.E. Woolley	10
M.R. Ramprakash	11
D.L. Amiss	16
A. Sandham	21
J.H. Edrich	22
W.R. Hammond	24
T.W. Hayward	47

G.A. Hick scored his 99th and 100th hundreds in the same match.

10

Andrew Sandham

'With Andy, it was simply a case of bowl and wish'
(Jack Mercer)

Andrew Sandham

Born

Streatham, London

6 July 1890

Died

Westminster, London

20 April 1982

First hundred

196   Surrey v Sussex, The Oval, 1913
Age: 22 years 359 days

100th hundred

132   Surrey v Hampshire, Basingstoke, 1935
Age: 44 years 355 days

Last hundred

102   Surrey v Sussex, Hove, 1937
Age: 47 years 58 days

Career record

M	Inn	NO	HS	Runs	Average	100s	50s
643	1,000	79	325	41,284	44.82	107	207

Test record

M	Inn	NO	HS	Runs	Average	100s	50s
14	23	0	325	879	38.21	2	3

The picture in the Oval pavilion just about says it all concerning the career of Andrew Sandham. It is dated 1925, and the adoring crowds are welcoming back Jack Hobbs in his first game at The Oval since breaking W.G. Grace's record of centuries. The Master is walking out to bat, shyly acknowledging the acclaim with that endearingly modest way of his. His partner, Andrew Sandham, can be spotted behind a knot of spectators who have dared to get that little bit nearer to Hobbs. Sandham is quietly fastening on his batting gloves, getting ready for the business of the day once all the fuss has died down. He was always one step behind Jack Hobbs.

A batsman who scored 107 centuries, more runs than Compton and Hutton and who once held the record for the highest score in Test cricket would, by all the canons of fairness, be expected to enjoy a few slaps on the back from his home crowd. It never happened to Sandham; he even contrived to score his hundredth century at Basingstoke, away from The Oval ground he adorned for so long. He was overshadowed too long by Hobbs to be called a great batsman, but he never allowed the fact to obscure his wry, balanced view of life. At The Oval in 1931, Hobbs had the rare experience of a first-ball dismissal against Leicestershire. Stan Squires went to the next ball – Surrey 0 for 2. Sandham batted five hours for a skilful, composed century and as he walked out of The Oval that evening, reasonably content with his labours, he noticed the newspaper placard: 'Hobbs 0 at The Oval'. Sandham grinned and said: 'Well, I suppose you've got to be a pretty good player to get a placard like that when you get a duck.'

If he ever felt irritation at being pigeonholed as Hobbs' partner, he did not show it. He once said: 'He was a great man, Jack. It used to annoy my wife, who didn't know anything about cricket at all. She'd say there were ten other people playing besides Jack Hobbs.' There was never any rivalry between the two men, just a bond of mutual respect and affection. Sandham knew the needs of the side, and he was content to run the singles that Hobbs wanted and to take the bowling when necessary. They ran beautifully between the wickets; Sandham was always ready to run for the last ball of the over and no calling was needed. He could see the humour in the situation, particularly the time when he faced one ball in a quarter of an hour and was criticised in the press box for being slow. They had 63 partnerships of a hundred to their credit – six behind Holmes and Sutcliffe – and during their fifteen-year association they ran each other out just once. Reg Sinfield had painful memories of the speed between the wickets of Hobbs and Sandham; Gloucestershire came to The Oval and fielded first on a typical featherbed. Sinfield fielded at short leg in those days and opened the bowling. His first over at short leg did not equip him for a long stint with the new ball: 'Jack pushed the first one past me, and I had to chase after it because we had a few slips and other fielders behind the wicket. On that vast Oval outfield, they ran five. I came puffing back for the second ball, and Andy pushed it past me – they ran another five! Ten runs in two balls, all run, and they were both no youngsters. My word, they could run!'

It was always Hobbs and Sandham, never the other way round; it could not be otherwise, for Hobbs was the greatest player of his generation. Sandham, however, was a delightful batsman – the word 'dapper' might have been coined with him in mind. He was small, wiry and beautifully balanced, a player with an on-drive as good as that of the Master and a darting late cut that was not in his partner's wondrous repertoire. Sandham was a touch player: a deflector of fast, rising deliveries, a glider of the break-backs. Like W.G. Grace, he cocked his left foot in the air as the bowler braced himself for the delivery. He executed exquisite wristy shots, played the hook with disarming ease and at all times looked poised, unyielding and efficient. R.C. Robertson-Glasgow described him as 'a first fiddle who, for most of his time, played second fiddle in the orchestra.' Sandham would be the last man to suggest a roll of drums on his behalf.

R.E.S. Wyatt, who toured the West Indies and India with Sandham, told me how much he had learned from him by batting at the other end. 'He never moved too soon, his head was always so still. He was a most beautiful player who would walk into the England side today. His cutting and hooking would plunder all this short-pitched stuff.' Even when he retired at the age of 47, Sandham was still playing immaculately straight, the result of learning his trade on good, hard wickets. One day at The Oval Hobbs and Sandham were moving elegantly towards yet another big stand against Sussex. Hobbs was content to coast along for a time, while Sandham saw an unusual proportion of the strike. It all became too much for Maurice Tate, who spluttered: 'For heaven's sake, let me have a go at Jack! At least he gives you a half a chance!' Jack Mercer, a great friend of both openers, agreed: 'I'd always prefer to bowl at Jack, because he had so many shots that he might just play one too many. With Andy, it was simply a case of bowl and wish!' Barring accidents, Hobbs was usually the first to go – normally as soon as he had reached his hundred and picked out an old friend to be the lucky bowler – but Sandham would invariably be still there after tea, inscrutably clocking up the runs at forty an hour. He knew how to rattle a fast bowler; within earshot, he would say, 'He's lost a yard of pace since last season, hasn't he?' and then wait for the inevitable bouncers on which to feed his peerless hook shot. He really loved batting against fast bowling, relishing the demands placed on his superb footwork, his orderly technique. Harold Larwood maintained that no one played him better than Sandham.

He was, of course, lucky to assess the methods of Hobbs at the other end and adapt them accordingly. He also admitted his indebtedness to Tom Hayward before the Great War. When still at school, Sandham – who lived just a few miles away from The Oval – idolised Hayward. After he joined the staff, he would spend every available moment watching him and analysing his technique, especially against fast bowling. Whenever he was twelfth man, one of Andy's duties was to go to the Members' Bar and buy a large whisky for Hayward when he was out. He could never recall being reimbursed for his pains by Hayward and the young pro was too much in awe of him to cavil. After Sandham established himself in the Surrey side, he displayed much of Hayward's soundness – and none of his fielding defects. He became one of the finest outfielders in the world, with blistering speed and a marvellous pick-up and throw.

His apprenticeship was a long one. He first played for Surrey in 1911 at the age of 21 and, although *Wisden* said kind things about him, he had to be content with three games in two years. In 1913 he scored his first century and a good one it was – 196 against Sussex after his side had slumped to 64 for four. But it was not enough to keep him in the first team. Donald Knight, the captain of Malvern College, was available during the school holidays and in those days the amateurs were chosen ahead of promising young professionals. Sandham managed just nine matches that season and five in 1914.

During the war he was invalided home from the front line after being badly injured. When cricket resumed in 1919 he was still kept out by Knight once he had finished his term at Oxford. Despite one innings of 175 not out against Middlesex, Sandham was still on trial at the age of 29. The following season, he gained a regular place and, when Jack Hobbs missed most of the 1921 season through illness and injury, Sandham made over 2,000 runs and looked a high-class player. The England selectors agreed, although they hedged their bets. He was picked just for the final Test at The Oval and made a modest enough 21 before Ted MacDonald bowled him. His chief merit was to keep Phil Mead loyal company while he soldiered on to his 182 not out. Sandham had to play second fiddle for more than just Surrey.

He played in just one more Test at home, against South Africa in 1924, and had to tour to pick up 12 further caps. He played twice against Australia on Arthur Gilligan's tour but, for some reason, batted number six in the first innings and seven in the second. As he watched Herbert Sutcliffe consolidate a partnership with Hobbs that became a byword for reliability and temperament, Sandham knew he would never be centre stage for England. He never opened for England with Hobbs, whereas Sutcliffe and his splendid partner Holmes did manage it against India in 1932. Technically, Sandham was a better player than Sutcliffe, but the Yorkshireman was so positive, such a competitor, that there was only one man who could open with Hobbs against the best in the world. A total of 49 runs in five innings against Australia did not recommend Sandham for the task.

Sandham knew he would never need a special cabinet to hold all his England caps, but his last game for England amused him greatly. He remains the only man to score a triple hundred in his last Test. His 325 at Kingston in 1930 took him ten hours; he used his captain's long-handled bat (he had sold or broken all his own) and batted in Patsy Hendren's shoes, which occasionally slipped off as he scampered a single. He started off with sore feet and shins, a legacy of the hard grounds, and as the day wore on he was near to exhaustion. The bat did not suit him, it was too hot and, at the end of a hard tour, he wanted to put his feet up. Sandham swore till his dying day that he only stayed out at the crease to keep Joe Hardstaff Snr happy; Hardstaff, who was on the county umpires' list, had been brought over to show the West Indians the rudiments of umpiring. When Sandham reached his century, he told Hardstaff he was going to get out. 'Don't do that, Andy,' the umpire replied. 'I don't know anybody out here, and I'll feel lonely. Stay a little longer, try for two hundred!' Throughout the day Hardstaff prevailed on Sandham – 'Hang on till tea now', 'Go for your three hundred, you've never scored one, you know.' And he lasted till the close, unbeaten on 300. He faced two additional hazards: Patsy Hendren and Les Ames. Both men came out to bat, breathing aggression and demanding quick singles. On each occasion Sandham had to call a halt to the frenzy. Les Ames remembered Sandham's words of wisdom: 'He said to me, "Young man, do you see that scoreboard up there? It says I've got 220, and it feels like it. I'm not having any youngster coming in and running me off my feet. Run when you're told to!" He said it all with a poker face, and I did what I was told.'

Sandham was bowled the next day for 325, yet he still had not finished batting in that Test. He came in at number seven in the second innings, cursing his stiffness and wincing during the singles. He made 50 and his total of runs in one Test remained a record until beaten by Greg Chappell in 1974. Sandham's 325 did not last quite so long as the record for an innings – six months later, Don Bradman made 334 at Leeds. Somehow it seemed typical of Sandham's self-effacing batting that his record would not stand for any length of time; he was the second fiddler, not the cymbals crasher.

In the last few years of the Hobbs/Sandham partnership, the older man was carefully nursed through some sticky moments by his devoted junior partner. Sandham would notice when fatigue had gripped Hobbs and, calmly and quietly, he would take the bowling for a while. Hobbs always lauded the unselfishness of his friend and often pointed to Taunton in 1925 as a great example. In the first innings Hobbs had gratified the tastes of the mass media and his own fretting supporters by scoring the century needed to equal the record of W.G. Grace. The posse of cameramen, news reporters and sensation-seekers had moved on by the time Surrey's second innings had started. Hobbs batted without care for an hour until Sandham confidently hazarded that another hundred was there for the taking. Surrey needed 183 to win, and Sandham ensured that his own score would not threaten the pursuit of Hobbs' century. It was reached within nine runs of victory, Grace had been caught and passed within three days and, although the laurels were placed on the head of a superb batsman, much of the credit goes to the unselfish Sandham.

He was to have his own day of glory, and it came on 26 June 1935 when he scored 103 against Hampshire at Basingstoke, his hundredth hundred.

He was a worthy successor to his partner, Hobbs, and the idol of his youth, Hayward. Nearly fifty years later, Sandham could remember the stroke that brought him the hundred – a push off his legs for a couple of runs. Typically deft, typically safe. That night, over a celebratory drink, he allowed himself the rare luxury of basking in his glory and quipped: 'I ran a lot for old Jack as well, you know!'

Sandham did not outlast his usefulness on the field of play. He retired in 1937 while still a good player, proving that with a hundred in his last championship match. He finished his career on exactly 1,000 innings, a neat, well-rounded end in keeping with the methodical precision of his batting.

His association with Surrey cricket was to last till 1970, a round total of sixty years. He ran a cricket school with Alf Gover at Wandsworth – he never strayed far from South London – then returned to The Oval as coach. The Surrey captain, Stuart Surridge, called him 'Mr Producer' as he turned out class substitutes for the household names who were called away on England duty. He did much for Ken Barrington and John Edrich in their formative years at The Oval, instilling in them the virtues of playing straight and building an innings. He was proud and delighted when they became England regulars, and Barrington and Edrich always called him 'Mr Sandham' with a touching blend of respect and warmth. He was a whimsical man with the same sort of dry humour associated with Jack Hobbs. Once Stuart Surridge returned to the dressing-room after picking up several respectable wickets, and he was looking for some praise from his coach. In front of the rest of the side, Surridge said: 'Well, coach, what do you think of that?' Sandham sipped his tea, winked at the other players and said, 'You bowled two very good balls – and they hit 'em both for four!' He did not lose his timing when he put his bat in mothballs.

Alec Bedser recalls his kindness as a coach: 'He was so pleasant, yet authoritative. He spoke rich common sense about the game; I can hear him now saying "Make your elbow hit the sky when you play back" to the young professionals. A great man for the basic principles of cricket.' He had no time for the biff-bang style of batting; he liked to see class in the nets. He would say: 'Now come on, my son, let's have a bit of ease and grace.' Alf Gover remembered Sandham's frustration at one cricketer who visited the indoor school at Wandsworth. 'Andy used to say to me, "This bloke can't bat. Why does he keep coming here?" Andy would try his darndest to get him to play properly, but he just wanted to whack it all the time. Finally Andy got fed up of the ball whizzing back at him, he threw down his box of balls and walked out of the net for good. His version of the art of batting was being insulted in his eyes.'

He loved Surrey cricket with a touching devotion. After retiring as coach, he became the first-team scorer, a well-loved, kindly figure always delighted to talk about the old times and forever speaking up for the latest addition to the Surrey first team. The tea room at The Oval was redesigned and named

'The Sandham Tea Room': Hobbs had his gates at The Oval, Sandham the tea room. He left the scorebox in 1970, but he was not finished with Surrey; he would often be found watching the Club and Ground side, hoping to be able to put a word in for some promising youngster.

He lost part of his sight in his last years but bore his affliction with stoicism and dignity. He enjoyed the Centenary Test in 1980, meeting up with so many old friends and modestly fending off media questions such as: 'Mr Sandham, why didn't you play more times for England?' Les Ames saw him for the last time in December 1981, when the Master's Club convened to pay its annual homage to Jack Hobbs. He seemed cheerful enough, although frail, and his last words to Ames were poignant: 'Les, don't ever live till ninety.'

He died in April 1982 at the age of 91. Generations of cricketers mourned him and his former captain Percy Fender told me: 'He was a very great batsman and an even greater gentleman.' Few cricketers can have been so popular or given such distinction to the game for such a long period of time.

11

Sir Donald Bradman

'My feet feel tired when I think of him'
(Joe Hardstaff)

Donald George Bradman

Born

Cootamundra, New South Wales, Australia

27 August 1908

Died

Adelaide, South Australia, Australia

25 February 2001

First hundred

118   New South Wales v South Australia, Adelaide, 1927
Age: 19 years 111 days

100th hundred

172   Australian XI v Indians, Sydney, 1947
Age: 39 years 80 days

Last hundred

123   D.G. Bradman's XI v A.L. Hassett's XI, Melbourne, 1948
Age: 40 years 99 days

Career record

M	Inn	NO	HS	Runs	Average	100s	50s
234	338	43	452*	28,067	95.14	117	69

Test record

M	Inn	NO	HS	Runs	Average	100s	50s
52	80	10	334	6,996	99.94	29	13

When considering the batting record of Sir Donald George Bradman, it is almost impossible to still a sense of wonder. His figures are quite staggering, but so is his impact on modern batsmanship. He was the third link in the chain that began with W.G. Grace. The Doctor evolved the basics of back and forward play against new styles of bowling, then Jack Hobbs developed those principles and adapted them to the demands of new bowling methods. After Hobbs top-class batsmen aimed for quantity on predominantly good pitches. But then came Bradman. He was a batsman who could score more runs than anyone else – but also at a faster pace. His genius lay in the art of doing things simply, clinically and with phenomenal success; his detractors thought he was unorthodox in technique, but it was his attitude that was unorthodox.

Don Bradman was just too good. He destroyed the contest between bat and ball that had always been one of the chief attractions of cricket. From 1930 – his first tour of England – till his retirement in 1949, Bradman was in the driving seat, and the rest nowhere. By his deeds he changed the emphasis of Test cricket. In 1930 the attitude was still fairly Corinthian; England, under the uncomplicated, optimistic captaincy of Percy Chapman, tried to bowl Bradman out, even when he was scoring at forty runs an hour. When Maurice Tate was asked why he had failed to curb Bradman's scoring rate, he replied with engaging ingenuousness: 'Pin him down? Of course not! I bowled every ball to get the little devil out.' On the first day of the Leeds Test, Bradman scored 309 not out; no less than 46 overs were bowled before lunch, and the hourly average for the day was 22. Chapman's field placing during the series was, in retrospect, foolhardy; he should not have attacked such a devastating batsman. It was the last time a Test series was conducted in the spirit of the pre-1914 code; Chapman lost the captaincy for the final Test and the pragmatic R.E.S. Wyatt ushered in a new era of sensible, ultra-professional captaincy. Never again would a series in England see so much leg-spin bowling from so many: 300 overs from Peebles, Robins and Tyldesley for England and nearly 350 from Grimmett. Douglas Jardine and Wyatt realised they could not curb Bradman with leg-spin, so 'Bodyline' was born for the 1932/33 series. It was specifically designed to bring down Bradman to the status of ordinary mortals, and it remains the greatest compliment ever paid to one player. At no other stage in cricket history has a tactical innovation been aimed at a single cricketer.

The scope of Bradman's achievements is so wide that a sense of perspective is needed: the eyes easily dull when confronted with page after page of statistics. I have always felt that the statistical evaluation of his career has unfairly overshadowed his genius, his certainty of strokeplay, speed of scoring and impact on generations of cricket-lovers. A few comments from whose who played with and against Bradman may redress the balance somewhat:

G.O. ALLEN: He had two shots for every ball when he was going well.

ALEC BEDSER: The more I bowled at him, the more I learned about bowling!

JIM LAKER: The only batsman who ever gave me an inferiority complex.

ALF GOVER: He would get runs off your best deliveries and murder your bad ones.

JACK FINGLETON: Music to him was the crash of the ball against the fence. His bat was an axe dripping with the bowler's blood and agony. He knew no pity.

JOE HARDSTAFF: My feet feel tired when I think of him.

LES AMES: If he came back today, he'd be streets ahead of anyone else.

I can hear the modern first-class cricketers scoffing at that remark by Les Ames, a man who was intimately involved in first-class cricket for more than sixty years. Of course, the fielding is better (although catchers like Hammond, Woolley and Duleepsinjhi, and outfielders such as Bradman and Sandham would have glittered at any age), of course today's wickets are inferior, and indeed the turgid over-rates would clip Bradman's scoring rate. Yet I cannot believe that a man whose footwork was so dazzling, a man whose powers of concentration were legendary, a batsman who co-ordinated mind, feet and bat to such an astonishing degree, would not still dominate today. His mastery of length meant that he was stumped just 22 times in a twenty-year career, even though against slow bowlers the crease to him was just a place to take guard. Today's cricketers rightly set great score on speed between the wickets, running two to third man if necessary and putting pressure on the deep fielders. Bradman was run out four times in first-class cricket, and three of those came before he was 22. Bill Bowes told me how masterful Bradman was at placing the ball from where a fielder had just been moved: 'He just toyed with the field.'

No batsman has been more likely to despatch a bad ball to the boundary, or with such certainty. Bradman did not believe in lofting the ball: on his triumphant 1930 tour to England, he scored 2,960 runs, yet hit only two sixes, one off a no-ball. He expected to score off every ball; at Southend in 1948 he scored 187 in just over two hours against Essex and the last over before lunch was classic Bradman. Frank Vigar bowled it (leg-breaks) and Bradman hit five of the six deliveries to the boundary. The odd one out was hammered straight to mid-off and Bradman punched the palm of his hand with irritation. The old hunger was still there, at the age of 40.

His attention to detail would surprise the modern sceptics who feel this 'action replay' age is the zenith of thinking, 'scientific' cricket. In 1930 Bradman began his first tour of England's unfamiliar, slow wickets with 236 at

Worcester. Fred Root, one of the Worcestershire bowlers who toiled in vain, congratulated Bradman after his innings and was astounded to be asked: 'Does George Geary turn the ball much on English wickets?' He was due to face Geary and Leicestershire in the next match. He made 185 not out.

Those bowlers of the 1930s were not unsophisticated; Bill Bowes called for some scoring charts of Bradman's innings before the 'Bodyline' tour, hoping that he and his fellow-sufferers might glean some comfort. His strokes on the chart looked like the spokes of a bicycle wheel. Bradman always scored all round the wicket. Wilfred Rhodes, a great slow bowler, canny Yorkshireman and hard taskmaster, played twice against Bradman in 1930, his last season in a wonderful career that began in 1898. The man who had been captained by Grace in his first Test, who had enjoyed many thrilling duels with Victor Trumper and admired the beautiful craftsmanship of his opening partner, Jack Hobbs – he had no doubt that Bradman was the greatest batsman he had seen. 'I once saw him come in and put his first ball straight back past the bowler for four. And the second. And the third. Just like that. Without getting his eye in or anything. Every one an offensive stroke off a good ball.'

Sir Pelham Warner captained England and enjoyed an association with first-class cricket that lasted seventy years, from Grace to Dexter. He likened bowling at Bradman to 'casting pebbles at the Rock of Gibraltar'. Victor Richardson, splendid Australian batsman of Bradman's era, thought that captains should offer Bradman a century before he batted, provided he was out as soon as he reached that target.

If Richardson's whimsical notion had been adopted, the results would have been instructive – after all, Bradman's average century was 174. If you took away his tally of 43 not-out innings, his career average would still be 83.13, the best by any accredited batsman in the history of the game. If he were to be robbed of his centuries, he would still average 58.20 in his other innings – eight points more than Hobbs, seven more than Sutcliffe and two more than Hammond, with all their centuries included. Bradman made nought in just sixteen of his 338 innings, and not one in a sequence of 70 innings between December 1936 and January 1940. On 27 occasions he scored 200 or more in a day, and he batted for more than six hours on just twelve occasions. The slowest hundred of his career took 253 minutes, a perfectly respectable time for modern cricket. His runs were scored at a devastating rate, yet – according to one of his biographers, B.J. Wakley – he gave just 93 chances that were not accepted throughout his career. Just one more statistic: of his 117 centuries, only eight were for a losing side. Bradman influenced the result of a cricket match more than any other player.

His temperament was as impressive as his statistical prowess. At Melbourne in 1933 Bradman walked out to bat in the second innings of the Second Test with immense pressures on him. He had missed the First Test through illness, yet he was already well aware that Larwood and Voce were aiming to intimidate him by fast, short-pitched bowling to a legside field. He was embroiled in a dispute with the Australian Board of Control over his right to play for Australia and also comment on the game in a daily newspaper; the Board had already fined him £50 for alleged breach of contract following the publication of a book under his own name after the 1930 tour to England. Bradman had hinted that, unless the imbroglio was happily resolved, he might have to give up cricket to earn a living. On the first day he had issued a statement to the effect that his newspaper had released him from his contract so that he could play in the series, but the atmosphere between Bradman and the Board was a little strained. The public interest in his comeback Test was frightening; during his illness, bulletins on his condition had been posted up in shop windows. The Australian public was willing him to be the man to combat this terrifying 'Bodyline' attack and Bradman was trying to come to terms with living a normal life amid the hysteria. On top of all that, he was on a 'king pair', having been bowled first ball by Bowes in the first innings. A new world record crowd of 68,188 watched Bradman take guard, with humiliation a distinct prospect. His first ball from Larwood was a bouncer, a supreme test of nerve and reactions on those fast, unreliable wickets of that season: Bradman hooked him to the boundary with a crack like a rifle shot. He made 103 not out in a second innings total of 191 and Australia won by 111 runs. For the moment the public's craving for revenge had been assuaged. In the circumstances it was one of the greatest innings of his career.

At Leeds in 1934 he had to dig deep into his reserves of stamina and iron will to salvage his reputation. He had batted frenetically so far in the series – 29, 25, 36, 13 and 30 were most unlike him. He had been troubled by ill-health and the cynics were having a lovely time. In the Fourth Test Bradman went in with the score 39 for three, all the wickets having fallen to Bowes. Bradman drove the first two balls past the bowler to the boundary and the next wicket fell at 427. Bradman made 304 – at 42 an hour – and in the final Test 244 and 77. He not only had to contend with indifferent form; his health had been poor for some weeks. Finally it broke in September and he underwent an emergency operation. His appendix was almost gangrenous, he lost a lot of blood and, at the height of his crisis, five bulletins a day were issued. He almost died. Skilful surgery, the presence of his wife at his bedside and his own blend of stamina and mental fitness pulled him through, but it placed his achievements on the cricket pitch into a new perspective. He had played for two months when he should have been in bed, but he carried on through sheer willpower to average 94.75 in the series.

In the following series against England Bradman again had to prove himself. It was his first series as captain, and he lost the first two Tests. He made two successive noughts and left the Brisbane ground in dark glasses to avoid public scrutiny. He had suffered a personal tragedy just before the series started – the loss of his new-born son. In the Third Test at Melbourne Bradman dropped himself down the order while the effects of a thunderstorm turned batting into a lottery, but when he came out – at 97 for five – the match was delicately poised. He made 270, followed that up with 212 and 169 and Australia became the first side to win a series three-two after being two down. Once again Bradman's personal example had been crucial.

The pressures on him were immense when he tried to resume his Test career after the Second World War. He had been discharged from the Army because of fibrositis; at one stage he could not lift his right arm to comb his hair and his wife had to shave him. When Hammond's England team arrived in Australia in October 1946, they were shocked to see the change in Bradman: he was frail and far from fit. At 38, dogged by gastric troubles and slowly recovering from five years of fibrositis, he was far from the concept of the strong Australian sporting hero. The general consensus was that, if Bradman failed in the early games of the forthcoming series, he would stand down and announce his retirement. One incident on the first morning of that opening Test altered the course of the series. When he had scratched together an unimpressive 28, Bradman played a ball from Voce hard to Jack Ikin at slip; while the England players appealed for the catch, Bradman stood his ground and waited for the umpire to rule in his favour. At the end of the over Hammond growled to Bradman, 'That's a fine bloody way to start the series!' and certainly the majority opinion of the England players was that it was a clean catch, not a bump ball. Doug Wright, Alec Bedser and Norman Yardley all confirmed their certainties to me. Afterwards, Bradman told the press he would have walked if he had thought it a clean catch. Whatever the opinions, Bradman batted through his bad form and made 187. In the next Test he scored 234; another personal crisis had been weathered, and his triumphant final tour of England was set up.

There is no doubt he was not the same player as pre-war, yet his performances were still massively certain after that Brisbane Test. He played straighter than ever before, eliminating all risks yet still scoring very quickly. He played closer to the ball, still using his feet to the spinners, but playing his shots when the ball was between his legs to ensure perfect balance. When Alec Bedser rattled him temporarily with the 'caught Hutton, bowled Bedser' ploy (caught at backward short leg off deliveries of a full length that moved in to him late), his reaction was typically thorough: he went into the nets and ordered his bowlers to bowl that type of delivery until he had mastered it. Bedser never got him out again that way.

On being told that the pre-war Bradman was an even more frightening proposition, Alec Bedser and Jim Laker would just count their blessings. Both great bowlers affirm he was the best batsman they ever bowled at. Bedser said: 'No matter the setting of the field, he couldn't be tied down. At such an age, his speed between the wickets was amazing. He could alter the angle from which the ball left the bat with a slight change of grip and he left the bowlers with no margin of error.' Jim Laker conceded nearly a thousand runs against the Australians in 1948 without ever getting Bradman's wicket: 'I can never remember Bradman letting a ball go by without playing a shot. He was streets ahead of anyone else and just couldn't be rattled. In the Lord's Test, I beat him with almost every ball of one over; he looked up at me and said, "Well bowled, Jim – now you've got that out of your system we can get on with the game." He went on to score 89.' Laker remembered a shot Bradman played in the match against Surrey: 'Jack Parker was bowling medium pace and he sent down one that was a little short. Bradman hit it so hard off the back foot through the bowler and mid-on that the ball had bounced back off the pavilion rails as Jack was finishing his run-up.'

Bradman brought to his batting a strength of mind and purpose that was rock-solid and pitiless. He did not espouse stylish play for the sake of it, he was interested in results. He knew that bowlers hate to see the full face of the bat and good-length deliveries turned into half volleys and long hops by use of twinkling footwork. When he came into first-class cricket at the age of 19, he seemed astonishingly mature as a batsman. He had worked out the mechanics of batting for himself and was largely self-taught. The remarkable footwork and reflexes had been honed by practising a little game he devised as a boy: he would throw a golf ball at the brick base of an old water tank and then try to hit the rebound with the stump of a gum tree. The ball would come back at different angles and speeds, which of course developed his footwork. Unless he achieved 75 per cent success, he would keep plugging away.

At the age of 12, he was taken to the Sydney Cricket Ground to see the visiting England team in the fifth Test. He watched the dazzling Charles Macartney score 170 for Australia and calmly informed his father: 'I shall never be satisfied until I play on this ground.' A lonely childhood, albeit within a loving family, had equipped him with that practical, calculating streak he later showed in all facets of life and when he made his debut for New South Wales in first-class cricket the resultant hundred seems, in retrospect, a formality. His opening boundary and the one that brought up his hundred were pull shots – the stroke that became his trademark. He had worked out the grip that suited his fondness for the pull; both hands were turned over the handle, which rested against the ball of the right thumb. That enabled him to close the face of the bat over the ball, enabling him to hook, pull and cut down rather than uppishly. The right hand emphasis meant his onside play was stronger than on the offside, but he compensated with venomous straight driving. Everything else was textbook and remained so for the next twenty years.

His orderly mind played a vital role in his batting. He treated it like a business, something to be approached with dedication and professionalism. Jack Fingleton, a colleague many times in the Australian side, gave a fascinating insight into the personal habits of Bradman during a lunch interval when he was not out. Fingleton wrote that he would place his pads, gloves and bat on the table, have a wash, then take off his trousers, put a towel round his waist and sit down to a light lunch of rice custard, stewed fruit and milk. 'Each slow mouthful was an essay in method, in digestion, in relaxation, in cold planning and contemplation of the real feast soon to follow in the middle.'

One can only guess if Bradman would have been so ruthless if he had started his first-class career in a more encouraging, tolerant environment. The hard-nosed leg-pullers of the New South Wales team soon found Bradman a fertile source of amusement: the farmer's son from the outback was 19 before he ventured outside the state of New South Wales and his gaucheness and naivety stood out. On his first trip to Adelaide one of the players sent him on a fruitless errand to a suburb eight miles from his hotel; when the team discovered he had musical talent, he was made to play the piano with his shirt off, so they could examine his back muscles as he tinkled the keyboard. Bradman swallowed the 'country boy' jibes and vowed to answer back in the most satisfying way: on the cricket field. After his debut century he was never again a laughing-stock.

Then he had to convince the Test selectors that he was the genuine article. From this distance it seems one of the great misjudgements of all time to drop Don Bradman after just one Test against England in 1928 – yet he only made 18 and 1 and did not look at all comfortable on a rain-affected wicket in the second innings. He was back for the Third Test, scoring a hundred, but there were still doubts about his technique. Maurice Tate called him his 'rabbit', Warwick Armstrong thought he was not, at present, Test class and Charles Kelleway, a team-mate in that series, said he would be found out in England, because he used a cross-bat. All this steeled Bradman even more to greater deeds, and his subsequent career is a triumph of will-power as much as natural ability.

The envy and pettiness of others inevitably kept pace with Bradman's burgeoning prestige. On his ascent to cricketing greatness he seemed to attract a motley assortment of denigrators, eager to misjudge an imagined slight, exacerbate differences of opinion and accept damaging rumours. The press did not always acquit itself nobly, and the strain on Bradman's private life must have been unimaginable. Much was made of the night at Leeds, in 1930, when Bradman retired to his hotel room to play classical music after he had scored his marvellous unbeaten triple hundred. Some of his team-mates felt he should have bought them a drink and joined in an orgy of back-slapping. Bradman's retort: 'What did they expect me to do? Parade around Leeds?' may have seemed tactless, but there is no playing regulation that ensures that a star batsman should spend his social hours in a way foreign to his nature.

His early, triumphal return to Australia at the end of that 1930 tour also irritated his team-mates. The sports manufacturing company that employed Bradman swiftly assessed he was now a hot commercial property – 'the Bradman brand' in modern parlance. They arranged his journey home by plane and then train as the rest of the tour party took the long way home, by boat. Bradman then took the hysterical plaudits from doting fans at public functions in the major Australian cities and, although he never failed to praise his captain and team-mates, envy naturally took hold on some of those players. At the age of 22 his commercial worth had soared in just the space of a few months, but over the next decade a few of his contemporaries nurtured resentment towards him. Not until the 1946/47 series against England did Bradman lead a fully supportive unit.

Bradman was a Protestant, eventually became a Freemason, working diligently in business circles as his cricketing prestige prospered. He embodied the link between Australia and Britain – allies in the Great War, suffering enormous casualties, closely aligned to the Monarchy, of lower-middle class stock. Bradman's team-mates such as Bill O'Reilly and Jack Fingleton were Irish-Catholic, embodying working-class republicanism, disinclined to respect traditional values. They hadn't forgotten the dreadful Australian losses at Gallipoli in 1915, in their view at the dictate of the British First Lord of the Admiralty, Winston Churchill.

They never shared Bradman's fondness for Great Britain, nor the Establishment.

Years after all three had retired, the anarchic views of O'Reilly and Fingleton about Bradman added greatly to the entertainment in press boxes, where the two great iconoclasts had carved out fine careers. E.W. Swanton, friend and admirer of Bradman for seventy years, never forgot the moment when he was bowled second ball for nought in his final Test by Eric Hollies at The Oval in 1948. 'There were two Australians in the press box, who nearly died laughing. They were, of course, O'Reilly and Fingleton.'

His successful business ventures while still a player attracted disparaging remarks from some with inferior financial acumen and playing ability. Certainly he seems to have been a tough negotiator with those desirous of his services and name, but there were never any criticisms of his integrity. His relationship with the Australian Board was a fluctuating one, but he never dissembled and would stick out on a principle that was important to him – like the row over his book on the 1930 tour and the fact that he was barred from making newspaper pronouncements on the 1932/33 series, while some of his team-mates were allowed to broadcast their views every night on radio. To Bradman's logical and clear mind, that was nonsense and it is difficult to disagree with him.

His greatness as a public performer inevitably meant that his shy, reserved persona would occasionally be stripped bare of defence against the demands of a mass media age. Jack Fingleton, no lover of Bradman, has paid tribute to his remarkable tolerance with the hordes of autograph hunters who besieged him for two decades. On one England tour a former Test captain who had drunk rather too much was refused entry to see Bradman at Lord's because of his condition; he took his feelings of outrage to Fleet Street, who gleefully printed the story without seeking the view of Bradman. In the first year of

Bradman's touchingly happy marriage, his wife overheard a conversation about their alleged pending divorce.

The flame of publicity also burned his son John. In 1954 John booked into a guest house in South Wales; when he signed his name in the residents' book, he immediately attracted interest. The guests never left him alone that night, quizzing him about his father. Finally, in 1972, John could stand it not longer, changing his surname by deed poll to Bradsen. Happily for his father, John reverted to his original surname in 2000. As late as 1980 Bradman attracted ill-informed publicity over his decision not to attend the Centenary Test celebrations in London. The Fleet Street whisper was that he did not wish to share the limelight with the other eminent cricketers of yesteryear. A couple of phone calls to sources close to Bradman would have yielded the truth – he was worried about the health of his wife, who had undergone open-heart surgery in recent years, his daughter Shirley (a sufferer from cerebral palsy since early childhood) and his son John (who had contracted polio at the age of thirteen). All that was enough to tax the morale of even Bradman.

I am happy to acknowledge innumerable acts of kindness by Bradman to the famous and the insignificant. G.O. Allen told me Bradman was the most sporting captain and gracious loser he had played against – despite his toughness on the field. Bill Edrich became the last Englishman to reach a thousand runs in May due to Bradman's willingness to share the spotlight of glory. It was in 1938 and on the last day of May the Australians were playing Middlesex. Bradman reached his thousand runs in May and then declared twenty minutes from the close to give Edrich the chance to follow suit. He needed ten runs, opened the innings and Bradman was the first man to congratulate him. Edrich's great partner, Denis Compton, also had a fond memory of Bradman from that 1938 season; it came during the Lord's Test, when the 20-year-old Compton played an innings of genius on a damp pitch. As Compton walked off the field – unbeaten on 76 – Bradman walked over to him, shook his hand and said: 'Denis, that was one of the finest innings I've seen.' Alec Bedser remembers two warm gestures – producing a sack of chilled beer for the England party as they prepared for yet another hot, sticky train journey in Australia, and bundling Bedser off to bed in his Adelaide home when he arrived in the city with 'flu and his hotel room not yet ready. Bill Bowes treasured the moment when, after beating Bradman all ends up, he was told: 'Well bowled, Bill – that's one up to you.' Reg Sinfield's first wicket in Test cricket was that of Bradman, caught behind by Les Ames at Nottingham in 1938; as he walked away, he said to Sinfield: 'Well done, Reg – I give you best.' Nor did he hog the limelight when Australia batted. His exhortation to the rest of his side ('Come and watch this, you'll never see the like again') during Stan McCabe's priceless 232 at Trent Bridge in 1938 reflected great credit on both captain and batsman. Neil Harvey will not readily forget the way Bradman blocked an over from Dick Pollard, so that young Harvey could hit the winning run in his first Test, at Leeds in 1948, nor the way his captain ran to him with congratulations, oblivious of his own 173 not out that had set up that victory.

He did not confine spontaneous acts of human decency to the great and the good. At Trent Bridge in 1934 Bradman was on his way into the ground when he noticed a man standing outside the gates looking wistful. Bradman stopped for a word, discovered he was an unemployed miner and invited him into the ground, paying his admission, finding a good seat and handing over some spending money. When he discovered he had a wife and eight children to feed, Bradman organised a collection for him in the Australian dressing-room and topped the list with his own contribution. On that same tour he was walking along the Embankment in London, reasonably pleased with life; he had scored 244 that day in the Oval Test and then enjoyed a pleasant evening at the theatre. He spotted some tramps and was visibly moved by their condition; he took them to a coffee stall, forced food and drink on them and when one hungry tramp said suspiciously, 'Who are yer?' Bradman wordlessly put a half crown in his hand.

All these were hardly the actions of a ruthless automaton, a man who carried the same merciless principles of his batting into his private life. He simply seems a person who knew his own mind, whom to trust and whom to avoid. Like any other member of the human race, his adult life was shaped by the circumstances of youth; because he had to play a lot on his own, he developed into a self-sufficient, wary individual. Yet he never forgot his family, writing every week to his mother from England in 1930, and making characteristically thorough financial provision for her future as his own prospects improved out of all recognition.

Surely no other sports personality has responded more diligently to letters than Bradman over such a prolonged period of time – in his case seventy years, right up to his death. Cricket writers down the years had cause to be grateful for the innumerable forewords he readily wrote. I have personal experience of his kindness. In 1982, while researching the first edition of this book, I sent him a list of twenty questions in an attempt to gain extra insight into his remarkable career and life. He responded in full by return post, in his own immaculate hand. He did not know me and had no reason to respond so generously.

When he came to London in 1974 to speak at a charity dinner for the Lord's Taverners' Fund, he signed every one of the 900 menus the day before, after being assured that this would appreciably swell the amount raised at the dinner.

After he retired Bradman's services to cricket were outstanding. A Test selector for two decades, he was twice Chairman of the Australian Cricket Board, playing a decisive part in clearing up the controversy over throwing in the late 1950s and early 60s. His book, *The Art of Cricket*, remains a seminal work, analytical, clear-headed and inspirational. Reading it, you are struck how quickly Bradman worked out the best batting method for himself and the importance of a strong mental approach.

So much for Bradman the man. The batsman has only one worthwhile charge to answer when his claims to pre-eminence are considered: his performances on bad wickets. It is generally held that Bradman did not see why he should be expected to bat on surfaces that made the game a lottery and this is why Jack Hobbs remains the *nonpareil* in the eyes of many good judges. It is true that Bradman looked very unimpressive in 'Verity's Match' in 1934, when he slogged the spinner up in the air soon after he came in on a turning wicket. Woodfull, his captain, gave him a schoolmasterly stare as he walked from the wicket, and the legend of Bradman and damaged wickets was born on that day. Closer scrutiny of his record in England does not substantiate the allegation; he came on four tours to England and scored more than 2,000 runs each time. One-third of his total career innings was therefore played in England. Surely in such a climate, with the wickets uncovered, surely he faced wickets that were occasionally as tricky as Lord's in 1934? He did and acquitted himself well. Norman Yardley recalled his superb hundred on a turner that won the Leeds Test of 1938: 'No one could have played better – wonderful footwork, immaculate defence and impeccable stroke selection.' Hedley Verity, the unwilling agent of the slurs on Bradman, would not agree that he was susceptible on unreliable wickets and he would cite Bramall Lane 1938 as an example. On an authentic 'sticky' wicket, Bradman batted for nearly four hours to total 59 and 42, playing most deliveries in the middle of the bat and living off his considerable wits. Again in that season his performance on a dry, dusty wicket in the Trent Bridge Test won high praise; on the last day Verity and Wright spun the ball sharply, yet Bradman scored 144 not out in an innings of judicious defence and clean striking of the bad ball.

Bradman played most of his Sheffield Shield career on covered wickets, and on the rare occasions when he came up against a 'sticky' wicket during Tests in Australia he did not fare well. It seems he had cashed in his psychological chips by the time he came out to bat on these uncertain, physically dangerous surfaces, but I believe he would have adapted if necessary. The man who improvised against the terrifying 'Bodyline' onslaught to average 56.57 (better than Sutcliffe or Hammond) in that series need have no qualms about any other type of bowling or cricketing surface. Jack Hobbs thought he would have been the best in the world if given the opportunity to play regularly on rain-affected wickets and, with his gifts of timing, concentration and footwork, it is hard to disagree.

When he died, aged 92, in February 2001, England was playing a Test in Sri Lanka. The requisite courtesies were accorded him – black armbands worn by both sides, a minute's silence before the start of play, suitably reverent quotes from both captains. But this was a rare occasion when contemporary cricketers knew the merit of someone who had not been seen on the field for more than fifty years. The modern player respects results and relevance above style and charisma, and the England players didn't need any extra insight into the colossal career of Bradman. They simply whistled at the scale of his achievements. Scoring a century every 2.88 innings and a double hundred every 9.13 innings automatically stilled any caveats they might have from seeing fielding frailties and bowling weaknesses on flickering newsreels when the Don was in his pomp.

He was simply the most effective batsman the game has known. Geoffrey Boycott, another practitioner of the art of effectiveness, is a keeper of the Bradman flame. When asked to comment on Sachin Tendulkar's elevation to the top of the run-scorer's list in Test cricket, Boycott didn't stint in his praise of the Indian maestro. But when it was put to him that Tendulkar might be the greatest of all time, Boycott snorted derisively and rasped: 'Don't be daft, that's Bradman – and the rest are nowhere.' For true cricketing perspective it's hard to beat a curmudgeonly Yorkshireman who doesn't usually dole out the superlatives.

Don Bradman was a marvel. Other batsmen of his age would make more charming hundreds (McCabe, Woolley), others were more thrilling (Hammond, Compton), more resolute in unfavourable conditions (Sutcliffe, Hutton), but Bradman's was always the wicket to prize. Alec Bedser, bluff, unsentimental veteran of countless Tests as player and selector, still treasures the ball that bowled Bradman for nought at Adelaide in 1947. Ian Peebles used to recount the newspaper placard that greeted him after he dismissed Bradman for 14 in the 1930 Old Trafford Test – PEEBLES DOES IT!

It was left to a hale and hearty in-swing bowler from Somerset to put Bradman's prestige in a nutshell. Bill Andrews was a splendid character with an engaging raconteur's wit, an enviable ability to remember the punchline and an endearing way of beginning a sentence with 'Did I ever tell you ...' At Taunton in 1938 he sent down one delivery that has kept him in after-dinner stories for the next fifty-one years: he clean bowled Don Bradman. He had made 202 at the time and had relaxed his customary vigilance at the end of the Test series, but no matter. In 1973 Bill Andrews' book of reminiscences was published, entitled *The Hand that Bowled Bradman.* All because of one carefree shot at a time when Neville Chamberlain still believed Herr Hitler was a man of honour. A Bradman dismissal really was that special.

12

Les Ames

'Taking on the bowlers was my idea of cricket,
not worrying about dropping a catch'

Leslie Ethelbert George Ames

Born

Elham, Kent

3 December 1905

Died

Canterbury, Kent

27 February 1990

First hundred

111   Kent v Hampshire, Southampton, 1927
Age: 21 years 185 days

100th hundred

131   Kent v Middlesex, Canterbury, 1950
Age: 44 years 251 days

Last hundred

116*   Commonwealth XI v Indian Prime Minister's XI, Bombay, 1951
Age: 45 years 91 days

Career record

M	Inn	NO	HS	Runs	Average	100s	50s
593	951	96	295	37,248	43.51	102	176

Test record

M	Inn	NO	HS	Runs	Average	100s	50s
47	72	12	149	2,434	40.56	8	7

Of the twenty-five batsmen who have scored a hundred centuries, four can be classified as all-rounders. W.G. Grace, Frank Woolley and Walter Hammond were all match-winning bowlers at some stage in their career, but there is a strong case for nominating Les Ames as the best all-rounder in the pack. Adam Gilchrist, over a short period, may have his supporters, but Ames was the outstanding wicket-keeper/batsman of all time and, if I concentrate on his orthodox, attractive batting for the bulk of this chapter, his abilities on the other side of the stumps should never be forgotten.

He made 102 centuries, most of them in aggressive, hard-driving style. His temperament was excellent, as eight Test hundreds testify. A little matter of 37,248 runs (average 43.51), a hundred in each innings on three occasions and 3,000 runs in one season – all these qualify Ames for honourable mention in any assessment of the premier batsmen of his time. When his wicket-keeping is considered, one can only marvel at his consistency and fitness.

Three seasons in particular demonstrate the all-round talents of Ames. In 1928 he took 121 victims behind the stumps and supplemented that with 1,919 runs; the following year 127 and 1,795; in 1932, 100 victims and 2,482 runs. The 1928 and 1929 totals of victims have never been beaten. Only J.T. Murray has also combined 100 victims and 1,000 runs in a season – and then just once. Ames did it three times.

The breakdown of Ames' victims graphically demonstrates the kind of cricket played by Kent in the 1920s and 1930s: challenging batting, geared to making enough runs to give 'Tich' Freeman sufficient time to bowl out the opposition twice with his leg-breaks. What fun it must have been to watch Kent in those days! Woolley, Chapman, Ashdown, Valentine and Ames would attack the bowling in their various styles, then Freeman, Marriott, Woolley and Hardinge would bowl assorted degrees of spin. Ames fitted to the manner born into this atmosphere; he needed no second bidding to play his shots, and what could be more enjoyable for a wicket-keeper than to stand up at the stumps for ninety per cent of one's career, picking Freeman's googly and enjoying the abortive attempts of callow amateurs to discern which way the ball would break? Today's top keepers would give their leather inners to learn their wicket-keeping trade at such a time.

A casual leaf through *Wisden* gives a flavour of Kentish cricket during the Ames/Freeman partnership. 'Stumped Ames, bowled Freeman' leaps out of the pages – four of them against Glamorgan in one innings (later, 130 runs from Ames), five against Northants (Ames 149), another four in one innings against Warwickshire and even four of the dour men of Lancashire perishing to the combination. In 1932 Ames stumped 64 of his 100 victims – a record that will only be threatened when wickets are better prepared, when spin bowlers are encouraged to bowl properly in long spells and batsmen go down the pitch to play them. In other words, never. Nor is Ames' career record of 415 stumpings likely to be surpassed, nor the 259 times that the Kent scorer wrote in his book: 'stumped Ames, bowled Freeman'.

So much, for the time being, on Ames the wicket-keeper. Ames the batsman is worthwhile enough to examine. His method was disarmingly simple; he believed in hitting the ball, on the ground or in the air, as hard and as often as possible. With Ames in the side, a run chase was always on – twice he won the trophy for the fastest hundred of the season during the 1930s. Essentially he played 'through the V', showing the full face of the bat to the bowler. He liked to settle in for the first half hour or so, then press on. Of all the batsmen who scored a hundred centuries, I would have thought that Ames played further down the wicket than anyone. Godfrey Evans, who kept wicket after the war with Ames in the side as a batsman, recalled: 'He used to go yards to get to the pitch of the ball. He'd love to play a low skimmer over cover point, like a three-iron golf shot. I called him "twinkletoes" and I've never seen a major batsman play so far out of his crease.' Doug Wright, another team-mate, admired his footwork immensely: 'As a quickish leg-spinner, I never had many batsmen give me the charge, but I'm sure Les would have tried it if we hadn't been in the same side. He was fantastic on his feet and played the same way through his forties.' Norman Yardley, who toured South Africa with Ames in 1938/39, felt Ames was never given his just deserts as a batsman: 'In his early England days, there was Sutcliffe, Hammond, Woolley and the rest, then later Compton, Hutton, Edrich and Leyland. Les was always a little overshadowed by them, yet his record was first-class. He was a beautiful striker of the ball.'

As one of just three batsmen to hit Larwood for six, Ames could fairly be said to be comfortable against the pace – with characteristic candour, Ames told me that he simply followed Larwood's delivery round on the legside, helped it on its way and the strong wind did the rest! His most glorious displays, however, were against the slow bowlers; Reg Sinfield told me how much Ames enjoyed wading into himself, Goddard and Parker whenever Kent played Gloucestershire: 'I remember the time when Tom Goddard had him caught in the deep – Les walked past me and grinned: "Well, I'd rather be caught out there than at short leg." That's the way Les played his cricket.' It is generally acknowledged that Ames played Goddard better than anyone after the lbw law was revised in 1935; afterwards, Goddard reaped a harvest of wickets because the right-hander just had to play the ball coming in on him. Ames counteracted that by splendid footwork and the courage to attack Goddard. He told me: 'It was either me or Tom who would win. I reckoned that if I stayed in the crease he would dictate the length to me. Tom didn't like the long handle at the best of times, and I loved to see his reaction if I got hold of him. Mind you, he made a fool out of me a few times!'

Both Jim Laker and Tom Graveney assured me that the post-war Les Ames played essentially the same way as a decade earlier. Graveney recalls four hundreds in a row by Ames against Gloucestershire when Ames was well over forty, dogged by lumbago and putting on weight. 'I couldn't believe it when I first saw him,' says Graveney. 'He gave our spinners some terrible hammer. I envied his footwork and confidence.' Jim Laker's cricket education was occasionally rudely interrupted by violent assaults from Ames in county matches: 'I think perhaps he couldn't pick my flight, but it made no difference to the way he attacked me. He'd take a chance, get down the pitch and crack me all over the place. He told me that was the method he used against Tom Goddard, so it would do for all the other spinners.'

G.O. Allen recalled affectionately his partnership with Ames against the 1931 New Zealanders – not for the achievement of adding 246 for the eighth wicket (a record for England against all countries), but for the attitude of Ames to a crisis. When Allen joined Ames, England were 190 for seven, still 34 behind. Ames discussed Bill Merritt with Allen and said of that very good leg-spinner: 'He doesn't like the tap, Gubby, let's go after him.' They added 246 in just under three hours, and Allen recalls: 'That remark was typical of Les. He believed in getting at them.'

Even when becalmed, Ames could always pick up ones and two by dint of his speed between the wickets. He was a wonderful judge of a run – Frank Woolley was happy to leave the calling to his junior partner – and he was one of the first batsmen to realise how to put pressure on a fielder. He would run the first one as quickly as possible, in the hope of getting another if the fielder fumbled the ball by taking his eye off it or panicked. Both Godfrey Evans and Doug Wright thought Ames the best runner between the wickets of their time, and that quality must have been invaluable during the many thrilling run-chases he guided. Alf Gover told an amusing story that sums up his own lack of fielding mobility and the effervescence of Ames: 'It was at Blackheath and I turned from mid-on to chase his shot. I thought I'd kid him to try for the second run, so I trotted after the ball, ready to turn round, whip it in and get him stranded going for the second run. It all worked according to plan, except that when I turned round with the ball in my hand, Les had run three! He laughed about that for years . . .'

Ames believed his ability as a soccer player was more central to his batting success than his wicket-keeping. He played on the wing for Second Division Clapton Orient, and shared with Denis Compton the fleet-footed skills of both the winger and the dashing batsman. He did not feel that standing up to the wicket for the bulk of an innings helped give him an insight into the pitch's condition when it was his turn to bat. 'I always separated the two in my mind. When I kept wicket, I concentrated on the batsmen and worked out what our bowlers were trying to achieve. I didn't have time to think about how I would play during our innings.' He did agree that his success behind the stumps gave him extra confidence: 'When you're double-barrelled, you can console yourself when you do badly early in the game. If I made nought with the bat, I'd think "Ah well, I've been picked as a keeper," and vice-versa.'

He became grateful for the advice given him by Gerry Weighall, the captain of the Kent Second Eleven when Ames joined the staff in 1926.

Before then he had kept wicket just twice at school and had no ambitions in that direction. In his first Club and Ground game, Ames was sent in to open the innings and did reasonably well. Weighall asked him if he could bowl and, when Ames said no, he was told in no uncertain terms: 'When you take up this game, you must have two strings to your bow – you'll keep wicket.' To his great embarrassment Ames was handed the regular wicket-keeper's gloves and told to get on with it. He had to keep on a turning wicket, with two slow left-handers in the side, but the Ames temperament showed its mettle for the first time: he took five victims.

He never thought of himself as a natural wicket-keeper and compares himself unfavourably with his brilliant successors in the Kent and England sides, Godfrey Evans and Alan Knott. At five feet nine inches, with a strong physique, Ames always looked a little out of place behind the stumps, yet he prospered by dint of an unfussy technique. W.H.V. ('Hopper') Levett, who deputised on occasions for Ames in the Kent side, told me: 'He was quiet, unspectacular and extremely competent. "Tich" Freeman got him many victims, of course, but he also pulled off some brilliant stumpings.' Godfrey Evans believed that the style of wicket-keeping in those days suited Ames – 'They never believed in throwing themselves around as we did. If a throw was wide, they would leave it to the fielders to gather it. Les was one of the very best of those kind. He was no goalkeeper, but he missed very little.'

'Gubby' Allen said Ames did not really like keeping wicket: 'In his heart he would love to have been a number four batsman, brilliant outfielder and occasional leg-spinner. When we played together for England, it was clear that Les preferred batting. When we came off the field, Les would be out of his wicket-keeper's gear very swiftly, getting himself prepared to bat, even if he was low down in the order.' Ames agreed: 'I never thought of myself as a natural keeper, but I loved to bat. Taking on the bowlers was my idea of cricket, not worrying about dropping a catch. You've no idea what it was like keeping to Bradman, all the time thinking, "Gosh, I can't afford to drop this fellow." It was much more fun when I let their keeper do the worrying.'

For all his modesty, Ames was the first choice for England as wicket-keeper from 1931 to 1939 as well as an authentic batsman. His work behind the stumps on two Australian tours drew high praise, and the team was fortunate to have such a splendid player going in at number seven. When necessary he would play within himself for the side. At Lord's in 1938 Ames played second fiddle to Hammond as his captain compiled one of the greatest double hundreds of his career. When he joined Hammond, the England score was 271 for five – almost a crisis against an Australian side containing Bradman and McCabe. Ames settled in to play for the morrow, giving the strike to Hammond, taking his measure of the bowlers. The next day he took his score to 83, the partnership added 186 and England thereafter could not be threatened by Bradman.

He was even more obdurate against the Australians at Lord's in 1934. Posterity has accorded this Test as 'Verity's Match' but, without the solidity of Leyland and Ames, England would not have won so resoundingly. They came together at 182 for five, with O'Reilly and Grimmett smacking their lips. England, already one down in the series, needed a large total to thwart the run-making greed of Woodfull, Bradman and McCabe. Leyland and Ames both batted through for centuries, Ames then encouraging Geary to add 48 precious runs and putting on another 50 with Verity. Ames did remind me that he was badly missed by Bertie Oldfield on 96, but that was his only mistake in an innings of 120 that took him nearly four-and-a-half hours, slow going for such a natural stroke-maker, but, in the circumstances, an invaluable performance. When he caught Bradman off a skier in the second innings, Les Ames thought Christmas had come early.

Lord's 1934 was his most memorable match, but there were many other moments to treasure. Another Test hundred that gave him particular pleasure came at Kingston in 1935; England lost the Test but without Ames they would have been ignominiously brushed aside. Overnight, five men including Leyland and Hammond had gone and the captain, Wyatt, had a broken jaw, courtesy of a fast delivery from Martindale. Ames scored 126 of the bravest runs imaginable, against fearsome fast bowling from Constantine, Martindale and Hylton on a very quick wicket. He did not just hammer slow bowlers.

His all-round skills were devastatingly revealed at Brentwood in 1934. Kent slaughtered the Essex bowling for 803 for four declared – 632 runs coming on the first day – and Ames made 202 not out in two hours and fifty minutes. That would be enough in one match for a normal man but, as Essex succumbed twice to the spin of Wright and Freeman, Ames picked up seven victims – including four more stumpings off Freeman. When he won the trophy for the fastest hundred of the 1939 season, it was made in typical style to win a county match. Surrey asked Kent to make 231 in 145 minutes and Ames – 136 not out – saw them home after reaching his hundred in 67 minutes. Other batsmen may have relaxed and played their shots in festival games at the season's end, light-hearted affairs when a bowler could always get the handful of wickets to reach his hundred for the season, or a batsman was able to get enough to reach a personal milestone; Les Ames played his shots right through the season, whatever the opposition and state of the wicket. He was a festival cricketer all year round.

The manner in which he achieved his century of centuries was quintessentially Ames. It came in Canterbury Week 1950, an appropriate venue for such a happy, colourful cricketer and achieved in the best possible manner. Middlesex asked Kent to score 237 at about eighty an hour, and Ames went in with the score 0 for one. He scored 131 in two hours, driving the spin of Jack Young and Jim Sims to all parts of the ground and handing out a thrashing to John Warr, who was deemed good enough to tour Australia with England that winter. He was dismissed in the most satisfactory way

– caught in the deep, going for another big hit. Kent won a marvellous match by seven wickets. For good measure Ames kept wicket in the second innings while Evans rested an injured hand. He was in his 45th year and surely good for a few more run chases.

He never played again for Kent after that season. The dreaded lumbago struck with a vengeance when he returned from a tour to India, and that was that. Typically he could see the funny side to his retirement: 'If I hadn't got a move on at Canterbury that day against Middlesex, I might have died on 99 hundreds! The two centuries I got in India were later ranked as first-class, but I didn't know that at the time so when I retired I thought I was on exactly a hundred. I shall always be grateful to Jack Young for slipping me one down the legside for a free hit.'

Cricket never stopped being fun for Les Ames. If you talked cricket with him for any length of time, he would tell you how lucky he was to play for Kent: 'All our captains had the right idea – get the runs quickly and attractively. We were never given a rollicking if we got out playing shots, and no one dared play for his average.' His top score of 295 is proof of that – 'It was against Gloucestershire and when one of our tail-enders came in, I was told to get a move on, because the skipper wanted to declare as soon as I got my three hundred. I only needed five more, so I tried to get down the other end with a quick single. I went to turn Charlie Parker to leg, it spun a little and I was dismissed by the old firm – caught Hammond, bowled Parker. No regrets though. When you saw Frank Woolley carry on playing his shots when he reached the nineties, you followed suit.'

Long after his retirement, Les Ames remained one of the most balanced and thoughtful of judges and a highly respected bridge between generations. He kept in touch with modern trends, as England selector and manager of MCC teams abroad and secretary-manager of Kent until 1974. He gave invaluable assistance in coaching at Canterbury after his retirement and then became the first former professional to be president of the county. Even in his eighties he could still be found at the ground every day during the Canterbury Festival, those twinkling feet carrying him from one group of friends to another, a perennial smile on that cheerful, freckled face. When pressed, he would pay due homage to the players of his day, but he was no *laudator temporis acti*; he marvelled at the fitness and consistency of Alan Knott, and no one was keener to see Kent prosper. His view of cricket over an active participation of more than sixty years was unprejudiced, sensible and charitable. He conceded that the paucity of slow bowling would perturb him if he had played his cricket in subsequent decades, but concluded that he would probably get by reasonably enough. Les Ames, the Mr Micawber of cricket, invariably ensured something would turn up.

13

Sir Leonard Hutton

'You've got to think it through, you know'

Leonard Hutton

Born

Fulneck, Pudsey, Yorkshire

23 June 1916

Died

Norbiton, Kingston-upon-Thames, Surrey

6 September 1990

First hundred

196   Yorkshire v Worcestershire, Worcester, 1934
Age: 18 years 33 days

100th hundred

151   Yorkshire v Surrey, The Oval, 1951
Age: 35 years 23 days

Last hundred

194   Yorkshire v Nottinghamshire, Trent Bridge, 1955
Age: 39 years 4 days

Career record

M	Inn	NO	HS	Runs	Average	100s	50s
513	814	91	364	40,140	55.51	129	179

Test record

M	Inn	NO	HS	Runs	Average	100s	50s
79	138	15	364	6,971	56.67	19	33

They did not waste words in the Yorkshire cricket hierarchy of the 1930s: no need, they had the best side in the land. When George Hirst, the county's great coach, saw a slender sixteen-year-old play in the nets for the first time, he contented himself with four words: 'Keep on wi' that.' George Hirst knew a great player when he walked into his nets, and Leonard Hutton did not let him down. Bill Bowes, fresh from bowling Bradman first ball, was asked by Hirst to assess the boy; apart from a slight technical defect on the leg stump that was soon rectified, Bowes pronounced him perfect. Herbert Sutcliffe, legendary opening batsman and a meagre singer of praises of other batsmen, could not contain himself. He wrote; 'He is a marvel – the discovery of a generation. At the age of 14 he was good enough to play for most county sides.'

If Hutton was disturbed by such uncharacteristic eulogy, he did not show it. He became one of the greatest opening batsmen in history, a man who carried innumerable weak England batting sides after the war. Few batsmen have been more technically perfect, more interesting to watch even when scoring slowly. He had as many shots as Hammond and Bradman and, if he kept them on a tighter rein, the occasions when he unfurled his flag of batsmanship have never been forgotten by those who witnessed them. He was a natural and worthy successor to the honourable line of famous batsmen who have gone in first for England – Shrewsbury, Hayward, Hobbs and Sutcliffe. There was a professional certainty about his batting, an elegance that beguiled and a quiet determination that compelled admiration. Colin Cowdrey said he was the most complete batsman he saw, Brian Close, Ray Illingworth and Johnny Wardle would not be shaken from the same opinion and Fred Trueman called him 'a batsman whose bat had no edges'. When Hutton was dismissed, it came as a jolt to the system, an affront to the well-ordered nature of things. On the opening morning of the Leeds Test of 1953, Ray Lindwall bowled him second ball with a classic yorker; the crowd and the England batting seemed to go into mourning. England laboured to 142 for seven on the first day, and the shadow of one delivery hung over the day's proceedings. No one seemed to give Lindwall credit for such a magnificent delivery. Hutton's dismissal in the first over was the big story.

He did not often fail the public that expected far too much of him. Just seven batsmen have scored more runs for England, although all but Hammond played at least 29 more Tests than Hutton, while eight have surpassed his 129 centuries. Hammond and Boycott are the only English batsmen to surpass his career average of 55.51. All this despite the loss of six years through war, an injury to his left arm that hampered his post-war batting and an early retirement at 39.

If batting mastery in the nets came easily to young Hutton, little else did. He was overawed by the great men in the Yorkshire side of the 1930s, by the achievements of players who came from his home town of Pudsey – men like John Tunnicliffe, Major Booth and Herbert Sutcliffe. At the age of ten he was reading M.A. Noble's book on captaincy and before he had needed to shave he was opening the batting for Pudsey St Lawrence with Edgar Oldroyd, a fine, bad-wicket player who had scored 37 hundreds for Yorkshire. As a wide-eyed teenager Hutton would give anything just to carry out the drinks for Yorkshire, and Bill Bowes remembered the youngster with great affection: 'He was a slow-speaking, naïve lad who found it hard to believe what he was watching. He would say something like "Eeh Bill, doesn't Hammond hit 'em a mile off his back foot?" The next time he batted, he tried the same shot and trod on his wicket. It didn't matter – he wanted to learn.' Others in the Yorkshire side were less approachable than Bowes; in one of his early games for the first team, Hutton was sent to field alongside Arthur Mitchell in the slips. Mitchell, a man who played the role of the stage Yorkshireman to perfection, growled, 'What's tha' doin' here?' Nor did he mellow on the occasions when he partnered Hutton. Once the youngster essayed a rather ambitious cut that missed the ball by several inches; from down the wicket came the familiar Mitchell grunt: 'Nay, nay, nay – you're not playin' for Pudsey Prims now. You'd 'a wanted a clothes peg to reach yon.'

Fortunately better batsmen than Mitchell knew how to encourage the shy Hutton. When he followed his debut duck for the second eleven with another on his debut for the first team, Maurice Leyland consoled him with: 'Never mind, lad, tha's started at the bottom.' Herbert Sutcliffe billed and cooed about his protégé out of Hutton's earshot and, when they batted together, the great man did everything possible to help – taking the difficult bowlers at strategic times, advising him what shots to play, praising his defensive technique. Hutton was always grateful that he was not expected to crash the ball all over the field in his early days in first-class cricket. Sutcliffe encouraged him to take his time and learn how to build an innings: he never forgot the formative years of his cricket education. Just after his first Test in 1937, Hutton was ushered into the presence of Bobby Peel, the slow left-arm bowler whose drunken exit from first-class cricket at the behest of Lord Hawke never obscured the memory of his classical bowling. Peel, then aged 81, told Hutton: 'Once you start thinking about getting quick runs you're finished. We don't expect fireworks from an opening batsman.' Hutton, conscious of the cricket heritage of Yorkshire, drank in such advice avidly.

When he started his England career with 0 and 1, it was simply one of those aberrations that seemed to dog Hutton on every debut; by the end of that New Zealand series of 1937, he had scored his first Test hundred, and Sutcliffe's successor for both Yorkshire and England was triumphantly confirmed. The Australian team of 1938 felt the brunt of a technique now classically moulded and a temperament secure and rocklike. A century in the First Test was followed by an innings at The Oval that dogged him for the rest of his life – 364, a new record for Test cricket. It took him 13 hours 20 minutes during eight sessions of play, and the first Australian to congratulate Hutton was the man he watched set up the old record of 334 in 1930 – Don

Bradman. As he observed Bradman from the stands at Leeds, Hutton did not cherish any particular ambition to topple that score – fourteen-year-olds from Yorkshire tend to aim for respectability before they climb the slopes of Olympus. Hutton's main memory of that Oval marathon was one of tiredness and nightmares about Bill O'Reilly on the night before he walked out to bat against him, needing just 35 to beat Bradman's record. His Yorkshire team-mates, Bill Bowes, Hedley Verity, Maurice Leyland and Arthur Wood, kept him going while his captain, Walter Hammond, forbade him to play loosely. 'I remember I had got to about 130 when I started to play freely, to hit Bill O'Reilly over the top. Hammond came on to the balcony and gestured to me to quieten down. He wanted to grind them into the dust.'

Joe Hardstaff was at the other end when Hutton chopped Fleetwood-Smith through the gully to establish the record. He recalls a conversation with Hutton just before: 'Len said to me, "Will you take O'Reilly for me? I don't fancy him." Well, I looked at the scoreboard, saw about 340 against his name and said, "You've taken a long time to discover that, Len." But I did as he asked because he looked all in by then.' Bill O'Reilly said that Hutton was so grooved in his concentration that he did not take advantage of a no-ball from him when his score was 333. Denis Compton – who made only one after sitting with his pads on for over a day – recalled how calm Hutton seemed at the end of it all. 'As the champagne was flowing, Len just stood there, saying "Thank you very much" to all the well-wishers. He had an old head on his shoulders even at 22.'

Compton told me that he had never seen anyone less likely to get out in that Oval innings, yet Hutton would not dwell very long on it. He said that the wicket was far too good, that the Australian attack was unbalanced – just three regular bowlers – and that he would have preferred to play his shots. It all seemed an ordeal to him, and the relentless demands of the media after that innings unnerved a young man who was trying to broaden his social as well as his cricket education. Hutton pointed out that he played a lot of shots in the last couple of years before the war and that the Oval marathon had overshadowed them. Compton agreed; he vividly remembered Hutton's glorious strokeplay at Lord's in 1939 against the West Indies. He and Hutton added 248 in 140 minutes and Hutton actually outscored the young genius during his 196. Norman Yardley, who toured with Hutton on the England trip to South Africa in 1938/39, remembered his commanding batting on those beautiful wickets. By 1939 Hutton was the best batsman in the world after Bradman. He was just 23. War came at a cruel time.

Hutton believed he was never quite the same batsman after the war. The responsibility of opening for England became far greater because, apart from Compton and the rugged professionalism of Edrich and Washbrook, there was little in the batting larder until May and Cowdrey came along nearly a decade after the resumption of Test cricket. Hutton knew that, if he was dismissed early, the batting was vulnerable; a conscientious man to a fault, he was always imbued with the necessary team spirit. He was also hampered by a wartime injury that meant his left arm was an inch shorter than the other. At one stage there were grave doubts whether he would play again; twelve plaster casts were needed. He mastered the disability with characteristic determination, but a right-hand batsman with a left arm that does not function satisfactorily is at a disadvantage. That was not lost on Lindwall and Miller when they bowled intimidatingly at him in Australia in 1946/47; they knew he was struggling to come to terms with the lifting ball. The Australian wickets were hard and lively and Hutton, the best batsman in the side, was the main target. The barrage continued in 1948, and it is a measure of Hutton's greatness that his reputation survived intact, apart from the occasion when the England selectors, in their infinite wisdom, dropped him for one Test in 1948 because they felt he had not acquitted himself well enough against the bouncing ball at Lord's. They presumably took little account of the fact that Hutton had to use the lightest possible bat to counteract his disabled arm, and that the regulations allowed one new ball every 55 overs in 1948 so that Lindwall and Miller never lacked incentive. Any England batsman who scored fifty against Bradman's side that series had acquitted himself nobly. Hutton managed it four times, plus a heroic 30 in England's all-out total of 52 at The Oval.

On occasions he would slip the leash and take apart a high-class attack with a breathtaking range of shots. It happened in the Sydney Test of 1946, when he scored 37 out of 49 in the first twenty minutes. Veterans on the ground babbled about Victor Trumper as Hutton put together a cameo innings that was ended cruelly when he lost control of the bat – that arm again! – and it fell on his stumps. Hutton conceded, with his familiar caution: 'Yes, I played well that day. I decided to go at them, and I played a series of judicious shots.' In the same series, he and Washbrook put on 87 in 57 minutes (Hutton 50) against another bumper barrage. In the opinion of Alec Bedser, Denis Compton and Bill Edrich – men who played during that fierce intimidatory atmosphere – not enough credit has been laid at the door of Hutton for coming through the ordeal with such quiet tenacity. One bad match – at Lord's in 1948 – was enough to see him dropped. Norman Yardley, the England captain at the time, eventually conceded that it was, on reflection, a ridiculous decision, but that must have been no consolation to Hutton after his buffetings. It only served to drive a reserved man further in on himself.

By 1950 Hutton had weathered the fast bowling barrage and re-established himself as the world's best player. He had come to terms with the ball that dipped late into him to trouble a technique getting used to a shortened left arm. He had made the necessary technical adjustment, and off-spinners and in-swingers no longer perturbed him greatly. The rest of the technical equipment that had delighted Sutcliffe was still there, even if the left shoulder now pointed a little towards mid-on to thwart the ball that came into him.

Everything was under control; the ball was played astonishingly late, and his balance when playing the delivery was a model. To the fast bowlers he would play half-forward, with the weight easily balanced and they just could not get him out of position, turn him round with a seaming or swinging ball, and make him vulnerable to late movement. He allowed the ball to come to him and could delay the shot by opening the face of the bat and running it down into areas where there were no fielders. Johnny Wardle remembered the match at Wellingborough, when the Northants captain, F.R. Brown, bowled seamers at Hutton: 'He had nine men on the offside, including two on the third-man boundary, yet he was still piercing the field. Freddie Brown got annoyed, bowled him a beamer, and Len just leaned back and cut it away close to the keeper to the boundary.' R.O. ('Roley') Jenkins was a brilliant cover point in his days with Worcestershire, yet he could never outwit Hutton's mastery of placement. He told me: 'Once at Sheffield I was busy watching Len's footwork from cover, trying to work out where he was going to play his off-drive. I managed to stop a magnificent drive on my right side, but to the next half-volley he played a little inside out and it screamed past my left hand. So I moved a shade towards my left, and next time it went whistling past my right hand. He just used his left arm to manipulate the ball away from me. A craftsman.'

Hutton was a master on bad wickets because of this ability to fashion runs, to manufacture them by deft manipulation of the bat face. If the bowler over-pitched, the most beautiful cover drive in the game would be brought into play, and in defence his masterly use of the dead bat would frustrate. Norman Yardley remembered his knack of playing the ball and deadening it at the same instant. He favoured playing with the bat rather than the pads, and from the crease rather than down the wicket – his rationale was that he was not a hitter of sixes and that he wanted to leave his stroke till the very last instant, so why go down the pitch? At all times he was elegant and utterly composed, a master on surfaces that exposed the lesser players. His innings of 62 not out in a total of 122 on a foul Brisbane pitch was a classic which even pleased Hutton: 'I made them without an acknowledged batsman at the other end, as I went in at number six. Yes, that was a good knock.'

One innings at The Oval in the early 1950s made a deep impression on so many players that it is worth a closer analysis. Hutton made 79 out of 130 all out on a wicket made for the spinning talents of Jim Laker and Tony Lock. Ray Illingworth remembers he and the other batsmen playing and missing three times an over, while Hutton did so twice in his entire innings. Illingworth said: 'At the moment of contact with the ball, he was so relaxed. He picked the length of the ball up remarkably quickly. Without him we'd have been pushed to make 30 that day.' Johnny Wardle, no mean performer himself on turning wickets, was also in the Yorkshire side and said: 'I defy anyone to have ever played better. He was playing Lock's quicker ones off his chest, yet somehow keeping it away from the leg-trap.' Jim Laker, one of the suffering bowlers, described it as one of the great bad-wicket innings he has seen. 'He just toyed with Tony Lock, hitting him that little bit squarer on the offside, just out of reach of the fielder. And he placed my off-breaks with uncanny precision.'

He had the capacity to surprise even his Yorkshire team-mates accustomed to his mastery. Just now and again he would play an innings of genius, when bowlers could not contain him. Ray Illingworth recalls a hundred in seventy minutes against Derbyshire's seam attack of Gladwin, Jackson and Pope on a green wicket; it included a six over square cover off an astonished Jackson, one of the best post-war seam bowlers in English conditions. Johnny Wardle remembered the day when Hutton gritted his teeth and decided to play his shots. 'We were coming back from Northampton, and we were due to play the South Africans at Sheffield. There had been some criticism about Len's batting against them in the Tests that year, and it had clearly got on top of him. He told me in the car, "I just hope the sun shines tomorrow, because I'm going to show the boogers I can play." He was 93 not out at lunch the following day. He just toyed with them.'

By 1952 the England captaincy was available and Hutton was clearly the best equipped for the job. He had stood in the slips alongside Freddie Brown during the 1950/51 Australian tour, and his captain had been vastly impressed by his tactical acumen. Some antediluvian members of the Lord's hierarchy baulked at the idea of England having a professional as captain, preferring to quote Lord Hawke's famous dictum ('pray God no professional ever captains England!') while ignoring the fact that the remark had been taken grossly out of context. Hutton made it clear – politely yet firmly – that he would not emulate Walter Hammond and turn amateur to secure his ambition. He was a proud professional and would stay that way. He won the day but, for the next three years, was acutely conscious that one or two sharpened knives had been placed on some tables in the district of Marylebone. This innate distrust of the Establishment, his own native caution and the quality of the players at his disposal inclined Hutton to a style of captaincy that was shrewd, realistic and unexciting. He unashamedly slowed down the over rate in Australia in 1954/55, and his success in that sphere has ruined many a day's cricket in later years as imitators perfected the ruses to avoid bowling too often. Apart from that Hutton cannot be faulted, except for an emphasis on pace that stemmed from the days when he was battered by Lindwall and Miller: a keen desire to get one's own back is a human trait. Whatever the moralities, Hutton's means justified the end and he never lost a series. Nor – until that exhausting Australian tour – did his batting suffer the responsibilities of captaincy. The 1953/54 tour of the West Indies was a monumental strain, not just for cricketing reasons, yet amid all the political disturbances, riots at the grounds, ill-discipline of some England players and ludicrous umpiring decisions, Hutton stood firm. By his own example, he turned a two-nil deficit into parity by the end of the series. His 169 and 205 were innings of the highest class and character – as Tom Graveney shrewdly observed to me, 'Tests aren't usually won by batsmen on good wickets, but Len did it twice in one series.'

Even after such an inspiring performance Hutton still was not sure of taking the side to Australia in the following winter. Out of action with a bad back, he was replaced by David Sheppard as captain for two of the home Tests against the Pakistanis in 1954, and some at Lord's were keen to return to an amateur captain for the Australian tour. Eventually, however, common sense prevailed, and Hutton had his last triumphant hurrah as England captain, winning the series in Australia three-one. Victory was achieved at a cost. The tour finished Len Hutton as a cricketer. The strain was too much – he won the toss at Brisbane, put Australia in and somehow lost by an innings. He shepherded Tyson and Statham through the early part of the tour, and they repaid his encouragement with a series of match-winning performances. Yet Hutton could not relax; he was still on guard against press criticism, ever conscious that he only had to slip slightly from his standards to lose both the captaincy and his place as batsman. He was so distracted that he forgot to take Alec Bedser to one side and explain why he had not been selected for the Third Test, harsh treatment to such a great, willing bowler who had just recovered from shingles. On the morning of the Melbourne Test, he refused to get out of bed; Godfrey Evans, Bill Edrich and the tour manager Geoffrey Howard had to plead with him to come down to the ground. 'Don't feel much like it,' he would only reply. Finally they cajoled him into playing. In the Fourth Test, he told Denis Compton, 'Pad up, Denis, I don't feel much like going in again,' when England needed just 94 to retain the Ashes. Compton did as he was told and then noticed Hutton putting on his own pads. Compton asked if he had changed his mind and was told, 'Ah yes, I'll be going in first.'

By the end of the tour Hutton was shattered. He was a sick man, and the fibrositis that had plagued him for years was taking its toll. He was suffering from occasional black-outs; he revealed that during the Oval Test of 1953 he had suffered an attack of temporary blindness and literally could not see the ball after the bowler had brought over his arm. Hutton was ready to go; he had done more than enough and, with typical hard-headed clarity, he realised that there was now only one way his career could go – down. His retirement showed the natural timing that characterised his batting. His knighthood for services to cricket was fitting reward for a great cricketer, a highly successful captain, a model team man and a supreme professional. One can only wonder why he never gained the captaincy of Yorkshire, but perhaps it is best to leave that particular hot potato to cool.

His colleagues and friends have confirmed the enormity of the pressure he seemed to feel. At times it was self-inflicted; Trevor Bailey says that Hutton genuinely believed that anything less than a century from him would bring press criticism raining down. Bill Bowes remembered being told by him:

'It gets increasingly difficult, this game. I have to get 40 for the spectators because of my reputation, and only then can I think of playing properly.' Tom Graveney recalls: 'Len wasn't on this earth when he batted, he was in a trance. During an interval he would just sit down, drink his tea while someone unbuckled his pads and just look into space.' During the Lord's Test of 1953 Hutton was about to introduce Graveney to the Queen when he realised he'd quite forgotten his name. 'I wouldn't have minded but we'd just shared a partnership of 168! Then, when we toured West Indies a few months later, Len introduced me as Tom Goddard! I didn't mind, Len put his heart and soul into his captaincy. But he could be odd at times.'

Norman Yardley remembers the day towards the end of his career when the strain was starting to show; he scored a hundred and when he came back to the dressing-room, he said: 'I never thought I'd see the day when I got tired of batting.' When Richie Benaud came in to bat for Australia, Hutton would always greet him with a cheery quip of 'Here comes the festival cricketer,' a reference to Benaud's fondness for attacking batting. Benaud feels Hutton's remark was made wistfully, with a sense of envy. Certainly Hutton's attention to detail and scrupulous concentration would have satisfied even Geoffrey Boycott, as Trevor Bailey will confirm. One morning, Bailey came across Hutton in the nets trying to eradicate an imaginary fault in his cover-drive: this from a man who was unbeaten overnight on a century! His memory, like most Yorkshire and England cricketers, was faultless. When I asked him about the game when he scored his hundredth century, he gave me a potted summary instantly: 'Surrey v Yorkshire at The Oval in 1951. A cover drive for four off Owen Waite. He couldn't have bowled me a better one, you know. My favourite stroke. He was a Cambridge Blue, was Waite. Died young. Cancer, I believe.' He had slight regrets that he could not play his shots more often but pointed out that he never had a sturdy physique, even before the war: 'I found it all very exhausting, you know. In a lot of cases I've lost interest after I got to a hundred.' He gently demurred that he would not have fancied modern short-pitched bowling, pointing out that a lot of half-volleys go unpunished with the batsman in position instead for the short one. Godfrey Evans felt that Hutton would have enjoyed himself: 'Don't forget that Lindwall and Miller were allowed to bowl plenty of bouncers. Len was used to quicks, alright.' Johnny Wardle was adamant that Hutton would have been a boon in limited-overs cricket, because of his ability to place the ball wide of fielders and his faultless judge of a run.

Hutton's former colleagues are immensely loyal to his good name, partly because of his classical batting gifts but also because of the quiet, unfussy way he carried on batting under the most trying of circumstances. It seems that the fear of letting down the side, rather than himself, was never far from his mind. Hutton told me how much admired Sutcliffe's conviction that luck was on his side and gives a game against Leicestershire in 1937 as an example. 'When we walked out to bat after tea-time, we had put on 315 and

Herbert said, 'We only want 240 more, Leonard.' I didn't know what he was on about and he explained – the record of 555 that he and Percy Holmes had set up five years before. I couldn't get over his confidence, and I was out within a couple of minutes. My concentration had been shattered by Herbert's conviction.'

If Hutton lacked the *sangfroid* of a Sutcliffe, he had a dry humour that his mentor lacked. Hutton could see the whimsical side of life as Denis Compton recalled. 'It was during a particularly tense moment in the Lord's Test of 1953, when we were hanging on for dear life. Lindwall and Miller were giving us a terrible old time and, at the end of an over, Len motioned me towards him. I expected some sort of technical discussion with my captain, yet he said: "What are we doing here, Denis? We could have better jobs than this!" At that stage I couldn't disagree.' Hutton had a droll way of dealing with fatuous questions from cricket journalists; once he was asked in a rather long-winded fashion why he had been dismissed by a particular delivery, and his reply was succinct: 'I missed it.' At the Centenary Test celebrations in Melbourne in 1977 he whispered to Joe Hardstaff, his partner during a record stand in the 1938 Oval Test: 'Joe, I've caught O'Reilly's eye several times, and I think he's ignoring me! What have I done to him?' When an earnest young cricket writer asked Hutton the best way to play fast bowling, he was told 'from the other end'. In 1957 Hutton, on one of his earliest excursions into the press box, was covering a match on the West Indies tour. Their two opening batsmen got into a fearful muddle, each was stranded and either could have been run out. Hutton, his sense of propriety outraged at the waste of a wicket, surveyed the West Indian recriminations with a mordant eye and said with resignation: 'Ay, and they want self-goovernment as well.' Once he was taken to task by Brian Sellers, his former captain, for not giving his young son Richard a very impressive bat with which to learn his trade. Hutton agreed it was not a very good bat, adding, 'But he's not a very good player is he, Brian?'

Well, Richard was good enough to play five times for England, watched by his father in the press box, but the stature of Hutton Senior was not threatened. Nothing could alter that. An instinctive, natural stylist who believed in stroking rather than hitting the ball, he was a batsman for the connoisseur. Resilient, undemonstrative and physically brave, he remains the hero of men like Ray Illingworth, who watched him as a boy, admired him as a playing colleague and wishes fervently that another of his ilk would walk into Headingley from Pudsey with his Herbert Sutcliffe bat under his arm.

Hutton always seemed to know what to do with his feet and his bat. Once he walked out to open with a young partner, recognised as an attractive player, but a little slapdash in his approach. 'What are you thinking about?' Hutton asked him. 'Nothing,' came the reply. Hutton persisted. 'Well, let me tell you what I'm thinking. I'm thinking about how the wicket's going to play, which bowler will have the breeze, what shots I should not try in the first hour, which fielders aren't too quick on their feet and I'm wondering about those sightscreens.' The learned discourse had lasted till the batsmen were almost at the wicket. As they parted to go to their respective positions, Hutton delivered the sting in the tail – 'You've got to think it through, you know.' No one thought it through better than Leonard Hutton.

14

Denis Compton

'He played cricket for fun and made it look fun'
(Godfrey Evans)

Denis Charles Scott Compton

Born

Hendon, Middlesex

23 May 1918

Died

Windsor, Berkshire

23 April 1997

First hundred

100*   Middlesex v Northamptonshire, Northampton, 1936
Age: 18 years 26 days

100th hundred

107   Middlesex v Northamptonshire, Lord's, 1952
Age: 34 years 19 days

Last hundred

103   International Cavaliers v Jamaica, Kingston, 1964
Age: 45 years 232 days

Career record

M	Inn	NO	HS	Runs	Average	100s	50s
515	839	88	300	38,942	51.85	123	183

Test record

M	Inn	NO	HS	Runs	Average	100s	50s
78	131	15	278	5,807	50.06	17	28

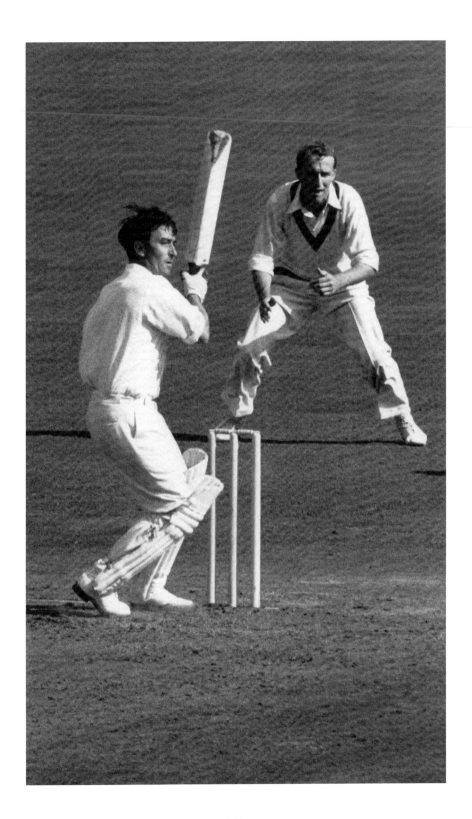

The very mention of Denis Compton's name is always good for a positive reaction from his contemporaries. They lean back, the features soften, the eyes mist over a shade, they smile and chuckle, 'Ah, Denis . . .' Two words that speak volumes. Denis Compton had that effect on everyone; he made you care for him. Anyone who ever watched him for an hour can remember at least one outrageous stroke, a moment of daring. When Denis Compton's genius was channelled in the right direction, no one went for an early tea or burrowed into the crossword. I am surprised that no government of his day thought of slapping an Entertainment Tax on him; he would have cleared the national debt in just one season.

It was always 'Denis', not 'Compton'. The great Leonard Hutton would sometimes be dubbed 'Len', even though his classic batting and demeanour marked him out as a 'Leonard'. Denis was always on first-name terms with the crowd, communicating his sense of enjoyment, gulling the spectators into believing it really was quite an easy game. Hutton, his only contemporary rival as a great batsman, would sometimes look careworn, racked by responsibility. Denis, on the other hand, brought cricket into the lives of many who had no knowledge of the game's technical niceties; he made it seem fun, an utterly natural way of passing the time. The shrill schoolboy cries of delight, the positive way their elders folded up their newspapers – that was the reaction Denis got when he walked out to bat. The crowd agonised if it was one of the days when his gifts had deserted him; they knew that the currency of genius can sometimes be devalued, when mundane bowlers enjoy one satisfying day to warm their memories in retirement. When that happened, the account in the bank of goodwill marked 'Compton, D.C.S.' was stamped with the imprimatur of tolerance. He would make up for it.

He was the cheekiest of the great batsmen. His gifts of improvisation against slow bowlers are well documented, but the way he tackled the fast bowlers was astonishing. He played Lindwall, Miller, Adcock, Heine and the rest from several yards down the wicket when the Muse of inspiration was with him. Tom Graveney, an England colleague and keen observer of today's style of batting, told me: 'The players today just wouldn't believe you if you told them how Denis played the short-pitched stuff from down the track. He made everything look so easy.' Fred Titmus, who batted many times with Denis for Middlesex, says he was the only English genius he encountered in cricket – 'I'd be batting at the other end, watching him do things I could hardly believe. You'd think, "No, he can't get away with that" and he usually did. I once saw him take Mel Ryan apart when we played Yorkshire. Mel took the new ball, and Denis hit the first two through the covers for four. The next ball was delivered in the same area, and it went through mid-wicket. Mel said to me, "How the hell do you bowl at him?" and I confess I didn't know.'

Denis was the scourge of slow bowlers. His reflexes and resourcefulness were so astonishing that he could not be contained when the fires of genius had been lit. His duels with Tom Goddard were vastly amusing to those who knew that bowling was no laughing matter to Goddard. At The Oval in 1947 Denis made 246 against the Rest of England, and during this innings he played a shot that has become legendary; he advanced towards Goddard, fell over and as his knee gave way, swept the ball to the square leg boundary. Goddard growled: 'One of these bloody days, Denis, there'll be no return ticket.' Goddard had his revenge, incidentally, in a subsequent season. Denis was left stranded, stumped by yards and Goddard pulled out a crumpled piece of paper and gave it to him. 'Off ye' go, Denis,' he said, and as he walked back to the pavilion he opened up the piece of paper. It was a bus ticket. Single fare.

Tom Goddard was not the only spinner to suffer from the Compton gift of improvisation. Doug Wright told me he once cut him to the boundary after falling over, and John Langridge remembered him doing exactly the same to his brother, James. He was irresistible on his good days; somehow he seemed to be making it up as he went along. No one could copy Denis's method – Jack Robertson was the coaching-manual batsman in his time at Lord's – but we could all identify with him. He was the eternal schoolboy, no matter what the hour glass indicated. Before the war he walked onto a cricket ground with a cheerful Cockney swagger and batted like an errand boy who winked at the lady of the house while delivering the groceries. Denis was always worth a tip. He was 28 when Test cricket resumed in 1946 and, if the figure had thickened, he still played enchantingly for the next three seasons. A chronic knee injury restricted him thereafter, but the way he adapted to his disability only accentuated his greatness. He managed to carry on until 1957 by guts and resilience but also due to a technique that was fundamentally orthodox. Denis was lucky enough to learn how to bat on pre-war wickets at Lord's that were hard, fast and true; he developed a confidence from those good wickets that enabled him to play his shots later on. Much has been made of the 'Compton sweep', the stroke that will always be associated with him – but he only swept the deliveries that were on middle or leg stumps. The ones that pitched on the off-stump were driven peerlessly square through the covers with a beautifully delayed stroke. He had a high backlift, but he brought it down straight and played impeccably through the line of the ball. Like the great overseas batsmen who were brought up on good wickets, he was quickly into position even for a defensive shot. Back and across with the back leg covering the leg stump, he would always get behind the ball. When playing back defensively his deft footwork would take him almost back onto his stumps. Perhaps there was a little too much right hand in his cover driving, so that it would resemble a square slash, rather than a drive, but he could play the shot very late and guide it into the open space in the manner of Hutton. His strong right hand meant he could on-drive superbly and he was a magnificent puller and hooker, often delaying the hook until the ball was almost on his nose. He played the sweep shot perfectly – only when the delivery was just fuller than a good length – and he would always roll the bat over the top of the ball, making sure he kept it down. Denis told me that he discovered he could play the sweep when he was about fifteen; he practised hard at it and he believes it got him out just three times in his career. His mastery of the shot spawned a clutch of imitators in the 1950s and 1960s, but none could master it because they did not observe the basic principles. Denis Compton, despite the excesses of imagination and audacity, always had the basic principles in mind when he batted.

Those who warm to the entertainers of cricket must feel there really was a sense of destiny about Denis Compton. It was a delightful coincidence that saw him begin his career as Patsy Hendren was ending his in the Middlesex side. Patsy saw Denis as his logical successor as prolific batsman and darling of the crowd, and he delighted in his success. He would guide him through technical teething problems – 'Sit on the ball when you sweep,' and 'Never duck when hooking,' he would tell him – and encouraged him to keep the crowd happy. When they batted together, Denis would watch how the old master would play 'Tich' Freeman or Tom Goddard, and he soon realised with great pleasure that he was being encouraged to play his natural game. When we glory in the career of Denis Compton, we owe a genial glance in the direction of Patsy Hendren, Walter Robins and the other influential members of the attractive Middlesex side. Many other senior players would have tried to coach the genius out of him; one can only imagine what Arthur Mitchell would have thought of him.

In those uncomplicated pre-war days, the main problem for Denis seemed to be staying awake on the field when not batting. More than once his captain, Walter Robins, had to bawl him out because he was not concentrating on the task. Alf Gover remembered Denis's first Test against New Zealand in 1937: 'Denis misfielded about four times and finally Robins roared: "Compton, I shall make it my business to make sure you never play for England again!" Typical Denis – he was always in the clouds, without a care in the world.'

He also batted in the same vein; before he was 22, he had made Test hundreds against Australia and New Zealand. Life was good and easy to this natural athlete: his soccer skills were so impressive that he was allowed to miss the England tour to South Africa to play a winter's First Division football with Arsenal. Joe Hardstaff told a story from the 1938 Australia series that epitomises the carefree Compton of that period – for that matter, the Compton of maturity and middle age as well. At Leeds Hardstaff was due to bat at number five, with Compton at six. With two England wickets down Hardstaff was on edge, expecting to have to go in at any moment. Batsmen of all standards know the feeling and, not surprisingly, Hardstaff suddenly felt the call of nature. As he walked towards the toilet, he saw Denis sitting reading the paper, fully clothed, without any cricket gear on. Hardstaff spluttered: 'Denis, you could be in any minute!' but Denis smiled and said: 'Don't worry, Joe, you'll be alright, I've got great faith in you.'

Those blissful days of 1938 seemed light years away when Denis and the other first-class cricketers tried to bring some enjoyment to a war-ravaged county in 1946. For the next few years cricket enjoyed tremendous prosperity, and Denis Compton, of all players, must take credit for this. The summer of 1947 is burned deep into the memories of those cricket-lovers who lived though that season. With the brilliant support of Bill Edrich, Denis Compton made people realise what they had been missing for six years. Statistically no batsman has enjoyed a better season than Compton or Edrich in 1947, but the joy of their batting and the challenging cricket played by Middlesex are what people remember most. Day after day the sun shone gloriously, and Compton and Edrich hammered bowlers all over the country. They enjoyed six stands of over 200 and for good measure helped win Middlesex the championship by honouring Walter Robins' instructions that quick runs were essential. The crowds loved it. At one stage in that summer the secretary of the MCC, Colonel R.S. Rait Kerr, was summoned to Downing Street to answer allegations that cricket popularity was hampering industrial production. One can only assume that Prime Minister Attlee – himself a great cricket fan – realised what Compton and Edrich were doing for the morale of a nation starved of thrills and honest sporting combat, a country rationed of food, petrol and all the other things we now take for granted. There were no rations when Compton and Edrich batted in 1947 and, if they had retired at the end of that season, they would never be forgotten by a generation for what they did. It did not matter that the bowlers were rather inferior, that the sun-burnt wickets were made for batting or that the field-placings were unimaginative and unsophisticated; Edrich and Compton reminded a nation of the contagious pleasure gained from watching fit, young men excelling at a sport and enjoying themselves in the process. Compton's tally of 3,816 runs (average 90.86) for 1947 will never be surpassed in first-class cricket, nor his 18 centuries in that unforgettable summer.

For good measure Compton learned how to bowl left-arm 'chinamen' in that 1947 season. Jack Walsh, the splendid spinner with Leicestershire, took him out to the nets one morning and demonstrated the art. In just over half the season Denis took 73 wickets with his new toy. Natural talent is not circumscribed by mundanities like apprenticeships.

Although Compton played like Victor Trumper, he had the backbone of Herbert Sutcliffe, even if he did not flaunt his competitive streak in the shameless manner of the modern, clench-fisted cricketer. He played two wonderful innings in a crisis against the 1948 Australians to demonstrate that a 'festival' batsman can also battle it out if he has the necessary temperament and bravery. At Trent Bridge he made 184 in seven hours against a rampant Lindwall and Miller. He had to play himself in no less than nine times due to intermittent rain and appalling light; he was dismissed when he slipped on the wet grass, avoiding a Miller bouncer, and fell on his wicket. Not one spectator had been bored by an innings that, by his usual standard, had been positively ascetic. It was resourceful, at times punishing, always full of character, and it proved that the Cavalier had steel beneath his finery. Two Tests later, at Manchester, he showed his class and temperament again. He scored 145 not out in five hours twenty minutes, after being knocked out of the fray by Lindwall when he top-edged a hook into his face. He retired to have some stitches inserted and returned with England 119 for five; not once did he flinch, or avoid playing the hook shot. It was a stern, unyielding effort, against the odds and in the face of deadly fast bowling.

By this time Denis was getting used to battling against the odds: the knee that he first injured while bowling in 1947 was beginning to cause him pain. Three minor operations and one major one eventually robbed him of a kneecap, and the remaining years were a story of grit, frustration and compromise with a body that had seemed certain to defy the march of time. He began to experience devastating periods of bad form – in the 1950/51 series in Australia he scored 53 runs at an average of 7.57, choosing the most remarkable ways to be dismissed. Even the pragmatic Australians tried to give him one off the mark, and Sir Donald Bradman took time out to give Denis some technical advice. It was a bad time for Denis; the news of his impending divorce was splashed all over the Australian newspapers and there were some snide remarks about his social life, remarks that were never forthcoming during his 'good old Denis' days of plenty. As vice-captain he wanted desperately to succeed, and he was acutely conscious that a consistent series from him would have altered the shape of that four-one defeat. Freddie Brown, the England captain on that tour, told me that such a low period in Denis's life did not affect his relationship with the rest of the side. 'He was the same lovable Denis, a little bit quieter on occasions but never out to make excuses for himself or wrap himself up in his own misery.' I wonder how many other batsmen would react the same way?

Occasionally he would roll back the years, and the old Compton – the unfettered, natural Compton – would come storming through. There was the astonishing 62 in 40 minutes against Lock and Laker on a vicious Oval pitch; the 278 against Pakistan in 1954 when the bowlers just did not know where to propel the ball at him; a hundred at Lord's against Worcestershire when Reg Perks swung the ball prodigiously in the humid conditions and Denis attacked him from a long way down the pitch; the mellow 94 against Australia at The Oval in 1956, his first Test after having his kneecap removed. Yet the tour of South Africa in 1956/57 convinced Denis he had to retire: he could not get Trevor Goddard's nagging medium pace away, while Tayfield's off-spin tied him down and the South Africans were pushed back in the field when he was on strike, because they knew he could not take quick singles. He knew that, in his palmy days, Goddard and Tayfield would have suffered the same fate as all the other bowlers; to his intense disappointment, he just could not do it any more. He had been given everything by the gods in his youth, and now, at an age when Jack Hobbs was still to score 98

156

centuries, Denis was reduced to the ranks of the mortals. Typically he ended his championship career with a century in his last match in 1957.

If only that knee has been whole; the surgeon said that it looked as if it had been gnawed by a rat when he opened it up. Johnny Wardle said he had never seen a sportsman's knee swell up so alarmingly when it gave Denis pain. Yet he never complained about his disability, never used it as an excuse for spells of bad form. It had been fun, and he could remember England team-mates such as Hedley Verity and Ken Farnes who had not survived the war. Denis had come through it, so how could he bemoan the fact that nature had decided to make a 39-year-old limp like a pensioner?

After his retirement he watched innumerable Tests in his capacity first as television commentator, then as newspaper columnist. Bombast was not part of his make-up, and he insisted that he would still go down the pitch to the fast men if he had played in later decades – 'Imran Khan wouldn't know where to bowl if you gave him the charge,' he told me as we watched the Pakistan captain make the English batsmen duck and weave. He felt there was too much emphasis on training and net practice: 'If you have the basic ability, all you need is the feel of the bat on ball just before the start of play. I only had a long net before the season began.' Of all his performances he singled out two where he feels he could not have played any better: at Lord's in 1938, when he made 76 not out for England on a damp pitch against Australia, and at Lord's in 1947 when Kent asked Middlesex to get 395 at more than ninety an hour. Denis made 168, and his duel with Doug Wright was a thrilling, challenging highlight of that dazzling summer. Middlesex lost by 75 runs, but the game of cricket was even more triumphant.

He laughed resignedly about his running between the wickets and agreed that he never really knew how to judge singles. Bill Edrich felt Denis was unjustly criticised and pointed out that he merely forgot where the good fielders were stationed: 'He would play one straight to Neil Harvey, call for one and then suddenly remember that Neil was a great fielder. It all stemmed from Denis's attitude that every ball had the potential of at least one run.' Nevertheless Denis did run out his brother Leslie in his benefit match – not the most fraternal of actions and one about which he winced for the rest of his days. Fred Titmus was another casualty of the 'yes, no' Compton style that day, and he recalls the pressure he felt when he partnered Denis: 'You'd get keyed up because he was such a great player and you knew you mustn't run him out, even if it was his own fault. There was no malice about it; he was just forgetful.'

It seems that the legendary stories about Denis's forgetfulness are also deeply rooted in fact – he did often forget his gear, borrow a bat and go out to make a hundred with it. He invariably forgot his passport when going on overseas tours with England, and his living quarters on tour were a perennial shambles and a nightmare for the cleaners. He did turn up half-an-hour late for a Test once because he had forgotten that play started earlier on the last day: it was the 1949 Oval Test, and he was sitting in a traffic queue in London when a taxi driver leaned out of his cab and shouted at him: ''Ere, Denis, the radio says England are just going out on the field. What's going on?' a question echoed by his captain, Freddie Brown later that morning. Bill Edrich also had cause to recall the famous Compton mental torpor; the game was the Bank Holiday fixture with Sussex at Hove. Edrich declared Denis in his side before the captains tossed for innings, even though there was no sign of him. After over an hour's play he came running onto the field, easing himself into his sweater (not his own, of course) and spluttering: 'I'm terribly sorry, it was my wedding anniversary last night and the telephone people forgot to ring me!' Edrich, shaking his head with due solemnity, put Denis on to bowl as a punishment – and he grabbed three wickets before lunch. Typical Denis.

I know of no other player held in greater affection by his former playing colleagues than Denis Compton. Not one person I interviewed uttered a breath of criticism of him as a person and all were united in their admiration at his brilliance as a player. Here are just a few random reflections on Denis . . .

> ALEC BEDSER: I can't think of anyone of such class who enjoyed himself more in the game and got away with so much.
>
> 'ROLEY' JENKINS: I toured South Africa with him and Denis, the star, was wonderful to Jenkins, the novice. If I were the spectator, he'd be the man I would want to watch above all.
>
> JOE HARDSTAFF: Such a lovely, unaffected bloke. He'd shun the limelight and just be one of the boys.
>
> GODFREY EVANS: I've never seen a man go down the wicket so far to the fast bowlers. He played cricket for fun and made it look fun.
>
> ALF GOVER: I caught and bowled him when he was close to a hundred, after a rare old battle of wits. As he walked past me he said, "Well bowled, Alf – I enjoyed that!" No word about not getting 100.
>
> BILL EDRICH: His tremendous sense of adventure rubbed off on me. He would have played cricket for nothing if necessary, he loved it so much.

Perhaps the most impressive tribute to Denis came from G.O. Allen, who batted with him on his first appearance for Middlesex. Denis was picked against Sussex as a slow bowler who batted number eleven, and Allen had to shepherd him through some testing overs from Maurice Tate. The composure of Denis impressed everyone and, although he made just 14, Allen's prognosis that Middlesex had unearthed a great player was soon confirmed. 'Gubby' Allen – England captain, chairman of the selectors and influential administrator – was not the man to toss eulogies around for no real purpose, yet he said that, if he had the chance to see just one batsman again, it would be Denis. 'He had this capacity to entertain. He was an authentic genius. Once Walter Robins told Denis at tea-time that he had never seen him hit a straight six. Denis said, "Watch the third ball after tea." Well, he took two steps up the wicket, hit a long, straight six and turned and waved to Robins. I call that genius.' This from the man who captained Hammond, played against Bradman and McCabe, selected May and Cowdrey for England teams, bowled against Jack Hobbs and saw Frank Woolley make those two immortal nineties against Armstrong's Australians in 1921.

Given Denis's active social life and the roistering that seemed to increase as he got older – often in tandem with his great friends, Keith Miller and Bill Edrich – it remains a minor miracle that he lived till he was 78. In the end complications from a hip operation claimed him in April 1997. He breezed through his hectic life with an insouciant good nature and charm that beguiled everyone. There were more applications to attend his memorial service at Westminster Abbey than for anyone else in the previous thirty years. E.W. Swanton captured the essential Denis Compton and his importance to post-war Britain when he wrote: 'I doubt if any game at any period has thrown up anyone to match his popular appeal in the England of 1947 to 1949.' Swanton may have been a snob, exercising undue influence through his media work on many an England selector, but he understood the attractions of chivalry, daring and joy in a cricketer like Compton.

The statistics of Compton, D.C.S., cannot compare with the pleasure he gave in such generous portions, but they will certainly act as an impressive adjunct to a glorious career. Twelfth in the list of centurions with 123 hundreds, including 17 in Tests, a batting average of nearly 52, and the fastest triple century in history – 181 minutes. Only Bradman – in 295 innings – got to his century of centuries in fewer innings than Compton – 552 – a stunning achievement for such a dashing batsman, who never coveted runs or hundreds for their own sake. If he had possessed two good knees after the age of thirty and a greedier attitude to batting, then those figures would have been much more impressive, yet the scorebook was never the gazetteer of a Compton innings. Denis traded in shining faces, sore palms and unread newspapers. If he had had his way, every year would have been like 1947.

15

Tom Graveney

'He would never have been out of an Australian side
during *my* Test career' (Richie Benaud)

Thomas William Graveney

Born

Riding Mill, Northumberland
16 June 1927

First hundred

114 Gloucestershire v Combined Services, Gloucester, 1948
Age: 21 years 72 days

100th hundred

132 Worcestershire v Northamptonshire, Worcester, 1964
Age: 37 years 50 days

Last hundred

100* Worcestershire v Yorkshire, Worcester, 1970
Age: 43 years 62 days

Career record

M	Inn	NO	HS	Runs	Average	100s	50s
732	1,223	159	258	47,793	44.91	122	233

Test record

M	Inn	NO	HS	Runs	Average	100s	50s
79	123	13	258	4,882	44.38	11	20

Tom Graveney of Gloucestershire and Worcestershire. There, that looks and sounds right, as fitting as Frank Woolley of Kent and Geoffrey Boycott of Yorkshire. I could never really visualise Tom Graveney plying his elegant trade for twenty years under the soccer floodlights at that utilitarian ground in Northampton, or caressing those sumptuous cover drives around the vast wastes of The Oval. Both the man and his batting were made for that lovely Cheltenham ground, where the tents blend with the Cotswold stone of the college during Festival Week, or Worcester, with that picture-postcard setting dominated by the most famous cathedral known to cricket lovers. And how appropriate that he now lives close to that delightful ground in Cheltenham, attending conscientiously to his duties as president of the town's Cricket Society.

Tom Graveney summed up all the aesthetic delights of cricket; even his name seemed to fit the image. A name that conjured up visions of tributaries winding gently into the main river of batsmanship, where all the artists of different eras merge into a cornucopia of quality. Graveney is in that exclusive river by right: he had to swim against the tide of functionalism for most of his career, to learn how to play with elegance against in-swingers and balls that whip in off the seam, making batsmen hop about on green wickets, thankful to jab it through the packed cordon of fielders close in on the legside. Men like Les Jackson and Brian Statham and off-spinners such as Jim Laker, Roy Tattersall and Don Shepherd gave Graveney precious little opportunity to indulge in his beautiful offside play. When he started just after the war, the absence of quick bowlers and the abundance of top-class spin bowling meant he could concentrate on the offside, to the delight of himself and his many admirers. During his 23 years in the game, the angle of attack changed drastically: batsmen in the 1950s and 1960s prospered if they could play off middle and leg. Peter May was the best English batsman of that decade, partly through his own supreme ability but also because his onside play was prodigious. It is to the great credit of Tom Graveney that he learned how to play the 'bread and butter' shots on the legside, to 'milk' the ball off middle stump through midwicket or ease a leg-stump yorker past square leg's left hand. He did not jettison his easy elegance in the learning process, and his batting had a bloom that was never surpassed in post-war England. May, Cowdrey and Dexter were equally delightful in their differing styles, but they had the good fortune to hone their skills on good university wickets. Tom Graveney learned how to bat on the slow, low wickets of Bristol, where the ball turned sharply and offside indulgences were limited to the occasional punishment of a bad ball before returning to the grind of chiselling out runs by the use of a strong right hand. Arthur Milton grew up with Graveney at Bristol and admired his work on those wickets: 'Those pitches produced poor players. They were so bad that you were out of form for half the season. Tom's attitude was far better than mine; he'd graft away, whereas I would shrug my shoulders and complain about the ball not coming onto the bat.'

Graveney always looked a cricketer: tanned, smiling, relaxed. His critics in the early days thought he was too convivial with the fielders and contrasted the taciturnity of the great Hammond when he batted. Len Hutton could never get on his wavelength when he captained him for England, unsurprisingly when you consider their different backgrounds and attitudes to the game. Graveney's high backlift allowed him to bat elegantly, and he would be deluged with praise when he played well; if he was dismissed early, it would be judged carelessness and the fault of that ridiculously extravagant pick-up of the bat. The implication that he played cricket for fun did not help, either; he did not believe in parading his misery after a bad day, preferring to enjoy a few pints with both colleagues and opposition. Did he not realise that cricket was a serious business?

Yes, he did; but it was not the fulcrum of his life. He could have played golf for a living, and he was naturally talented at all sports. He had drifted into county cricket and did not play for the first team until he was 21. Young men of his age were thankful to be alive in the immediate post-war years, and so the rigours of professional cricket could easily be held at bay with the right attitude. Graveney was lucky: natural talent, allied to a recommendation from his elder brother who was already on the Gloucestershire staff, brought him to Bristol. He was on leave from his army job as a physical training officer in the Middle East and he turned out in a few benefit matches for Gloucestershire players in and around the Cotswolds. He recalls: 'No one wanted to open in those games so I went in first. I got about thirty against the new ball in one game and thought I'd done rather well. Billy Neale, the batsman at the other end, was still on Gloucestershire's books, and he put a good word in for me. I still had no thoughts of playing cricket for a living; I loved the life in the Army.'

His early matches for Gloucestershire did nothing to wean him away from his fondness for the Army. He made nought on his first-class debut and scraped together about 250 runs in his first 25 innings. He was dropped from the first team and, in despair, turned to golf – the committee had earlier warned him off golf, fearing that it would distort his batting style. He was resigned to the sack when Don Bradman played a crucial part. With England being swept away by Bradman's Australians, the England selectors turned in desperation to the Gloucestershire batsmen, George Emmett and Jack Crapp. At that time Gloucestershire had just twelve professionals and a handful of amateurs. They had to turn to this young chancer Graveney again. In his first game back in the side he made an impressive 47 on a turning wicket against Hampshire; in the month of August, he made over 700 runs, and he was soon established as the most promising young batsman in the land.

Comparisons with Hammond were made. Apart from the silkiness of Graveney's off-driving, it is difficult to see any similarity; Hammond was equally awesome off the back foot, whereas Graveney played forward almost constantly to combat the low bounce of the wickets in Gloucestershire.

163

Hammond was a glorious medium-pace bowler in his youth; Graveney bowled occasional leg-breaks that sometimes pitched. The arguments about their respective merits raged for years, but Graveney never took them seriously: 'I had such a bad start to my career that I could never be judged in Hammond's class, quite apart from the fact that we batted differently. I relied on timing, he combined power with timing. I saw him bat once and that was enough; he was magnificent, scoring a hundred against Yorkshire in 1946. I don't count that awful comeback of his in 1951. I could only watch him play two balls. It was so sad.'

Nevertheless Hammond's former team-mates who were still in the Gloucestershire side realised that young Graveney could become a major batsman, a man who would score 2,000 runs a season for the county for the next twenty years if handled properly. Graveney acknowledges the help he got from those elder players, as he struggled to come to terms with challenges that were foreign to his affable temperament. 'I remember the first time we played Kent. I had never seen Doug Wright bowl, and he frightened me out of my wits as he bounded in off his long run and bowled unplayable fast leg-breaks. Jack Crapp was batting with me and said: "Just stay up the other end, watch him bowl and then play a few shots when you feel comfortable." That's the way to encourage a youngster – no waffle, just solid common sense.'

He longed for such encouragement when he first played for England. A succession of beautiful innings had whetted the public's appetite for a new batting star; the comparisons with Hammond would not go away, even though Graveney remained unperturbed by them. He was more concerned about the inferiority complex he felt when batting for England: 'I'd sit in the dressing room, look around at Compton, Hutton and May and think, "What the hell am I doing here? I'll never be as good as them!" I don't think Len Hutton believed I was up to much, he couldn't understand my attitude. As far as I was concerned, I played no differently in a Test than I did in a county match. I was a poor man's Compton – enjoy the game, have a laugh with the fielders and a drink with them afterwards. Len couldn't believe it.'

A partnership with Hutton at Lord's in 1953 hardened the captain's mind over Graveney. He was bowled in the first over of the morning by a Lindwall yorker. On the previous day he and Hutton had added 168 with batting of the highest pedigree and Graveney – on 78 – was expected to coast home to his hundred. Hutton (of course) went to his century, but he had been bitterly disappointed at Graveney's early dismissal. Richie Benaud, who was on the field that day, told me that not enough credit has been given to the bowler and that Graveney had unluckily deflected the ball onto his stumps. No matter – the dismissal had confirmed Hutton's view that Graveney lacked substance, and an incident in their partnership confirmed that feeling, as Graveney recounts: 'I'd scored about thirty when Bill Johnston bowled one to me that was fairly well up. It swung across me, and I followed it and flat-batted it square to the boundary. I laughed out loud at my good fortune, thinking it was going to be my day – but Len, at the other end, frowned and looked at me as if I was off my rocker.'

Graveney also blotted his copybook with F.R. Brown, the chairman of selectors. Brown, who was playing in that Lord's Test, was very pleased with Graveney's unbeaten innings and he told him to be at the ground early the following morning for a net. Brown – like Hutton – had a long memory of Australian dominance, and this was England's chance to grind away for a victory. The next morning Graveney was late and Brown was furious: 'He turned up just in time to pad up. He told me that he'd taken his wife shopping, and he got a rocket for that. So he goes out and gets dismissed in the first over with his mind not attuned to the job. That was typical of Tom in his early days with England: all the ease and grace, but he never got stuck in.'

That opinion was echoed by G.O. Allen, who succeeded F.R. Brown as chairman of the selectors. He told me: 'Of course, Graveney was very graceful but, you know, elegance can hide faults. His record for England wasn't really all that good in those early years.' Yet inferior players kept him out on several occasions, as Jim Laker remembered: 'They said he wasn't as good as Hammond, because he averaged forty to Hammond's sixty – then they'd pick someone who averaged 25! It didn't make sense to me. Tom Graveney was class and should've been in the side as a regular.' He did not achieve that until 1957 and, in the meantime, he was shuffled up and down the batting order and jettisoned intermittently. May and Cowdrey justifiably held the prime batting positions, but it does seem that Graveney never enjoyed the confidence of the selectors during that period in the mid-1950s. He missed the 1956/57 tour to South Africa, despite topping the averages in the 1956 season; his place was taken by the likeable Alan Oakman, a man not remotely in Graveney's class. Jim Parks – a fine, free batsman, even though inconsistent – was also selected ahead of him for that trip. Graveney feels the reason why he missed out stemmed from the Old Trafford Test, Laker's Match, when he pulled out with a damaged hand. Oakman played instead and caught some brilliant catches in the leg-trap. The following week Graveney had recovered and played one of the greatest innings of his career – 200 out of 298 all out on a turning wicket at Newport against the spin of Don Shepherd and Jim McConnon. As Graveney walked back to the pavilion he heard a comment from the Glamorgan captain, Wilf Wooller: 'That was the worst double hundred I've seen in my life.' Wooller was also an England selector at that time. Players who saw that innings tell me Wooller could not possibly have meant what he said, and Graveney thinks that Wooller was merely articulating the disapproval of the selectors at his withdrawal from the Old Trafford Test. That innings remains a record in first-class cricket, the lowest innings total that includes a double century.

Graveney has a whimsical reason for being out of favour with the England selectors for so long. He'd once beaten G.O. Allen at golf and the chairman of selectors was far from impressed. 'I had an unorthodox grip on the clubs and that annoyed Gubby Allen, because I still managed to get the golf ball into the right areas. That offended his purist notions. Gubby ran English cricket with a rod of iron in those days, and he would take offence at all sorts of things. Perhaps he didn't like the way I played golf. Or the fact that, if there was something on my mind, I'd speak out.'

For a couple of years Graveney gained a foothold in the England team but, after the disastrous tour to Australia in 1958/59, he was cast aside, along with Evans and Bailey. He assumed his England career had finished at the age of 32 and his detractors rested on their laurels: they agreed his hundred in the Sydney Test of 1955 had been dazzling but pointed out that Graveney had not played well when it mattered, when the rubber was at stake. They dismissed his 258 against the West Indies in 1957 as a cosy innings on a dead wicket, but they had more trouble over his 164 at The Oval in the same series, on a turning wicket that later saw the West Indies bowled out for 89 and 86.

The blossoming of Tom Graveney into a mature technician would probably never have happened without the unwitting help of the Gloucestershire committee. When they sacked him from the county captaincy in 1960, Graveney packed his bags and walked out on the club in much the same way as W.G. Grace in 1899. Graveney insists it was not caused by the loss of the captaincy – 'I wasn't all that good at the job, I was too close to the players I'd grown up with. I had an unbalanced attack with three class off-spinners jostling with each other, and I wasn't a great disciplinarian.' What upset him was the way the matter was handled and that his successor, the Old Etonian Tom Pugh, was not worth his place in the side. Graveney was accused of being a bad loser, and attitudes hardened on both sides. He gratefully transferred allegiance to Worcestershire, and his former county obdurately insisted on him serving a one-year qualification period before he could play county cricket.

Graveney was therefore 35 before he played a championship match for his new team. It proved to be the best thing he ever did in his career: 'The challenge was just what I had needed. I had become stale at Bristol, and the year out of the game put some steel into my soul. I came back refreshed and determined to make Gloucestershire sorry.' He was treated with respect at Worcester, and he responded to the different environment. It was made clear to him that his job was to score a lot of runs on wickets that favoured the county's strong bowling attack; as the best player in the side, his responsibility was to play major innings. There was an extra incentive – Worcestershire were genuine championship contenders, and Graveney desperately wanted to win something after all the years of dilettante enjoyment. The professional respect afforded him by his team-mates at Worcester was graphically illustrated by that fine swing bowler Len Coldwell, who told him, 'You used to play for Gloucestershire, but you worked for Worcestershire.' He had become a masterful batsman away from those turgid Bristol wickets and made it all count for almost a decade at New Road.

In his first season Worcestershire just missed out on the championship but secured it in 1964 and in the following year. Graveney made 2,385 runs and 1,768 runs in those two seasons, in the process playing some innings of majestic certainty on bad wickets. The one that gave him greatest pleasure was at Cheltenham in 1965 against his former county. On a spiteful wicket Worcestershire needed 130 to win against the highly professional off-spin of David Allen and John Mortimore; they lost three wickets before the score had reached twenty and, with a long tail, Worcestershire looked finished. Graveney and Basil D'Oliveira played everything off the back foot, while Graveney moved forward at every opportunity to hit Allen and Mortimore back over their heads. They both made unbeaten fifties to win the match. D'Oliveira modestly told me that Graveney's innings was the greatest he saw, while Norman Gifford, who watched the stand from the players' balcony, called it the most fascinating piece of cricket he has witnessed in his career.

D'Oliveira's presence in the Worcestershire side also acted as a spur to Graveney; he knew that the remarkable South African was determined to prove himself the best player at the club and Graveney had to keep nudging ahead of him. 'Basil was great for me. I loved batting with him, and he brought out a competitive streak in me that I didn't know I possessed. I was very annoyed, though, that he was better looking than me. I couldn't do much about that!'

No one was more pleased than Graveney at the selection of D'Oliveira for the England team against the 1966 West Indians; little did he realise that he too was about to enter a final, productive period in Test cricket. Graveney is convinced that if M.J.K. Smith had won the toss at Old Trafford in the First Test, then he would have played out the rest of his career exclusively with Worcestershire. The ball turned sharply for Lance Gibbs on the third day at Old Trafford and, when England lost by an innings, the captain was dropped and a vacancy in the middle order appeared. Graveney was selected for Lord's, made 96 in his usual, unhurried manner and he stayed in the side until 1969. The reception at Lord's as he walked out to bat was moving and unnerving: 'I was frightened stiff – they started clapping me as I came through the Long Room! In the circumstances, that was one of my best innings. Hall and Griffith didn't exactly say "welcome back" to me!' It was Graveney's 39th birthday, and the manner of his dismissal, four short of his century, still rankles. 'The previous ball I'd hit Wes square to the boundary, so he moved third man round, much squarer. He made the next one bounce a little more, and I was committed to the steer past second slip to benefit from the space down at fine third man. Caught behind. Annoying!'

At last Graveney was a reassuring fixture in the England side at the age of 39. His batting had reached a well-rounded maturity, and he felt content: 'It was so much better for me when May, Hutton and the others had gone.

I then felt I could compete on equal terms with the rest! Batting at number three or four gave me the responsibility I needed, and I no longer felt inferior, with the great players of the fifties gone.' As Graveney began the 1969 series against the West Indies, there seemed no reason why he should not be good enough for another season or two; the limited-overs game was causing him some technical problems and a few stiff limbs, but he was ideally equipped for the longer Test match game. He made an accomplished 75 in the first innings at Old Trafford to underline his suitability for the series but then took a conscious decision to end his England career. Graveney had told the selectors that he wanted to play in a match at Luton on the Sunday – it was his benefit season and he had been promised £1,000 if he played. He advised Alec Bedser, the chairman, about the Luton offer before the Test team was picked so, when he was selected, Graveney assumed that he was going to be allowed to go to Luton on the rest day of the Test. Bedser told him he could not go after the end of the first day at Old Trafford, but Graveney went ahead with the game at Luton. He was banned for the next four Tests, which effectively meant the end of his Test career. As Keith Fletcher, John Hampshire, Mike Denness and Peter Parfitt shuffled in and out of Graveney's place for the rest of that summer, lovers of class batsmanship cursed the benefit system and berated the intransigence that did not trust a mature professional to keep out of the way of physical danger during a Sunday beer match at Luton. In that benefit year he made just £7,500, so more than ten per cent was raised from that one match which ended his Test career. He points out that he had played four years for England before he could afford to buy a car: a Ford Anglia for £645. So who can blame Graveney for playing in that benefit match at the age of 42?

Graveney accepts his share of the blame and says he knew what he was doing. Within a year he was lost to English first-class cricket, terrified that his powers might possibly be on the wane. 'I didn't want to hear the kids saying, "Why is he still in the side?" and I was finding the Sunday League hard going. Looking back on it now, I packed up two seasons early.' In his last season, he was second in the national averages (62.66), with only Sobers ahead of him.

He emigrated to Australia for three years, to coach Queensland, and, against his better judgement, played a handful of Sheffield Shield matches and a few one-day games. 'Playing in that humidity out there at the age of 44 wasn't such a great idea!' He then returned home to run a pub at Prestbury, near Cheltenham's Racecourse, for a decade. Over a fourteen-year period he provided expert analysis for BBC TV's coverage of Tests and one-day internationals. In that period he would watch batsmen ducking against the barrage of short-pitched bowling and wonder how he would have avoided being killed when he had batted with such a pronounced forward emphasis – and without a protective helmet. He concludes that his head must have been in the right position and confirms that Lindwall, Miller, Adcock, Heine,

Hall and Griffith were every bit as hostile as the present breed of fast bowlers. Alan Knott and Dennis Amiss, who both played for England with Graveney, feel that he would be forced onto the back foot today and that his front-foot style would be his undoing. I wonder. Wickets have got even slower in England since Graveney's retirement, and most batsmen play forward to avoid lbw decisions against deliveries that keep low. David Brown, the former England fast bowler, agrees: 'Tom was always pretty good at getting out of the way of the short-pitched stuff. His head position was marvellous; he wouldn't take his eye off the ball, as some current England batsmen do. He never seemed to miss much around his legs when I bowled at him, and those wristy, late dabs were very productive. They'd have to pitch it up eventually, because they'd get fed up with Tom swaying out of harm's way. If they pitched it up, he would drive them on both sides of the wicket without any problems at all.'

The modern batsmen would be surprised at the amount of net practice Graveney took; only Geoffrey Boycott has emulated him since he retired. With Graveney, it was an article of faith to have a net every day at Worcester; he would arrive at the ground early and take his practice very seriously. Len Coldwell and Jack Flavell would take the new ball against him, and Norman Gifford always aimed for Graveney's net: 'You could bowl properly at Tom in the nets, because he would bat properly – no slogging, just a sensible attitude to finding his touch. He treated a net like an innings in a match, and you could learn to bowl accordingly. At the end he'd walk out with the sweat pouring off him – last night's beer! He had great pride in his performance at Worcester; years after he left Worcestershire, if he had to play in a charity match he'd pop down to the nets and get the feel of the bat in his hands.'

A strange paradox in some ways, Tom Graveney. A player who had many run-ins with the hierarchy at Lord's, yet a proud President of the MCC in 2004/05, the first professional cricketer to fill that post. 'If you love Lord's as I do, it has to be the greatest honour for a former pro cricketer. And we got the Ashes back in my year!' He was a dedicated practiser, even though he played with refreshing freedom of expression and sense of enjoyment. A man of immense natural talent, yet highly superstitious – he always sat in the same seat on the Worcester balcony when waiting to bat and he would use the same piece of chewing gum throughout his innings, placing it neatly on top of his bat handle at close of play and then popping it in his mouth when he resumed the next morning. When fielding, he always wanted to touch the ball; if the wicket-keeper missed him out at slip, he would fret as the ball made its way back to the bowler. A chivalrous opponent, delighted to chat about the achievements of others, yet his memory of his own performances smacks of Boycott. His recall of precise dates, locations, appropriate bowlers and the state of the wickets is as precise as his memory of his exact score at any stage in his career. Not surprisingly, the match which saw him reach a hundred hundreds is easily recalled: Worcestershire against Northants at

Worcester in 1964. He reminded me that he got 132 – correct – and went on: 'I knew all about those who had got a hundred centuries, and I was thrilled at the chance to be one of them. I loved moving up that list in *Wisden*! When I got to 99 against Northants, their wicket-keeper Keith Andrew said to me, 'We don't want to make it easy for you, do we?' and I wanted to say 'Yes!' David Larter bowled me a bouncer, I tried to hook it, got a bottom edge and it plopped just over short-leg's head for a single. Achieved in the grand manner!'

An articulate talker on the technique of batsmanship, he can remember the occasions when he worked out how to play certain shots – that little push on the bounce through the offside that got so many 'bread and butter' runs, the half-cock stroke on the front foot that allowed him to defend so skilfully on turning wickets. His weight distribution was always excellent; even though he played almost everything off the front foot – including the hook – he never seemed off-balance. As Tony Brown, a colleague at Bristol, recalls, 'Tom never seemed at odds with his game. If he was dismissed, we would assume it was a very good ball. He never had a bad run in my experience, his technique and timing were so good.' Fred Titmus told me that Graveney was the best player of off-spin he ever saw: 'He was always so far over the ball that you couldn't get him off balance. He would work you away on the legside, then if you bowled a little outside the line of middle and leg, out would come that superb cover-drive!'

He remains a compelling talker about the art of batsmanship, even in his eighties. He says he would hit in the air more often if he played today – 'I used to think that going for sixes was another way of getting yourself out.' He bemoans the use of heavy bats, recalling that his weighed around 2lbs 3oz. 'Many modern players don't pick the bat up straight because of those heavy bats, which means they're playing towards mid-on rather than straight. And when the ball's doing a bit, you'll struggle if you're not bringing the bat down straight.' The basics of batting haven't changed since his palmy days – 'although some of the shots that blokes like Kevin Pietersen play are fantastic. He's an amazing player, with fantastic hand-eye co-ordination.'

He must have missed out on around thirty England caps. He should have gone to South Africa in 1956/57 and again in 1964/65 and to Australia the following winter. Although recalled in 1966, he was just as good in 1964, when his batting prowess – five hundreds, sixteen fifties – put him in a class of his own, fully twenty runs an innings ahead of the next batsman in the side. He was considered good enough for the Rest of the World side in Barbados in 1967, yet not for England until the previous season. Richie Benaud told me that the Australians could never believe that Graveney was not rated highly enough by England's selectors in successive years: 'We never sung Tom's praises unless we were asked, and then we said he should be in the England team. A lot of people thought that was a double-bluff, a piece of Australian sharp practice, so Tom missed out a lot. There was a definite prejudice against his style of batting. He would never have been out of an Australian side during *my* Test career.'

Graveney has no regrets about the way he batted. 'I couldn't help being a front-foot player, not playing the game in a certain way. I always felt sorry for David Gower; he went through the same wall of criticism that I faced. If he played a lovely shot, he got all the praise but, if a stump went out of the ground, they'd say "what a terrible shot" without giving any credit to the bowler. You simply have to play the way that suits you as a person and as a batsman.'

He believes he would find it very hard not being able to play at least four championship innings every week if he was around today. 'My game was based on timing, and I needed to be out there in the middle. Batting's all about what's given to you, but I do think that today's players have missed out by not playing on uncovered wickets and surfaces that varied from county to county. When you play on consistently dry wickets, technique becomes less vital. Anybody decent can get runs on a flat pitch.'

We can only be grateful for Graveney's independence of mind, for he gave great pleasure consistently for twenty years. Those who accuse him of inconsistency should know that he scored more runs in the 1950s than anyone, that his Test average was 44 and that he scored more runs than Cowdrey, Hayward, Hutton and Gooch. He was the first to reach a hundred centuries and 30,000 first-class runs in purely post-war cricket. A reasonable effort from a man who did not play serious cricket till he was 21, a batsman who was a bit of a dasher until he was 35. How he would have flourished in the pre-1914 era! The very thought of Wilfred Rhodes bowling at Tom Graveney with seven men on the offside makes me long for a time machine.

16

Colin Cowdrey

'When Colin was in that sort of mood, you could take your
pads off for the rest of the day'   (M.J.K. Smith)

Michael Colin Cowdrey

Born

Bangalore, Karnataka, India

24 December 1932

Died

Littlehampton, Sussex

4 December 2000

First hundred

143   Free Foresters v Oxford University, Oxford, 1951

Age: 18 years 160 days

100th hundred

100*   Kent v Surrey, Maidstone, 1973

Age: 40 years 193 days

Last hundred

119*   Kent v Gloucestershire, Cheltenham, 1975

Age: 42 years 217 days

Career record

M	Inn	NO	HS	Runs	Average	100s	50s
692	1,130	134	307	42,719	42.89	107	231

Test record

M	Inn	NO	HS	Runs	Average	100s	50s
114	188	15	182	7,624	44.06	22	38

The career of Colin Cowdrey is cogent proof of the maxim that cricket is a matter of inches – those between your ears. When his mind was clear, he was peerless: an effortless timer of the ball, a batsman with so much time to spare that he made the game look a case of men against boys. He would caress the fastest bowlers around the field with the paternal air of an indulgent father amusing his brood on the beach. The contrast in Cowdrey on his introspective days was striking and sad to anyone who admires class: he would scratch away diffidently against bowlers who should never have troubled him, the penalty of all 'touch' players, those who rely on instinctive timing. Jim Laker neatly summed up the enigma of Colin Cowdrey when he told me: 'I always felt you could bowl a maiden over at him when he'd scored 120.' M.J.K. Smith, a contemporary at Oxford and former England colleague who captained Cowdrey, assessed him equally succinctly: 'The word to describe Colin's batting is frustration.'

Before delving too deeply into the Freudian and estimating why Colin Cowdrey sometimes complicated the game to his own detriment, it is important to emphasise his class and record as a batsman. For 25 years his name was synonymous with grace and charm, yet he was also an extremely prolific batsman. Only Grace and Woolley have surpassed his tally of a thousand runs in a season (27), he is thirteenth in the list of run-scorers (42,719), and only Hammond and Boycott among Englishman have equalled his tally of Test hundreds (22). He also scored 107 first-class hundreds and, in doing so, left indelible memories of a glorious batsman who possessed every shot and the tactical intelligence to alter his style to the prevailing trends of the game. He is also acknowledged as a chivalrous opponent, an unselfish team-mate and one of the most impressive representatives of the game.

And yet, and yet; both Les Ames and Doug Wright thought he should have scored two hundred centuries, opinions based on the prodigious natural talent he displayed when those two veterans first played with him for Kent. Fred Trueman pitched his estimate a little lower: around 150 hundreds. M.J.K. Smith's tribute is impressive: 'He made batting look easier than anyone I've ever seen,' and F.R. Brown, a man associated with first-class cricket for over fifty years, said: 'If I had to assemble a coaching film on the art of batting, the man I would choose from my time would be Colin Cowdrey.' Jim Laker considered he had more natural ability than his great partner, Peter May, and Ray Illingworth judges him the nearest technical equivalent to his hero, Sir Leonard Hutton. Despite his lavish gifts he only topped 2,000 first-class runs in a season twice.

Cowdrey was the ideal number four, a man capable of playing on any wicket against all varieties of bowling, yet such was his vast ability that he performed superbly as an opener. He hated opening – 'I used to dread getting out early and having no further part to play for the rest of the day' – but he had a wonderful tour of the West Indies in 1959/60, when his hooking of Wes Hall was masterful. Cowdrey, acknowledging that some of his best innings were played on that tour, recognised the anomaly that they were made from a batting position he did not like; yet his adaptability was one of his greatest assets and the brave, composed way he stood up to Lillee and Thomson as the age of 42 in wholly disconcerting circumstances crystallised his multifarious, enduring talent.

Perhaps his choice of Hutton as his mentor when young gives a clue to Cowdrey's occasional batting schizophrenia. Cowdrey, a keen cricket historian, had imbued himself with the knowledge of Hutton's deeds before meeting him on the cricket field: then he fell under the spell of Hutton's poise and perfection of style. It seemed that Hutton batted like a master every time Cowdrey saw him in his early days as a first-class cricketer. Cowdrey admitted that he became a committed disciple of the Hutton style and temperament. Crashing the ball to the boundary fence was 'infra dig'; the ball had had to be persuaded away, with just enough speed on it to beat the pursuing fielder. When Cowdrey first toured Australia under Hutton's captaincy, he was deeply impressed by his tactical grasp, his beautiful batting art and the kind, thoughtful way he helped the young man recover from the shock of his father's death. Hutton had told Cowdrey Senior, 'I'll look after him,' on the day the England team left for Australia; when they arrived in Perth to learn of the bereavement, Hutton was as good as his word. That made a deep impression on Cowdrey and may partly explain why he was such a kind counsellor and sympathetic friend to so many young cricketers for the rest of his life. To return to the influence on him of Hutton's batting: there can have been no finer mentor to copy at that stage, yet something of Hutton's innate caution must have rubbed off on him. 'You've got to think it out,' Hutton would say – and perhaps Cowdrey did too much of that in subsequent years.

Cowdrey admitted he used to fret during an innings if he thought he had lost the thread of consistent timing that was crucial to him. He had made a conscious decision not to rely on strength, to play like Hutton and not May or Dexter, and therefore he needed to feel 'in touch'. Certain wickets do not favour the effortless strokemaker who likes to use the pace of the ball, to open the bat's face and glide a delivery away with deceptive speed and certainty. Cowdrey needed pace in the wicket to be at his best and would watch with a certain amount of admiration someone like M.J.K. Smith, a scourge of off-spinners on slow wickets, who used a strong right hand to punch the ball with the spin through the legside. Smith never compared with Cowdrey as an all-round batsman or in his ability to play the fast bowlers, but there is no doubt that during their careers many slow wickets favoured the Smith pragmatism rather than the Cowdrey delicacy. When Cowdrey went out to bat, he had attuned his mind and body to the exigencies of the situation: the wicket, the appropriate bowlers and the tactical needs. He admits he could be thrown off course by an inspired bowling spell or his inability to stroke a half-volley to the boundary; he would enjoy the need to delve into his store of temperament and technical ability to combat the bowler, but he would worry more about the placement of his shots. Why was he hitting a half-volley straight at mid-off, rather than five yards to his left? On such days he would seemingly potter around after racing to a fluent fifty and take stock of his game, wondering whether to tinker a little with the system. 'Batting always fascinated me,' he said. 'Life becomes a bore if you've nothing left to prove, if you're not stretched. I relished the challenge of surviving at the wicket, of trying a few experiments.' He was inordinately proud of developing the 'paddle' shot – that curious sweep he played from an almost erect position which sent the ball to the wicket-keeper's left, at a very fine angle. Cowdrey perfected that shot to thwart the legside line which Richie Benaud once used to tie him down: 'The next time England played Australia, I was ready for him. It proved that I was not just an offside player but, more importantly, that I was justified in thinking about my game to an exact degree. I had kept pace with an evolving tactic of a bowler.'

Such a capacity for a technical adaptability led to periods when a new method was in the gestation stage; at such times Cowdrey could be maddeningly passive. Even though an excellent judge of a run, he occasionally allowed himself to be subjugated by bowlers whose only merit was nagging accuracy. Many of his former team-mates could not understand the depth of technical conundra that swirled around in his brain; several of them have told me that, if Cowdrey's ability could have been fused with the ruthlessness of Peter May, then the game of cricket would have seen the perfect batsman. Godfrey Evans said: 'Colin had all these heroes, but why couldn't he just bat like himself? That would have been world-class.'

At Melbourne in 1966 Cowdrey was caught at the wicket off the bowling of Doug Walters for a lovely 79. He returned to the dressing-room, acknowledged the congratulations and sympathies with his customary modesty and admitted the dismissal was his own fault: 'I knew as soon as he let go of the ball that I could have hit it past cover's left hand, but I thought I'd run it down through the slips for four instead.' Cowdrey could not understand why that remark was greeted with such mirth by less talented but more realistic team-mates; he was enjoying the battle so much that he had reached the stage where he could play two shots to each delivery. Such a range of options is only available to batsmen of the highest class, yet his unconscious attempt to over-complicate a simple manner of stroke selection had got him out.

Fred Titmus recalls occasions when Cowdrey would amuse the fielders at certain stages of the game with virtuoso displays of mastery: 'Sometimes, if a game was drifting to a draw, we'd say, "Come on, play us some shots," and John Murray behind the stumps would nominate a particular stroke and he'd play it whatever the delivery. Amazing talent, done without showing off – he was just amusing himself.' Dennis Amiss remembers being captivated by a duel between Cowdrey and Tom Cartwright on a green wicket at Gravesend; at that time, Cartwright was supreme on green wickets with his subtle medium pace and Amiss admits that he could not be certain about Cartwright's delivery from his position at slip. 'Colin had no such problems. He kept going down the pitch to Tom, saying, "I can read you from the hand now, Tom." No one else could lay a bat on him. In the second innings he got a brilliant hundred against the spinners with the wicket changed in character. His versatility was amazing.'

In the Oval Test in 1960 Cowdrey was opening the batting with Geoff Pullar, against South Africa's Neil Adcock, a splendidly hostile, genuinely fast bowler. Cowdrey calmly announced: 'I'm going to go out there and play him as if the ball isn't moving at all.' Adcock's first delivery was stroked through cover by Cowdrey and he went onto make 175 as England, following on, easily avoided defeat. Mike Smith was due to bat number five that day but recalls: 'When Colin was in that sort of mood, you could take your pads off for the rest of the day.' Adcock had already dismissed Cowdrey five times that series, and he had returned a string of low scores but, once he worked out the technical answer, he exuded an aura of omnipotence that day at The Oval.

Yet there were times when Cowdrey could not unlock the technical door, when he would retreat into his shell in the manner of a southern Hutton. On the 1956/57 tour of South Africa Peter May, the captain, and his manager, F.R. Brown, spent a long time trying to persuade Cowdrey to attack that splendid off-spinner, Hugh Tayfield. They felt that Cowdrey's range of strokes and nimble footwork were the right answer to Tayfield's wiles and, with May out of luck in the Tests, it was becoming an urgent matter. Brown remembered vividly the Durban Test: 'Colin went in with our instructions ringing in his ears, and soon he hit Tayfield for an effortless six over long-on. The next ball was played in the direction of mid-off, who made a great stop but couldn't prevent the batsmen running three. After that, Colin hardly played a shot at Tayfield for the next ten overs and eventually got out. I said "What happened, you had him!" He replied: "I was dropped and felt I had to stay in." Tayfield, who couldn't bowl at him, was allowed to get back on top.' He took eight for 69, and 37 wickets in the series.

Ten years earlier, life must have seemed much less complicated to Colin Cowdrey, as the small, rotund schoolboy impressed the harshest judges. He was marked down early for greatness; at the age of 13 he stood out at Alf Gover's cricket school and he dominated cricket at Tonbridge School for five years. At 17 he was in the Kent side, two years later he was capped (the youngest in the county's history) and at 21 an England player. Trevor Bailey saw him score a hundred for the Gentlemen against the Players at 18 and judged that he looked more like a 30-year-old craftsman than a mere boy. In 1953 he played two innings of remarkable maturity against Surrey on an Oval wicket that was ideal for Laker and Lock's diverse spinning talents. Cowdrey made 154 out of 270 and 34 out of 63, and Jim Laker – eight wickets in the match – told me: 'He played me better than any young player did at any time in my career. I was certain he was an England batsman for the next twenty years.'

An innings of grandeur in the Melbourne Test eighteen months later added to his glittering reputation. Keith Miller, bowling with inspiration on an unreliable pitch, had reduced England to 41 for four: Cowdrey scored a sumptuous 102 out of 191, and the crowd of 63,000 forgot their impartiality to roar him home to the pavilion at its end. Only three other batsmen reached double figures and Cowdrey, while at the crease, scored 100 out of 158. Bill O'Reilly described it as the finest innings he had seen in a Test match and whether or not that was Irish hyperbole, it did not matter: O'Reilly knew a high-class innings when he saw one. At 22 years of age, Cowdrey had proved himself at the highest level and seemed set fair for greatness.

That matchless performance became an albatross around the neck of his career. During his uninspired efforts his critics would call on Melbourne as proof that he had the quality but not the vital spark of consistency. If he could do it once, he should be able to repeat the dosage at will, they said. Cowdrey was well aware that his great innings raised expectations too early – 'After that, I was judged by a different yardstick, even though circumstances change so often from day to day. At Melbourne everything went right – I had some luck, and also played to my full capacity – but that was something people took for granted. I used to feel sorry for David Gower: he'd looked a class player since he was 21 at Test level, yet people expected him to turn in great innings irrespective of the quality of the bowlers and the wicket.'

The England captaincy cannot have helped Cowdrey's peace of mind: at various stages, he lost it to Dexter, Close, Illingworth and May. The selection of Ray Illingworth to captain the England tour to Australia in 1970/71 caused Cowdrey some heartache; he hesitated before accepting the vice-captaincy and he never did himself justice on that trip. Cowdrey insisted that the distractions of the England captaincy never consciously affected him, but the general feeling among his contemporaries is that he was indecisive and lacked sufficient dynamism. His many kindnesses are acknowledged, but his fondness for cricketers seems to have militated against a course of action that would possibly upset anyone. He did manage to cast aside the air of diffidence on the tour of West Indies in 1967/68, when he won the series by a mixture of team-spirit, tough out-cricket that did not baulk at slow over-rates, a generous declaration by Gary Sobers, batting depth and excellent fast bowling by John Snow. Cowdrey batted magnificently on that tour and his innings of 71 that won the Test at Port of Spain was a masterpiece of calm, controlled batting. Even then, the old diffidence reappeared; at tea on the final day John Edrich and Tom Graveney had to take their captain into a corner and persuade him the match was there for the taking.

No matter who was captain, Cowdrey served England loyally. Halfway through his career, he learned to battle it out at the crease, to graft for his runs even though they were not coming with their usual facility. Edgbaston 1957 was a turning point in his development as a major batsman, the first time he had scored a Test hundred by occupation of the crease rather than strokeplay. The situation of the game demanded that Cowdrey stay in with Peter May, but they both realised that they also had to quell the menace of Sonny Ramadhin for the series. They dominated the little leg-spinner in differing ways – May stroked the ball cleanly while Cowdrey played forward, padding the ball away for ever after. Ramadhin appealed himself hoarse, but on a slow wicket with little bounce, he had no chance of an lbw decision with Cowdrey a long way down the pitch. It was not pretty batting from one of the game's great stylists, but it worked. May and Cowdrey added 411, till recently the record in Tests for the fourth wicket, and Ramadhin was never the same bowler again. Cowdrey's success with the pad/bat method was to be imitated by a generation of less talented English batsmen, with distressing results, but he had proved that he had the stomach for the fight underneath the veneer of elegance.

Alan Knott, who played for a decade with Cowdrey, likens him to Ken Barrington in the way he would pick up runs by unostentatious shots. 'He would accumulate like Kenny – a tickle off his legs early in the innings or a little dab down to third man, just to judge the pace of the wicket. Of course, when he established himself, he was a much more fluent player than Kenny, but he really got stuck in during my time with him. He would be really disappointed at getting dismissed cheaply. He may not have looked it, but Colin was a real competitor.'

The competitive instinct led him to accept an invitation which he instinctively knew he should refuse. It came one morning in December 1974 when his morning ablutions at home were rudely shattered by a phone call from Mike Denness in Australia. The England captain explained that injuries had disrupted his tour party and that he wanted Colin to fly out to join them. As a batsman. At 42 years of age. Against Lillee and Thomson. On lightning fast, unreliable wickets that had reduced the England batsmen to nervous wrecks. Cowdrey forgot about his disappointment at not being originally selected after a fine season and agreed to go. Five days later he was playing in the Perth Test, on the fastest wicket in Australia, against bowlers who had broken one of Amiss's thumbs and one of Edrich's hands. At Perth he was sent in first wicket down and then, in the second innings, he had to open after Brian Luckhurst broke a hand. Cowdrey made 22 and 41 and gave an astonishing display of defensive batting. Dennis Amiss, one of the men who suffered most on that horrific tour, told me: 'It gave us so much confidence to see how fast bowling could be played. Colin would drop his wrists to anything short of a length and take his bat down and across his body, away from the ball. That casual sway of the head while the rest of us were all arms and legs and undignified scuttling – a wonderful technical effort.' Unfortunately Cowdrey had to opt for survival. Very few deliveries were pitched in an area that favoured his front-foot driving, even if he had acclimatised himself to the bounce. Bob Willis remembers feeling desperately sorry for Cowdrey: 'He could survive through his wonderful technique but he couldn't score runs. He'd battle away to get twelve in an hour and a half, then watch Tony Greig come in at the other end and carve three boundaries over the slips in an over. But the fact that we wanted him out there is a great tribute to the guy.'

Six months later, on a balmy June evening, Cowdrey paid back some of the dues to the Australians, when an innings of 151 not out steered Kent – chasing 354 – to a four-wicket victory. Ian Chappell, with his usual tact, had ordered the coach driver to be ready to take the Australians off to Southampton at four o'clock; they arrived at midnight after a thrashing from the master. Brian Luckhurst, the Kent captain that day, never forgot that innings: 'He was absolutely in control as he tore Lillee apart. After the battering I had taken in the previous winter, it was a delight to beat them by a vintage Cowdrey innings. At the age of 43, he was hooking Lillee in front of square!' It was a wonderful way to end Cowdrey's career; he had already decided to retire at the end of the 1975 season and he longed for one more good innings at Canterbury, the ground he loved. Now, another ambition fulfilled, he was content to leave the stage to others.

Few cricketers did more for the game on retirement than Colin Cowdrey. Only that great man of rugby union, Cliff Morgan, could match Cowdrey's readiness to travel up and down the country to speak to club societies and schools, at no cost. He devoted himself to the welfare of cricket until his death in December 2000 from a heart attack. He was just 67.

He was a tireless President of the Lord's Taverners for three years and a tenacious, strong-minded MCC President. As Chairman of the ICC he strove manfully to overcome the divisions between various countries and their boards, and he was proud to supervise the re-introduction of South Africa into international cricket, a cause long close to his heart.

Many sceptics had denounced Cowdrey's bridge-building stance towards South Africa in previous decades, believing this was a policy at odds with his declared Christian principles. But he never wavered. He was, at heart, a conciliator rather than a radical. We will never know if he did let Basil D'Oliveira down in that fateful selectors' meeting in August 1968 which ultimately led to South Africa's expulsion from Test cricket for 22 years. As the England captain Cowdrey would surely have had a key part in D'Oliveira's original omission, but the Establishment at Lord's closed ranks and collective responsibility has shrouded Cowdrey's role in ambiguity. He was – unashamedly – an Establishment man, friend and confidant of more than one Prime Minister. His second marriage to the daughter of the Duke of Norfolk and subsequent pleasure from mixing in august horse-racing circles only added to the consensual character of the man christened in homage to the Marylebone Cricket Club.

But Colin Cowdrey was no snob, unlike some he mixed with at Lord's. He loved cricketers and the game too much to have ideas above his station. Over the course of several arranged interviews for the BBC and many impromptu meetings at cricket functions, I can vouch for his kind nature and devotion to cricket.

For the rest of his life he missed the game desperately. He had regrets: that he was not fit enough to do himself justice on his final Australian tour, that he waited until halfway through his career before realising the need to adapt and improvise. He wished he could have played more against the spinners: 'That part of cricket was always special to me. In my early days, I would happily watch Hutton and Compton playing the spinners in their different ways. It was wonderful to be in the same side as a man like Doug Wright, such an inspirational leg-spinner.' Perhaps Cowdrey would have batted differently if he'd had his time over again: 'Yes, I think I'd smash it a bit more now. I was coming to terms with that in the one-day games towards the end. Perhaps I overdid the delicacies a little, but that was my style, the way I was brought up to play.' Gently he took issue with the modern fad of net practice: 'Roger Bannister wouldn't have run the four-minute mile if he'd trained that morning. I never wanted to lose what I had within me, I wanted to bring out everything in the middle.'

Fred Titmus believes Cowdrey would have been an even greater player if he had not been an amateur: 'If he had to earn his money as a pro, Colin would've been more practical and got rid of all the theory. He could afford to experiment, because his job didn't depend on it.' There may be some truth in that – Cowdrey admitted he played the game for fun. After marrying in 1956 the daughter of a Kent committee member who owned a chain of department stores in the county, Cowdrey became a director of the company. So he no longer had to worry about financial matters, the sort that forced other brilliant amateurs such as May and Dexter to leave the game early to gain security. The influence of his father was profound: he insisted young Colin's initials would be MCC, and one night in March 1938 he ensured his son would be hooked on the game for the rest of his life. The Cowdrey family was sailing back from India to England and six-year-old Colin was dragged from his bunk by his father to observe a ship passing three miles away. Reverentially Cowdrey Senior told his son: 'Don Bradman is on board that ship. He's bringing the Australian team to try and beat England.' Thereafter cricket fired the imagination of young Cowdrey and towards the premature end of his life – after a goodly crop of personal disappointments – he inclined towards an optimistic, romantic opinion on cricket, refreshingly free from the jaundiced, unsentimental stance of many former players.

He was properly proud of scoring a hundred hundreds, and paid due homage to the keenness of Asif Iqbal to scamper the necessary single from a push to cover in the Surrey match at Maidstone in 1973. He told me he felt that he had a pretty good temperament to play first-class cricket for 25 years and to surmount reverses such as a broken arm and a snapped Achilles tendon that ruined his chances of captaining an England tour to Australia. Strange how an ambition like that should be rooted in such a modest man, a player who never courted the England captaincy; yet the choice of Illingworth for the 1970/71 tour proved to be one of his greatest disappointments. Nevertheless he touched greatness many times. His unobtrusive yet brilliant slip catching brought him 120 Test catches, an England record he shares with another outstanding slipper, Ian Botham. Cowdrey was the first to play in 100 Tests, and he marked the occasion with a century against Australia. He was the first batsman to score centuries against every other Test-playing country of his time.

Equations like 'May's steel plus Cowdrey's natural ability plus Botham's self-belief equal a great player' are, in the end, self-defeating. Cowdrey's batting was like the man: charming, prone to self-doubt, civilised and human. We should be grateful for the privilege of watching him unravel the complexities of a game that fascinated him. He was rare value when the jigsaw fitted.

They also bowled ...

Wickets

W.G. Grace	2,876
F.E. Woolley	2,068
W.R. Hammond	732
D.C.S. Compton	622
T.W. Hayward	481
C.P. Mead	277
G.A. Gooch	246
G.A. Hick	232
I.V.A. Richards	223
L. Hutton	173
J.B. Hobbs	107
T.W. Graveney	80
M.C. Cowdrey	65
E.H. Hendren	47
G. Boycott	45
D.G. Bradman	36
M.R. Ramprakash	34
Zaheer Abbas	30
L.E.G. Ames	24
D.L. Amiss	18
A. Sandham	18
H. Sutcliffe	10
G.E. Tyldesley	6
G.M. Turner	5
J.H. Edrich	0

and fielded

Catches and stumpings

L.E.G. Ames *(703ct, 418st)*	1,121
F.E. Woolley	1,018
W.G. Grace *(887ct, 5st)*	892
W.R. Hammond *(819 ct, 3st)*	822
E.H. Hendren	754
G.A. Hick	709
C.P. Mead	675
M.C. Cowdrey	638
G.A. Gooch	555
T.W. Graveney *(553ct, 1st)*	554
T.W. Hayward	493
H. Sutcliffe	473
I.V.A. Richards *(464ct, 1st)*	465
D.L. Amiss	417
D.C.S. Compton	416
G.M. Turner	409
L. Hutton	401
J.B. Hobbs	337
J.H. Edrich	310
G.E. Tyldesley	296
Zaheer Abbas	278
G. Boycott	264
M.R. Ramprakash	239
A. Sandham	159
D.G. Bradman *(131ct, 1st)*	132

17

John Edrich

'It's not the hundredth one that counts,
it's the previous 99'

John Hugh Edrich

Born
Blofield, Norfolk
21 June 1937

First hundred
112   Surrey v Nottinghamshire, Trent Bridge, 1959
Age: 21 years 329 days

100th hundred
101*   Surrey v Derbyshire, The Oval, 1977
Age: 40 years 21 days

Last hundred
114   Surrey v Gloucestershire, Guildford, 1978
Age: 41 years 10 days

Career record
M	Inn	NO	HS	Runs	Average	100s	50s
564	979	104	310*	39,790	45.47	103	188

Test record
M	Inn	NO	HS	Runs	Average	100s	50s
77	127	9	310*	5,138	43.54	12	24

In the summer of 1977 Geoffrey Boycott reached the milestone of a hundred hundreds amid the emotion of a Test match, capturing the attention of the whole cricket world. A month before, the feat had been quietly reached by an unassuming left-hander in front of the metaphorical three men and a dog. John Edrich of Surrey, one of Boycott's favourite opening partners, made it at the fag-end of a fairly meaningless last day in the Derbyshire match at The Oval. If the event lacked the stage-managed qualities of the Boycott spectacular, that was wholly in keeping with the career of the admirable Edrich.

Edrich had got used to second billing. Indeed, a place on the poster was sufficient for him throughout most of his time in first-class cricket. Unheralded and reticent, he was greatly admired by his fellow-professionals. Like Boycott, he was a limited player; unlike Boycott, he went about his business with the minimum of fuss. Of his 103 centuries, twelve were made in Tests and seven against Australia – only Hobbs, Hammond, Gower and Sutcliffe scored more against the traditional enemy. His average of nearly 49 against Australia was four points better than his career average, the kind of statistic appreciated by Herbert Sutcliffe, the man Edrich resembled most in terms of temperament. Edrich would sell his soul dearly. Fred Titmus neatly encapsulated the frustrations bowlers experienced at the hands of Edrich: 'I got fed up conceding eight runs in an over after beating him four times in it. He was the best hitter of the slightly bad ball I can remember.' Micky Stewart, who opened the batting with Edrich for more than a decade at Surrey, said: 'If I were asked to nominate three batsmen to play for my life, I'd go for Geoffrey Boycott, Graham Gooch and John. If you were in trouble or chasing a total on a bad pitch, John would come up with the goods, time and again. He was excellent at punishing the bad ball.'

At the end of his career Edrich would have won no prizes for displaying the aesthetic delights of batting. He was an even worse sight twenty years earlier. One day a member of the Surrey first team encouraged the rest of the squad to walk over to the nets where the second team were practising. He said, 'Come and look at this bloke, I can't make out whether he's supposed to be a bowler or a wicket-keeper. He's certainly not a batsman.' John Edrich was in that net, trying his utmost to do himself justice: he looked stiff and mechanical, his footwork was minimal and he seemed to follow the ball hypnotically. The Surrey first-teamers had a quiet snigger at him for about a quarter of an hour, then the voice of the highly respected Bernie Constable interrupted the levity: 'I don't know what you're all sniggering at, he hasn't missed a ball yet.' For the rest of his career Edrich continued to confound his critics.

He was lucky enough to be born into a famous cricketing family. His cousin, Bill, had played with great distinction for Middlesex and England, and cousins Geoff, Eric and Brian had all played county cricket. Bill bowled at young John when he was about eleven but, apart from that, the illustrious

186

quartet played no real part in his development. John's father was the early influence; he bowled at him on a concrete pitch on the family farm in Norfolk, in between the back-breaking stints of pulling up sugar beet that toughened up John's impressive physique. John was very disappointed that Norfolk was not a first-class county, and he set out to prove himself elsewhere. Cousin Bill had suggested he try his luck with Middlesex, but John sensibly opted for Surrey, not least to duck allegations of nepotism at Lord's.

Andrew Sandham takes the major credit for Edrich's development once he arrived at The Oval. Sandham knew enough about batting to realise that the youngster's determination was of priceless value. He would tell him, 'You can't get hundreds sitting in the pavilion,' and the sturdy young man would take it all in. Edrich speaks with great fondness about Sandham: 'We had just one little skirmish early on when he threw down his cap in frustration at my efforts in the nets. I told him I had to work things out my own way, and after that he was marvellous. He was very good at the mental side of batting; he told me it didn't matter how I got my runs, just to get them. Once I got to forty, I had to go on to get a hundred.' Sandham, an unselfish partner for the great Jack Hobbs, also instilled in Edrich the importance of team spirit, of playing for the side: 'He said I had to make things happen, to learn to judge quick singles to keep the score ticking over. At no stage must I play exclusively for myself.' One of the features of Edrich's career was his unselfishness: his readiness to take the strike against dangerous bowling or to support a free-scoring partner. He also learned how to increase the tempo at strategic moments, especially in limited-overs cricket. It is a happy coincidence that, of the five Surrey batsmen to score a hundred hundreds, two of them should have played such important roles in the success of the others: Tom Hayward for Jack Hobbs and Andrew Sandham with John Edrich.

Under Sandham's guidance Edrich made impressive strides, even if he was never to win any garlands for elegance. Edrich was happy with runs in the book and, in his first game as an opener for Surrey, he scored a hundred in each innings at the start of the 1959 season. In the same summer he came up against Fred Trueman and Frank Tyson, who both managed to break an Edrich finger. An orthopaedic surgeon solved the problem during that winter by grafting a piece of leg bone into his hand to strengthen him against buffeting from fast bowlers. It was the start of Edrich's association with the pain barrier; no player in recent years has gone deeper into that barrier without flinching. For the rest of his career his name was synonymous with bravery, and no fast bowler could rattle him. The England selectors in the early part of his Test career were more of a problem than any hostile fast bowling. In 1963, with Wes Hall, Charlie Griffith and Garry Sobers forming a potent fast-bowling unit, England turned to the Surrey pair of Edrich and Stewart to combat the West Indies. Walter Robins, the chairman of selectors, told them they would play in at least the first three Tests of the series. On the first morning of the First Test Robins burst into the room shared by the Surrey pair and confided, 'I couldn't sleep for thinking about you poor buggers facing that pace attack.' A ringing endorsement, indeed. Edrich was dropped after the Second Test. He soon learned never to take anything for granted when playing for England, least of all the support of the selectors. Yet he willingly continued to take his punishment at the top of the order. When Peter Pollock hit him a sickening blow on the head in 1965, he was back in the middle a week later, battling away against Les Jackson on a dangerous seamers' wicket, steeling himself to get in line. On the 1974/75 Australian tour Edrich broke a hand on the unreliable Brisbane wicket, then picked up two broken ribs at Sydney. After being patched up, he insisted on going out again to bat and remained unbeaten on 33 as England were swept aside. It was ten days before Edrich discovered he had broken two ribs; he felt discomfort sleeping and found difficulty in bending down in the gully. Many other players would have been only too pleased to accept they were badly injured to avoid facing Lillee and Thomson in that series. Edrich's attitude to pain was as simple and uncomplicated as his batting: 'I was brought up not to show pain. We'd be out in all weathers, working long hours at harvest time and, for me, playing cricket in the sunshine for my country was a huge bonus after working on a farm. That's what I called hard work.'

Hard work never frightened John Edrich. He grafted away in the nets to work out his selection of shots and settled on his armoury of strokes very early. He says he often got confused with the theorising of the older players. 'Far too many cricketers try to do the things they can't manage; they go out of their depth. I reckoned I could get away with about three main shots, plus the knack of being able to pick up ones and twos here and there. I learned how to use the pace of the ball against the quick bowlers, to glide it away off the face of the bat.' When Edrich reached 30,000 runs in his career, his colleague Robin Jackman kidded him that 28,000 of them had come through the third man area!

There was far more to his batting than just guiding the ball easily through the gap between gully and the slips. Those strong forearms enabled him to punch the ball from a short backlift; when established in his innings, Edrich was not averse to lofting a few sixes. He was a splendid driver square on the offside, from front and back foot. He was adroit at slackening the grip on his bat if the ball found the edge, so that it would invariably drop in front of the close fielders behind the wicket. For a fairly short man he played the quick bowlers in front of his face remarkably well. Alan Knott modelled his defensive technique on Edrich: 'We were about the same height, and I always admired the way he got his bat up so high to play the short-pitched stuff down at his feet. It might be heading for his chin, but he'd get the middle of the bat to it.' Against the spin bowlers Edrich would advance a couple of paces and loft the ball over mid-on with a fully extended swing of the bat. Norman Gifford bowled for many years at Edrich and cannot remember ever thinking he would get him out: 'He was such a good worker of the ball.

He would slide it away off a slightly open face and, if I bowled at middle and leg, he'd find the gaps on the legside. On slow wickets his enormous strength of forearm would help him play forcing shots.'

As a left-hander he was vulnerable to the ball slanted across him by the right-arm bowler coming over the wicket, but Edrich worked out a method to combat the late swing. He played wicket to wicket, ignoring the slant of the ball if he was set to play defensively. If the ball was straight, then he would hit it; if he missed it, he would do so by a long way. Edrich only followed the ball that slanted away if he was either out of form and unsure of his position, or seeing the ball so well that he could afford to estimate the amount of late swing. David Brown opened the bowling for Warwickshire, to be frustrated regularly by the method of Edrich: 'Quite simply, he would play it if it was a bad ball; if it was a good ball, he'd contrive to miss it. It was all a matter of nerve. He had stacks of that, and he'd stand his ground and play down one line, instead of hopping around to follow the ball.'

Thus Edrich was an extremely frustrating man to bowl at, because he always looked as if you had a chance with him. Yet he played and missed so often that it could not just be a matter of luck; he had worked out the mechanics of batting with precision. His serene temperament allowed him to ignore the gestures and imprecations of the long-suffering bowler. 'I saw it as a direct challenge between me and the bowler. Cricket is like any other walk of life in that you are faced with a series of challenges. I relished them. Being brought up on a farm, I enjoyed being out in the sunshine, rather than sitting in the pavilion, feeling sorry for myself. I was lucky because I saw things in perspective; I learned that every day is a new day and that you can do absolutely nothing about what has gone before – either the previous day or the ball you've just missed.' Edrich learned to conceal his doubts under a façade of unflappability, but I learned from Micky Stewart that he was not always so phlegmatic. 'Sometimes he'd come up to me at the end of the over and whisper, "What the bloody hell's going on?" He never let the bowler know he was worried.' Dennis Amiss, who opened for England with Edrich, remembers that he used to enjoy a little moan before getting down to the business of the day: 'He was a bit of a Job's Comforter. On tour he'd say something like "Oh hell, we've got so-and-so tomorrow and he's really quick." On the way out to bat, he'd jib a little about something or other, but I think that was just to get it out of his system. Some players talk themselves out of an innings once they get out there, but John would love a scrap.'

Robin Jackman used to enjoy Edrich's phlegmatic attitude just before he went out to bat: 'We'd all be in the dressing-room and he'd have a little dig about something like the dark clouds or that he didn't fancy a particular bowler. It would be a green wicket and we'd lost the toss and had to bat, with immense pressure obviously on John. As he went out, I'd say "Good luck," and he'd smile and say, "We'll see what happens." He always seemed to be in charge mentally; he didn't appear to be frightened of failure, as most of us are.'

One innings at Headingley in 1965 demonstrated Edrich's rock-like temperament. He scored 310 not out against New Zealand in a truly remarkable manner; on average he played at and missed one ball an over but never lost an opportunity to hit the bad ball to the boundary. One could not imagine England making 300 on that pitch, never mind one batsman scoring that amount – it was grassy and every time the ball pitched, it left a lush green mark. New Zealand were well equipped with good seamers – Motz, Collinge and Taylor – and they all moved the ball around over two days. Batsmen of the class of Barber and Cowdrey were nonplussed by the tricky conditions, but Edrich kept banging the bowlers over long-on, thrashing them through the covers and whacking them past midwicket. Edrich whimsically points out that he stopped playing and missing after he passed the 200 mark but agrees that he gave the bowlers heart failure. 'They obviously thought I'd get a touch eventually, but they didn't realise I was having a great season. I had played on excellent wickets in South Africa during the previous winter, and I returned to England bang on form. I had decided to hit the medium pacers straight back over their heads, and I hit a lot of sixes that season. That day at Leeds I never thought I'd get out.' That triple hundred was part of a sequence of scores by Edrich that were positively Bradmanesque: in nine innings, containing three not-outs, he score 1,311 runs at an average of 218.5.

The following winter, Edrich scored two hundreds against Australia, to add to the one he made against them on his debut in 1964 at Lord's. David Brown recalls with a smile how baffled the Australian journalists were at Edrich's style of batting: 'The papers were full of opinions that Edrich must be dropped through lack of form, yet he was averaging sixty at the time. The Aussie players learned quicker than their writers that Edrich didn't worry too much about style.' Like a good team man Edrich also agreed to bat number three to allow the dashing Bob Barber to partner Boycott; on his next tour of Australia Edrich agreed to do the same because Brian Luckhurst was unhappy waiting to go in to bat. Edrich typically made no fuss: 'I wasn't a great waiter either, but I reckoned I was lucky to get a game for England.' When Edrich partnered Boycott, they were an impressive pairing for England, averaging 55 for the first wicket.

By the time the Australians visited England in 1968, Edrich was at last an automatic choice after several disappointments. A series of brave innings in the West Indies against Hall and Griffith had cemented his place in the side; 554 runs in the 1968 series confirmed his worth and 648 runs on Illingworth's tour was further proof of his fondness for the Australian bowling. After that triumphant effort for Illingworth, things went rather flat for Edrich for the next three seasons. He was a little jaded after several England tours, the captaincy of Surrey distracted him somewhat and he took a little time to adapt to the demands of the Sunday League. He slipped into some bad habits in the three-day games that he had picked up on Sundays and his record declined for a couple of seasons. By 1974 he was rejuvenated and the England selectors, mindful of his excellent temperament and the imminent tour of Australia, brought him back for the India series. At 37 he was appointed vice-captain of the Australian tour party and, although the trip was a painful one for England, he achieved one personal ambition by captaining the side in the Fourth Test when Mike Denness stood down because of his poor form. Edrich averaged 43 in that series of broken limbs and ribs – a great effort against fast bowlers who were allowed to bowl up to four bouncers an over on dangerously uneven wickets.

With Boycott in exile, and Amiss in eclipse, Edrich was again invaluable for England. He made 175 against Australia in the Lord's Test of 1975, and this gave him greater pleasure than any of his other innings: 'It was great to see Lillee on his knees after the hammering we had taken from him a few months earlier.'

A year later Edrich had become sickened of Test cricket. For some time he had been concerned at the latitude allowed fast bowlers, as they intimidated batsmen with short-pitched deliveries which remained unchecked. One hour of batting in the Old Trafford Test against the West Indies convinced Edrich that it was time to go; he and Brian Close were subjected to a most vicious barrage of bouncers by Michael Holding, Andy Roberts and Wayne Daniel. It was a tribute to the remarkable courage of Close and Edrich that they survived on that Saturday night, but Edrich knew he was playing in his last Test: 'I wasn't scared, just frustrated that blatant intimidation was not curbed by the umpires. I couldn't see the point in standing out there for hours, waiting to get my head knocked off and wondering if I'd ever get a chance to score. I calculated that the amount of short-pitched bowling allowed me about six deliveries an hour to have a chance of runs. I was fed up with being a target man, with no hope of taking the fight to the bowlers. It was the last straw, after the way Lillee and Thomson had been allowed to bowl.'

Even though England needed his example and guts, Edrich would not be swayed from his decision; to him cricket had to have some sort of purpose, and he could see no sign of an overdue crackdown on intimidation. Such was his bravery and sheer competence that no one could impugn his motives. John Edrich never walked out on a fair challenge within the spirit of the game. At the age of 39 he saw no reason why he should waste his time doing something that bored him.

Two years later he was through with first-class cricket: it was important to him to go before he was pushed. A profitable business career loomed, so one chapter of his life closed with no regrets or sentimental rhetoric. 'I have to have challenge in life, and cricket was no longer providing too many of them. You have to make the best of your life, rather than sitting around expecting things to happen to you.'

So many of his contemporaries speak of Edrich with immense respect. Robin Jackman praises his fielding: 'He'd try like a demon in the field if he was having a bad run with the bat. He had such strong hands; he took some blinding catches in the gully.' Jackman admires the way he'd graft for his runs: 'I've watched him score a hundred, and that night I couldn't remember a shot he'd played. But the runs were in the book, and he hadn't taken all day getting them.' Bob Willis calls Edrich 'my kind of batsman – brave, unselfish, he knew his limitations. And he didn't get out.' Derek Underwood says Edrich was more respected by the Australian players than Boycott, while Fred Titmus observes with amusement: 'All the quick bowlers fancied their chances against him, yet he got a hundred hundreds, most of them as an opener. It's a funny game, isn't it?' M.J.K. Smith says he was a less predictable player than Boycott and therefore more value in limited-overs cricket, and David Brown positively drools at his solidity: 'I used to think for the first few years after he retired that, if John came back and batted with a runner, he'd still be better than most of those who opened for England. And he wouldn't wear a helmet.' Norman Gifford sums up the Edrich unflappability thus: 'He didn't play and miss. We bowlers didn't hit his bat.'

Edrich chuckles at the memory of his hundredth century against Derbyshire: 'Eddie Barlow said he liked a glass of champers now and again, and he didn't mind staying on the field. The game was as dead as a doornail, you know.' He assessed this achievement shrewdly: 'It's not the hundredth one that counts, it's the previous 99.' Edrich is content to be in illustrious company and thinks fondly of Andrew Sandham, the kindly little coach who died in 1982. 'He and I soon realised I was no Cowdrey. I set out to be more like a Barrington. I realised that to play for England I would need to perform to the absolute limit of my capabilities, and Andrew helped me achieve that.'

Despite carving out an impressive business career after retirement, John Edrich has had to face several daunting tests of his tough character. His son Jonathan was killed in a car crash and then, in 1999, he was diagnosed with leukaemia. He was told he had up to seven years left for a decent quality of life, but after that there were no guarantees. After gruelling chemotherapy, then alternative treatments, he remains active, travelling to parts of the world with his wife Sue that he never visited as a cricketer. John took a full role in the Presidency of Surrey CCC as he neared his 70th birthday and still keeps in touch with his old Surrey team-mates. In facing the biggest challenge of his life, John Edrich continues to demonstrate the tenacity that illuminated his outstanding cricket career.

Conversion rate of 50s into 100s

For the purpose of calculating the percentage of innings in which a batsman turned a 50 into a 100, those not-out innings between 50 and 99 are excluded.

	50s	*50-99 **	*100s*	*%*
D.G. Bradman	186	9	117	66.1
W.R. Hammond	352	27	167	51.4
G.A. Hick	294	17	136	49.1
M.R. Ramprakash	238	21	103	47.5
L. Hutton	308	25	129	45.6
J.B. Hobbs	467	29	197	45.0
G.M. Turner	251	20	103	44.6
Zaheer Abbas	266	21	108	44.1
D.C.S. Compton	306	26	123	43.9
I.V.A. Richards	276	13	114	43.3
C.P. Mead	411	55	153	43.0
G. Boycott	389	37	151	42.9
H. Sutcliffe	376	26	149	42.6
E.H. Hendren	445	42	170	42.2
L.E.G. Ames	278	21	102	39.7
J.H. Edrich	291	30	103	39.5
T.W. Graveney	355	40	122	38.7
G.A. Gooch	345	14	128	38.7
G.E. Tyldesley	293	28	102	38.5
D.L. Amiss	314	26	102	35.4
M.C. Cowdrey	338	41	107	36.0
A. Sandham	314	16	107	35.9
W.G. Grace	380	29	126	35.9
T.W. Hayward	322	22	104	34.7
F.E. Woolley	440	19	145	34.4

18

Geoffrey Boycott

'I wish he'd opened when I played for England. We would have won a few more Tests!' (Jim Laker)

Geoffrey Boycott

Born

Fitzwilliam, Yorkshire

21 October 1940

First hundred

145 Yorkshire v Lancashire, Sheffield, 1963
Age: 22 years 224 days

100th hundred

191 England v Australia, Headingley, 1977
Age: 36 years 294 days

Last hundred

135* Yorkshire v Surrey, Headingley, 1986
Age: 45 years 272 days

Career record

M	Inn	NO	HS	Runs	Average	100s	50s
609	1,014	162	261*	48,426	56.83	151	238

Test record

M	Inn	NO	HS	Runs	Average	100s	50s
108	193	23	246*	8,114	47.72	22	42

He remembers the moment vividly, almost a quarter of a century on. It was 5.21 on the afternoon of September the 12th 1986, at Scarborough's North Marine Road ground. The last time Geoffrey Boycott ever stood on a cricket pitch as a player.

The county championship match against Northamptonshire had long dwindled to a draw as the visitors, having followed on, batted staunchly for the draw. Boycott was the last to leave the field – deliberately drinking in all the paraphernalia of a cricket ground, filing it all away in that most retentive of memory banks.

Just a month away from his 46th birthday, he knew his time was up. He didn't want to go, he was still deeply in love with the game but the internecine politics that had bedevilled Yorkshire CCC for nearly a decade, with Boycott at its epicentre, had claimed him. He was not going to be offered a new contract, and one of the most controversial playing careers was over.

As a batsman it had ended on the first day of that Northants match, in ironic fashion. Run out for 61, by a direct throw from the third man boundary by the Huddersfield-born Allan Walker. Boycott had been sent back by his partner, Jim Love, looking for a second run and the arrowed throw left him stranded by two yards. Boycott's formidable memory instantly sparked into play, all those years on: 'I should have got a hundred that day. That Walker lad had a strong throw.'

Boycott's many critics, some of whom had suffered from his selective and partial judge of a run, would guffaw at his last innings being ended by a run-out. But even those who carped about him must grudgingly admit that ending just eight runs short of his thousand for the season, at an average of 52.21, was a considerable achievement at his age. For others it was especially piquant that a Yorkshireman should end for good Boycott's occupation of the crease. It was perhaps a fitting end to the civil war of those years.

He knew he would never play again. Not even in a charity match or as a favour to one of his friends. 'I needed that air of finality. All my career had been one of complete professionalism and doing my very best. Playing second best would have meant diminishing everything. Did I really want to be second or third best?

'So on that last day at Scarborough, I had a feeling of emptiness when it dawned on me I wasn't going to get another bat. At the end I took my time getting changed, and I was the last to leave the dressing-room. Then I walked around the ground, committing it all to memory – even the litter! – trying to think through the previous 25 years as a Yorkshire player.'

He took comfort in the advice given to him years earlier by one of his biggest admirers and another Yorkshireman who divided opinion in sport. 'Brian Clough told me to play as long as I could, so long as I was still doing well, because it would be the best time of my life. Considering that his playing career ended early through injury, and despite his brilliance as a football manager, I could tell how much he missed playing.

'I loved the game so much, you know. Still do. Getting up in the morning, feeling so fit and healthy, opening the curtains, seeing the sun shining, making a cuppa tea, telling myself it was a great day to be opening the batting – nothing like it for me in sport. It was a wonderful feeling, anticipating a day's play.'

Geoffrey Boycott's preferred judgement on his career would be 'Judge me by what I've done, not what some people would say about me.' On that basis, history will be favourable. He is eighth in the list of run-scorers (48,426); just four batsmen have bettered his 151 centuries.

It is a record of which he can be justifiably proud. It has been achieved by technical skill and dedication of the highest order, and none of Boycott's many detractors should forget how much of himself he gave to the game. He performed wonders on short rations, on a frugal diet of strokeplay; a hundred by Boycott was a triumph of will-power, when a lonely man could find freedom of expression in the way that suited his own character. For most of his career he prospered through a defensive technique of great class and a quiver of about five shots. Whether or not he was capable of playing more shots is a matter for conjecture; he did not wish to, and he should therefore be judged on the means he chose to reach his goals.

Boycott was one of those batsmen who subscribed to the axiom that 'It's a sideways-on game': he played beautifully straight with an initial 'back and across' movement that gave him time to decide whether to play forward or get back on his heels. Alan Knott, an expert on the physical attributes needed for cricket, points out that Boycott had a very flexible, supple body, which enabled him to get his elbow pointing up at the sky when he played a defensive stroke. Says Knott, 'This helped him get on top of the bouncing ball, simply because he could get his bat so high that he could bring it down a long way. His superb fitness was geared to making him a better batsman.' Boycott's head and feet positioning were faultless, apart from a traumatic tour of Australia in 1978/79, and his placement of strokes was shrewdly productive. His best shots were the cover drive, the on-drive to the left of mid-wicket and a back-foot force square on the offside which brought his strong right hand into play. He gave up the hook shot, after a brief flirtation with the stroke in the early 1970s – it got him out a number of times, because he played it in the air. He never forgot the opprobrium that rained down on his head after getting out to the hook shot in the Lord's Test against the 1973 West Indians. 'It was the only time I got cross at the crease. It was the last over of the day, and Brian Luckhurst refused me an easy single. I was angry at Brian – God rest his soul – and not focused. Keith Boyce was the bowler – I used to hit his short stuff out of the park in county matches – and he bowled me a short one that drew me into the hook and got caught. Never again. I got slated in the press for that.' Boycott never forgot the times when he gave away his wicket.

His footwork against the spinners was excellent, and his forward defensive shot, with the hands loose on the handle, was exemplary. Mike Brearley, who opened for England with Boycott, is a great admirer of his defensive technique: 'He held the bat so loose when playing defensively that the ball would drop short of the slips if he got an edge. I take my hat off to him for his survival instincts; perhaps he'd be in trouble with the bouncer, but next ball he'd be back in line, still battling away.'

Geoffrey Boycott's most admirable quality was that he made himself into an opening batsman from the top drawer. I make the distinction about his place in the batting order, because his obsession with occupying the crease served Yorkshire and England well due to his being an opener. He played in a succession of weak batting sides, and his view that he had to stay in the middle was generally compatible with the needs of his side. Differences of opinion arose when something other than the anchor role was needed. He was a product of an environment that valued efficiency and achievement. Fancy cameo innings used to be regarded with deep suspicion by the good folk of Yorkshire, especially when they felt that a batsman could have done better for himself with a little more backbone and professionalism. Mike Brearley appreciated the difference in attitudes to batting, compared with southern counties: 'At a place like Hove they love to see the ball crashed through the covers. The Yorkshireman likes to see things done correctly: the full face of the bat, playing "through the V", the bent knee in forward defensive strokes, etc etc. To play a correct defensive innings is admirable to them, as it is to Geoff Boycott.'

I believe that Boycott would have scored many more runs in a more attractive style if he had contrived to play his cricket for a southern county. Yorkshire to the marrow, his many batting virtues were essentially those that stemmed from his upbringing, but life is easier for a batsman in the south of England. The wickets are faster, the boundaries shorter and spin bowlers are more readily used, a style of bowling against which Boycott was a master; in Yorkshire, the wickets are greener and they seam and lift for the quicker bowlers. You have to graft for your runs on Yorkshire wickets, a point acknowledged by a man from that county, Barry Wood: 'Boycott really had to work hard up there. He would have got about twenty per cent more runs if he'd played in the south.' Bob Willis estimates the difference to be about fifteen per cent. Whatever the figure, there was a genuine admiration in the game for the scope of Boycott's achievements in the light of his lack of outstanding natural ability. Norman Gifford told me: 'You can say to a youngster, "Now look at Boycott, just see what he's done with himself," and to that extent Boycott was good for the game. There's nothing wrong with working hard to better yourself.' Ray Illingworth remembers his reaction when he saw the young Boycott more than forty years ago: 'I wasn't very impressed. He couldn't seem to hit the ball off the square. I thought someone like Titmus would just bottle him up all day. He worked and worked at his game, and he deserves tremendous credit for achieving so much.'

Boycott was a late developer, compared with other Yorkshire players with more natural talent. He was 20 before establishing himself in the Yorkshire colts side and played his earliest championship matches in his 22nd year. He had practised and practised for years before that; his uncle Albert and the former leg-spinner, Johnny Lawrence, were the two props on which the bespectacled introvert leaned. They consoled him on the many occasions when the Yorkshire Club reacted non-committally to his advance as a batsman in league cricket. Boycott stuck at his clerical job with the Ministry of Pensions throughout the frustrating years of his youth: where he came from, a living wage was a bonus compared with fancy notions of becoming a Yorkshire cricketer. One of Boycott's favourite sayings to any querulous team-mate was 'It's better than being down the pit,' and there is no doubt that his early struggles amid that close-knit mining community of South Yorkshire toughened him mentally for the challenges ahead. He might fail through lack of top-class ability, but no one would chide him for not trying. His relentless ambition and self-absorption astonished the first-team players at Yorkshire in his early days and led to innumerable personality clashes; more than one established player was run out by the intense young man immersed in his struggle for survival and self-respect. He was determined to make up for lost time; John Hampshire, who came into the first team at about the same time, may have looked the freer, more impressive batsman but Boycott would outshine him in the end. Boycott's style of batting was bound to cause tension in a team that prided itself on an unselfish attitude towards scoring quick runs, a side captained by Brian Close in a daring, imaginative manner. Close solved the problem by suggesting to the young man that he should open the batting rather than bat in the middle order. Close told me: 'There was no room for him down below because of his attitude to occupying the crease. As a restricted player, that was the best place for him.'

Boycott's first appearance for Yorkshire at Lord's revealed the self-imposed tensions from which he suffered. On a rain-affected wicket, he scored a magnificent 90 out of an all-out 144; it was the innings of a mature player, ended only by an unplayable delivery from Alan Moss that he was good enough to follow and touch. It was not good enough for Boycott; as he rushed blindly past well-wishers at the top of the pavilion stairs, he ignored a 'well played, lad' from a slight silvery-haired gentleman, walked into the dressing-room, put a towel over his head and wept. He had desperately wanted a hundred in his first game at Lord's. The man who had tried to congratulate him was Sir Leonard Hutton.

Don Mosey, the BBC radio cricket commentator, vividly recalled the pressure that the young Boycott piled upon himself. At that time Mosey was a cricket writer on the *Daily Mail*, and his brief was to cover Yorkshire's matches; he used to drive Boycott to the various games in those early days.

199

Mosey described him as shy, intense and very conscious of the fact that he was having to battle for everything in his life. He remembered stumbling upon a weeping Boycott in the Bradford dressing-room in 1962. 'I said to him, "Whatever's the matter, lad?" and he sobbed, "They've left me out, Mr Mosey. The day will come when I decide who gets left out." Some senior players had properly been brought back into the first team, and he had to drop out. He couldn't understand the reasoning.'

The Yorkshire captain, Brian Close, says he treated Boycott with a mixture of tolerance and discipline in those days: 'In some respects, he was immature, which stemmed from this burning desire for success. He would ask me where I was eating that night, so he could join me and discuss cricket. I was impressed by his keenness to learn, but he had some funny ways.'

Boycott impressively made up for lost time. Within a year of being capped by his county, he was scoring a Test hundred – the first of 22 – against Australia. On successive tours to South Africa, he alienated some England colleagues by his running between the wickets, an inclination to hog the strike even though a more talented strokeplayer was fretting at the other end, and his tendency to say the first thing that came into his head, no matter how justified or ill-advised the sentiments. Boycott at least was clear-sighted in his objectives: to be the most consistent, heaviest run-scorer in the side. No one could ever accuse Geoffrey Boycott of duplicity; he felt that his interest and those of his team ran concurrently. His job was to stay in as long as possible and to present himself for cricket in a supremely fit, mentally clear state. Within these constraints his career has been a model of consistency.

He is convinced he was at his best between 1968 and 1974. 'I had a little problem adjusting to contact lenses in 1969, but I was soon back on track. I was lucky being born with the ability to concentrate. And my reflexes were sharper, I wasn't living off my wits as I had to do later in my career when I was slowing up. And don't forget we played on uncovered wickets in those days. Derek Underwood on a wet one! Now that was a challenge! Not like the pitches at The Oval where Mark Ramprakash has piled up all those hundreds lately, on covered wickets. You could get runs with a stick of rhubarb there now!'

By 1970 Boycott was the best opener in the world. The England batting order of the late 1960s – including Cowdrey, Edrich, Graveney, D'Oliveira, Barrington – was strong enough to make up for any dilatoriness on his part. On the 1970/71 tour to Australia he batted magnificently, playing some fine shots on good wickets. Ray Illingworth, his captain on that tour, feels he got closer to him than at any subsequent stage: 'Geoff respects ability in others, as long as they try to the utmost. What he can't stand is incompetence or someone who doesn't do himself justice through his own fault. We came from similar backgrounds and, on that tour, talked the same language.'

At the height of Boycott's eminence on that trip, a decision was taken 12,000 miles away that gave him initial pleasure but ultimate sadness. Brian

Close was sacked from the Yorkshire captaincy, and Boycott was appointed successor. On the face of it, that was a tremendous compliment to a man who had crammed so much experience into a short career: after all, Close had played for England at 18, an age which saw Boycott still at the Ministry of Pensions, still grafting away in league cricket. The affairs of Yorkshire County Cricket Club after Boycott's appointment as captain took on a quality that would be recognised by Lucretia Borgia, and it would be wrong for someone like myself to try to unravel its complexities, treacheries and heady moments of farce. More than one eminent cricketer was handed a loaded revolver and ushered towards cricket's equivalent of a forest; lawyers prospered as writs, extraordinary meetings and press statements fluttered in the air like ticker-tape. The rumour machine picked up many a productivity bonus as claim and counter-claim permeated committee rooms, bars and dressing-rooms. For more than a decade Yorkshire County Cricket Club was a laughing-stock in the game, a matter of sadness to those of us who believed that the club's basic principles on cricket are sound.

Since the intriguing began in the first year of Boycott's captaincy, one man remained in the eye of the hurricane: Geoffrey Boycott. Committee chairmen may have come and gone, other captains may have dipped in and out of controversies, but Yorkshire's best batsman was a constant presence. If you accept that premise, then Boycott must bear some responsibility for the shambles. Other major batsmen in cricket history have had a highly developed sense of their own importance, but how many have also been insecure? Boycott's prickly, self-justifying persona stemmed partly from his hard upbringing, partly a reaction to those dissemblers who falsified the facts and partly a feeling that some influential people were out to get him. His ambivalence to the media was typical: he would lose no opportunity for castigating the media for fanning the flames of controversy, yet blithely appeared on the Michael Parkinson show to indulge in an orgy of recrimination that was ultimately self-defeating. No one was more adept at backing reluctantly into the spotlight, then discovering that the water of publicity was not that chilling to the toes. He is a splendidly articulate framer of his own point of view; no one in my journalistic experience had said 'no comment' so often without meaning it. The views that have been readily coaxed from him have not been the doings of the dastardly media, they represented the willing involvement of Geoffrey Boycott in situations he felt demanded some good, honest, Yorkshire plain speaking. He had a flair for self-destruction that makes a moth near a flame seem like a canny investor: in January 1982, upon his controversial early return from the Indian tour, he allowed himself to be interviewed by David Coleman on BBC *Grandstand* and, in doing so, did his cause no favour. Clearly he was not himself – but his rambling, disparate remarks smacked of a persecution complex. He had been badly advised: just once, he should have kept his own counsel and tried to recover his health.

Boycott's willing excursions into publicity in the 1970s harmed Yorkshire CCC. The supporters, accustomed to success, needed a hero in the absence of a team to admire and laud; Boycott was happy to oblige. The individual became bigger than the team by dint of supreme individual cricket ability and the media's complicity in building up Boycott as a cult figure, the 'good guy' boxed in by the machinations of jealous team-mates and administrators with long memories. The 'them and us' syndrome will always enjoy a healthy run in Yorkshire, and Geoffrey Boycott was as skilful as his opponents in drawing up his battalions. His playing prestige inevitably attracted some sycophants who just wanted to be seen in his corner of the ring, while others joined him after being bruised by other bouts of in-fighting. Reform Groups flourished, players' polls were bandied about and the activities of one batsman seemed more important than the fortunes of a great cricketing county. John Hampshire, a proud Yorkshireman, was so sickened by events that he did the unthinkable – he walked out and joined Derbyshire. Anyone who knew the fierce pride of John Hampshire in following his father into the Yorkshire eleven will appreciate the depths to which the farce had sunk. John Hampshire found it painful to talk about the tensions and the factions that drove him from Yorkshire. He accepted that Boycott's personality was just one of many contributory factors and stressed that at no stage would he align himself with groups either for or against Boycott. Hampshire blamed the people who put Boycott on a pedestal, rather than the man himself – 'Geoff just wasn't suited for the job of captain when he was appointed,' Hampshire told me. 'He was completely absorbed in his cricket. He could never, it seemed, relax for a moment and somehow he couldn't really talk to us except on his own terms.'

Hampshire felt Boycott was at his best during his years in exile from the England team: he encouraged the players to bring their wives to Yorkshire's matches and he appeared more outgoing in every way. When he returned to the England fold in 1977, Boycott reverted to his old ways, according to Hampshire. 'His conversation was all about Test cricket, money, records and the England captaincy. The more pressing matters at hand seemed to have no real place in his thoughts.'

Hampshire blamed Boycott for much of the melodrama at Scarborough at the end of the 1981 season which precipitated his move to Derbyshire. Boycott had been suspended by Ray Illingworth for making allegedly unauthorised comments to the media, and the atmosphere at the ground was charged with tension as the various pressure groups made their vociferous presence felt. John Hampshire, an undemonstrative, disciplined person, was appalled to see Boycott linger on the ground after being told to go home: 'He stood there, signing autographs and generally holding court while signatures calling for Illingworth's sacking were being collected alongside him. Out in the middle Yorkshire were trying to play a county championship match. I was sick to the depths of my soul.' Hampshire could take no more of the squalid personality clashes, and this proudest of Yorkshiremen left. He took to Derbyshire painful memories of, in his own words, 'supporters torn apart by a cult which regarded one man as greater than the club and even the game itself, and of a committee that made a terrible mistake and didn't try to put things right until it was too late.'

Ray Illingworth, who stepped into the hornets' nest on being appointed team manager in 1978, felt the various pressure groups caused untold damage to the club's prestige and to Boycott: 'Because of his cult following, it was harder for him with Yorkshire than it was with England. He just had to succeed. A team should be the first priority for the supporters, not an individual. If Geoff Boycott had played for another county, there would have been none of this fuss, but in Yorkshire cricket's a religion and everyone had a positive view about Geoff Boycott.'

Illingworth believed that Boycott should have been given the captaincy a decade after the sacking of Close. He thought that Boycott should have been appointed vice-captain for the 1970/71 Australian tour, so that he could have started cutting his teeth on responsibility for players and the differing ways of handling them. One can see that he would have learned much from Illingworth, an acknowledged expert at fostering team spirit at the expense of individual ambition. Jim Laker thought that Boycott did a good job as Yorkshire's captain: 'Not even Brian Sellers would've won anything with that lot, they weren't good enough.' In eight seasons under Boycott's captaincy they finished twice in the top four, yet never won a trophy.

Boycott also allowed himself to be side-tracked by the issue of the England captaincy as his eminence as a Test batsman increased. Ray Illingworth phoned Boycott to tell him that Mike Denness had been chosen England captain after Illingworth's sacking in 1973: 'Geoff was very disappointed, I think he really thought he would get it after me.' When Boycott pulled out of the 1974/75 trip to Australia, he cited personal reasons that did not equip him for the pressure of Test cricket – he was embroiled in his benefit season, his mother's illness was a worry, the intrigues at Yorkshire were ticking over at a merry pace, and he had been embarrassed at being dismissed several times in May and June by the innocuous Indian left-arm seamer Eknath Solkar.

Boycott went into purdah for the next three years, concentrating his energies on Yorkshire cricket. Alec Bedser – great cricketer, uncomplicated patriot who would have played for England on one leg if necessary – had to keep the lines of communication open in his capacity as chairman of selectors. He knew that an England team containing Boycott was automatically a more difficult one to beat, but he had to indulge in an extraordinary amount of wooing before the Yorkshireman graciously allowed himself to be selected in 1977. He returned to play two innings of immense character and guts in the Trent Bridge Test against the Australians – running out the local hero, Derek Randall, and remaining strokeless and prone to self-doubt for three hours, before Alan Knott galvanised him to play some fine strokes. Boycott believes that Trent Bridge hundred was his best innings. 'It was a test of my ability, character and mental strength. I was coming back into Test cricket at an age when the likes of Steve Waugh and Allan Border were retiring. Three years out is a long time. We were struggling, it was against the Aussies and I'd just run out Randall. The locals were baying for my blood, but I turned it round.' In the following Test he scored his hundredth hundred – the first man to achieve it in a Test (Zaheer was the second). For good measure it came on his home ground, and the crowd euphoria moved him greatly. He admits he was uncharacteristically nervous on the first morning of that match. 'I barely slept that night, which wasn't like me and I got to Headingley late. I had to beg the groundsman, Keith Boyce, to keep one net up, so that I could have just a few minutes before the toss. I was praying we'd lose it and field first so I could sort myself out. When Mike Brearley went early, that woke me up and I felt fine after twenty minutes or so. Getting the milestone on my home ground and beating the Aussies as well just made it even more memorable for me.' He had proved overwhelmingly that he was still a major batsman at Test level, and he proceeded to do so until his exile in 1982 after going to South Africa to play in a series of 'unofficial' Tests.

Boycott played some splendid innings for England from 1977 to 1982, but I think he was at his most impressive in Australia in 1979/80 and against the West Indies in two series a year later. He went to Australia with a score to settle: in the previous year he had played badly under the weight of losing the Yorkshire captaincy and the death of his mother. This time he reverted to his orthodox stance and played staunchly in the Tests and excellently in the one-day internationals against Australia and the West Indies. Mike Brearley, his captain on that tour, was full of admiration for the way Boycott coped: 'We dropped him from one of the early one-day games and told him he had to step up the tempo. He was a revelation – playing the West Indian quickies off the back foot through the covers and going down the wicket to hit people like Max Walker over the top. All this, plus his immense skill at placing the ball and getting twos instead of ones.'

Against the West Indies his wicket was always the most prized one: Graham Gooch was the most exciting player, but Boycott sold his wicket dearly against a quartet of intimidating fast bowlers, who were allowed to pitch short by weak umpires. In the summer of 1980 and the winter of 1980/81 Boycott triumphantly doused the slurs of Tony Greig that he did not fancy quick bowlers, a reference to his non-availability for the 1974/75 tour. Boycott showed his character and tenacity in the Antigua Test with an unbeaten hundred, a stark contrast to his innings of 0 and 1 in the previous Test at Bridgetown. Michael Holding bowled him at the end of an opening over that has become a legend: the first five deliveries reared steeply and sharply off a length and there was Boycott – firmly in line – dropping the wrists on them. The sixth ball was too fast even for Boycott, taking out his off-stump. Graham Gooch, watching from the other end, says it was the fastest and best over he has seen. Clive Lloyd, the West Indies captain, told me that Holding's over was exactly what he had ordered: 'I made Michael get warmed up in the nets just before the innings began. I wanted him to steam in at Boycott right from the first ball, rather than just ease himself in gently. The result was the best over from a fast bowler I've ever seen.' In its own way it was a great compliment to Boycott and that night, after watching endless re-runs of that historic over on the BBC's video machine, Boycott pronounced himself satisfied that he could have done nothing about the delivery which bowled him. A fortnight later he scored 104 not out in the Third Test, and, as the West Indies players applauded Boycott's century, Viv Richards paid him a generous and well-deserved tribute. He turned to Clive Lloyd in the slips and said, 'You've got to hand it to this guy, he never gives it away.'

How right Richards was. Boycott would settle for that as a memorial to his career. He triumphed remarkably over his limitations of ability and eyesight – only Zaheer has scored a hundred hundreds with such poor eyesight. Mike Brearley says that he found Boycott's batting at its most fascinating when the conditions were against him: 'I wouldn't want to watch him on a slow wicket against a second-rate attack, but he was excellent when keeping out Lillee if the wicket was helping the bowler. They say attacking batsmen win you matches, but so does Boycott if he scores 100 out of 220 when you could have been bowled out for 120.' Dennis Amiss, who partnered Boycott many times for England, pays tribute to his judgement of when to leave the ball that starts near the off-stump and moves away: 'Some of us would nibble at them, but he always knew where his stumps were.' John Edrich, another of Boycott's illustrious partners, recalls how he would regularly draw comfort from watching him play properly, and with confidence. Jim Laker's praise was heartfelt: 'I wish he'd opened when I played for England. We would have won a few more Tests!' Sunil Gavaskar, the Indian captain in Boycott's last series, rated him very highly. He told me in 1982: 'In India we are still temperamentally suited to Test cricket, rather than the one-day slogging, and that is why we respect Boycott so much. He is the best defensive batsman in the world, who has adapted brilliantly to the different bowling strategies of his career.' One statistic from Boycott's Test career summarises his excellent defence: he was bowled only thirty times in 193 innings, a percentage of 17.65, compared with the average of 22.

He ended up proud of the respect of his fellow professionals and the public awareness that he was in the top flight of opening batsmen. The occasions when his behaviour embarrassed his colleagues have faded into the mists of time; they will be embroidered in the telling and therefore lose their impact. Here is just one anecdote, and it comes from a man I consider speaks the truth just as easily as Geoffrey Boycott, albeit in a more personable manner. Dennis Amiss partnered Boycott in the opening Test of the 1973 summer against New Zealand with the words of his county captain, Mike

Smith, ringing in his ears: 'There are enough ways of getting out, so don't be run out by Boycott.' In the second innings Amiss and Boycott had an early misunderstanding: Amiss, unlike previous openers, was not to be overawed by his senior partner and he made good his ground. Boycott was run out for one and Amiss compounded the felony in his eyes by scoring 138 not out. Amiss told me, 'Boycott thought I'd done it on purpose and wouldn't speak to me for the rest of the game. I met him in the lift at our hotel, said "Good morning" and he ignored me. It wasn't until our team talk on the eve of the Lord's Test that Ray Illingworth got us both talking again. Boycott fired off at me, but Ray was very fair and told him that unless he sorted it out we'd both be dropped.' In that Lord's Test Boycott and Amiss put on 112, but the relationship was still uneasy. In subsequent Tests Amiss – always conscious that his senior partner would want to lead the way out of the pavilion gate – would wish him 'good luck' as they reached the middle, only to be told sniffily, 'It's not luck that matters, it's ability.' Dennis Amiss had enough of the latter quality to secure his place in the England side and to prosper as Boycott's batting partner. In the Trinidad Test of 1974, as Boycott and Amiss tried to shore up the England innings, Amiss was given another insight into the Yorkshireman's character. 'He suddenly said to me, "I've just realised that you're not trying to run me out." He had finally accepted me, even if it meant deluding himself that I was after him in the early days.'

Such vignettes would fill the whole of this book if I recounted every one I have unearthed. Ultimately it matters not one jot whether Brian Close really did bully him to play that wonderful Gillette Cup final innings in 1965 or if Boycott was responsible for it himself. They are both former England captains with detailed differing knowledge of the circumstances, and one can only guess whether Boycott deservers all the credit for that knock or whether Close did effect the transformation with a few well-chosen words when he joined him at the wicket. Everyone seems to have a story about Boycott, an inevitable corollary to his prolific record over forty years in the game, the fame that he has enjoyed and the chip on the shoulder beloved of so many Yorkshiremen. I agree with Mike Brearley, the son of a Yorkshireman but a different animal from Boycott, when he said to me in 1982: 'It really is extraordinary how anything to do with him is inflated out of all proportion.' It is equally strange to me that a 'percentage player' like Geoffrey Boycott is such a crowd-puller – a man like John Edrich had an equally good record over the same period, yet he never appeared on chat shows or fended off journalists anxious for his side of the latest story. I suppose there is a part in all of us that enjoys hearing the old emotive stuff about 'old school tie', 'public school cronies' and 'enemies in high places' – good knockabout rhetoric that never fails to sell papers or strike a chord in disaffected breasts. Bob Willis remembers Boycott once telling him: 'They want my runs, not me,' and this sense of alienation seemed central to Boycott's character. 'The public understands,' he appeared to be saying, 'they've been sold down the river in their lives. They can identify with me.'

For Boycott the challenge was his *raison d'etre*, proving himself against the best. 'That's why those two series against the West Indies when I was 40 meant a lot to me. That was the toughest you could ever get, with Colin Croft targeting me, giving me the short ball four times an over, with them bowling twelve overs an hour. They really tested our mettle, and I came through it. You couldn't have a Flash Harry crashing them through the covers off the front foot, it was a question of having the bottle. I wish I could have had a go at them in my prime. It was like a middle-weight up against a heavy-weight, but I enjoyed the challenge as well as the occasional triumph against them.'

Was Boycott a great player? His record would say so, emphatically. Over the years any carping about his self-absorption has faded, especially when you consider the many palsied efforts of England opening batsmen against bowling attacks and pitches a good deal less testing than when he was in the sere and yellow of his England days. The fact is that any side containing Boycott was more difficult to beat for his presence. At Test level you had to dismiss him twice to have a chance of winning, and few players made it more difficult for the bowler than Geoffrey Boycott. Many other batsmen have been considered great despite a reluctance to unfurl many shots. Boycott always appeared to know what he was doing. Cussed, tenacious, with a massive pride in performance, he set up many victories by his obduracy early in the game. The top players aren't always dashers. I believe he was a great batsman, and he will probably be content with this verdict from another Yorkshireman who respected him, but also despaired of him at times. Ray Illingworth, never one for fancy notions, a pragmatist to his bootlaces, can't help but admire Boycott: 'I reckon Geoffrey's epitaph should be that he would always do you a solid, professional job. You can't ask for more than that.'

Indeed – and since his retirement Boycott has given more entertainment than he invariably did with the bat. He has become the most distinctive commentator on the game, displaying an incisive, honest assessment that is rare among former players who still cleave to a Masonic, consensual take on punditry, in case their erstwhile colleagues still in the various dressing-rooms take offence.

Boycott has no truck with such niceties. Sometimes it appears contrived, as he bustles into the commentary box with a trenchant 'Coom on, let me at 'em, where's that microphone!' and he is at times rather prolix – but he fulfils the key criterion of any sports summariser. He makes you listen. You turn up the volume, just as football fans did when Brian Clough was pontificating. To some he is maddeningly egotistical and insufferably brutal while others cherish his clarity of opinion, his grasp of facts to justify it and his refusal to gild the lily. He is, at heart, a Yorkshireman and sees no reason why someone of his playing eminence should deal in platitudes. It may make for uncomfortable listening for modern players, but they should know that Boycott is more generous when praise is deserved than many would acknowledge. He just believes that such praise has to be earned. Context of the game, the state of the pitch and the quality of opposition are the currencies that Boycott deals in, and a cricketer who gets the Boycott accolade should respect it rather than sneer at someone who played in another era. His eminence as a player qualifies him for whatever judgements he feels are necessary.

It could easily have been the late Geoffrey Boycott we are now analysing. In 2002 he was diagnosed with throat cancer, and the prognosis was not favourable. It was the biggest challenge he had yet faced and he came through in familiar bloody-minded, brave manner – this time backed devotedly by Rachael, who subsequently became his wife, and their daughter Becky. Those of us who have known Boycott down the years, occasionally despairing of him, accept that his cancer has smoothed off a few of his flintier edges, and he agrees: 'It was a death sentence, and I got reprieved. It affected me greatly, and I was lucky. My friends and family all say it's mellowed me. It certainly changed my life and made me realise what is really important.'

And cricket remains one of those. He is still daft about the game. 'I was lucky, because, unlike millions who don't enjoy their jobs, I absolutely loved mine. Playing cricket in the fresh air for a living when you come from a mining community was a joy. Mind you, I wish I'd had the foresight to know when I was going to get nought – I'd never have got out of bed on those days!'

Innings per hundred

	Inns	100s	Inns per 100
D.G. Bradman	338	117	2.9
W.R. Hammond	1,005	167	6.0
L. Hutton	814	129	6.3
G.A. Hick	871	136	6.4
M.R. Ramprakash	684	103	6.6
J.B. Hobbs	1,315	197	6.7
G. Boycott	1,014	151	6.7
D.C.S. Compton	839	123	6.8
I.V.A. Richards	796	114	7.0
Zaheer Abbas	768	108	7.1
H. Sutcliffe	1,088	149	7.3
E.H. Hendren	1,300	170	7.6
G.M. Turner	792	103	7.7
G.A. Gooch	990	128	7.7
C.P. Mead	1,340	153	8.8
L.E.G. Ames	951	102	9.3
A. Sandham	1,000	107	9.3
G.E. Tyldesley	961	102	9.4
J.H. Edrich	979	103	9.5
T.W. Graveney	1,223	122	10.0
M.C. Cowdrey	1,130	107	10.6
F.E. Woolley	1,532	145	10.6
T.W. Hayward	1,138	104	10.9
D.L. Amiss	1,139	102	11.2
W.G. Grace	1,493	126	11.8

19

Glenn Turner

'I realised just in time that unless I put bat to ball
I'd have to change in another dressing room!'

Glenn Maitland Turner

Born

Dunedin, New Zealand

26 May 1947

First hundred

106*   Worcestershire v Middlesex, Worcester, 1968
Age: 21 years 84 days

100th hundred

311*   Worcestershire v Warwickshire, Worcester, 1982
Age: 35 years 3 days

Last hundred

118   Worcestershire v Kent, Hereford, 1982
Age: 35 years 57 days

Career record

M	Inn	NO	HS	Runs	Average	100s	50s
455	792	101	311*	34,346	49.70	103	148

Test record

M	Inn	NO	HS	Runs	Average	100s	50s
41	73	6	259	2,991	44.64	7	14

In one way Glenn Turner is unique among the batsmen in this book. He started as a stonewaller, then halfway through his career he became a dashing strokemaker. Others such as Hobbs, Hammond and Graveney learned to curb their aggression while remaining masterful all-round players, but Turner took a conscious decision to enjoy himself, to lose the tag of being 'New Zealand's Boycott' and play shots that he did not really know he possessed. The last fifty of his hundreds were glorious, flowing affairs: if you walked on the ground at lunchtime, and discovered that Turner was undefeated, then he would certainly be near or past the hundred mark. In county cricket during the late seventies and early eighties, only Vivian Richards and Ian Botham rivalled him for destructive strokeplay, but, unlike the two Somerset batsmen, Turner had to contend with the new ball as an opening batsman.

He was just 35 when he left Worcestershire and county cricket for good, to return to New Zealand. The education of his children had become more and more important, and Turner wanted to consolidate his business interests and put down roots back home. He left behind warm memories of his uninhibited batting and an impressive list of achievements. He was the second non-English player to score a hundred hundreds, the first to reach that landmark with a triple century and, with 24,562 runs in the 1970s, he was the most prolific batsman in that decade. He was the first batsman to score a thousand runs in May since the Second World War. And by happy coincidence it has only been achieved since by another Worcestershire batsman, Graeme Hick.

It was typical Turner that he would become the first batsman to reach a century of centuries by scoring a hundred before lunch. He went on to make 311 not out that day against Warwickshire, and it could have been 400 such was his cool mastery of the bowling. That innings had all the hallmarks of the Turner of his last few seasons – calculated belligerence, perfect timing and a calm certainty that made him look invulnerable. His fellow New Zealander, Richard Hadlee, called him 'the run-a-ball man', and one can understand what he meant; when Turner was in the mood, it seemed impossible to set a field to thwart his variety of strokeplay. He won countless matches for Worcestershire by cool supervision of the run-chase. His ability to pace an innings was matchless. All this with a slight physique totally unsuited to buffeting from fast bowlers and long days in the middle; Turner amply demonstrated the value of timing to those who lacked the muscular stature of a Botham.

He was even more physically unimpressive when striving painfully to get a toehold on first-class cricket back home. Growing up in Dunedin, a rugged part of the South Island where the climate can be distinctly inhospitable, Turner's self-sufficient character was not unusual. Many from that area hail from stern, Scottish farming stock and, although his father was English, Turner wasn't given to self-indulgent exhibitionism while trying to come to terms with batting. He came from a family of high achievers. Brian, his elder brother, was a distinguished hockey player and cyclist and became a poet of great repute, holding prestigious positions at Dunedin University, while Greg was a top-class golfer, a serial winner of tournaments on the professional circuit. Glenn's family was a voluble, supportive yet self-confident unit. Getting the best out of yourself in your chosen profession was their mantra. Young Glenn was to display an infinite capacity for taking pains as he strove for a measure of cricketing competence as a teenager. He was expected to shine. He played for Otago while still at school, and all he had to offer was a good defence and a huge inferiority complex. In his first game he opened the batting against Dick Motz, the experienced international seamer, and Turner remembers his embarrassment: 'He couldn't get me out and I couldn't understand why. I was just a schoolboy, petrified at the occasion, and he was bouncing me and I kept blocking him. I thought to myself, "Surely these guys are so much better than me, what am I doing here?" But they still couldn't get me out.' Motz was the first of many bowlers to know that feeling. Jeremy Coney, later to play for New Zealand alongside Turner, recalls him scoring just three runs in an entire session for Otago against Central Districts and a turgid century against Wellington. 'It was such a tortuous affair when Glenn batted in those days, but the boy had yet to become a man. I never saw a batsman watch the line of the ball so closely, even when he was a teenager. He was learning the basics of batting, and it mattered nothing about how long it would all take him. There was no emotion; he was clinical, so driven.' Turner's immaculate defence had been the one thing to impress his school coach, Billy Ibadulla, the former Warwickshire player who was coaching that winter in New Zealand. Ibadulla recalls his first impressions: 'I watched this pale, skinny little lad getting behind the line of the ball, trying desperately hard. All he could do was block it, but he wanted to do well, and that's half the battle. I thought that things could be grafted on to his immaculate defence. Above all, he wanted to learn; he asked intelligent questions.'

Ibadulla believed Turner could prosper in county cricket, and he recommended him to his old county, Warwickshire. They asked him over for a trial, but then Turner came up against a slight problem – he had no money. With the determination that became a characteristic of his batting, he set out to earn his air fare. He worked on the night-shift at a bakery for the next eighteen months and scraped enough together for a one-way ticket. A couple of days before he left for England, he received a letter from Warwickshire, informing him that the club now had its quota of overseas players and that he would be wasting his time coming over. Other teenagers would have cut their losses, shrugged their shoulders and blown the money on a week of hedonism somewhere. Not Turner: he got on the plane, went to Birmingham and asked Warwickshire to arrange trials for him with other counties.

Turner's impact when he appeared in the Edgbaston nets was extraordinary. He batted against the Warwickshire first team, and he stunned them by his reluctance to do anything but block the ball. David Brown, at that time an England opening bowler, recalls: 'All he did was hit the ball back to me.

Mentally he was on the back foot – defence was everything. I thought he hadn't a hope of playing county cricket.' Worcestershire must have seen something extra, because they were sufficiently impressed to take him on the staff. He made his debut for them in 1967 and proceeded to play a succession of dull, careworn innings that contrasted with the elegance of Graveney, the aggression of D'Oliveira and the dash of Headley. Yet he stayed in: Turner had to be prised out. He demonstrated that limpet tenacity for his country on the 1969 tour to England, carrying his bat for 43 at Lord's as Underwood devastated the rest in an all-out total of 131. Geoffrey Boycott, not a cricketer easily impressed, liked what he saw in the 22-year-old Turner: 'When Deadly Derek got you on a turning pitch, you'd got serious problems, believe me, but Glenn handled everything thrown at him.'

He was beginning to earn respect in the county game for an iron will, impenetrable defence and rocklike temperament, but no more than that. There seemed no reason to doubt that, in a couple more years, Glenn Turner would slip back to the mediocrity of New Zealand cricket, having earned nothing but the ire of countless, bored spectators. He used to go to bed at nine o'clock, playing over in his mind his latest blocking innings that day. He was saved by the John Player League, that bane of classical batsmanship, the home of the slogger. Initially, Turner could not adapt to its 40-over demands: hard hitters like D'Oliveira would sit fretting in the dressing-room, waiting to get in while Turner studiously played the ball to mid-off and the fielding side hoped fondly he would not get out. The turning point came after one match against Northamptonshire when Turner took 34 overs to make 40, an incredible effort in hindsight. The Worcestershire players doled out a few home truths in a locked dressing-room: he was heading for oblivion unless he played some shots. The following Sunday he made 60 against Essex, including five boundaries back over the bowler's head. Tom Graveney, his captain that day, recalls the turning point: 'He knew what was needed, yet after seven overs, we were seven for nought! He saw me pacing up and down, looking furious, and he made fifty in the next ten overs, an amazing transformation. Before then everything about his batting had been basically right, but all he needed to do was unlock the key. After that he was a brilliant player in the Sunday League.' Turner became the first man to top 6,000 runs in John Player cricket.

If Turner had discovered the secret of Sunday cricket, such freedom still eluded him in the longer games. In the West Indies on the 1971/72 tour, he scored four double hundreds – including two in Tests – but he became frustrated by the attrition of the performances. He says: 'At that time New Zealand looked on a draw as a bonus, and my job was just to stay there and wear the bowlers down. I was beginning to realise there was more to batting than a watertight defence.' The strain of carrying a weak batting side began to tell on him during that tour: after a long innings, he found it almost impossible to sleep.

Turner decided to get his relaxation from the game itself. From 1973 onwards, he started to play with great freedom and an increasing amount of risk. Cricket became a pleasure, rather than a chore. On the 1973 New Zealand tour of England he scored a thousand runs in May: he says he was lucky to bat against some friendly bowling on good wickets in favourable weather, but it remains a staggering effort from a man with a reputation as a stonewaller. To score a thousand runs in May you need to be a fast scorer as well as a fine player. Glenn Turner was now both. Typically he thought little of the record until he got near to it: 'I've never really bothered about statistical achievements, but in the end everyone else was so wound up about it that I tried hard to do it. I reacted to the outside influences on me.' He reached the landmark figure off the bowling of Bishen Bedi at Northampton, with a steer behind square on the offside. All he can remember by way of celebration is a congratulatory cake, and that suited Turner. 'Back in Southern New Zealand one doesn't make a fuss. That tends to be the way it is; one plays things down.' No doubt his family approved of that attitude. That 1973 season began and ended magnificently for Turner but, in between, he suffered failure in the three-Test series, averaging just 23. If he had made a reasonable contribution to the Trent Bridge Test, New Zealand would have triumphed, instead of going down by 38 runs – Turner made 20 in the match. He just could not get going; Geoff Arnold, his *bête noire*, troubled him as usual. Derek Underwood remembers Arnold's dominance over Turner in Tests: 'Geoff was the best new-ball opener in the world at that time, and Glenn was good enough to get a touch to his late swing.'

That Test series left its mark on Turner. It was not enough to average 62 for the overall tour, or 74 for Worcestershire at the season's end: he had failed in the vital games. Despite his great performances on tour, his reputation dipped in New Zealand; the whisper was that Turner had lost his old steel after deciding to enjoy his batting. Even after scoring two hundreds in the Christchurch Test to secure New Zealand's first win over Australia, he was still the victim of carping comments about his worth to the team. That was the start of the downward spiral in his relationship with the New Zealand Board – Turner eventually became captain and resented having no say in the selection of the side. An articulate man with a clear, hard mind, Turner ruffled some feathers in the New Zealand dressing-room by dispensing a few lectures about the inferiority complexes. He took on the legendary Walter Hadlee, the New Zealand Board's chairman, over the derisory fees paid to the players for Tests. Jeremy Coney, by then established in the national side, was grateful for Turner's leadership: 'I got nine dollars a day when I first got capped, and Glenn definitely assisted our development as players by getting us more money. But Walter Hadlee was as strong a personality as Glenn, and in the end the captain lost out. Glenn was just too honest for his own good at times.' In his own subborn way Turner was just as visionary as Tony Greig and the other key international cricketers who threw in their lot with Kerry Packer around the same time. By 1977 he was disenchanted with the administrators in New Zealand. He decided to stay in Worcester during the winter of 1977 to prepare for his benefit season, thereby ruling himself out of three Tests against England. Turner was disenchanted with the new harshness creeping into Test cricket and he deplored the 'sledging' tactics of Ian Chappell's Australian team. In the 1974 Christchurch Test Australia were about to lose to New Zealand for the first time and Turner was nearing his second hundred of the match when Chappell made a derogatory comment to Turner about his Indian wife, Suki. Jeremy Coney, who was playing in that Test, will never forget the cold fury of Turner at close of play after that incident. 'Glenn stormed into our dressing-room, eyes ablaze with anger. He was looking beyond us in his fury, generated by a reference to Suki that he couldn't comprehend. He believed this was outside the realms of decency. Glenn saw cricket as part of a civilising process and, after that Test, I always felt an abrasiveness from him towards Australian cricketers, almost as if he felt he was representing the civilised world against the barbarians. Glenn felt too many of us had a feeling of inferiority as cricketers towards the Aussies, but he would never tug his forelock at them. He believed in himself.' A proud man, at odds with the Board, Turner felt a prophet without honour in his own country and wondered what he had to do to instil a sense of professionalism into the make-up of the Test side. He was also tired of continuous cricket throughout the year. 'I reasoned that I would make more money by playing county cricket for a fair amount of time, rather than burn myself out all the year round. I felt I owed it to Worcestershire to return fresh and eager every season, and I could only do that by resting for a few months and getting away from cricket.' He confined himself to radio and television commentaries on New Zealand's home Tests, a decision that rankled with several players and officials. Not for the first time Turner would not be swayed from a course of action he had mapped out.

Turner's absence from the Test arena for five years when in his prime is the main reason why some of his opponents refuse to recognise him as a great player. Alan Knott told me: 'It's much easier taking on an overseas fast bowler in county cricket, when you can get runs at the other end. It's a different game when you have to battle through against four of them at the same time. Test cricket changed drastically in the last few years of my time – there were hardly any spinners and it was all about quick bowlers.' Bob Willis agrees and points out that Turner scored only one hundred against England. Willis felt that Turner had a bit of an obsession about fast bowlers taking an unfair advantage by indulging in too much short-pitched bowling and concludes: 'There were few better players when the ball was not deviating off the wicket.' Sunil Gavaskar, on the other hand, feels that Turner would have been as prolific a Test run-scorer as himself and Geoffrey Boycott if he had stayed around.

For the last five seasons of his career in England Turner had to live with the jibes that 'he doesn't fancy the quicks'. His short answer to that was that nobody does, that some batsmen show it and others do not. Jeremy Coney agrees. He saw at first hand the way that Turner organised his game, the analysis that went into meeting the challenge on a particular day. 'It was grossly unfair to suggest that Glenn didn't fancy the quicks. He had his game worked out, using a forward press movement while others would go back and across. After transferring slightly his weight onto his back foot, he was ready to go forward quickly. Holding the line was the bedrock of his game. What do you want from your opening batsman? He must be well organised, know where his off-stump is, and instantly alive to either letting the ball go or having a crack at it. Glenn was a master of all that. In English county cricket, there were lots of West Indian fast bowlers, plus the likes of Clive Rice, Garth le Roux and Imran Khan. Glenn had a terrific record against them once he decided to attack them in his own unorthodox fashion.' Turner's remarkable way of playing quick bowlers may have contributed to the generalisation. He perfected the knack of stepping away from his stumps and steering the ball over the slips, or smashing it through square cover with a flat bat. He decided to play championship matches like the John Player League. 'I was fed up with getting into line, playing correctly, taking the knocks and getting hardly any runs. Umpires allowed quick bowlers to get away with murder in the last few years of my career, and I found the only way to combat the short-pitched stuff was to step back and take a free swing at it. Does that mean I was scared? I've gone out and taken apart all the top fast bowlers at some stage – sometimes on wickets nowhere near as good as Test tracks – yet some felt I didn't fancy it. I thought the early part of my career proved I could stand and take the knocks.' There was no doubt that the protective helmet helped Turner's confidence; in common with most modern professionals, he had become increasingly worried about the uneven bounce on English wickets.

If Turner's method of combating the fast bowlers was unique among batsmen of his era, so was his grip on the bat. He wrapped his left hand round the top of the handle, so that the back of the left hand faced the bowler. That high grip enabled him to bring the bat down straight; the top hand guided and the bottom hand eased it through the shots. He used a very heavy bat and concentrated on a free flow of it with a powerful follow-through. The bat came up and down straight like a pendulum, which gave him great power from such a slight physique. He stroked the ball through a very wide arc, and the variety of shots at his disposal enabled him to play a series of unpredictable strokes to areas containing no fielders. He had two shots that carried the Turner trademark – the 'flat bat' and the 'chip'. The first one was played off the front foot to a ball of any length that was in his driving area; he hit it square with an uninhibited swing of that heavy bat. It was a shot that drove slow left-arm bowlers to distraction as he waited for the precise moment, then smashed it away with amazing power. Turner's mastery of the 'chip' shot was a boon in a run chase when several fielders were positioned on the boundary. He would advance down the wicket, chip the ball over the inner ring and run two while the ball landed safely some way from the deep fielders. Other players would either be caught on the boundary or get frustrated as they smashed the ball direct to the inner ring: Turner's gift of timing was so sharp that he could play the shot as if he was chipping out of a bunker on the golf course. Norman Gifford remembers how the Turner of later years would approach early-season nets after his lay-off: 'All he worried about was getting his hands working properly on the bat. Lesser players would have to worry about timing and footwork, but Glenn had those naturally. He worked at keeping his bottom hand out of his game, so that he followed through correctly and played straight. A light bat would wander in his hands, and the heavier versions helped him with that swing like a pendulum.' Alan Ormrod, Turner's opening partner for many years at Worcester, had the fascination of observing his unique technique at close quarters: 'I've never known a player hit the ball so consistently in the drive area of the bat. That's why he hit so many boundaries. Unlike other great batsmen he didn't need to pinch the strike with quick singles; he got enough boundaries to score quickly.'

That point was amply demonstrated at Swansea in 1977, when Turner's ability to score at will enabled him to create a new world record for monopolising a complete innings. He scored 141 not out in Worcestershire's total of 169 – 83.4 per cent of the total score. No other player reached double figures, and the other ten batsmen made fourteen scoring shots between them. Norman Gifford, second top scorer with seven, helped Turner add 57 for the ninth wicket – he remembers being staggered at the way Turner would play the ball and call for a run in the same instant. 'He was so much in command that he knew not only where the ball was going but that no fielder was there. We'd got used to his dominance by then, but that was the first time he'd done it all the way through an innings.' Turner, with characteristic candour, says he had got drunk the night before with an old friend from New Zealand and, as far as he was concerned, he was still a little groggy at the start of play. 'I concentrated harder as a result, and soon the top order had gone and I was left with the tail. We had to avoid the follow-on so the lower order just played for me and blocked it. The wicket wasn't a bad one and, although I played well, the circumstances created the record.'

The circumstances were equally propitious on that sunlit Saturday in May 1982 when Turner reached his century of centuries in great style. He had long developed a fondness for the Warwickshire bowling – eleven championship hundreds in all – which partly stemmed from the disappointments of 1967, and the slow wicket for the Bank Holiday match at Worcester was ideal for him. He was due a big innings – his previous six knocks had totalled 45 runs – and he was getting fed up with everyone talking about the missing hundred. The day before the Warwickshire match I reminded him that he averaged 71 against them in first-class cricket; he said he would try to get another 29 as well. The first ball of the innings, a short one from Willis, was pulled to the square-leg boundary, and in the next over he hit Gladstone Small for six over long-on. He reached his century in 114 minutes with a legside flick for three and celebrated with a gin and tonic at the wicket. Fittingly the man who brought out the drink was Billy Ibadulla, his old coach, now a first-class umpire but without a game that day. Turner did not stop there; in 342 minutes he made 311 not out and the declaration robbed him of the chance of toppling Macartney's record of 345 in a day in England. Not that Turner knew of the record or even cared: 'I was pleased to reach the target stylishly, in fine weather, in front of my home crowd in a local derby. Somehow it all felt right.' Alan Ormrod, who helped Turner add 291 that day, thought he was looking for a big score: 'He had that look in his eyes early on. I wasn't at all surprised that he made 300. Glenn was a very aggressive thinker, and he could be very determined.' Dennis Amiss was sufficiently impressed by Turner's mastery that he sidled up to him after half-an-hour's batting and whispered, 'Bet you can't get 300 in a day.' Turner smiled and carried on looking at the pitch. Amiss says: 'Our lads weren't too pleased with me when I said that, but I didn't think he would carry on in the same vein. He just battered us to death, taking a fresh guard when he reached the next fifty. Eventually he was just coasting along.'

It is true that Warwickshire bowled badly on a flat wicket, but that cannot really detract from Turner's display. The only surprise is that he did not reach his hundred with a boundary. Turner pronounced himself 'fairly pleased' at attaining the landmark reached by just 18 other batsmen at that time. A touch of the old inferiority complex surfaces when he says, 'It's one of the few ways a New Zealander can be compared to the top batsmen from other countries. Rugby will always be the sporting religion back home, so I had to gain some prestige elsewhere in the world. I suppose I was most pleased by the way I got the latter half of my hundreds, once I decided to stop boring the pants off myself and the spectators.'

By the 1982 season Glenn Turner had worked out his game and his aspirations to precision. He still loved a challenge – he was disappointed that an appendix operation robbed him of scoring 2,000 runs, or bowing out with an average of over a hundred – but no longer was cricket the dominating force in his life. 'I used to hate getting out; I'd mope and sulk for hours. Suddenly I realised it was time to change the way I played, to cram more enjoyment into a shorter stay at the crease. I was cheesed off with my style of batting, so heaven knows about the poor spectators. It dawned on me that there were other things to do: write some letters, read a book, broaden my mind. Occupation of the crease for the sake of it is self-destructive, you end up knowing nothing but cricket.' Conversations I have enjoyed with Turner over the years confirm his diverse mind: he sets out to acquire an understanding of a topic and only then will he speak on it with authority and clarity of thought. I find his self-deprecating humour amusing – he still laughs at the comment of a Dunedin taxi-driver to a friend of his during the 1976 series against India: 'That guy Turner, he's boring to watch!' First impressions take a long time to die. His appendix operation during the summer of 1982 gave Turner further comic potential – he was being whisked to the operating theatre at high speed and, just before be passed out, the porter asked him for his autograph. 'Perhaps he thought he would be the last guy to get it before I snuffed it,' smiles Turner. 'It seemed a funny time to ask for my autograph.' Jeremy Coney recalls Turner's professional approach to the chore of signing autographs. 'He got pleasure from doing it properly. He made sure he had a clean page to sign, and he'd do so deliberately. Glenn was fastidious in so many areas. He left nothing to chance. On our tour to Australia in 1973/74 he'd clean his knife and fork thoroughly at the dinner table and then, after asking for the fruit to be removed from his bowl of ice cream, he'd ask, 'Are you sure the fruit hasn't touched this ice cream?' These days you'd call it Obsessive Compulsion Disorder. It was the same when he was batting – before going out, he'd brush his hair immaculately, not a hair out of place, then put his collar up and be ready to go to work. He wanted to be in control. But I had immense time for Glenn. Despite his rather solitary, self-sufficient air, he was very good to me, both as team-mate, then my coach when I became New Zealand's captain. I never knew anyone who could read a match situation as well as Glenn. I found him compelling on cricket tactics.'

When he finished with Worcestershire, Turner felt that English county captains were killing the game by negative tactics and that Test cricket was even more spartan. He agreed to return to the Test fold in Australia early in 1983 but admitted the attraction of night cricket was the magnet. 'I couldn't have one or the other, so I played Test cricket to try something different. Playing under the lights in front of an emotional crowd was exciting.' His restless, enquiring mind wasn't done with cricket, though. He had two spells as national coach, the first more successful than the second when some of the younger New Zealand players lacked the discipline of Turner at a similar age and were disconcerted at the coach's reluctance to praise unless it was truly deserved. Turner appeared happier to work with grown adults who wanted to improve without making a fuss or briefing the press in hostile fashion. He also coached provincial sides, served as a national selector and impressed many as an honest, incisive TV pundit. He is now the chairman of New Zealand's selectors, and it's a given that Turner will approach that task fearlessly. His family background and fierce self-confidence mean he can deal with the job no other way. Significantly he has always been a huge fan of Frank Sinatra and his first autobiography was titled *My Way*.

In his time Glenn Turner was not the most popular man in cricket for a variety of reasons, some of them reflecting no credit on his detractors. He was very much his own man and would not compromise when he felt he was right; in this, he resembled Geoffrey Boycott, another prolific opener who went into voluntary exile from the Test arena for a time in the 1970s. When Turner felt he had been wronged, he was not slow to say so, as the New Zealand Cricket Board discovered. When Ian Chappell disconcerted him with a string of abuse during the Christchurch Test of 1974, Turner demanded a public apology: it never came. Turner's sense of fair play was also outraged by the West Indies team that came to New Zealand in 1980. From his seat in the commentary box he was disgusted at the boorish behaviour of some of the West Indians as they crashed to defeat in the Dunedin Test. He also felt that they behaved unsportingly at certain post-match social functions. When Turner batted against them a few months later at Worcester, he tried to teach them a lesson in a bizarre way. He cross-batted every ball, made 45 off 24 deliveries, then deliberately sat on his wicket after playing a shot to mid-off. The West Indies team and the Worcester crowd were bewildered at Turner's antics, but he says he did it to show his contempt for cricketers who could not take defeat in the proper manner or handle themselves with dignity in public. 'I didn't want them to get any pleasure at all from my dismissal. I know it seems childish to everyone else, but I made my protest in the best way I knew.'

Glenn Turner remains nothing if not positive, even when registering disapproval. His strength of character saw him through enough disappointments to hamper lesser men, while his strong beliefs rubbed more than one influential person up the wrong way. Sport in New Zealand broadly revolves around rugby union and the mighty deeds of the All Blacks, where the team ethic and the concept of 'mateship' prevails. But Turner could never see the point in propping up the bar with his team-mates all night and indulging in juvenile pranks like electing the Pillock of the Day. He was independent-minded enough to go off on more challenging pursuits. Unsurprisingly he enjoyed trout fishing near his Dunedin home. He often appeared on the periphery, giving his very best as an individual, preparing himself assiduously. He didn't run with the herd conversationally and didn't see why he should agree just for a quiet life. Turner polarised opinion in New Zealand because of his independent streak, but not even his harshest detractors could deny that he deserved immense respect for his batting prowess and struggles to improve the lot of other cricketers. At Worcester, in contrast, he was generally popular with the players because he no longer took himself seriously; when he was dismissed, he walked calmly back to the dressing-room and switched on to some other interest almost immediately. Cricket was only a part of his life, and we can be grateful that he saw the advantages of enjoying his game: 'I realised just in time that, unless I put bat to ball, I'd have to change in another dressing-room!'

Was he a great player? Was he too unorthodox to be ranked in the top bracket? That maverick streak offended the fastidious side of Mike Brearley's nature: 'I'd much rather have seen him fight it out like Boycott and show the youngsters how to play properly, rather than slogging it around.' John Emburey feels he was a great player – 'the best timer of the ball I've ever bowled at, and perfectly happy against the fast bowlers. He saw the ball so quickly from the hand, the sign of a great player.' Richard Hadlee, Turner's compatriot, makes the valid point that he was lucky to bat on good wickets at Worcester but conceded that he could see off the new ball in about five overs, thereby altering the shape of an innings. David Brown, the Warwickshire manager, thought him unique: 'I've never seen anyone play so fluently with such an amazing grip. The way he picked up the ball was fantastic.'

When Tom Graveney retired at Worcester in 1970, he forecast in his farewell speech that Glenn Turner would be the batsman of the 1970s. Statistically, he was – but just seven Test centuries with an average of 45 does not suggest greatness. He was a great player in county cricket because of his adaptability – he turned his game upside down and worked out a unique method of batting against top-class bowlers from all over the world. A man who can play an innings like the Swansea one in 1977, a batsman who toyed with county attacks in the last five years of his time in England and dominated defensive field placings in limited-overs cricket – such a player should not have had to fear batting on a flat wicket in an Edgbaston Test or churning out the hundreds in Pakistan and India. He should not be denied his eminence just because he was brave enough to say that he found Test cricket boring. The challenge in Glenn Turner's batting brought him close to greatness. One of the qualifications of a great batsman is that on his day, the bowlers are helpless to stem the tide of fast runs. For enough years before retiring comparatively young, Turner went out to bat with that aim in mind and he consistently succeeded. When necessary his bat was as straight as Boycott's: the spectators who came to relish him were delighted his aspirations went much higher than that.

Going on after 100

	100s	150s	200s	250s	300s
J.B. Hobbs	197	52	16	3	1
E.H. Hendren	170	56	22	4	1
W.R. Hammond	167	66	36	13	4
C.P. Mead	153	47	13	1	-
G. Boycott	151	43	10	2	-
H. Sutcliffe	149	49	16	3	1
F.E. Woolley	145	41	9	2	1
G.A. Hick	136	52	16	5	3
L. Hutton	129	47	11	5	1
G.A. Gooch	128	36	16	3	1
W.G. Grace	126	47	14	7	3
D.C.S. Compton	123	30	9	3	1
T.W. Graveney	122	33	7	1	-
D.G. Bradman	117	58	37	16	6
I.V.A. Richards	114	31	10	2	1
Zaheer Abbas	108	36	10	1	-
M.C. Cowdrey	107	22	3	2	1
A. Sandham	107	36	11	3	1
T.W. Hayward	104	28	8	2	1
J.H. Edrich	103	22	4	1	1
M.R. Ramprakash	103	36	14	5	1
G.M. Turner	103	33	10	3	1
L.E.G. Ames	102	19	9	1	-
D.L. Amiss	102	32	3	1	-
G.E. Tyldesley	102	26	7	1	-

350s: D.G. Bradman (3), G.A. Hick (1) and L. Hutton (1).
400s: D.G. Bradman (1) and G.A. Hick (1).
450s: D. G. Bradman (1).

20

Zaheer Abbas

'If only I could bat all the time'

Syed Zaheer Abbas

Born

Sialkot, Pakistan

24 July 1947

First hundred

197   Karachi v East Pakistan, Karachi, 1968

Age: 21 years 127 days

100th hundred

215   Pakistan v India, Lahore, 1982

Age: 35 years 140 days

Last hundred

119*   Pakistan International Airlines v Lahore City, Lahore, 1987

Age: 39 years 185 days

Career record

M	Inn	NO	HS	Runs	Average	100s	50s
459	768	92	274	34,843	51.54	108	158

Test record

M	Inn	NO	HS	Runs	Average	100s	50s
78	124	11	274	5,062	44.79	12	20

Few batsmen have combined an insatiable appetite for runs with shimmering brilliance, that butterfly elegance which suggests transience at the crease. With Zaheer Abbas the aesthetic demands were invariably met – unless the wicket was juicy and the fast bowlers were on top – and his air of wristy delicacy beguiled the most partisan of spectators. When Zaheer batted, newspapers were folded up and put away and the picnic hamper remained closed.

His slim physique and glasses contributed to an air of fragility, accentuated when the ball was flying around his ears at pace. Zaheer was never particularly comfortable against sustained hostility. Learning his trade on flat wickets in Pakistan, then the ersatz beach of the pitches at Bristol hardly equipped him to tough it out in the manner of a Border, a Gooch or an Atherton.

Yet his sheer weight of runs underlines his eminence, despite that caveat offered by all of his admirers. He has scored more runs than any other Asian – 34,843, at an average of 51.54 – a country mile ahead of Mushtaq Mohammad, Javed Miandad, Majid Khan and Sachin Tendulkar, all batsmen of longevity. In terms of centuries Javed (80), Majid (73) and Mushtaq (72) lag far behind Zaheer's tally of 108.

On eight occasions Zaheer scored two separate hundreds in a match, a record shared with Ricky Ponting. How many in a cricket quiz would have plumped for Hammond, Bradman, Hick or Hobbs as the answer? Even more remarkably, Zaheer holds the record for scoring a double hundred and a century in the same game no less than four times. He was not out in all eight innings. No other batsman has done this more than twice.

And this was no grinding accumulator. It would be almost impossible in researching Zaheer's career of 21 years to find a hundred lacking his characteristic wristy charm. He was one of those Asian batsmen who conformed to the stereotype, a matchless driver of steely elegance and a masterful manipulator of the ball into vacant areas. All with just enough force to reach the boundary rope. No wonder Zaheer loved Gloucestershire's matches at the Cheltenham College Ground, a compact arena. When he leaned on the ball with his customary sublime timing, it was invariably a boundary once it passed the diving fielder. Zaheer believed in conserving his energies for the long haul; hasty, despairing singles were viewed with disdain.

Chris Broad, former county colleague, fine Test batsman and now a respected international match referee, has seen enough top players over the past thirty years to pass rational judgement on someone like Zaheer. He simply purrs when assessing him: 'He could hit the same ball to three different places – past the bowler, legside or offside, all with a late flick of the wrists. For a batsman who wore glasses, he had a magnificent eye. Zed was the last word in elegance. And didn't he love batting!'

All of Zaheer's contemporaries with Gloucestershire focus on his prowess against spin bowlers. David Graveney, later county captain and then chairman of the England selectors, struggles to nominate a batsman who was equally adroit. 'An unbelievable player of spinners. His ability to find the gaps was his forte. He would toy with the very best of them. And for someone like me, pre-season nets were an absolute nightmare. He'd have a sighter against me, then just launch me miles, ball after ball. I used to take a long time walking back to the net after finding my ball!'

Playing at Bristol, where sand was often mixed into the surface to aid the home spinners, was ideal for Zaheer, where the lack of pace meant the Nevil Road wickets were a reasonable facsimile of a typical Pakistani pitch. But he was equally pre-eminent elsewhere. He loved the firm, true wickets at The Oval where he made a stack of runs, and at Canterbury he usually came out on top against the great Derek Underwood, then one of the supreme challenges to a batsman in English cricket, especially on a damp, drying surface.

Underwood rates Zaheer as one of the three best batsmen he bowled against: 'He was so wristy, deflecting the ball at the moment of impact into open spaces.' In one match at Canterbury Underwood set out to frustrate Zaheer, using the sort of defensive tactic Ashley Giles tried against Sachin Tendulkar years later – packing legside and firing the ball outside leg-stump, in the vain hope that Zaheer would get bored. He kept kicking the ball away, finally telling Underwood that if he would revert to a proper game, bowling on the offside, then he would back himself to get his strokes through. Very few players had the dexterity and touch to do that to Underwood, but the Pakistani did. He wanted to be tested by a great bowler, rather than get strangled down legside. Zaheer scored yet another hundred to win the battle of minds. In his county career, he averaged more than 80 against Kent.

Zaheer hated sitting in the dressing-room after getting out, while lesser lights made batting appear such a taxing exercise. Even in warm-up matches he would not give away his wicket. In 1982 he scored a routine century in the Parks against Oxford University. His captain, David Graveney, had reminded him of the convention that once you reach three figures against the callow undergraduates, you get out to give others some early-season practice. Zaheer proceeded to ignore or forget his captain's instructions and took fresh guard. Eventually Graveney had to position himself alongside the sightscreen, trying to distract Zaheer. Finally, and reluctantly, he allowed himself to be bowled for 144.

When in full flow Zaheer expected to take the bulk of the bowling. That led to some hairy calls near the end of the over and some ignominious run-outs. But Zaheer rarely was run out. He told David Graveney, 'You run when I tell you' and 'If there's a mix-up, I won't be the one who's run out.' Just for good measure, he would add, 'When I say 'no' I sometimes mean 'yes', so be ready.' Graveney eventually reached an accord with his batting partner: 'The first four balls of the over would find me just leaning on my bat, because Zed would either block it or hit it for two or four, so he could keep the strike. For the last two balls I was ready for the quick single because he would want the strike. All part of his charm! But we all loved Zed – a top bloke and a loyal man to Gloucestershire. When he played like he could, you forgot about his little ways.' Team-mates of Denis Compton were saying something similar decades earlier.

Zaheer's determination to cash in when the batting omens were favourable stemmed from his father's advice as he was starting his cricket career. 'One day he took me to the railway station at Karachi and pointed to all the sweating masses in the overcrowded third-class compartments. He then showed me the air-conditioned compartments in first-class and told me that would be my reward if I worked hard. He didn't think I'd get there by playing cricket!' He promised his father he would give up his cricket ambitions if he failed on the 1971 tour to England.

An innings of 274 in the First Test at Edgbaston soon stilled those paternal doubts. Already he was a big-innings man, aware that he had to capitalise when it was his day and the wicket favoured him. Three years later, in the Oval Test, it was again his stage as he fashioned a beautiful 240. The toiling and persevering Derek Underwood, wicketless at Edgbaston in 1971, finally nailed him at The Oval, but Zaheer had again demonstrated he was currently the best in the world at cashing in when the wicket was flat.

He once told me, 'Batting is my religion, after being a Muslim. I'm of the same mind as Geoffrey Boycott, whose religion is to get runs.' You could see similarities with the Sage of Fitzwilliam, whose family coat of arms would be the boot on an opponent's windpipe. Although Boycott batted with more resolution and defensive excellence than Zaheer, they shared a conviction that you should never give a sucker an even break while batting, and that the game was a desirable social passport if you achieved eminence. Then there was the running between the wickets to consider and their genuine despair at being dismissed.

Zaheer was eventually delighted to be bracketed alongside Boycott, a player he deeply admired. They are the only members of the Hundred Hundreds Club to achieve the milestone in a Test match. Boycott's innings, in the Leeds Test of 1977 against Australia, is the stuff of legend. Zaheer had told me early in 1982 that he wanted to get there in a Test against England, the opponents for whom he had the greatest respect. Doing it at Lord's would be perfect. It was not to be. His highest score in the 1982 Test series in England was 75. But he made amends later that year.

Zaheer made it against India, Pakistan's fiercest opponents, at Lahore. It was a typically slow pitch and, with Kapil Dev the only bowler operating above medium pace, it was perfectly set up for Zaheer, as he resumed his love affair with the Indian bowlers. He had dominated them in 1978, and in this 1982/83 series he scored three more centuries.

Just after lunch on the second day in Lahore, he arrived at the landmark with one of his speciality strokes, flicking Madan Lal off his pads through midwicket for three runs. Typically he took fresh guard and went on to score

215. It meant a great deal to him to become the first Asian to score a hundred centuries. 'I have always wanted to be respected in the cricket world and by its historians in later years. I want to be like Don Bradman and Jack Hobbs, to be talked about long after I've finished.'

That status cannot be awarded to Zaheer Abbas, despite batting with such charm and distinction for so many years. He managed the dichotomy of being an unashamed seeker of batting records while being a lovely player, incapable of being dull. He was still scoring hundreds for Pakistan International Airways in his fortieth year in domestic first-class cricket, so he was no flashing meteor, no cameo batsman.

But his Test record does not admit him into the pantheon of top batsmen. Given the flat wickets on the sub-continent, where he played so many of his 78 Tests, a total of 5,062 runs at an average of 44.79, with 12 hundreds, is highly commendable but, judged by rigorous standards, not that impressive. Among Pakistanis Javed Miandad, Inzamam-ul-Haq and Mohammad Yousuf outstrip him, with twenty-odd centuries and averages in the fifties. Indian batsmen such as Sachin Tendulkar, Rahul Dravid and Sunil Gavaskar are also far ahead of Zaheer.

And Zaheer never scored a Test hundred against the West Indies, the outstanding bowling unit in his pomp as a batsman. He averaged 17 against the West Indies in Tests. Fast bowlers rattled Zaheer. He said as much when he told me in 1982, 'It's very difficult to score against men like Holding, Croft and Willis. The standard of batting is deteriorating because of the quality of quick bowling.' Yet contemporaries and team-mates such as Allan Border, David Gower, Graham Gooch, Geoffrey Boycott, Javed Miandad, Imran Khan, Allan Lamb and David Boon battled through against the West Indian juggernaut to post hundreds.

Bob Willis put it pithily when he said, 'The place to bowl at Zaheer on bouncy wickets is his nose – he doesn't fancy that at all.' Under Willis' captaincy in 1982, Zaheer was also tactically outwitted in the Test series, in which he averaged just 26. England had done their homework on Zaheer, as Willis recalls: 'We had a square cover and a normal cover, just ten yards apart, to combat that wristy stroke of his that went square. The place to bowl at him on slow wickets was about a foot outside his off-stump to encourage him to play his shots. He rarely worked you to mid-off, preferring to take his right leg back towards leg-stump to force you squarer. If you bowled straight at him, he'd murder you through legside.'

And against sheer speed, Zaheer was 'iffy', giving the bowler a chance. Even more so after his experience playing in World Series Cricket between 1977 and 1979. David Graveney recalls the impact a diet of short-pitched fast bowling had on Zaheer: 'Before Packer came along he was never out of position, but he was then subjected to high pace aimed purely at his body. His courage was tested and certain bad habits stayed – like showing more of his chest to the fast bowler in order to get quickly into a position for the hook.'

Graveney remembers Sylvester Clarke working Zaheer over at The Oval in the post-Packer period, and a match against the 1980 West Indians when, against Holding, Roberts and Garner, Zaheer was twice caught at fly slip, failing to get into line. Malcolm Marshall disconcerted him at Portsmouth on one of the quickest wickets on the county circuit at the time. He may have scored 87 but, in Graveney's words, 'It wasn't the bravest innings; he didn't duck but just stood there and hopped about. All that gladiatorial Packer stuff, with six bouncers an over sometimes, took its toll on Zed. The first time he came back from World Series Cricket his stance was more like a baseball player, with his bat above his head, rather than the elegant batsmen we all knew. He was never the same against the quicks after Packer.' Zaheer always believed that the runs he scored in World Series Cricket should have been included in his first-class tally because they really had to be earned. It was the toughest cricket he ever played.

Ian Botham resolutely maintained that Zaheer could be bounced out, even on flat wickets – admittedly a policy embraced by Botham in his halcyon, bullish years against most batsmen. But he had a point with Zaheer and he prevailed in one county match at Taunton. Botham knew that Zaheer hooked in the air and often failed to get over the pull shot. So he peppered him with the short ball and Zaheer struggled. Yet he kept despatching Botham to the short boundaries at Taunton, with some of his top-edged hooks clearing the wicket-keeper for one-bounce boundaries. When umpire Bill Alley warned Botham for excessive use of the bouncer, Botham expostulated, pointing out that the batsman was scoring enough boundaries and did not need any protection. He finally got his man but not before Zaheer had made a fortuitous but thrilling 140 out of 198 while at the crease. Yet Botham, in the summer after the first season of World Series Cricket, had exposed Zaheer's Achilles heel.

Lest these reservations about Zaheer's claim to greatness appear carping, the ledger is comfortably in the black when assessing the sheer grandeur of his batting, the serene way he gorged on bowlers when he had booked in for a long innings. He took pains to assess bowlers that he had not encountered before. He would watch a new bowler intently, checking if they did anything unusual to indicate what sort of delivery would follow. He would tell the Gloucestershire bowlers that he knew what sort of ball they were about to send down, because he had noticed their particular mannerisms while turning at the start of their run-up, or how they placed the ball in their hand just before delivery. David Graveney was astonished at such attention to detail: 'He was convinced he'd spot a tell-tale sign. He could tell me what I was going to bowl halfway through my run-up when he stood at slip. That sort of insight was so useful when he walked out to bat; he had a sixth sense. And don't forget that he knew all about the complexities of batting against reverse swing before it became so fashionable, because he'd played with Sarfraz and Imran for Pakistan, when it was being developed. So reverse swing didn't faze Zed.'

Graveney chuckles at the memory of a visit to Zaheer's house in Karachi. While the host attended to his various responsibilities, he invited his county colleague to watch some cricket videos. They were all of Zaheer batting, and the tape ended when he was out. 'I never knew anyone who loved batting as much as Zed, and it wasn't his ego working overtime. He was just fascinated at watching how he batted, hoping he could pick up some tip that would help him stay out there even longer.'

Anything to delay having to field. Zaheer was a safe catcher at slip, but often he would languidly patrol the outfield with a distracted air, much to the despair of the Gloucestershire bowlers. The first few weeks of a cool English summer would test his resolve, and he would often conjure up an imaginary strain to return to the comparative warmth of the dressing-room. Les Bardsley, the Gloucestershire physiotherapist, was used to all the excuses from his time working with professional footballers at Bristol City, and he would threaten Zaheer with a bucket of ice-cold water, standing at the top of the pavilion stairs, if he escaped from the field.

He once told me with feeling: 'If only I could bat all the time. You know, I hated fielding. Someone once said to me, "We've come here to see you bat and not field," as I stood at third man. I couldn't help agreeing with him!' Zaheer was always a batsman with his priorities in the right order. It was a boon for cricket lovers that he eschewed the bored attitude of a great player like Barry Richards and that he never got tired of charming runs out of tired bowling. That air of fallibility only added to the massive pleasure he gave, because there was often the prospect that his sumptuous talent might have to blossom on another day. But not on a flat pitch when the bowlers would be caressed to exhausted impotence. Chris Broad will never forget Zaheer's dominance over spinners: 'It was dreamlike to watch him dance down the pitch and flick them away. His movement was fantastic, the execution of the shots so crisp and flowing. I wonder if he would play the reverse sweep against the spinners if he was playing today. I doubt if he would have needed to, because his range of shots was so wide. No one skipped down the pitch as quickly as Zed, to hit the off-spinner between mid-on and mid-wicket.'

Zaheer is still spoken of with great reverence and affection in Gloucestershire cricket circles. Like so many overseas players of his era, he gave more than a decade of service, and club and player were good for each other. Zaheer's professional pride drove him on, and his one regret is that he didn't manage 3,000 first-class runs in a season. He fell 446 short in the 1976 summer, a remarkable effort considering the first-class programme had been curtailed several years earlier and opportunities were correspondingly limited. But he kept churning out big scores with little apparent effort, including 21 first-class centuries in just two seasons of county cricket. Porridge would keep him going while on the county grind, building up his stamina. Because his physique was slight, he had to psych himself up mentally for a long innings. He was no Viv Richards, able to stride in and unleash a fusillade of impossibly bold shots that smacked of macho certainty. Zaheer would lie on the dressing-room floor during intervals to harbour his resources. That was the preparation for his two monumental innings against Surrey at The Oval in 1976, when he scored 372 without being dismissed. Relax, then focus a couple of minutes before the bell sounded for resumption. His team-mates were astonished at his mental strength, especially as he would then proceed to make batting appear so easy.

After retiring from the game he dabbled in TV punditry and then developed property interests in Pakistan, before branching out in Dubai. With his thick, steely-grey hair, relaxed smile and air of prosperity, he looks a good deal younger than his official birth suggests – not always the case with Pakistani cricketers. He has served in a number of official administrative capacities in Pakistan cricket, including manager of the 2006 tour to England. That was a sad experience for such a confirmed Anglophile, as the Oval Test was abandoned a day early, due to the Pakistani captain refusing to accept the ruling of the umpires that the fielders had been tampering with the ball.

In the bitter aftermath, in such a febrile atmosphere, Zaheer did his best to hold the ring with his customary good manners and quiet diplomacy, but those who had known him long enough knew that he was hurting at such an acrimonious fissure. It made it even worse that the match referee involved in awarding the Test to England was Mike Procter, for so long his inspirational Gloucestershire captain. Zaheer had never been one of those cricketers to challenge the accepted behaviour of the game, and he always praised the integrity of English umpires, proclaiming them to be the best in the world. Confrontation was not part of his psyche, and the graceless impasse at The Oval hurt him.

Class and grace had always been the hallmark of Zaheer Abbas, and memories of his bewitching batsmanship will linger after more prolific and greater players have faded into sepia-tinted obscurity. Style has its own innate durability. He made you wish you could play like him.

County cricket   and elsewhere

T.W. Graveney: 50 for Gloucestershire, 27 for Worcestershire
I.V.A. Richards: 47 for Somerset, 10 for Glamorgan
M.R. Ramprakash: 46 for Middlesex, 50 for Surrey

Other than Bradman and Grace, only three batsmen have scored 70 centuries when not playing for English counties:
S.M. Gavaskar (79), G.S. Chappell (71) and S.R. Waugh (70).

Five batsmen have scored 60 centuries outside the British Isles:
D.G. Bradman (76), S.M. Gavaskar (67), R.T. Ponting (61), M.L. Hayden (60) and S.R. Tendulkar (60).

Three English batsmen have scored 30 centuries outside the British Isles:
W.R. Hammond (33), D.C.S. Compton (31) and T.W. Graveney (31).

21

Dennis Amiss

'Once he gets in, he doesn't get out'
(Alan Knott)

Dennis Leslie Amiss

Born
Harborne, Birmingham
7 April 1943

First hundred
114   Warwickshire v Oxford University, Edgbaston, 1964
Age: 21 years 86 days

100th hundred
101*   Warwickshire v Lancashire, Edgbaston, 1986
Age: 43 years 113 days

Last hundred
120   Warwickshire v Leicestershire, Hinckley, 1987
Age: 44 years 126 days

Career record

M	Inn	NO	HS	Runs	Average	100s	50s
658	1,139	126	262*	43,423	42.86	102	212

Test record

M	Inn	NO	HS	Runs	Average	100s	50s
50	88	10	262*	3,612	46.30	11	11

When the gods were handing out unspectacular qualities like guts and determination, they lingered long at the door of Dennis Leslie Amiss. If ever a man embodied the strength of character needed to score a hundred hundreds, it is the affable Amiss. This is not to decry Amiss's talent: few contemporary English players could match his ability to churn out big scores elegantly and masterfully. In a career spanning 28 seasons he ended up with 43,423 first-class runs, twelfth in the list, ahead of players such as Hutton, Cowdrey and Compton. In 23 of those seasons he topped 1,000 runs, including his final season when he was 44. Unlike Geoffrey Boycott, Amiss was always an aesthetic pleasure, the master craftsman, at home in any form of cricket – technically adept to graft through troubled waters, yet ready to hit over the top in limited-overs games. Yet Dennis Amiss would never have lasted as long in the game if he had not abundantly possessed the ability to grit his teeth and fight his way through a host of crises.

On at least five occasions in his career Dennis Amiss considered packing up the game that he loved deeply. He once had to face the wounding fact that his county did not wish to retain his services because of his association with Kerry Packer, and he never really mastered the demands of short-pitched fast bowling. At no time could Amiss ever be considered the supreme batsman in the Warwickshire side, with the likes of Rohan Kanhai and Alvin Kallicharran alongside him. He did not crave for pre-eminence at any stage; all he ever wanted was to play cricket for Warwickshire, and for more than a quarter of a century he was an object lesson in how to utilise natural ability. Dennis Amiss was one of the supreme professionals of cricket since the war, and his stature increased as the laurel wreaths were modestly accepted.

Dennis was too diffident ever to dream of a century of centuries. As a boy he set his ambitions at nothing higher than a place in the Warwickshire team. Born and bred in Birmingham, his father, Vic, was a good club cricketer and very supportive of his son's ambitions. The talent was obvious very early on, a fact confirmed by M.J.K. Smith, who was then Warwickshire's captain: 'He was always around the indoor nets at Edgbaston at the age of fourteen or so – and he looked a class above the other boys of his age. I never had any doubt that we would be taking him on the staff.' David Brown, Warwickshire's fast bowler and later the cricket manager, recalls the promise of the tyro: 'Even as a kid he looked a complete player. He used to score millions, even though he was tiny.'

Dennis was taken on the staff at Edgbaston at the age of 15, the youngest player ever to be chosen for the county. Initially he was out of his depth – a shy lad, ill at ease with the worldly elders on the staff. But now Dennis agrees that those painful early days were typical of later challenges: 'I've never been at my best in a new situation. I need to come to terms with changes. Throughout my cricket career I had to get used to reverses and come back with my teeth gritted.' Those are not chip-on-the-shoulder sentiments, more an acknowledgement of nerves from a man who is still naturally shy and modest. His achievements are the more admirable because he admitted to psychological defects. Some outstanding batsmen need to create an aura of invincibility, to let the bowler think their dismissal was simply an aberration. Not Amiss: his steely resolution did not preclude a gracious acceptance that he had been worked over by good bowling.

That mental strength was fostered early on at Edgbaston by one of the legendary figures in Warwickshire cricket, E.J. ('Tiger') Smith. Now 'Tiger' had been the quintessential old-style professional cricketer: tough, independent-minded, with exacting standards of behaviour on and off the pitch. He recognised the talent of the young Amiss and proceeded to drum home the basics: 'He always told me that you learn to bat once you're past the century mark. 'Tiger' was great on mental attitude and making the best of your resources. I remember how he had me in tears when I couldn't play the ball off my legs, but he sorted me out.' In doing so, 'Tiger' contributed to a scene that has become part of Edgbaston folklore. Despairing of Dennis's attempts to play the ball off his legs, he took his bat and proceeded to order two bowlers to bowl at him. The first delivery was played beautifully away and Dennis was impressed. 'Tiger' then ordered the two bowlers (Roley Thompson and Jack Bannister, two fast-medium bowlers) to bowl at their fastest. They did not protest that 'Tiger' had no pads on, that he was over seventy and should beware the curse of failing eyesight and slowing reactions – they knew the old boy too well. The next ball cracked him on the shin, and he went down like a sack of potatoes. Waving away the ministrations of Amiss, he got to his feet and rasped, 'It doesn't matter about hitting the ball; that's the way to play the shot.' Dennis still chuckles affectionately about 'Tiger' when he tells that story but admits that the shot which has become his trademark – the clip through midwicket – was honed and perfected under the baleful eye of that hard old taskmaster.

Despite his obvious promise things did not run too smoothly for Amiss during his apprenticeship. Those who suffered at the hands of his erratic calling will not be surprised to learn that, on his debut for the second team, he was run out without facing a ball and the same fate befell him in 1960, when he first batted for Warwickshire in a championship match. As Dennis struggled to establish himself in the harsh, unyielding world of county cricket, he developed a bit of a 'drawbridge mentality' about running between the wickets. Instinctively he would protect himself, with the result that on several occasions senior players were run out when they should have been leading the chase for batting bonus points. More than once Dennis was involved in heated arguments in the dressing-room, and the calming influence of M.J.K. Smith was vital. Smith also took the youngster's side as he grafted out in the middle, accumulating twenties and thirties when a more positive attitude was needed. The captain's view that 'He's got to learn somewhere' and Smith's standing in the side were such that grumblings among the senior players were at least muted.

Although Dennis was shedding his shyness layer by layer as the seasons slipped by, he did not feel fulfilled. He was not doing himself justice in county cricket, even though he drank in every morsel of advice that was offered and toughened up mentally. By 1965 he was a capped player at the age of 22, yet the runs were not coming in any impressive amount. The lure of the family tyre business became stronger and stronger as his batting marked time. Dennis worked for his father's firm every winter (humping around enough tyres to develop those massive forearms that aided his batting so much), and he had enough self-respect to get out of first-class cricket if he felt he could go no further. Then came a surprising development: he was picked for England. Today it seems astonishing that a young man of little statistical prowess should be picked to bat against Hall, Griffith, Sobers and Gibbs when the likes of Cowdrey, Barrington, Mike Smith, Eric Russell and Jim Parks had been found wanting. Moreover, Amiss had never scored a championship hundred and his tally of first-class wickets (five) outnumbered his first-class hundreds (three). He was in illustrious company, though; neither Colin Cowdrey nor Ted Dexter had scored a championship century before playing for England. When former Test players decry modern batsmen from the comfort of the commentary box, they might care to ponder the case of Dennis Amiss in 1966. Predictably the occasion was too much for Dennis – he was lbw to Wes Hall for 17 after batting 43 minutes and, with England winning by an innings, a second chance to impress had gone.

At least the selectors kept faith with him for a time. He was sent to Pakistan in the winter of 1966 with the England Under-25 side, averaging 61 and returning with a growing self-belief. Five hundreds and 1,850 runs in 1967 indicated his quality, but he could never get started whenever the call came from England. A total of 108 in five innings against India and Pakistan in the summer of 1967 suggested he was out of his depth. He was. 'I was just like Mike Gatting in later years,' he recalls. 'I chose all sorts of daft ways to get out, and underneath I felt completely overawed with all these famous players in the side. I didn't feel I belonged at all.' When Ken Barrington came down the wicket for a chat in the final Test against Pakistan, that was the first time Amiss had ever received any help from an England colleague. Worse was to follow in 1968: the dreaded 'pair' in the Old Trafford Test against Australia. He was close to tears as he walked back up the pavilion steps past unsympathetic members. 'My frame of mind contributed to my downfall. I just couldn't come to terms with the special pressures of Test cricket.' At the age of 25 it seemed that the tag 'former England player' would soon be used by the Fleet Street scribes.

He went back to county cricket to re-learn his trade, experimenting with his technique, steeling himself to churn out the big hundreds that would make the selectors notice him again. In 1971 he played in four Tests against Pakistan and India, with little success. At the 13th time of asking he finally passed fifty in Tests, but there was no tangible evidence that Amiss had worked out how to play the game at the highest level. Every generation sees a talented batsman who dominates county cricket but cannot go up a vital gear in Tests. Amiss seemed the latest contender for that stereotype.

In 1972 his cup of misery overflowed. He was dropped from the Warwickshire side. At that time the team oozed batting class. John Jameson, that punishing striker of the ball, opened the batting with John Whitehouse, elected Young Cricketer of the Year in 1971. The great Rohan Kanhai was first wicket down, followed by Alvin Kallicharran, the latest West Indian sensation: at number five, Mike Smith, later to play for England again in 1972. The winter signing of Kallicharran meant there was no room for Amiss in the top five and the capture of Derryck Murray as wicket-keeper also stiffened the middle order. This would allow Warwickshire to select five bowlers and strengthen their push for the championship, which had faltered by just one point the previous year. Amiss could not be fitted in and Alan Smith, the captain that year, remembers the dilemma. 'Mike Smith, Rohan Kanhai and I sat in my car at Northampton, debating who to drop for an important Benson and Hedges match. As the windows steamed up, it was clear it could only be Amiss. We needed the extra bowler.' Amiss was hurt and worried. He was now in his 30th year, with a wife and young daughter to support. Nine caps for England meant nothing when languishing in the second eleven. A prolonged spell of second eleven cricket would ruin him. A move to another county seemed the only solution. Then the gods smiled on him and frowned on John Whitehouse; the man in possession completely lost his touch, and Amiss realised he could get back in the side if he volunteered to open. 'I had always thought of myself as a number four but, if it meant I could play for the first team again, I was happy to open. With so much limited-overs cricket around, there was always a good chance for the openers to get among the runs. I thought my technique would be good enough against the moving ball, and I would battle through against the bouncers.' Warwickshire agreed to give it a trial: in his first innings as opener, Amiss scored 151 not out and Middlesex were beaten by ten wickets. Amiss stayed as opener for the rest of the season and made five hundreds, with an average of 55. Warwickshire won the county championship and a superb opening pair came together. John Jameson was the belligerent cavalier, Amiss the majestic strokemaker with the patience to play second fiddle whenever the Muse of inspiration was upon Jameson. They were marvellous value for the next four seasons, and today Jameson says, 'We just gelled together, as simple as that. Our basic differences as batsmen meant the bowlers always had to alter their line. As for running between the wickets, we tried to deal in boundaries and avoid too much anguish. We had known each other for years, so that there were no problems in getting used to each other as blokes.'

Amiss's new lease of life was noticed by the England selectors, and they picked him for the Prudential one-day series against Australia at the end of the summer. A hundred at Old Trafford – partly exorcising the spectre of the 'pair' in 1968 – saw him selected for the England tour of India and Pakistan that winter. Tony Lewis, the captain, had no qualms about selecting Amiss, despite the vicissitudes of his career. 'I always thought he was a high-class player,' says Lewis. 'He got in ahead of me at The Oval in 1966, but I knew he was a better batsman than me and I could accept that. It's amusing to recall that Brian Close picked him ahead of me because he thought Dennis to be the better fielder! It wasn't exactly a clash of the giants in that department.' Certainly Dennis was never a fleet-footed athlete in the field (a slipped disc in his early days at Edgbaston restricted his mobility), but he set his stall out to score heavily on the 1972/73 tour. Yet again he had to show his determination after a nightmare series in India. He averaged just fifteen against their great spinners, and Tony Lewis had to drop him. 'Poor chap, he was in a dreadful state against Bedi, Chandra and co. I should have shown more courage and stuck with him, but I found myself wondering if I had only seen him play well at Edgbaston on flat wickets.' Characteristically Amiss practised his way back into the groove. At the deserted Brabourne Stadium in Bombay he took a net against Bishen Bedi, Venkat and Abid Ali and asked them to simulate match conditions and to appeal every time they thought they had him. To the eternal credit of the Indian bowlers they did just that, and Amiss learned how to combat the turning ball. When he returned four years later to India, he showed his gratitude by averaging 52 in the series!

When the Pakistan leg of the tour started, Amiss was far happier. On the flat wickets, he scored two hundreds and a 99 in three Tests. 'At long last I felt I had arrived. I'd come through the torments and honestly believed I could bat at Test level.' He was almost 30 before he scored his first Test hundred, but he was right: he was now an England player and the next eighteen months were golden ones for him. Back home in 1973 he showed his soaring self-confidence by running out one Geoffrey Boycott. It came in the Trent Bridge Test against New Zealand, when Amiss sent back Boycott after a mix-up over a second run. Boycott hurled a few expletives in Amiss's direction and stalked back to the pavilion. Amiss made 138 not out and Boycott did not speak to him for the rest of the game. When the sides reassembled for the next Test, the England opening batsmen were still ignoring each other and it took the good offices of the England captain, Ray Illingworth, to heal the rift. Boycott had met his match in the self-preservation stakes, and they settled down to a rewarding year as England openers.

They were among the few successes on England's tour to the West Indies in 1973/74, a series that England somehow managed to square, even though outplayed for much of the time. With three hundreds in the series, Amiss was outstanding. At Sabina Park he played the innings that all his England contemporaries refer to within five minutes of his name being mentioned. England had to bat the best part of two days in draining heat and humidity to avoid defeat – it was as simple, or as daunting, as that. Dennis Amiss managed to do just that, batting 9½ hours for 262 not out. He was just the man for the situation; by this time, he loved the tensions associated with Test cricket, and his confidence enabled him to take on the West Indies on equal terms. Yet he might not have lasted so long if his running between the wickets had been sounder. By the end of the penultimate day, England were 258 for six, just 28 runs ahead. Amiss was unbeaten with a hundred, but he had also run out Frank Hayes and Alan Knott. 'I was at fault each time, and I dreaded the reception from the dressing-room when I got back. I realised it was now my responsibility to stay there the next day.' Alan Knott, his room-mate, woke him up the next morning with, 'Come on, you've got to bat all day!' and he did not let him down. John Jameson recalls, 'He came in at tea-time with his eyes sunken in his cheeks, looking totally drained. We poured a brandy down his throat, pointed to the middle and pushed him out there again. Even in that state he was keen to keep batting.' The Test was saved, and back home in Birmingham, the *Evening Mail* reflected the current general election fever with pardonable parochial pride with the headline, 'Amiss for Prime Minister!'

By the time Dennis arrived in Australia later that year, he was acknowledged to be one of the world's best batsmen. He was to finish just short of the record for Test runs in a calendar year and, in the absence of Boycott, the Amiss scalp was the prized one for the Australians. Every one of the English batsmen was scarred by subsequent events, as they ran into Lillee and Thomson bowling frighteningly fast on green, under-prepared pitches. The series was lost 4-1, and Amiss found it a traumatic experience. He was stunned to receive a volley of loud-mouthed abuse from Lillee after steering him through the slips and admits that Lillee established a psychological stranglehold over him. 'All the sledging would not have bothered me if I had been playing well, but I wasn't. I kept worrying about my technique – why was he getting me out? It all got to me and I was totally unbalanced.' Lillee dismissed him three times in a row for nought – including two in the first over at Adelaide – and Amiss's decline was pathetic to watch. 'I got to the situation where I walked out to the middle, knowing it was virtually a waste of time carrying a bat. The physical and verbal intimidation wore me down.' Later Dennis came to appreciate that he was undone by fast bowling of the highest class. Lillee subsequently paid tribute to Amiss, saying that he was a good enough player to get a touch to some devastating deliveries, and the wicket-keeper Rodney Marsh said: 'We never gave him a chance; everything he touched we caught.' Alan Knott was on that tour and remembers how Amiss was scarred. 'He shouldn't have let it get to him, because he was our best player and the Aussies bowled wonderfully well at him.' Reasonably Knott points out that great players like Denis Compton (Australia 1950/51) and Peter May (South Africa 1956/57) had nightmare series but came back impressively – whereas Amiss was written off far too soon after such a frightening experience. Derek Underwood agrees: 'He just seemed to play a little half-cock – neither back nor forward – and the late movement and bounce did for him. But it was only a phase; he would have come through it. Dennis always did, you know.'

The Australians still had the upper hand on Amiss in 1975, when they toured England: a total of 19 runs in four innings meant it was kinder to send him back to county cricket for a rehabilitatory spell. He was beginning to look more and more uneasy against the short-pitched ball and, when Michael Holding hit him on the head in May 1976, it looked as if he would have to bow out of a game that was becoming increasingly harder. 'Today it isn't unusual to see someone hit on the head because we all wear helmets, but in 1976 it was very embarrassing. What made it worse was that I had turned my head away from the delivery, and it hit me on the back of the head. I've still got a lump today to remind me of my lowest ebb.' There was no question of Amiss's suitability to combat the pace of the West Indians; even in county cricket he looked terrible. David Brown, Warwickshire's captain at that time, says, 'He was bobbing and weaving against medium-pacers like Ken Higgs. He couldn't stand still and fight it out by orthodox means. His nerve had gone.' Amiss acknowledges that, if he had not survived that awful period, he would have retired that season at the age of 33. Always the theorist, he worked out a two-eyed stance to enable him to combat the pace bowlers by keeping his eyes on the ball. He tried the new stance against Sussex and heard Tony Greig shout to his fast bowler, John Snow: 'Okay, Snowy, let him have it!' Amiss withstood the bouncers and got a brave 87. Greig, by now the captain of England, was impressed and decided he wanted Amiss back in the England team. He rang Jill, Dennis's wife, and asked about his frame of mind. Could he fight it out again with the quicks aiming for the upper parts of his body, not the stumps? The pace barrage that summer had even worn down the likes of John Edrich and Brian Close. When Amiss was contacted, he said he could do it: the new stance gave him time to get onto the back foot and watch the ball. He wanted to play.

If Sabina Park showed Amiss's superb concentration, then The Oval 1976 demonstrated the man's guts. He knew he looked very odd as he moved onto the back foot from an exaggerated two-eyed stance. He knew that, in moving across his wicket, he was leaving his leg stump exposed. He admits he was very lucky early on, as Andy Roberts beat him with some superb out-swingers. Yet he stuck it out and scored 203 of the bravest runs imaginable, as England was swept away by some remarkable bowling from Michael Holding. 'I never thought I'd get out, once I got through that tricky early stage. From a professional point of view I was delighted to make such a good comeback, and it restored some of my confidence against the quicks. But I wished I'd scored that double hundred by playing properly, using my normal technique.' There speaks a craftsman.

With his Test career re-established, Dennis then took the decision that effectively ended it at the age of 34. He signed for Kerry Packer's World Series Cricket in the summer of 1977, a brand of cricket that set itself on an inevitable collision course with the established version. Dennis's involvement was a more rational one than the early crop of signatories: he had an extra month in which he watched the ferment raging in the game and heard about all the grim penalties facing the Packer players. Finally he signed during the one-day international series against the Australians. 'It was my own decision. When I came home and told Jill, she said, "Are you sure about this?" She was more cautious than me about it, but I was a little disillusioned. I felt we deserved better rewards for the incredible pressures of Test cricket. There was a lot of talk about Boycott coming back for England and I thought, "He's after my place." Apart from all that, there was my ego. When I first looked at the list, I thought, "Why haven't they asked me, aren't I good enough?" I wanted to be considered among the elite. And I was also attracted by the promise that the wives of Packer players could come on the tour with them.'

That decision plunged Dennis into the unhappiest period of his life. It lasted two years, and the divisions at Edgbaston hurt him deeply. He was an acknowledged supporter of the Establishment line at Lord's. He always understood that his England career would be in abeyance during the Packer period but could not see why Warwickshire felt they could dispense with his services. That was the decision reached by the club in 1978: he would not be retained because of his involvement with World Series Cricket. This despite Amiss's continuing prowess with the bat – he was the only man to score 2,000 first-class runs that summer. The Warwickshire dressing-room was not a harmonious place in 1978: for good or ill, the rest of the players were toeing the traditionalist line that Packer was harming Test and county cricket, while Amiss had given up trying to change their minds. On my visits to the dressing-room that summer, a sad sight would greet me – Amiss on his own, writing letters on World Series notepaper while the rest of the team watched the game at the far end of the viewing area. The previous summer the captain, David Brown, had taken the unprecedented step of moving Alvin Kallicharran into his home in the Worcestershire countryside to get away from the threat of Packer. Kallicharran had originally signed for Packer, then changed his mind, much to Warwickshire's relief. One day Packer rang the Warwickshire dressing-room at Chesterfield and asked to speak to Dennis Amiss. He told Amiss that he wanted to talk to Kallicharran, and Amiss conveyed that message. The rest of the players construed that as harassment by Amiss on behalf of Parker, and that led to the ridiculous sight of the little West Indian being escorted by hulking Warwickshire fast bowlers whenever he stepped out of the dressing-room. Amiss says, 'It was ridiculous to suggest that I was hassling Kalli. All I ever did was pass on the message from Kerry Packer. The whole thing was blown hopelessly out of context, and I kept out of everyone's way after that.'

Yet the mythology of Chesterfield lingered on, and the following summer the Warwickshire players stated in August that they felt Amiss should go in the wider interests of the game. The club then announced that Amiss was playing his last season. For a time affairs at Edgbaston resembled Yorkshire during one of its periodic bouts of blood-letting. There were calls for a special general meeting and assurances from the club that the decision was in the best interests of English cricket. Meanwhile Dennis Amiss soldiered on at the wicket: 'I realised the best thing to do was stay out there as long as possible, to get away from all the squabbling. It was coming all the way down from Lord's to the players, and I was very hurt at their attitude.'

Today David Brown admits he and the players over-reacted. 'I was also chairman of the Cricketers' Association at that time, and that body felt it was vital to preserve Test cricket because that is where a good proportion of the average county players get their wages from. Dennis was also very stubborn – I remember a big shouting match at his house. It was a very sad time.' Luckily the Cricketers' Association played a crucial part in the discussions that enabled Amiss to return to Warwickshire in 1979. The Association Executive talked to Lynton Taylor of World Series Cricket, who confirmed that Packer would be disposed to settle his dispute with the International Cricket Conference if Amiss was offered a new contract. In the eyes of Packer, Amiss has been the only player victimised by his county club, and he had always promised to protect his players. At the same time Warwickshire had learned that an accommodation was imminent between WSC and ICC and, when the tape of Taylor's phone conversation was played to some Edgbaston officials, it was clear that a rapprochement between club and player was possible. Over Easter Amiss announced he would accept a new contract, and he paid tribute to the Association's role in the peace formula – but it was a very close run thing. 'I just wasn't sure the slate could be wiped clean after all the trouble of the previous two years. I was on the point of packing it all in. I only wanted to play for Warwickshire. I even took up golf as a substitute in case I wasn't going to play cricket any more.'

Many of Dennis's friends in the game were convinced that his Packer involvement thwarted his chances of an England return once everybody was available for selection again in 1979. Certainly England caps have gone to inferior players, and his fielding no doubt told against him. Alan Knott says, 'Around the county circuit the pros all say that Dennis should have played a hundred Tests.' Mike Smith, hardly a Packer disciple, agrees: 'I've no idea why he didn't play after Packer's peace; he was in a class above several other selections.' Keith Fletcher fought hard for Dennis's inclusion on the 1981/82 tour to India that he captained – he was outvoted because the average age of the tour party would have risen. Derek Underwood went on that tour and says, 'Dennis would have made a stack of runs out there and in good time as well. He was as much in his pomp around that time as anyone.' Bob Willis would certainly have asked for Amiss if he had been England captain before 1982, by which time he had been banned again from Test cricket. The South African Breweries tour was an obvious attraction to Amiss, even though he knew a Test ban would follow. 'I hadn't been picked since 1977 for various reasons, and I had nothing to lose. It was a much simpler equation than signing for Packer.'

So Dennis Amiss didn't appear again on a Test pitch after the day in July 1977 when he cracked a ball from Kerry O'Keeffe to the offside boundary to earn England a nine-wicket victory at Old Trafford. As he anticipated, Geoffrey Boycott deigned to return to the fray at Trent Bridge and out went Amiss. An average of 46 underlines his class at Test level, despite those dreadful early forays. His biggest regret is his record against Australia – an average of 15 in eleven Tests, compared with one of 70 in ten Tests against the West Indians. 'Great players don't have the kind of problems I had against the Aussies,' he says – and it is hard to disagree. He was unlucky to come up against Lillee, Thomson and Walker in their prime, on wickets that did not suit an essentially front-foot player like Amiss. He did not favour the hook or the pull shots, and his cut was more of a dab than an authentic rasping shot. The glory of his offside play was never likely to flourish against fast bowlers intent on intimidation on unreliable pitches. Yet the Australians rated him highly; they thought he should have been spared the new ball and batted at number three or four. Alan Knott agrees: 'There was always the chance that Dennis would be done by a great delivery with the new ball, and he was too good a player to sacrifice early on. When the score was 200 for two and Dennis walked in, you thought, "Oh dear, we're in for some hard work."' As Derek Underwood puts it, 'He was the gaffer when he got in. He just loved to churn out the big scores. He was the greatest thinker and theorist on the game I've known. And no Englishman today played me better on a wicket that was helping me.' The match at Gravesend in 1970 convinced Underwood of Amiss's talent on a bad wicket. He took 14 wickets in the match, and Amiss made a superb 91 until Underwood stuck out a hand to an Amiss drive and was astonished to see the ball lodge there! 'Dennis played so late that he didn't commit himself on bad wickets,' says Underwood. 'He was a wonderful leaver of the ball, with enormous concentration. Those big forearms were handy when he wanted to ping you away if you over-pitched slightly. If there was a bloke I'd have picked to bat for my life, it was Dennis.' Alan Smith, former captain of Warwickshire and at one time a Test selector, points out that Amiss's manipulation of the bat was very deft for such a powerful man. 'He's the best I saw for adjusting his hands with smallish movements to combat the turning ball. He was a model for any young batsman.' A personal memory backs up those tributes. In the hot summer of 1983 Amiss gave a masterclass in bad-wicket batting at Edgbaston, against Middlesex, who possessed the most talented array of bowlers in the country. The pitch was too dry, breaking up on the first afternoon under the hot sun, and bowlers of all types were slavering to get at the batsmen. Against Daniel, Cowans, Williams, Emburey and Edmonds – all international bowlers – Amiss was top scorer in each innings with 25 and 57. Middlesex mustered 78 and 74 to lose heavily, and the next highest score in the game came from extras (38) in Warwickshire's second innings. Amiss's half-century, particularly against the spin of Emburey and Edmonds, was simply masterful. Even Mike Gatting, a notable player of spinners, struggled in that match.

Dennis admits he was very lucky to play at Edgbaston: 'When you're in a bad trot, it's not a bad place to come back to and sort out what's wrong.' He agrees that his constant fiddling around with his technique drove his team-mates to despair over the years, 'especially as I always came back to the original format after the experiments. But it motivated me to fiddle around; it kept me interested in the game. Apart from batting, I was a pretty ordinary cricketer. It was the one thing I did well, so I kept telling myself to get more than nought, then the target was fifty and after that, a hundred.' Significantly eight of his eleven Test hundreds were 150 and more: Amiss was always a big innings man. His technique was so sound that he could score very fast in limited-overs matches, without slogging. Unlike many modern batsmen he did not try to play 'inside out'; he adopted his normal, sound method and played 'through the V', with a penchant for skimming sixes. The years spent lugging around tyres in the sixties helped him dominate by sheer power when slow pitches frustrated the 'touch' players. Many players of Dennis's experience do not like the limited-over games – all that dashing around, those frantic finishes – but he loved it. 'There's nothing better than hitting it over the top and nudging quick singles to disconcert the bowler.' His team-mates would say that his calling for singles disconcerted everyone in his own dressing-room, and the grapevine was full of Amiss stories. When he ran out Gordon Lord for 199 against Yorkshire in 1985, it seemed he had lost none of his touch. 'It was my fault, I know. I called him for a quick single behind square leg, and he was run out at the bowler's end. Gordon hesitated when I called, and I admit it was a sharp run. The trouble was, I could see a single, but I wasn't always sure about my partners.' It is a tribute to Dennis's genial nature that none of his colleagues ever believed he ran people out deliberately. His popularity survived sterner tests than that.

I first alerted Dennis to the possibility of a century of centuries around 1980. At that stage he had made about 75 hundreds, and he said there wasn't a hope of it. I could tell, however, that he was intrigued by the prospect, and by 1983 he had changed his attitude to 'Perhaps if they let me bat with a runner all the time!' By 1984 he was sufficiently committed to be annoyed at a baffling sequence of innings that ended in the eighties rather than past the century mark. A testimonial season in 1985 gave him further incentive to keep going – a considerable feat for a man in his forties, in a sport where athleticism had become more important – and he approached the 1986 season with a degree of self-denial that astonished his friends and team-mates. Dennis had always liked a sociable drink and an enjoyable meal, yet with the new season more than a month away he was to be found sipping Perrier water – and contemplating where he could find another four centuries.

Dennis's professionalism was soon rewarded when he made his 97th century at the end of April against Essex. By mid-June he had added two more, both splendid efforts, against Gloucestershire and Glamorgan. He was playing so fluently that another century seemed imminent: yet he had to wait a further six weeks and 15 innings. The runs had not dried up – he made three 50s and averaged 31 between the 99th and 100th hundred – yet he was starting to fret as the weeks slipped away. Mark Ramprakash, 22 years later, could relate to that feeling of time slipping through his fingers.

Finally, on July 29th, in front of his home crowd, Dennis got there. He had Clive Lloyd to thank. The match against Lancashire was drifting to a draw when Amiss (not out 64) asked the opposition captain to stay out in the middle a while longer. Dennis promised that he would slog the runs and – the clincher – that copious bottles of champagne were available if the deed were done. In the next five overs he made 37. John Abrahams, plying his occasional off-spin, told him when he reached 99, 'short outside the off-stump and it's yours', and a delicate dab backward of point brought him two precious runs.

A year later Amiss had to give best at last to the creaking limbs and call it a day in first-class cricket. There were only so many times he could hide away in the slips or third man, watching those cheeky young pups run two to him, including one for the throw. If it had just been a case of batting, he'd have carried on for a few more years. But he wasn't done with the club that had meant so much to him. Within a few years of retiring as a player, he was back as Warwickshire's Chief Executive, presiding over the most successful period in the club's history. Eight trophies were garnered on Dennis's watch and he would be the first to admit that, compared with previous administrative heads at Edgbaston, he was lucky enough to inherit a first-class staff. Dennis's office was strategically placed to enable him to watch the action out in the middle, allowing him to rhapsodise about the glory of Brian Lara's batting. It's a measure of Amiss's essential humility that he would wax so lyrical about the genius of Lara. To hear him speak so fulsomely about Lara you would think the Chief Executive had been just a jobbing cricketer, instead of Warwickshire's greatest ever scorer of runs and centuries.

He may have finished full-time at Edgbaston in 2006, but Dennis is still part of the furniture there, as substantial an institution as his old mentor, 'Tiger' Smith. He'll always stop for a natter with anyone, practising his golf swing while chattering animatedly about his latest batting fad. Still crazy about both games, enjoying a love affair with the Edgbaston ground that began sixty years ago. It seems astonishing that the painful events of 1978 made him contemplate leaving a club that has meant so much to him, and he is pleased that younger Warwickshire supporters only recall the brilliance of Allan Donald and Brian Lara rather than the blood-letting of that sad, rainy summer.

Ask him about becoming the 21st to make a century of centuries and he'll try to change the subject, talking about Lara's amazing hand-eye co-ordination or Donald's athletic run-up. But, if you persist, he'll say it was many moons ago and then go on to praise the batsmanship of Rohan Kanhai on bad wickets. Eventually, though, if you pin him down, he'll say with characteristic modesty: 'There are many great players in that list, and I'm pleased to know I'm in the supporting cast.' It sums up the man. Dennis Amiss has always loved the game too much to over-estimate his own importance.

Most double hundreds

D.G. Bradman	37
W.R. Hammond	36
E.H. Hendren	22
H. Sutcliffe	17
C.B. Fry	16
G.A. Hick	16
J.B. Hobbs	16
C.G. Greenidge	14
M.R. Ramprakash	14
K.S. Ranjitsinhji	14
G.A. Gooch	13
W.G. Grace	13
B.C. Lara	13
C.P. Mead	13
W.H. Ponsford	13
J.T. Tyldesley	13

22

Sir Viv Richards

'When you bowled at Viv, you really needed to wear a helmet'
(Clive Lloyd)

Isaac Vivian Alexander Richards

Born

St John's, Antigua

7 March 1952

First hundred

102   Somerset v Gloucestershire, Bristol, 1974
Age: 22 years 79 days

100th hundred

101   West Indians v New South Wales, Sydney, 1988
Age: 36 years 251 days

Last hundred

224*   Glamorgan v Middlesex, Cardiff, 1993
Age: 41 years 117 days

Career record

M	Inn	NO	HS	Runs	Average	100s	50s
507	796	63	322	36,212	49.40	114	162

Test record

M	Inn	NO	HS	Runs	Average	100s	50s
121	182	12	291	8,540	50.23	24	45

It was the walk that defined the man. It was partly a saunter, partly a swagger. It heralded the arrival of a great batsman onto the stage.

Viv Richards would ensure the returning team-mate had left the field of play before announcing himself. He wanted to impose himself on the bowlers at his own languorous tempo. Always wearing a cap – he held out against a helmet right till his final season, in his 41st year – checking the light, examining his bat, flexing those massive shoulders. He knew that the bowlers would be wondering about his mood; if Viv Richards was in the groove, there was little they could do about it. They would just be page boys at another coronation of King Viv.

In living memory, only the languid sailor's roll of Garry Sobers could rival the menacing entrance of Viv Richards for sheer distinctiveness. As his former captain at Glamorgan, Hugh Morris, said, 'Was there ever a better swagger than Viv's?'

Surely that stately, measured arrival exceeded the maximum of two minutes, as demanded by the laws of the game? Why did no one ever have the gall to appeal for Richards to be 'timed out'? The spectators would have mobbed the relevant dressing-room, the umpires passed the buck to some official at Lord's – and Richards would have filed the moment away. He never forgot any slights, real or imaginary. When he had a cause to support, he was an even more majestic and daunting batsman. His main opponent in his prime was ennui or a lack of motivation. Richards was so brilliant that he transcended the conventional element of competitiveness between batsman and bowlers.

Gladstone Small, that fine England fast bowler, summed up the dominance of Richards graphically: 'If it was Viv's day, you had no chance.' In 1985 Richards scored 322 inside a day's play for Somerset against Warwickshire at Taunton, and Small maintains he bowled the best over of his career when Richards was nearing his double hundred. 'I bowled a maiden at him and Viv said, "You're bowling well, Smally." I was floating on air. Mind you, I then sent down the perfect middle-and-leg yorker that would have got anybody else out. Before I'd finished my follow-through, the ball was pinging off the boundary boards at mid-wicket.'

Geoffrey Boycott remains one of the most trenchant judges of a batsman, someone who rations his praise, recoiling from hyperbole like Dracula from the sight of a clove of garlic. Yet he calls Richards 'an astounding batsman' and cannot separate him from Sobers as the greatest batsman he has seen. When I asked three England contemporaries who had suffered at the hands of Richards over many series, the first sentences uttered by Mike Gatting, Derek Underwood and John Emburey all contained the same adjective – 'destructive'.

Geoff Miller, England off-spinner and now chairman of selectors, has this pithy assessment of Richards: 'Get it wrong against him, and you'd disappear. Get it right, and you'd still disappear.'

Many bowlers were overwhelmed by the sheer physical presence of Richards. He epitomised the ferocious nature of cricket in the seventies and eighties, a period when many of the traditional courtesies of the game disappeared for ever and fast bowling became more unrelenting, intimidatory and plentiful. It was remarkable that Richards spurned the use of a helmet throughout those years, when the psychological mettle of international batsmen was tested as never before in cricket's history.

He admits he would not have felt comfortable wearing a helmet. 'I was lucky, I had wonderful eyesight. My eyes were like mini-binoculars, I could pick up anyone in the crowd and see the ball that split second quicker.' Yet it was not just his natural physical assets that helped Richards prosper as the most charismatic and punishing of batsmen. He simply would not back down against a challenge. When Australia's fast bowler Rodney Hogg hit him on the head in the 1980 Melbourne Test, he hooked him for six next ball. His sporting hero was Joe Frazier, the world heavyweight boxing champion, nicknamed 'Smokin' Joe' for the way he exuded aggression, and there was something of that threat in Viv Richards. He was beautifully built – 5ft 10ins tall, the ideal height for a batsman to play off front and back foot. His wide, powerful shoulders helped him launch the ball out of the ground, his footwork was nimble, reflexes phenomenal and his remarkable eyesight allowed him to glide around the crease, never appearing to be out of position. Somehow he looked bigger at the crease, as John Emburey confirms: 'He looked wider and taller, so much so you thought you'd never get the ball past him. His bat certainly looked massive as well. But it was the physical presence of Viv that marked him out.'

His pyrotechnics should never overshadow the technical purity of his batting. The forward defensive stroke that he often played when bored or just coasting along was impeccable. A book I compiled with Viv Richards about the art of batting in 1987 is open as I write, and the photographic evidence of his mastery of the basics of batting is overwhelming. Viv Richards was in charge of all the technical fundamentals; you do not score a hundred first-class centuries unless you can defend.

Of the 25 batsmen who have reached that target, Richards is the only one to have done it by hitting a six – planting Greg Matthews over long-on at the Sydney Cricket Ground against New South Wales in November 1988. Never interested in statistical achievements for their own sake, he is proud to be the only West Indian on the list of 25, but he knows that that is because he played more than a decade of county cricket. He modestly acknowledges the many wonderful Caribbean batsmen and simply states that he represents them in the Hundred Hundreds Club.

Yet did any other West Indian batsman quicken the pulse in the manner of Viv Richards? Brian Lara, Gordon Greenidge, Everton Weekes, Clyde Walcott, Garry Sobers, Rohan Kanhai and Clive Lloyd could destroy any bowling attack while George Headley and Lawrence Rowe were technically masterful.

Indeed that shrewd judge Michael Holding nominates Rowe as the soundest West Indian batsman of his time. 'But Viv was the greatest. He had a great batting brain, he was the best hooker and puller I've seen and a big occasion batsman. Viv wasn't bothered about records, he was an unselfish team man who wanted to make it count when it was really needed.'

His record in big matches at Lord's bears that out. Richards imposed his will on matches there. 'When I was batting at Lord's, I wanted to make sure that no one else was going to come in. It was my stage.' He played in eight one-day finals there for Somerset and West Indies and only failed once with the bat. On that occasion he played a vital part in West Indies winning the 1975 World Cup by running out three Australians in dazzling, athletic manner. In the 1979 Gillette Cup final Somerset, bidding for the first trophy in its history, needed a key contribution from Richards. He obliged with a century and Somerset triumphed. That same year, in the World Cup final against England, he pulled his side round from the depths of 99 for four with 138 not out, in an innings of astonishing improvisation and cold-eyed certainty. They could not bowl at him by the end, and he secured the trophy.

He blitzed England again in 1984, at Old Trafford, in one of the greatest innings in a one-day international. West Indies were 166 for nine on a good pitch when Richards was joined by the last man, Michael Holding. Fifteen overs later, the innings ended at 272 for nine, with Holding twelve not out and Richards unbeaten on 189 off 170 balls. Time and again he would chassé down the pitch and hit Bob Willis, Neil Foster and Derek Pringle out of the ground, over long-off. It was the cleanest hitting imaginable, an assault rarely experienced by bowlers of that calibre at that time. It was Twenty20 batting, two decades earlier. No slogging, just effortless mastery. Geoff Miller, one of the bowlers that day, recalls: 'It was a typical Viv innings. His side needed him to bat through, and he did. If he'd got out, we would've won.' Holding remembers how thrilled Richards was at the end of the innings, when they walked off the field: 'He had hit them where he wanted, and I just made sure I ran when he called near the end of each over. I was careful not to back up too far, because the ball was coming back at me, very hard!' Colin Cowdrey, covering that match for the *Cricketer* magazine, was dazzled. 'This was true mastery,' he wrote. 'Yet, with it all, he conducted himself with a charm and gaiety that put me in mind of Denis Compton in his heyday.'

When Richards was going well, there was always one ominous sign for the bowlers. He would tap the top of the handle on his bat, making as loud a sound as possible. 'I'd do that when the rubber on the handle was getting a little loose, but it also sent out a great message. I wasn't trying to disrespect anyone on the field, it was just a case of me sending out a signal that I was feeling confident and positive. It was all about confidence for me; it was great to feel fit in mind and body. I knew I'd been blessed with a God-given natural talent, and I would back myself. My pride was a very important factor in my career.'

His father's unyielding yet tough support also shaped a combative nature that sometimes sat uncomfortably with his undoubted genius. Richards received little formal coaching as he grew up in Antigua, an island of around 75,000 souls, but his father inculcated the desire to capitalise on his prodigious talent. 'He was the biggest influence on my career. He'd been a very talented sportsman and was a very hard taskmaster with me. If I scored a double hundred, he'd ask why I didn't make it a triple. He had a solid wisdom and instilled in me the need to make it all count when necessary.'

At times that drive brought Richards into conflict with officialdom. Early in his first-class career, he refused to leave the crease when given out while batting for Antigua. Many spectators invaded the pitch, the match was held up for two hours and eventually Richards was suspended for two years from inter-island cricket. More than thirty years later, it would appear a swingeing, draconian sentence, but Richards has no complaints. 'I was wrong. If you do the crime, you expect to do the time. I was headstrong and confrontational, and that suspension made me think about cricket's disciplines and what I wanted to achieve.' It would not be the last time that he appeared to march to a different drumbeat, but genius is rarely contained within a cloak of plodding conformity.

His penance served, Richards gave notice of his stunning precocity with two delightful cameos for the Leeward Islands against the touring England players in 1974. There was no doubt about his gifts – *Wisden* remarked on the 'immense gusto' of his batting against the MCC – but he needed to build on a good start. The West Indies captain, Clive Lloyd, was impressed but told him, 'Nobody remembers a quick forty.' Lloyd felt that all that was missing was the need to concentrate: 'He was earmarked for greatness, it was just a matter of reining him in. Eventually, his forte was weighing up the match situation while at the crease. Adjusting to situations consistently is the hallmark of a great player.'

By the end of 1974, Richards was learning how to be a great batsman, eyeing up the building blocks, assessing how to build the necessary foundations. He was signed by Somerset, gained vital practical experience in batting on so many different wickets, then – to his touching pleasure and astonishment – was chosen for the West Indies' tour to India. It was a toss-up for the final place between Richards and Gordon Greenidge for the First Test and, after failing twice in Bangalore, Richards feared the worst. But Clive Lloyd backed him. In his second Test, he made 192 not out in just five hours against top-class spin bowling, and Lloyd – with 71 – gave him invaluable support. For a 22-year-old to handle spinners such as Bedi, Prasanna and Venkat with such aplomb, on unfamiliar surfaces, marked Richards out as a special talent.

That much was obvious in his first season with Somerset. Seasoned observers and old sweats on the staff soon realised they were watching the development of a remarkable batsman. He was, of course, rash at times – what young batsman with so many shots in his locker, brought up on excellent Antiguan pitches, would not be? – but one particular shot became his speciality. It remains a source of wonder.

Richards had worked out that playing the textbook on-drive would bring him little joy, because it would just sting the hands of mid-on and flatter the bowler. So he decided to wait that split second longer, turning the wrists to send the ball squarer. He would plant the front foot down the pitch and swing across his front pad, sending the ball through the mid-wicket area like a tracer bullet. Strong wrists, wonderful eyesight, a still head and immense chutzpah were essential ingredients in the package, and it became the trademark shot of Viv Richards.

Many frustrated bowlers down the years averred that Richards would often get away with strong lbw appeals on the rare occasions when he missed the ball, going for that murderous flick shot. Mike Gatting, no stranger himself to the pulverising on-drive, disagrees: 'He was clever enough to get outside the line, playing a shot, so he'd often get away with the lbw shout. Viv's hand-eye co-ordination was so amazing that he would get on the right side of the ball so quickly, and then he would either flick it past mid-on's right hand, or leave it if it was swinging away. If you bowled it wider, trying to eliminate his trademark on-drive, he'd just smash it through the offside. Even if you bowled it in the right place, he'd still whack it.'

Peter Roebuck, who joined the Somerset staff on the same day as Richards, was an obdurate batsman who counted it a privilege to witness the flowering of genius. 'Viv's custom of clipping the ball to leg was not as dangerous as it seemed. He straightened his front leg at impact, which allowed his bat to get to the ball easily. It was a flick, not a cross-batted hit. Also, it took him outside the ball, which reduced the chances of an edge to slip. And it brought into play the undermanned legside, opening up the entire field, forcing bowlers to aim wider. Then they were easy meat.'

Richards' rationale for this astonishing stroke is endearingly prosaic. 'My job was to get the ball past the fielders, not to hit them with the ball. It was all about avoiding the fielders, and I just thought about how to do it.'

One brash young team-mate of Richards' in that first season at Taunton knew straight away he was in the presence of greatness. Ian Botham's career was built on not only supreme all-round talent but also a refusal to bow the knee to any other opponent. Yet even though he dismissed Richards seven times in Tests – only Dennis Lillee, with nine, surpasses that – Botham concedes that Richards usually trumped him when on international duty. 'Both of us loved the full-on challenge. Every top sportsman has that mentality, and Viv hated getting out to me. I tried pushing mid-on wider and doing without a mid-wicket to see if I could get him playing for the empty space and get him done by the swinging ball, playing across the line. Usually, though, he hit me through mid-wicket, like he did every other bowler. Viv could do anything he wanted, there was no weakness. I would stay awake in the Somerset dressing-room to watch him bat – and any of my team-mates will tell you that I can't give any higher praise than that!'

Botham and Richards. Apart from Compton and Edrich in the immediate post-war years, has any other pair given so much entertainment and credibility to a county side for so many years? They also drove Somerset on to five trophies in five seasons, imbuing a winning mentality into a dressing-room that had perennially under-achieved. It would all end amid acrimony in 1986, with accusations that Richards and Botham were no longer receptive to conventional disciplines, but for more than a decade they were glorious value. Match-winners. A rare commodity.

By the end of 1976, Viv Richards was the best batsman in the world. He made 1,710 runs at an average of 90 in that calendar year – surpassed just once in history – and yet, in the early days of that year, he and his West Indies colleagues were dismissed as a bunch of dilettantes. They had been swept away by Australia, hammered 5-1 in the series, routed and demoralised by the unremitting hostility and pace of Dennis Lillee and Jeff Thomson. Richards had struggled, along with more senior team-mates. Batting in the middle order, he would usually make a start but then get blown away. It was a prolonged taste of the medicine that West Indies teams under Lloyd and Richards would be eventually handing out, but early in 1976 it was too much for the Caribbean dashers.

The imputation was that the West Indies batsmen lacked a certain intestinal fortitude in the face of the Lillee/Thomson blitzkrieg, but that slur could never be laid at the door of Viv Richards. He was thrust into the opener's slot for the last two Tests and responded with scores of 30, 101, 50 and 98. That ordeal by speed was to be the making of him. 'That was a tough baptism of fire for us, and we learned a hell of a lot on that tour. If you could make runs against Lillee and Thomson on those fast pitches, then you could be judged a decent player. They were a huge challenge. So many things clicked into place for me after that tour. It toughened me up. No challenge would ever be as hard as that one.'

His captain, Clive Lloyd, admired the sheer guts of Richards. 'That tour opened all our eyes. It gave Viv a precious insight into what he had to do to compete against great bowlers. He showed such bravado against them – no helmet, don't forget – and he never flinched for a second. A lot of other fine players were around for us at the time but, once Viv had stabilised himself and toughened up mentally, he was a great player. The Master Blaster.'

Michael Holding remembers how Richards soon calmed down in the dressing-room and exuded the aura of a great batsman, secure in himself. 'Initially he was very nervous in the dressing-room; he couldn't sit still as he waited to go out to bat. He used to disappear a lot to the bathroom. But then he seemed to get organised mentally, exuding such self-confidence without being egotistical or brash. He had taken runs off Lillee and Thomson, and his pride and intimidating character helped develop his batting.'

England's bowlers in that hot summer of 1976 could certainly vouch for Richards' greatness, as his scoring approached Bradmanesque proportions. Even though, to his chagrin, a virus ruled him out of the Lord's Test, he still managed 829 runs in four Tests, at an average of 118. His 291 at The Oval is recalled with a shudder by Geoff Miller. 'What a time to be making your Test debut! I can honestly say that my off-spinners made no impact whatsoever on a typical flat Oval pitch. Our attack was demoralised, and I'm sure Viv was angry at not getting his 300. I still can't work out how Tony Greig got him out. It was humiliating.'

By the time West Indies declared on 687 for eight, a perspiring, weary Derek Underwood was surveying an analysis that read 60.5–15–165–3, and he had become fed up with bowling at Richards in that series, getting his wicket just once. 'I had been made aware of his awesome talent at Taunton, when he hit my first delivery over long-off into the stand for six. No one had ever done that to me before. You'd usually hope he'd go for the wrong shot early in his innings, but he rarely did. My biggest regret of that 1976 summer was not bowling at the West Indies when the ball was turning, but Viv had such an amazing eye that he would have probably played me off the back foot, as all the other great players did.'

Underwood's suffering at the hands of Richards did not end there. 'In my last Test at Lord's in 1980, I bowled a maiden over at him and felt encouraged. Next over, he hit me for four boundaries. Viv played all forms of cricket as if it were a one-day game. One of the all-time greats.'

Further evidence of Richards' willingness to scrap against all-comers came in World Series Cricket, between 1977 and 1979. Purists cavilled at the more excessive aspects of a form of cricket designed to cater for a television audience in Australia but, by common consent, this was a highly competitive and combative challenge. Fast bowlers on all sides were encouraged to rain down as many bouncers as they liked, and casualty wards in hospitals became used to treating the broken bones of cricketers. In this gladiatorial atmosphere, one batsman reigned supreme, relishing the physical challenge. Richards made four hundreds and three fifties in the six 'Supertests' against Australia in the first season of WSC and he probably never surpassed such a scintillating standard. 'I needed that supreme test of nerve and skill against bowlers like Lillee. I loved that in-your-face attitude of World Series Cricket, standing toe to toe, not giving an inch. Perhaps I was foolish not to wear a helmet then, but God blessed me with wonderful eyesight and I backed myself.'

Statistically, Richards was not quite the same prolific batsman after 1980. In his first 40 Tests, he averaged 60.48, then from 1980 to 1986 (42 Tests) he averaged 47.98, ending up with an average of 41.42 in his final 39 Tests from 1986 to 1991. If that constitutes a decline, many a Test batsman would settle for that. Fatigue may have contributed to a slight inconsistency. He played all round the year for Somerset and the West Indies, barely missing a game in fifteen years, and even someone of his natural fitness and athleticism must have wearied of the routine. This is the slightest of quibbles, though. He was still a wonderful player as he entered his thirties and even in his 39th year, while captaining the West Indies in England, his remained the most coveted wicket. With Richards, the style and the impact he made transcended any caveats.

He craved a challenge, though, as the constant diet of cricket and travelling drained his competitive juices. Genius cannot be plentifully available on tap; it needs a context and a relevance to flourish over dogged competence. Richards could still stake his flag on the summit when necessary – and England's fatalistic bowlers usually suffered more than most. A glittering century in his first Test at Lord's in 1980, that astonishing 189 not out in the 1984 one-day international at Old Trafford and two historic centuries in Antigua Tests contributed to averages against England of 62.36 in Tests and 57.82 in one-day internationals.

The Antigua hundreds underlined how Richards would steel himself to perform at his best when a situation demanded it. In 1981, Antigua staged its first Test Match, a proud day for a region that had achieved cricketing eminence on the back of the achievements of Richards and Andy Roberts. Every native of Antigua appeared to assume Richards would automatically score a hundred to symbolise the growing stature of the island. He felt the pressure of expectation, scratching around early in his innings, picking up some streaky boundaries after coming in at 12 for one. He never really got out of third gear for the next five hours, playing with uncharacteristic introspection – but he made a century, a historic one.

Five years later, on the same ground, he scored 110 not out, an innings of joyous abandon and enormous panache. It remains the fastest Test century in terms of balls received – just 56 deliveries – and every England bowler still winces when they remember it. Three successive deliveries from Ian Botham went for 6, 4, 6 – the first a skimmer through long-off, then two fielders at fine leg were bisected, followed by an enormous blow over square leg. John Emburey was smashed one-handed over long-on, then plonked effortlessly over long-off from a low full toss outside leg-stump. Richards just jumped inside the ball and pinged it casually out of the ground, an astonishing shot. Emburey had warned his captain, David Gower, that Richards looked dangerous right from the start 'and soon the other bowlers were looking in the opposite direction as I got the treatment. Once or twice I did him in the flight, but he adjusted late and still hit me miles. His eye and timing were phenomenal.'

This brilliant dissection of England's bowling was vintage Richards. His side needed quick runs to set up a declaration, he wanted the fifth win in the Test series under his captaincy, and the Test was being played on his home ground. Once again, Richards delivered. Yet again, England reeled away from his punishment.

It was mooted at the time that Richards' dominance over England stemmed from the extra motivation of racial issues. Certainly the rise of the Black Consciousness movement in the Caribbean coincided with the supremacy of the West Indies in international cricket. Bob Marley became the musical mainstay of the West Indies dressing-room, as pride in the cricketing success became tangible throughout the Caribbean. For years Richards sported the Rastafarian sweatbands on the field and never looked the other way when racial abuse was being dished out. He and his team-mates in the 1976 West Indies tour party to England needed no extra motivation after the infamous 'grovel' comment from the South African-born captain of England, Tony Greig. There was never the remotest chance that Richards would follow some of his team-mates in signing up for any of the 'rebel' tours to South Africa in the 1980s. He was too proud to be a black man to compromise in that area.

Yet that does not mean he had a racist attitude. Perceived injustice fired his anger, not any animus towards white people. The enduring friendships he enjoyed at Taunton and subsequently at Cardiff with Glamorgan would rebut that notion. His closeness to Ian Botham – iconoclast, yet colour blind – is further overwhelming evidence. Michael Holding, that intelligent and dignified fast bowler, is clear: 'Too much was made of the Black Power thing when we were so dominant. Viv never wanted to prove that black was superior to white; he just wanted equality. His immense pride meant he would never shirk a challenge, but he wanted to get the job done. He liked to swagger and intimidate and that was sometimes enough for bowlers who lacked his mental strength.'

That steely determination was tested after Somerset dispensed with his services in 1986. Influential figures at the club, disturbed that the team had lost its winning ways, felt that Viv was losing his appetite for the county grind and that his influence on younger players was not as constructive as that of Martin Crowe, the accomplished New Zealand batsman who had filled in for him in the 1984 summer. In order to sign Crowe instead of Richards, the club had also to dispense with the services of their second overseas player, Joel Garner, and Ian Botham, loyal to a fault, walked out in support of his two friends. It drew an illustrious era of Somerset cricket to an inglorious and messy end. Peter Roebuck, captain at the time, was fingered by Botham as one of the prime architects of the palace revolution, and bitterness lingers to this day in the Botham/Richards camp.

This is not the place to revisit that sad period of internecine feuding, and supporters of Richards will wonder why Roebuck is allowed space to comment here on the great batsman. Yet Roebuck has a sound point in wondering just why it took another county so long to sign him before Glamorgan took the plunge for the 1990 season. 'Many counties must have felt he was too hot to handle, but I couldn't understand that. He had been ditched by Somerset, who were at the foot of the table and rife with wrangling, but a fresh start was exactly what he needed. Glamorgan saw the best of him as a man and a competitor. I think he had mellowed by then.'

Roebuck is fulsome in his praise of 'an awesome batsman and competitor. He respected fighters – for example Peter Denning at Somerset – and detested selfishness and the craven. Viv hated bad cricket, hated it when the field was spread out for him, treated it with contempt. He shared the West Indian scorn for arranged declarations and lob bowling. To him, cricket was man against man. He was the bravest batsman I ever saw. I remember Wayne Daniel hitting him on the chest with a beamer in a Sunday League match. He didn't blink, just stuck out his jaw.'

Those three seasons Richards spent with Glamorgan marked a mellow, fulfilling coda to the tempestuous earlier years. He craved a new challenge in a place where he could be valued. At Cardiff he became a revered, indeed loved figure. Tony Lewis, the Glamorgan chairman and former England captain, backed his judgement that Richards had one last relevant staging post left in his glittering career, and he was handsomely vindicated. Cardiff and the warm, emotional nature of its cricket supporters suited a proud man who needed nurturing, despite what his occasionally forbidding persona suggested. An instinctive, passionate person, Richards had always responded well to the hand of unconditional, generous friendship. Cardiff, like Antigua and Taunton, was small and intimate enough to provide him with a support system that did not threaten his privacy when he needed it.

Glamorgan CCC and Viv Richards were good for each other, and those who played alongside him still talk about his contributions with awe. He said he had joined them to try to win a trophy, and in 1993 he helped them land the Sunday League. The match which clinched the trophy, at Canterbury, proved the last of Richards' career. Hugh Morris, the captain, recalls their distinctly Welsh celebrations: 'Viv cried just as much as any lad from the valleys that day, as we sang our hearts out and he joined in. He loved being in a side that was the underdog, and his self-belief and passion for our team simply inspired our players. He turned us from a Cinderella county to the winners of the championship four years later. Viv was not just the best batsman I ever saw, not just my inspiration when I was growing up – he was a hero to all of us in Cardiff. Viv provided the glue and cement for the talented youngsters coming through from our Academy. He will always be loved down there.'

He could still bat in his final season, despite evidence that the fabled eyesight was not quite so sharp. He scored a wonderful double hundred against Middlesex, the eventual champions, and then was out first ball in the second innings. The successful bowler was Phil Tufnell, and it is a measure of the respect even this dedicated insubordinate held for Richards that he did not celebrate with the expected gusto. 'I was a cocky little sod when bowling, and I'd be happy to give a batsman a verbal serve when I got him out. But never with Viv. He'd stare you down and you'd think "Blimey

O'Reilly, I hope someone gets him out soon!" and you'd never think you'd be the one. He just got stuck into me for that double hundred and, when I got him out in the second innings with an unplayable ball, I just kept my mouth shut. You always thought that Viv would file it away if you gave it plenty and come back next time even harder.'

Intimidation. The word keeps recurring when assessing the majesty of Viv Richards. Other batsmen like Don Bradman have intimidated through utter certainty and elimination of risk. Some like Jack Hobbs would have bowlers despairing with their purity of technique. A wonderful player like Walter Hammond would subjugate bowlers on poor pitches when he was fully engaged in the challenge. The dominant personality of W.G. Grace often overwhelmed bowlers from impoverished backgrounds who knew their place in the social pecking order was a long way below that of such a famous Victorian gentleman. But was there ever such a physically intimidating batsman as Viv Richards?

Only Kapil Dev from Richards' era scored faster in Test cricket – 84.81 per 100 balls to 69.28 – and Kapil had his bowling as back-up if he failed with the bat. Richards, his side's best batsman, still played with dash and daring. No player of his generation approached his tally of 84 sixes in Tests. Botham and Greenidge are joint second with 67. Since then, Adam Gilchrist, Brian Lara and Chris Cairns have surpassed Richards' tally of sixes, but the wickets and fast bowling are less testing than in the period when Richards was pre-eminent.

Interestingly, Richards nominates two spinners, Chandrasekhar and Abdul Qadir, alongside Lillee as the best bowlers he faced. Some illustrious West Indian batsmen were deemed vulnerable against top-class spinners, because it was rarely seen in the Caribbean, but no one ever levelled that charge against Richards. At the age of 22 he was tested fully, and his 192 not out in the Delhi Test nipped any doubts in the bud. A tyro who had seen so little high-class spin bowling had announced his credentials in the grand manner.

One familiar discussion point about his wonderful batting concerns his good fortune in not facing regularly the illustrious battery of outstanding West Indian fast bowlers. Would he have scored so heavily if he had been born somewhere else and represented another country? Michael Holding thinks not. 'He would've perhaps got two centuries a series, because he was a great batsman – but not many got more than that against us, because as a unit we were so good. You didn't score quick runs against our attack when we were at our best.' Richards' record in first-class games in the Caribbean was patchy, by his illustrious standards. Against Barbados – with the likes of Malcolm Marshall, Joel Garner, Sylvester Clarke and Wayne Daniel in the attack – he averaged just 27.31. Yet that was in a mere 13 matches, and there so many imponderables involved in dissecting the statistics of performances that were substantially at the start of Richards' career, when he was still striving to assemble his approach to batting. Holding also concedes that Richards once made a glittering century against Jamaica, when he and Patrick Patterson were running in hard at him.

As further evidence of Richards' refusal to be cowed by fast bowling, Ian Botham cites a superb 189 at Southport in 1977, when he put the fearsome Colin Croft to the sword. Peter Roebuck nominates a duel with Jeff Thomson at Lord's in 1981, when Richards made 92 out of 132. 'It was the most exciting toe-to-toe battle I ever saw in county cricket. Thommo was lightning fast that day, and Viv just kept cutting him. He would not give an inch.'

Case dismissed, then. When assessing the whole package that makes a great batsman, no one could compare with Viv Richards in his halcyon years. Modestly he wants the phrase 'serious commitment' to describe his career. 'It's all about the collective,' he says, 'getting the job done for your side, hoping your team-mates will respond to you.' That is why winning the World Cup in 1979 was more important to him than the virtuoso century which set it up. That is why he has been so disappointed in the decline of the West Indies since he left international cricket.

Let us leave the impact of Viv Richards on cricket to a man who is hardly a dispassionate witness but knows a little about broadening the appeal of the game, about an individual shaping a match by sheer brilliance. Ian Botham simply will not accept there has ever been a better batsman. 'Ok, Bradman was amazing, but he didn't have to bat all round the world, year after year, on different wickets in England, playing so many different forms of the game. Unlike Bradman, he didn't mind playing on uncovered wickets early in his career – and he still sent it round the park. Viv imposed his mind games on opposition bowlers before they stepped onto the field. He had amazing bottle, presence, a sharp brain, huge ability and self-belief. The opposition would think, "Oh no, the man's in town!" And then they were beaten. What more do you want from a batsman?'

Always entertaining to argue with Botham when he is on a roll, but difficult to mount a coherent argument on this matter. Somehow it mattered little when your team was getting clattered by Viv Richards. He transcended partisanship, a major bonus if you love the game. Who did not relish seeing Richards walk out to bat?

23

Graham Gooch

'I scored a hundred hundreds because I loved
playing for Essex as much as for England'

Graham Alan Gooch

Born

Leytonstone, Essex

23 July 1953

First hundred

114* Essex v Leicestershire, Chelmsford, 1974
Age: 21 years 35 days

100th hundred

102* England XI v Indian Under-25s, Cuttack, 1993
Age: 39 years 184 days

Last hundred

170* Essex v Glamorgan, Chelmsford, 1996
Age: 43 years 59 days

Career record

M	Inn	NO	HS	Runs	Average	100s	50s
581	990	75	333	44,846	49.01	128	217

Test record

M	Inn	NO	HS	Runs	Average	100s	50s
118	215	6	333	8,900	42.58	20	46

Graham Gooch was as much an Essex man as a yeoman of England. Since the summer international calendar became so compressed two decades ago, no other England cricketer has been able to turn on the tap so productively for his county as soon as he returned from England duty.

He won more matches for Essex than any of the bowlers who adorned their succession of outstanding sides. While many of Gooch's contemporaries were shuffling off to the world of corporate hospitality or the commentary box, he was still putting in the hard yards of physical preparation to maximise his abilities, well into his forties.

Graham Gooch took responsibility for his career. He did not expect the team to be baled out by other players of supreme natural talent such as Ian Botham and David Gower; Gooch dedicated himself to improvement. With that increased self-esteem as an international batsman came a clear-headed assessment of what was needed to prosper at the highest level. His greatness also lay in the standards he set himself and the respect he never lost for Essex cricket, a love affair that began when he used to turn up to play for the Second XI on his second-hand scooter, then in a battered Vauxhall Victor, driven by John Lever, for his county debut.

To understand the stature of Graham Gooch it is necessary to appreciate what drove him on: how he was still playing county cricket in 1997, at the age of 44, and how in the previous summer he had scored eight first-class hundreds and finished just short of 2,000 runs. He felt he owed so much to Essex CCC, where the shy, unprepossessing youngster had been nurtured into a great player. The apprentice toolmaker from Leytonstone, with the sloping shoulders, knock-kneed gait and tendency to put on weight, did not look a natural athlete until he got on the cricket field. Then the introvert, socially gauche in the presence of the ready wit that characterised the Essex dressing-room, was transformed into a batsman of undeniable quality. As he developed and grew in confidence, Gooch's wry, ironic humour flourished, and his personal example ensured that, when he wished to hand out some overdue home truths in the dressing-room, he would be heard in silence. It is no coincidence that his sporting hero remains Bobby Moore, a football captain who led by example, the acme of dignity.

Gooch was a legend at Essex and, although he demurs at the description, his former team-mates have no doubts. Keith Fletcher, his county captain for so many years, then his coach with England and always one of his trusted confidants, cannot name another illustrious England cricketer who did so much for his county. 'When I played for England, I always found it very hard to up my game when I came back to Essex because I was mentally and physically shattered. But Goochie gave his absolute utmost for us the day after he got back – every time. If you add his under-rated swing bowling and his slip catching to his batting, there can't be an all-round contribution to match his. He won more matches for us than any other England player I can think of. Ian Botham, Bob Willis and David Gower all struggled when they got back to their counties – but it was incredible how Goochie remained so passionate for Essex.'

Gooch's grandeur as a cricketer was underpinned by a humility and drive that operated along parallel lines. That is why he could be as influential for both his county and country for so long. To him, professional cricket was his job, and he respected that he was handsomely remunerated for it. He became well aware of his standing and the value of money, but he saw that as fair reward for the amount of thought and hard physical work he had put into his profession. 'If you fail to prepare, prepare to fail' became one of his recurring mantras, and he fully utilised every ounce of his abundant talent. Another of his maxims is 'success in life is an inside job'. The motivation must come from inside the individual. 'That applies not just to sport, of course, but for me, there was never any trouble in getting up for county cricket as well as the internationals. You search for the truth inside yourself, no one else can do that for you – and you must drive yourself on. Many I've known in my career didn't understand the sacrifices involved to get the very best out of yourself. If you're not going to do your best, then why bother?'

John Emburey, his closest friend in cricket, tellingly recalls a conversation with Gooch at the end of the 1989 season, when Terry Alderman's late swing had exposed Gooch's sluggish footwork, trapping him lbw on too many occasions. Gooch's series average of just 20.33 contributed to England's 4-0 hammering and, amid all the recriminations and knee-jerk moralising, Gooch took a long, clinical look at his own defects. His career Test average at the end of that Ashes series stood at 36.90, with eight centuries from 73 Tests. He told Emburey, 'That's too low; I'm a better player than that.' At the age of 36 he steeled himself to improve. He played another 45 Tests, averaging 51.55 and scoring twelve more hundreds. Emburey feels that sums up Gooch's qualities. 'The older he got, the more he got from his game. Excelling against the better bowlers turned him on, and he became a really tough competitor. In those last few years for England, he was more or less on his own, the backbone of our batting. I don't think we've had a consistently great player since the Gooch of 1990-93. He once told me, "No one feels comfortable against the speed of the West Indies quicks, but it's my job to get runs off them." He was the ultimate professional and, after Ian Botham's decline, our only consistent match-winner.'

Gooch's career is a rare example of a batsman improving markedly as he enters accepted middle age. The impressive deeds of Hobbs, Hendren, Woolley, Sutcliffe and Grace as they entered their forties are well documented, but they operated in eras that were less physically stressful, with no drastic diversifications from the norm, such as one-day cricket in its various guises. That makes the triumphant march of Graham Gooch, as he neared middle age, even more admirable.

In his first decade of first-class cricket (leading up to his 30th birthday in July 1983), he compiled 15,216 runs at an average of 39.28, with 34 hundreds.

Over the next decade (ending when he was 40), his tally read 22,348 at 57.44, with 69 centuries. From his fortieth birthday till retirement, he scored 7,372 runs, average 51.19, including 25 hundreds. Bradman, Compton, Hutton, Hick and Cowdrey from the hundred hundreds club were out of their precocious blocks swiftly, but Gooch embraced the motto *festina lente*. He made haste slowly. As a lover of a good red wine himself, Gooch would appreciate any analogies about improving with age that an oenophile would care to make.

It also took him long enough to score his first Test century. It was timely and impressive – at Lord's against the 1980 West Indians – but it was his 38th innings in his 22nd Test. His England debut could not have been less auspicious, with two ducks in the defeat by Australia at Edgbaston in 1975. Yet he ended up England's heaviest run-scorer in Tests, and only Hammond, Cowdrey and Boycott surpassed his 20 centuries. He made five Test hundreds against the forbidding, ruthless West Indian fast bowlers, at that time the litmus paper test of high quality batsmanship. At least two of those hundreds rank amongst the greatest played against those bowlers over a period of fifteen years.

He is the only batsman to score a triple and a single hundred in the same first-class match – and it was in a Test, against India in 1990, at Lord's, his favourite ground. After he was dismissed for 333 in the first innings, he went for a run. That was partly through habit but also the need to put more energy back into the 37-year-old tank. That attitude served him well in the second innings. 'To me, there was no substitute for working at your talent. It all comes from inside. That's why players like Allan Border, Geoffrey Boycott, Javed Miandad, Ian Botham, Dennis Lillee and Viv Richards were so special. They made it happen by willpower.'

Once he had worked out his game, Gooch simply loved to bat on and on. Kenny Barrington, his much-loved mentor as England coach in his early days, used to tell him, 'Once you're in, you book in for bed and breakfast.' Gooch saw no merit for the team in getting out soon after reaching three figures. As long as he played with his side's interests in mind – and no one could ever criticise him on that score – he would roll along inexorably, utterly dominant, increasing his tempo of run-scoring. After the County Championship matches were reduced in 1969, it became increasingly rare for anyone to score 2,000 first-class runs in an English season. Gooch did it five times, two more than any other batsman has done. He was equally commanding in one-day games, winning nine NatWest and 22 Benson and Hedges Cup awards for Man-of-the-Match, both a record.

In fact, Graham Gooch is the most prolific batsman in cricket history, if you amalgamate his one-day record to his tally of 44,846 first-class runs. The grand total is 67,057 at an average of 45.81, including 170 hundreds. That puts him ahead of the first-class record of Jack Hobbs. Such a projection smacks of *lèse-majesté* when any cricket historian assesses the glory of Hobbs. In sport, you can only take on what is there at the time and, if the peerless Hobbs were somehow to be placed in the cricketing Tardis, there is ample evidence to suggest that he would be as brilliant in the shorter forms of the game as he was in Tests and three-day county cricket. Yet in Gooch's period, it became undeniably harder to score prolifically for a long period. Fielding improved dramatically, declining over rates meant batsmen had to extemporise more to score quickly, intimidation from fast bowlers became the norm, while a vast increase in overseas touring and the variety of matches in a hectic English summer meant batsmen had little time or energy to work on their techniques. Jack Hobbs would not have been able to score 98 first-class hundreds after the age of forty if he were around now. His legs and eyesight would have given up on him. With due obeisance to so many wonderful players from other eras, the durability and versatility of Graham Gooch qualify him at the very least to join the elite company of great batsmen.

Gooch also entertained hugely. He was not an impassive, limited accumulator of runs for their own sake. His batting was relevant, with his team's interests paramount. He would adapt to the exigencies of the match and, when in full, pulverising flow, he was majestic and valiant. Then only medium-pacers appeared to perturb him, probably because he had too much time to consider his scoring options and the adrenaline did not flow as much as when the fast bowlers were steaming in at him, or the spinners were gliding in, more in hope than expectation.

Keith Fletcher chuckles when recalling how Gooch treated the spinners. 'He just called them slow bowlers. They couldn't bowl at him on flat pitches – not even Derek Underwood. He would just hit through the line.' John Emburey, later an England off-spinner, bowled at him in schoolboy cricket and felt he was a little loose, too keen to hit through the offside on a turning wicket. 'But he soon started to dominate me when we graduated to county cricket. He developed a superb all-round game, eliminating mistakes and punishing the spinners, session after session. Goochie had such a strong mind. He used to say to me, "Batsmen get themselves out, eight times out of ten." I was struck by the way he matured into a batsman who would still crack boundaries, scoring at a fast rate, yet never looked like getting out.' Mike Gatting, a top-class gorger on spin bowling himself, always knew when Gooch was in good order. 'He'd just block it straight back past the bowler for four, with great timing. Or he'd whip it off his legs. His back-foot shots were superb, punching it with that heavy bat. When you saw him off the field, shambling around, you wouldn't believe he could be so light on his feet against the spinners.'

Keith Fletcher admits that, when Gooch first came into the Essex side, he thought he would be a good county player with no real prospects of an international career. 'He didn't say much, but he was a great listener, with a brilliant attitude to learning about the game. He started to work out where he could score his runs against particular types of bowling, and he was particularly good at looking at the bowler's hand as he ran in, so that he could assess whether it was going to be an out-swinger or an inner. That Test debut of his may seem to have been a nightmare, but it toughened him up. You can't get worse than a 'pair', but it was all too soon for him and it made him even more determined to improve.'

Two key developments within twelve months sparked Graham Gooch's career. In 1978 he was moved up the Essex order to open. He has always maintained that this is the best position. 'Ok, you can get seen off by a great delivery with the new ball early on, but there are a lot of loose deliveries around and you can impose yourself right from the off, against an attacking field, with plenty of gaps. What batsman wouldn't want to get out there straight away, with the prospect of filling your boots all day long? You've got to back yourself. And I loved the challenge of facing top bowlers.'

Gooch was restored to the England team that summer of '78, and it was after returning from the triumphant tour to Australia the following spring that he took a radical decision to change his batting style. In those days the forensic dissection of cricketing skills that is today available to the laptop brigade was not present in the England dressing-room. You had to trust the evidence of your own eyes in the nets, or that of your team-mates and coach. Fundamentally, technical matters were your own problem. Gooch had flattered to deceive in that triumphant series in Australia – averaging 22.36 – and he knew remedial work was necessary. He managed to watch the TV highlights of England's 5-1 victory when he returned home and was dismayed at his batting. 'I didn't like what I saw at all. I was playing across the line, falling over, my footwork poor. I needed to stand up straight, keep my head still and play through the line. So I decided to hold my bat aloft while the bowler was running in. That stopped me crouching, with my head straying towards the slips. Playing straight is a fundamental of batting.'

The second development was a decision that had an important impact on his career. Gooch realised he was not a natural athlete, that his slow metabolism meant he was prone to putting on extra pounds. He enjoyed his food, his pint of beer and a bottle of wine at the appropriate time. Yet he put on weight and felt lethargic in the season before getting back into the England side. So he took up running and also trained with West Ham FC – for a dedicated supporter of the Hammers, this was a clear case of mixing business with pleasure. Gooch wanted to be fit enough to concentrate all the time, to hammer the bowlers in the final hour's play when they were fatigued and fantasising about a hot shower and a few pints of beer. So began a relationship with running shoes that undoubtedly improved his batting, adding many years to his career.

So began the critique of Graham Gooch as a fitness obsessive, intolerant of those with a more *laissez faire* philosophy, mistrusting cricketers who believed that natural talent was the key to success. The two most talented England cricketers of Gooch's time did not subscribe to his work ethic. When he was England captain in the West Indies in 1981, Ian Botham would chide Gooch for nodding off over the dinner table, only to receive the withering response that he was out for an early-morning run on the beach at about the same time as Botham was returning from a party. David Gower was a great believer in detachment from the pressures of international cricket at certain key times on tour. For him, optional nets and the occasional trip to a winery helped clear the mind, equipping him mentally for the fray. Gooch disagreed and remained frustrated that he and the most gifted England batsman of his generation could not reach common accord towards the end of their careers. Their antipathy undoubtedly affected Gower's career prospects with England and scarred Gooch's reputation. He was categorised as a killjoy, obsessed with a desire for every player to work equally hard. Gower's many friends in the media enjoyed lampooning Gooch as the Roundhead who wanted his Cavalier to put in a thousand press-ups before breakfast and then run to the ground for a compulsory net lasting two hours.

As ever, the truth lies between the two generalisations, and there were faults on both sides. Gooch now admits he should have cut Gower some more slack, that he was too intolerant. 'David was an iconic figure, the most talented England batsman I played with, and I just wanted to get more from him, to set an example to the younger players. But I should have respected more that he had his own way of doing things and I should've relaxed. It was a fault in me, I now realise, but, when I was captain, I'd get impatient when others didn't strive to reach a higher standard.'

Yet that approach worked for Gooch. He was bewildered by team-mates who coasted along, resting on their laurels. Daley Thompson, the great Olympic decathlete, once told him that he wanted all his competitors to know that he was the first to arrive for training in the morning and the last to leave at night. Gooch sees it in simplistic terms: 'Throughout my career, I never saw a fitter, healthier and stronger cricketer become a worse cricketer.'

He had seen at close quarters the training sessions of the West Indies in the 1980s under their exacting physiotherapist, Dennis Waight, and felt that, if such commitment was good enough for the likes of Viv Richards, Clive Lloyd and their great fast bowlers, then England should not be so sniffy. Allan Border's Australian side of 1989 that swept away England under Gower was infinitely superior in physical preparation. Gooch could never understand why some England players believed that what worked for better sides did not suit them. Micky Stewart, the England coach when Gooch became captain, welcomed this new, tough attitude: 'We saw things very similarly, despite me being two decades older. You've got to work at it, that's what you're paid to do. Too many cricketers were turning up without doing the right preparation. So many hammered me and Goochie, but is there an international squad today that doesn't work seriously hard before the actual cricket starts?' John Emburey, hardly the most dedicated disciple of physical training among cricketers in his era, now accepts that his great friend was

271

ahead of his time: 'Many of the players and coaches weren't ready for all the physical work, but change was necessary. Gower saw cricket as a game, but Goochie saw it as a job that should be enjoyed. Later on, coaches like Australia's John Buchanan and South Africa's Bob Woolmer opened so many eyes – and Woolmer also did it at Warwickshire. But too many players under Goochie didn't want to change.' Gooch is wryly amused to see so many back-up staff helping the players prepare: 'All those hangers-on today, how many are there of them? We were the first to scratch the surface, and now you can't move for assistants.'

Gooch's willingness to make technical and lifestyle changes had helped to establish him in the England side by 1980, and in just under a year he was triumphantly vindicated in a series of defiant innings against one of the great bowling attacks in international cricket. To the chagrin of most England players, they had to play West Indies at home and abroad in 1980/81, and they posed severe questions of nerve, technique and concentration. Gooch came through it admirably, posting three Test hundreds. The most memorable came at Sabina Park, when he made a lacerating 153 out of 249 for five, reaching his century in only the 40th over. He was particularly severe on Colin Croft, the most intimidating fast bowler of that era, a pitiless explorer of a batsman's mettle, as he bowled around the wicket to the right-hander, peppering his body. Gooch stood four-square, pulling and hooking Croft so devastatingly that he disappeared for 56 in his first eight overs. It was the sort of indomitable, punishing innings that few played against those West Indian fast bowlers, and one of them, Michael Holding, recalls the respect they had for Gooch: 'That was very good going, to get two hundreds against us in that series. We never gave many opportunities for batsmen to drive us so he had to be sound against the short ball. Goochie certainly was good in that area, and he just didn't look to occupy the crease. He scored quickly, even when we were only bowling 12 overs an hour, and he could damage you. There was no chance of keeping attacking fields against him. His height helped him get over the short ball, and he had a great eye. Getting him out early was always a big boost.'

At the other end to Gooch, a gnarled old pro was relying on his own dogged method of combating Holding et al. Geoffrey Boycott, having turned forty, was still resourceful and brave enough to average over forty in those two series, and his experience of opening with Gooch turned him into an ardent admirer: 'I enjoyed Goochie, I liked his dry sense of humour and, along with John Edrich, he was my best opening partner for England. Goochie was always up for the challenge, and you need that with four quicks of that calibre coming at you. Deep down, a batsman needs positives in his head when the bowlers are trying to knock it off. He had that quality. We were good together.'

A year later, they were both lost to England. They signed to play for an England squad in South Africa for a handsome fee, proclaiming their right to play where British businessmen were free to ply their trade. Boycott never played again for England while Gooch was banned until the summer of 1985. The stubbornness that has been a feature of Gooch's life as well as his cricket career buttressed his conviction that it was the right thing to do for his financial security, and he never felt the need to apologise.

England missed him greatly, losing series against Pakistan (twice), Australia, New Zealand and the West Indies in his absence. Gooch became an even better batsman during that period. He played for Western Province for two seasons, finding time to work on his fitness and fine-tune his technique, and he became an even hungrier batsman. Essex benefited from his ban and, with such an inspirational figure regularly available, they were the best side in the land.

There was never any doubt that Gooch would slot easily back into the England team after serving his time, and for the next decade he was the best batsman, apart from a torrid experience in the Caribbean in 1986, when he was distracted by demonstrations over his South African connections and he struggled on some unreliable wickets. His torment at the hands of Terry Alderman was the only other aberration, until a tour too far to Australia in 1994/95. No doubt he could have added a couple of thousand runs to his record-breaking Test aggregate had he been available between 1982 and 1985, but that period away from the international game gave him valuable time with his family and helped him re-assess his cricketing priorities.

That clarity of mind, that meticulous approach, served his batting well when he finally became England captain in 1990. 'When you're the captain, you're the leader of the English game and that either inspires you or weighs on you. It gave me even greater responsibility as a player, and I thrived on it.' By then, rising 37, he had come to terms with his game. He would mutter to himself 'play late and straight' and 'no mistakes' as his innings progressed. To him, eighty per cent of dismissals are the fault of the batsman. 'There are exceptions – like when Jeff Thomson got me second ball on a wet wicket at Edgbaston in '75, when the ball just took off. And good, pressurised bowling can get you. But usually it's the batsman who screws up. When you're struggling with your timing, you can still make a hundred, rather than just score one when everything's in your favour.'

Gooch believes there are three fundamental parts of batting: technique, management and concentration. 'You need firstly to know what areas to hit the ball, the position of your head, your stance, your own style. Then you must know how to manage your innings. What knowledge have you picked up along the way to make the technique work? How do you play on a wet wicket or one that's turning square? You must listen to the great players as you mature. Kenny Barrington was like a father figure to me when he was England coach, a fantastic influence. Finally, overshadowing the other two, you must have concentration. Without that, the other two won't work for you. You must be able to switch on and off between overs, even between deliveries. The same at intervals. You're in your own little world, and you come in and out of it when necessary. Geoffrey Boycott was the best at this.'

Gooch has always maintained that batting must be relevant. How many games have you won for your team in a season? Five examples from Gooch's career after his ban serve to underline his value. Keith Fletcher will never forget the championship game against their closest rivals, Middlesex, at Lord's in 1985. Both teams were chasing the title and, when Essex were set a target of 210 in 33 overs, Fletcher considered their chances only academic. Gooch told his sceptical team-mates, 'Please your bloody selves what you think, I'm having a go at them.' He finished 105 not out, against an attack of four Test bowlers, and Essex won by four wickets with seven balls to spare. Says Fletcher, 'That's what you call leading from the front.'

A few months later, in Port-of-Spain, Trinidad, Gooch scored one of England's greatest hundreds in one-day international cricket. Viv Richards had limbered up with an astonishing 82 off 39 balls, yet even he was eclipsed by Gooch's 129 not out in a successful chase of 230 off 37 overs. He was there at the end, for the five-wicket victory, having taken apart Joel Garner, Patrick Patterson, Courtney Walsh and Malcolm Marshall. His strokeplay was controlled, majestic, and he gave no chance.

Another remarkable hundred in a one-day international came the following year, in the 1987 World Cup semi-final against India in Bombay. Gooch arrived at the ground, two days before the match, with a game plan. He knew that the safest way to combat the Indian spinners Maninder Singh and Ravi Shastri was to sweep them. He looked at the wicket and was certain that the ball would turn. So he rounded up as many left-arm spinners as he could find and practised only the sweep shot for the next two days. The result was 115 off 136 balls, an innings of immense security and control. England won by 35 runs. Gooch was the difference between the two sides.

That was the same at two Headingley Tests in 1991 and 1992, when centuries by Gooch decided two close contests. The first, against the West Indies, has credible claims to be the greatest Test innings played by an Englishman. The quality of the opposition bowling must always be judged when making such a bold statement, but Ambrose, Walsh, Patterson and Marshall were in the top bracket as a menacing, varied unit. England led by just 25 runs after two innings on a capricious pitch, where no one ever really felt they were in, and soon the match equation was clear. If Gooch went early, West Indies would win. Rain was never far away, the numerous stoppages in cold, cheerless conditions chipped away at the batsmen's concentration while refreshing the bowlers. The typical challenge of a Headingley Test – the ball swinging around disconcertingly and seaming off the green pitch – added up to a bonanza for Ambrose and company. Yet Gooch carried his bat for the first time in his career, making 154 not out from 252 all out. No one else got past 27. He himself faced 65 out of 106 overs, spread over seven hours. It was a masterpiece and set up a famous England victory. As deserved eulogies rained down on Gooch, an assessment by the cricket correspondent of *The Times* carried great resonance. John Woodcock had covered more than 400 Tests in the previous forty years and was never a writer to wrap himself up in the Union Jack. He said, 'Since the Second World War, no innings by an England captain has surpassed this. It stands out, not for artistic merit but for skill and courage against a very formidable attack in awkward conditions at a crucial time.'

That epic innings has eclipsed the memory of another wonderful effort by Gooch at Headingley, against Pakistan the following year. His serene century against the brilliant reverse swing of Wasim Akram and Waqar Younis and the wiles of the leg-spinner Mushtaq Ahmed set up a crucial lead of 123. Then, as England advanced nervously on a victory target of 99, Gooch's 37 was a cameo of self-control and judgement as the three superb Pakistani bowlers refused to bend the knee. At this stage of his career, Gooch was such a reassuring sight at the crease for England supporters that his early departure usually reverberated down the batting order and gave the opposition bowlers a fillip. If he had gone cheaply in that first innings, then surely Pakistan would have won.

Those two match-winning performances satisfied Gooch greatly, because he had been tested by the two finest bowling attacks in the world and triumphed. 'Testing yourself in bowler-friendly conditions, gritting your teeth, concentrating hard – all that was very satisfying.' Micky Stewart, England coach at the time, was hugely impressed by the way Gooch applied himself to the differing challenges: 'At Bombay he told me he wasn't going to go down the pitch to the spinners, he'd just lap and sweep them. He worked so hard in his preparation. At Headingley he'd built soft hands into his technique by then; that was crucial against the moving ball. And those Pakistanis were as big a challenge as the West Indies. He had to contend not just with the vagaries of the pitch but the devastating reverse swing of Wasim and Waqar. He showed such bravery and resource.'

Stewart's son Alec played in that 1992 Test. As a former England captain himself, he knows how the job can chip away at your effectiveness as a player. That did not apply to Gooch. 'His bat looked about five feet wide, and he looked so imposing at the crease. He was 39 when he played that fantastic innings against the Pakistanis; he proved that age is just a number. I'd follow him anywhere when he was captain because of the example he set us. It didn't bother me when he handed out some home truths. He was the best English player of my time, and I still hold him in the highest esteem.'

Gooch's imperturbability was also a factor in his dominance. The constant sledging of the Australian bowlers was never directed at him, because he just ignored its crassness. After Gooch had scored a hundred in the 1993 Old Trafford Test against Australia, the principal sledger Merv Hughes was asked in a press conference if he had learned anything from a good day for

Australia. 'Yup,' he said, 'there's just no point in sledging Goochie.' Even Shane Warne, having experienced Gooch scoring two centuries in his first Ashes series, addressed him as 'Mr Gooch' and the feeling was that the irreverent Warne meant the appellation as a mark of respect. John Emburey used to tell his Middlesex team-mates not to mouth off at him when they played Essex, because that would just fire Gooch up even more. 'If anyone got stuck into him, he'd stare him out, as if to say "Who the hell do you think you are?" So it was always best to keep quiet when Goochie came out to bat, and we'd try to bore him out. He had that air of massive self-confidence when he was at his peak, totally unlike his modest, shy self off the pitch.'

He was in his fortieth year when he reached his hundredth first-class century. I leave it to the statisticians to squabble over whether it came at Cuttack, against India Under-25, or against Cambridge University three months later. A hundred Gooch scored against South Africa on the 1981/82 'rebel' tour furrowed many a brow and, after the ICC had ruled that South Africa match was not first-class, he was back on 99. So the Cambridge students were caned for his fourth century against them for Essex, and he promptly retired his innings. His rationale was typically whimsical: 'I'd never had a 'retired' against my name before. Later that summer I copped a 'handled ball' in the Old Trafford Test, so I was on my way to the full set of dismissals.'

His parents were still around to celebrate. Alf and Rose were a delightful, warm-hearted East End couple who supported Graham totally from the time he first displayed sporting prowess. A personal memory is seeing their pride and pleasure in Australia in 1991, on their first tour there. They arrived just in time to savour a blistering century from their son in the Adelaide Test, and it would have taken the flintiest of hearts not to be moved by their unaffected happiness. Graham had enormous respect for his father's opinions and they did not always agree, especially over his South African experience, but he and Rose were the best kind of parents to an ambitious youngster who loved cricket. They were a regular sight at Essex's home matches, and Graham always looked for them around the boundary edge.

It was Alf Gooch who unwittingly provided a link between the third and the 23rd batsman to score a hundred hundreds. When he was eleven, young Graham was taken by Alf to Fleet Street, to the Jack Hobbs shop, where the great man had sold cricket bats. He had died by then, but Graham was told about Hobbs' towering reputation before he walked into the shop, and he was properly respectful. There his first bat was bought by his doting father. It was a link between two England batsmen who scored Test hundreds in their forties, separated by more than sixty years. The younger one, clutching his new bat, would end up scoring more runs in all first-team cricket than Hobbs, one of the immortals.

That does not make Graham Gooch a better player than Jack Hobbs. It simply marks a pleasing symmetry, a happy connection between two great batsmen.

Centuries in all forms of cricket

	f/c	1-day	T20	Total
J.B. Hobbs	197	-	-	**197**
G.A. Hick	136	40	2	**178**
G.A. Gooch	128	44	-	**172**
E.H. Hendren	170	-	-	**170**
W.R. Hammond	167	-	-	**167**
G. Boycott	151	8	-	**159**
C.P. Mead	153	-	-	**153**
H. Sutcliffe	149	-	-	**149**
F.E. Woolley	145	-	-	**145**
I.V.A. Richards	114	26	-	**140**
L. Hutton	129	-	-	**129**
Zaheer Abbas	108	19	-	**127**
W.G. Grace	126	-	-	**126**
C.G. Greenidge	92	33	-	**125**
D.C.S. Compton	123	-	-	**123**
T.W. Graveney	122	-	-	**122**
S.R. Tendulkar	68	53	-	**121**
D.L. Amiss	102	15	-	**117**
D.G. Bradman	117	-	-	**117**
M.R. Ramprakash	103	14	-	**117**
G.M. Turner	103	14	-	**117**
M.C. Cowdrey	107	3	-	**110**
A.J. Lamb	89	19	-	**108**
M.E. Waugh	81	27	-	**108**
A. Sandham	107	-	-	**107**
M.W. Gatting	94	12	-	**106**
M.L. Hayden	79	27	-	**106**
J.H. Edrich	103	1	-	**104**
T.W. Hayward	104	-	-	**104**
L.E.G. Ames	102	-	-	**102**
A.I. Kallicharran	87	15	-	**102**
E. Tyldesley	102	-	-	**102**
D.S. Lehmann	82	19	-	**101**
R.T. Ponting	71	30	-	**101**
S.G. Law	79	20	1	**100**

24

Graeme Hick

'I was never bothered by all those statistics.
I just batted. I never got bored with batting.'

Graeme Ashley Hick

Born

Salisbury, Rhodesia
23 May 1966

First hundred

230   Zimbabweans v Oxford University, Oxford, 1985
Age: 19 years 18 days

100th hundred

132   Worcestershire v Sussex, Worcester, 1998
Age: 32 years 8 days

Last hundred

149   Worcestershire v Derbyshire, Worcester, 2008
Age: 42 years 75 days

Career record

M	Inn	NO	HS	Runs	Average	100s	50s
526	871	84	405	41,112	52.23	136	158

Test record

M	Inn	NO	HS	Runs	Average	100s	50s
65	114	6	178	3,383	31.32	6	18

Graeme Hick may have hailed from Zimbabwe, but he became as much a part of Worcester and its glorious ground as the teas in the Ladies' Pavilion or newspaper photos in late spring of swans gliding serenely over the outfield as the River Severn again burst its banks. When he retired at the end of the 2008 season, it felt as if an institution had tumbled. He had played 25 years for Worcestershire, at a time when cricket careers were being shortened as a result of the physical demands of so many matches in different formats. But for Hick, no matter what colour of clothing he was wearing on the field, it was his job to score runs. The more, the better.

His final tally of statistical achievements is towering, even more so when every colleague would acknowledge he was the quintessential team man. He gained as much satisfaction from seeing a team-mate shape a victory as from his own success. No one enjoyed the dressing-room euphoria more. For him the essence of sport was being part of a team that won matches. 'I could never have been happy playing sport as an individual, much as I admire golfers. To me, sport teaches you proper values. I loved being part of a happy team.' That helps explain the widespread popularity of this unassuming man.

Yet as an individual cricketer he was immense. Statisticians will struggle filling their days now that Hick has finally had his time. He kept them enraptured for so long.

He amassed a total of 64,372 runs in all cricket (first-class and one-day games), putting him second to Gooch. With 178 hundreds he is only behind Jack Hobbs. He is eighth in the list of first-class hundreds (136) and played more matches in all forms of cricket than anyone else – 1,213 in all. He was the youngest to score 2,000 first-class runs in a season, to make fifty first-class hundreds and to reach 20,000 first-class runs. He is in the select band of eight batsmen who have scored 1,000 first-class runs by the end of May.

Yet the statistics that will dog him are 3,383 runs in 65 matches, with an average of 31.32 and six centuries. His Test record.

It means Hick will always be denied a place in the pantheon of great players. He can speak from bitter memory of the pain of being dropped eleven times in his batting career, the wariness with which he was greeted by some in the England dressing-room, the number of times he was shunted up and down the batting order. But he is not bitter. He is at ease with all aspects of his career. In a subsequent era, when central contracts gave England players a security that suggested it was harder to be dropped than get selected, Hick might easily have flourished. Certainly the management could have been more considerate towards a sensitive, shy person who knew nobody when he joined up with his new England team-mates at Headingley in June 1991, with the burden of expectation on the 25-year-old enormous.

Yet Hick refuses to blame others. 'Growing up and playing sport in Zimbabwe, I was taught to enjoy it and to respect the opposition, and that stayed with me the whole of my career. A huge part of your success at the highest level must come from within. When I look at the really outstanding players of my time – Viv Richards, Sachin Tendulkar, Brian Lara, Ricky Ponting – they had all the areas covered, especially temperament. Look at Steve Waugh. He often looked uncomfortable against high pace, getting into the wrong positions. But his attitude towards adversity was fantastic. That's what sets these guys apart.'

It did not help that he had to spend seven years qualifying for England, in the process pulverising so many bowlers and setting records. He had not come through the usual feeder system of England Under-19s and 'A' tours so missed out on developing friendships with other emerging players who were in that Headingley dressing-room for his first Test against the West Indies. 'Some of them just didn't know what to say to me because we'd never met and I was too shy to start up conversations. I felt like a foreigner in that dressing-room.' By then he had already scored 57 first-class hundreds, more than Mike Atherton, David Gower, Nasser Hussain and Alec Stewart scored in their entire careers. In those days insecurity was rife among England players. The idiosyncratic whim of the chairman of selectors Ted Dexter meant that most were unsure they would last an entire Test series unless they succeeded immediately. The motto was more *'sauve qui peut'* than 'all for one.' Hick was being sized up by his new team-mates. Was he as good as the hype suggested? On first examination, probably not. He was dropped before that 1991 season was over. The following year, he was also dropped in the Pakistan series.

Graham Gooch, the England captain at the time, accepts some responsibility for not ensuring Hick felt at home in his new, exacting surroundings. 'He was a shy bloke, but I liked him and his dry sense of humour. But we didn't really have any communication; he kept himself to himself in that area. But in batting I think you need to throw ideas around and broaden your knowledge, especially when things aren't happening for you. After such a fanfare, so much was expected of him but I thought he lacked presence at the crease; he didn't project himself enough.'

David Graveney, chairman of selectors in the latter half of Hick's Test career, believes he would have prospered if lucky enough to be at his peak a decade later, under the more enlightened captaincy of Michael Vaughan. 'One of Vaughan's greatest traits as England captain was the way he managed to make a new player comfortable in the dressing-room. He would have got the best out of Graeme. He was a victim of the selfishness of others when he first played for England, from both management and certain team-mates. I estimate Graeme's failure with England was only 30 per cent his fault. Eventually the scars were too deep; by the time I became chairman, he wasn't doing himself justice whenever we brought him back.'

Graveney winces as he recalls how Hick batted during that first careless rapture of youth, before he qualified for England. Gloucestershire invariably suffered from Hick's unerring ability to despatch the bad ball and Graveney remembers the sheer power of the strapping young man. 'He would play forward past you with a mixture of bat/pad for four. He never bothered with the hook shot, unless the ball was on the offside, and he was a brutal cutter. But the overwhelming impression was that of a massive presence at the crease with a heavy bat, who was outstanding off the front foot. We'd look at the fixture list and groan, "Oh no, we're going to get Hicked next week!" Yet there was no arrogance about him, even though he dominated.'

Having played for Zimbabwe as a seventeen-year-old, Hick had fetched up for a trial at Worcestershire and 'the suits' had doubts over taking him on. The overseas recruits in those days tended to be nasty fast bowlers, unless you were talking about greats like Richards or Lloyd. Worcestershire wavered; a season's scholarship was arranged. The coach Basil D'Oliveira had been convinced of Hick's talent by just one shot, in the nets in April 1984. He pulled a short ball from Paul Pridgeon towards the Cathedral, and everyone whistled. The general impression was summed up by D'Oliveira's 'Did you see that?' That one blow convinced the first team squad that this lad could bat. Phil Neale, the county's captain, recalls a checked straight drive from the same net session. 'That stopped the net, while everyone talked about him. When I first saw him walk over, I thought, "Hope he's a fast bowler, he's tall enough," but we soon knew where his talents lay.'

D'Oliveira took the young man under his wing and got him a season at Kidderminster, the club where he spent a happy year qualifying for Worcestershire in the 1960s. Hick butchered the Birmingham League bowlers for most of that hot summer and, in the last county game of the season, he made a significant first-class debut. Against Surrey's fearsome Sylvester Clarke, at the time the most hostile and dangerous bowler in county cricket, he came in at number nine and helped save the game with 82 not out. An admiring Neale shepherded him through his first fifty runs. Rain ruined Hick's chance of a championship hundred on debut, but Neale had seen enough. D'Oliveira was right about the boy, and coach and captain managed to persuade the committee to sign him up as next season's overseas player before the county grapevine set to work.

The legendary D'Oliveira was Hick's cricketing confidant as he proceeded to lay waste around the county circuit. At times, as the centuries piled up, Hick wondered why the old boy did not praise him more, but D'Oliveira was complimenting him by saying so little. He felt there was little he could teach him technically so he concentrated on attitude, on building up mental toughness, on how to manufacture a big innings when not timing the ball well. Just before Hick qualified for England, D'Oliveira told me, 'All Graeme needs is an early hundred for England; then we can all settle down and watch him become one of the greats. When he walks out to bat for England, I think only his family will be prouder than me.' Sadly, it did not pan out that way; perhaps Hick should have stuck to the simple principles of batting laid down by D'Oliveira, instead of listening to others working for various

England squads. Perhaps the one thing that D'Oliveira had in abundance – granite mental strength – was the main weapon missing in Hick's armoury. D'Oliveira remained angry that Hick had not done himself justice: 'They mucked him around too much. I kept telling him that it didn't matter how you looked when you scored your runs, it's how many you score. Graeme got confused with so much advice when he was with England.'

Micky Stewart, Hick's first England coach, disputes that. 'It was a great pity he didn't experience adversity till he arrived on the international stage; that was a big hurdle to negotiate. He was vulnerable at the crease, getting stuck there, a little stiff – like Gooch when he was out of touch. I sat Graeme down with the videos of his batting in that '91 series and showed him what I meant. I asked if Basil had worked with him on using more of the crease, particularly when playing back. He said Basil felt the individual should work it out himself, according to his ability. I didn't get through to Graeme; it was always difficult expecting a batsman to make major technical changes during a home series. It's much easier on tour, when you've got more time.'

Those misgivings about Hick's technique were absent during his productive years after qualifying for Worcestershire. His father, John – inveterate reader of the scrapbooks – calculated that Graeme had scored 23 hundreds in all forms of cricket by the time he arrived at New Road in 1984. Two years later, he was smashing Len Hutton's record by a year in becoming the youngest to score 2,000 first-class runs in a season. That was just an *hors d'oeuvre* to the 1988 season when, at the age of 22, he emulated Don Bradman to become the youngest to score 1,000 first-class runs before May.

Three very different innings stand out in that golden run. One was the 172 against the touring West Indians that took him past 1,000 runs. His parents had flown in from Harare that day, and they got to New Road in time to see their son battling it out against Walsh, Ambrose, Patterson and Bishop – four considerable fast bowlers, bending their backs with a purpose, aware that places were up for grabs for the first Test the following week. Hick did not think he would get to the necessary 153 on a typical New Road wicket that helped the seamers. He became only the second batsman to reach the landmark since the war, in an innings that should always be an exhibit for the defence when his mettle against West Indian fast bowlers is examined.

Before April was out, he had compiled a double hundred against Lancashire that many of his supporters claim to be his finest innings. On an Old Trafford pitch that turned on the first morning, he made 212. The next highest score in the game was 68, and Worcestershire won by ten wickets. It was a classic example of a top batsman winning a match, as he did so often for his county. Phil Neale shared a stand of 202, and he scored just 40 of them. 'He was the only batsman in the match strong enough on a slow, turning pitch to hit the ball down the ground, and he was the difference between the two sides.'

A fortnight later, Hick had almost doubled that score when making 405 not out at Taunton against Somerset. It was a Bradmanesque feat, yet as he walked off after batting for five sessions, not giving the semblance of a chance, he looked as if he was simply strolling back after facing one over. It was the highest first-class score in England since 1895, and I offer this morsel for the statisticians. On the first evening of the match Hick was 179 not out, and he dined in an Indian restaurant with his team-mates, fielding with his usual affability the suggestions that he could get a triple hundred. He added another 226 next day. It was his second first-class hundred of a season that ended with him posting eight more. Of those ten centuries, eight came after Hick had enjoyed a curry the night before.

Some felt that Worcestershire should have batted on to allow Hick the chance to get to 500, a new first-class individual record, but he would have none of it. Phil Neale had kept him abreast of the match situation, and he was content with the tea-time declaration. 'Graeme always batted with the team in mind. He never lost sight of the objectives; he was very committed to winning games for us. Because he always scored at a very good pace, there was never a time that anyone could accuse him of batting for himself. We wanted a dart at their batting that last session and, to complete a perfect day for Graeme, he nipped in with two wickets. He was laughing his head off at the close.'

Hick is typically modest about that Taunton innings. 'I was just batting on a good pitch with even bounce. Some four-day games in championship cricket had just started that season, and this was one of them. Perfect for any batsman to stay out there, session after session, clocking up the runs.' Yet the ball seamed around on that first day and, at one stage, Worcestershire were 132 for five. Hick mastered the conditions effortlessly to score 405 of the 550 runs added while he was at the crease. To many of the players in that historic match, there were two separate contests going on.

That was again the case in a vital championship game later that summer. Kent and Worcestershire were level on points, going into the last round of matches. Soon it was clear that Worcestershire had to get the full 24 points to win the title. That meant securing all four batting bonus points on a typically lively New Road pitch against Glamorgan. Hick obliged with 197 in a total of 423; Worcestershire won by an innings and secured the championship by a single point. A year later, he did it again. At the end of August Worcestershire simply had to beat Somerset to retain the title. Set a target of 300 off 57 overs, they got there with five balls to spare, and Hick was unbeaten with 136 off 120 balls. Worcestershire retained the championship, six points ahead of Essex.

On each occasion Hick was the match-winner. Phil Neale still marvels at Hick's coolness in a run chase. 'He was always talking to his batting partner about what we had to do, when the tempo had to change and when he would go all the way with his shots. Graeme never thought about himself when he batted, he would run his partner's runs as if they were his own. He was a huge team man.' Steve Rhodes, the wicket-keeper, remembers Hick's facility at putting away the bad ball. 'That's essential in a run chase, when the bowler's feeling the pressure as well. He seemed to miss nothing. He could score off good deliveries as well. Time and again he'd get the perfect yorker and jab down on it to send it rocketing straight to the boundary. The bowlers despaired so many times. And he seemed to breeze through the nineties, never seeming bothered about playing for his century.'

Rhodes is right about that. Of the 25 batsmen who scored a hundred centuries, only Bradman and Hammond converted a higher proportion of their fifties into hundreds than Hick. Usually, when he got in, he needed prising out, despite scoring at a fair old lick. No wonder bowlers felt intimidated by his remorseless power. John Emburey believes he was one of the finest players of spin bowling on the county circuit. 'I'd be bowling at him for a time, thinking I was keeping him quiet, then I'd look up at the scoreboard and see he was 40 not out! Then he'd go up a gear and start hitting you back over your head or slog-sweeping you. He loved batting against off-spinners.'

It was hardly surprising that Worcestershire won seven trophies during his time at New Road. Only Graham Gooch was more influential for his county in Hick's time. Yet Gooch also performed nobly for England. Why not Hick?

The burden of expectation in 1991 was not his fault, nor his shy disposition, away from the warmth of New Road where he belonged. Gooch, another shy man who struggled at times with his footwork, was out of his depth early on with England – you cannot do worse than a 'pair' in your first Test – but he worked at his game. Hick was unfortunate to come up against some outstanding bowling attacks in his first two years of Test cricket, with the '91 West Indians, the '92 Pakistanis and then the Australians with Shane Warne, Merv Hughes and Paul Reiffel. Micky Stewart sympathises but points out that he was still getting trapped lbw on the crease or bowled via the inside edge when he had played sixty Tests. 'He needed to be more arrogant at the crease. We saw him dominate at times for England, showing what he could do, but he just didn't react quickly enough. His footwork let him down.' Graham Gooch believes Hick's footwork was not as positive in defence as in attack: 'In his early days he would get on the front foot and marmelise bowlers, but at Test level they work you out. Compare Kevin Pietersen. He's got a great eye like Graeme had, but he's more solid in defence. He has the foundations right.' That superb coach Bob Woolmer had no doubt what was needed when he first saw Hick bat: 'He needs dancing lessons to get him moving quicker at the crease,' was his simple verdict. John Emburey believes the reservations about Hick's technique are harsh, feeling his early problems were psychological: 'I didn't see too much wrong with him, apart from getting a little too much square on at times. I remember Graeme saying that he wanted to be judged after a couple of years in the England side, and I wonder if that says a little bit about his character. Perhaps he didn't feel he was wanted because he was from Zimbabwe, and that would be unfair, because he was a lovely person and a great team man. But he wasn't thick-skinned like Pietersen. Both were billed as England's saviours, and Graeme struggled with that. Yet I always felt happy with Graeme in the team; he gave us substance.'

Alec Stewart could relate to feeling extra pressure in his early England days, because his father Micky was the coach. Yet, within two years of his England debut, he had scored four Test hundreds. He possessed what the Australians called 'a bit of mongrel', that innate readiness to scrap and eyeball the opposition. Stewart had played several years of grade cricket in Western Australia and was a different animal from the gentle soul who had breezed through all the previous challenges before hitting the buffers in 1991. 'I have great sympathy and respect for Graeme, because it was tough at the start for him. He didn't have a bad bone in his body and was almost too nice. He didn't have that killer instinct.'

Barry Richards has some sympathy with that assessment. The great former South African batsman was Chief Executive of Queensland when Hick went out to play a season of Shield cricket in the 1990/91 season. Richards thought it would toughen up the young man a little, with Test cricket just around the corner, and after a slow start – he needed to adjust to the extra bounce – he made three hundreds and came close to 1,000 first-class runs. Richards admired Hick's batsmanship and liked him immensely. 'But I don't think he believed enough in his own ability. I talked to him about the mental side of things, rather than the technical – about the need for greater self-belief. That was the one thing that held him back. You've got to remember his upbringing. At the time kids were brought up in Zimbabwe to be very respectful and well mannered, whereas in Australia brazen youth was more the norm. Look at someone like Shane Warne. Or Kevin Pietersen from South Africa from a later generation. They've got no doubts about themselves. I know Hicky was a little heavy on his feet, but that wasn't a major technical problem. Not every top batsman can dance at the crease like Ricky Ponting. If Hicky had possessed more self-belief, he would have been more alert to taking singles to get off strike when the pressure was on. Nothing wrong with a batsman keeping away from the firing line till he regroups.'

A photograph from Hick's first encounter with the Ashes encapsulated the concerns about his temperament. In the Old Trafford Test Merv Hughes had just got him caught behind and, as Hick left the crease, Hughes veered towards him to spray some oafish comment in his ear. Hick appeared impervious, but did such brutal sledging leave some sort of subconscious scar? Angus Fraser, a sincere admirer of Hick, wonders about such incidents. 'Unlike Graeme I was confrontational on the field at times. If Merv had given me that sort of abuse, I'd have said, "See you round the back of the pavilion later" before I left the crease, but Graeme wasn't like that. That's why so many of us warmed to him, he was so decent, one of my favourite England team-mates.'

So many comments about Hick the Test batsman are made in sorrow, rather than anger. This is partly through genuine affection for him and partly an awareness that there was an outstanding player lurking beneath the diffident persona. Also frustration at the times he should have capitalised when batting masterfully. In the 1993 Oval Test he was batting on a different plane from anyone else, reaching 80. The Australians did not know where to bowl at him. Then he slapped a long-hop to short third man, giving his detractors a field day. Great players do not get out so tamely when it is all set up for them. A few months later he made a magnificent 96 in the Sabina Park Test, against an accomplished West Indian attack. He stood up manfully to all the intimidatory fast bowling, played positively off the back foot, then nicked a good delivery. 'I was so disappointed not to get those extra four runs. That would've been a big tick in the box to get a hundred against those bowlers. Keith Fletcher, our coach, came and sat alongside me as I tried to get over my disappointment, and he told me that if I could score runs against that attack, then I could against anyone else. I appreciated that; I responded better to a quiet, sensitive word.'

Even when Hick batted superbly for England, it did not bring his side victory, always the most important aspect for him. None of his six Test hundreds led to a win. His first Test century, an imposing 178 – shepherding the tail against the Indian spinners in Bombay – was overshadowed by a heavy innings defeat. His best Test innings in his estimate was his magisterial 141 at Centurion Park in 1995, when he caned South Africa's Allan Donald and Shaun Pollock. It was hard to imagine a better exposition of how to punish top fast bowlers. Yet it was to no avail, other than to Hick's personal satisfaction. The game was washed away by severe thunderstorms. Who today remembers Graeme Hick's wonderful century in a Test that became simply a footnote? Only those lucky enough to have seen it.

Another of his substantial Test innings also came in a drawn match, but not before he was the beneficiary of widespread sympathy as the victim of his captain's intransigence. At Sydney in 1995 Mike Atherton declared on Hick when he was 98 not out. England were chasing quick runs to set up the declaration, but the captain thought Hick was being too tardy, putting his own interests ahead of that of his team and so he called a halt. The dressing-room was stunned and Hick was angry, refusing to speak to Atherton when England took the field for the final session. There is no doubt that Hick had slowed up as he entered the nineties, but Damian Fleming was bowling some excellent, swinging yorkers at him, and he had not received an update on the imminence of the declaration until Alec Stewart came out with a change of batting gloves. 'I told him he had to get as many as he could in the next five overs, and Hicky joked, "OK, as long as he doesn't declare on me!" I told him just to get his hundred, and then we'd declare.' Three overs later came the declaration. Graham Thorpe was batting with him: 'I was shocked and immediately put myself in his situation – a first Ashes hundred taken away from him, for the sake of two overs.' Stewart recalls Graham Gooch getting fidgety as Hick blocked several deliveries, saying to Atherton 'What's he doing?' and then Atherton stood up and called in the batsmen. Stewart, a great admirer of both Gooch and Atherton, still feels it was badly handled. 'Once the message goes out, it stays the same, but the declaration came with two overs left.' Angus Fraser was in that England dressing-room and could not believe what he saw. 'The Ashes had been lost, and we'd had a miserable time getting thumped. Here we were, at last in total control of a Test and enjoying a hugely popular member of our side possibly putting his demons to bed at last against the best side in the world. Think what that hundred might have done for Graeme's Test career.' Fraser and Atherton have been close friends for twenty years, yet whenever Fraser mentions Sydney '95 to him he refuses to talk about it – 'which is an obvious sign that he got it wrong.' Graham Gooch still sides with Atherton. 'The team's bigger than the individual, and we needed a declaration. Graeme knew the situation.' Fraser counters that: 'But you often get an individual starring with the help of the rest of the team or the captain. What about when he throws the ball to the guy who's got four wickets when the last pair are together? There's room for sentiment in sport. Another couple of overs would have made no difference.'

What is not in doubt is that the England team felt deflated at Atherton's decision, and they bowled without fire and passion in the last session, failing to take a wicket. Hick kept his own counsel at slip but, when he chased a ball to the third man boundary, Fraser realised how angry he still was. 'He threw the ball back to our keeper, Steve Rhodes, like an exocet. I've never seen a cricket ball hurled so strongly; it made a hell of a whack.'

That evening Atherton paid a call to Hick's hotel room, where he was relaxing with his wife and daughter. Legend has it that Hick told him he did not want to discuss the matter and sent his captain off with a flea in his ear. Not so. 'I respected Athers for coming to see me. We had a sensible chat and we agreed to disagree. Next morning it was a case of just move on, and I still have great respect for Athers. If I hadn't been angry, there'd have been something wrong with me. I just believed after the last message that I still had a couple of overs left. Damian Fleming was bowling really well, and I wasn't going to slog him, there was still time. Anyway Athers was paid to make those decisions, though it took him some time to hold his hand up. His dad was rather quicker, though. When it happened, Alan said to my wife Jackie, "I'd like to apologise for my son's decision," and walked off!' In Hick's defence England's total of 255 for two declared occupied 72 overs – despite a lead of 193 on first innings – and Atherton and Gooch had batted more slowly than Hick before they gave way to Thorpe and the thwarted Hick.

With Atherton and Ray Illingworth in charge of England at that time, there was hardly any sympathy or touchy-feely sentiment directed towards Hick. They both came from a tough, Northern school where you had to develop your own carapace of flintiness to survive international cricket. Illingworth, in particular, gave the impression that he felt Hick was a wimp. An incident just before the Old Trafford Test of 1995 demonstrated the differences between them. Illingworth told Hick he was dropped. He took it badly and left the ground in tears. That seemed to sum up the enigma that was Hick in the eyes of the taciturn Illingworth, who proceeded to criticise him in the press for being soft. Hick was angered by that. 'I called him up and asked why he said that, and he told me he'd been misquoted. I'm not embarrassed at being in tears – what did he expect me to say? That it was fine by me to be dropped, and I'm off down the pub? I'm an emotional guy and sometimes I can't hold it in, but what's wrong with that? I cared about my England place; I didn't like being dropped. But it happened so often. I never played an entire Test series at home. I eventually preferred playing Test series away from home, it seemed a more relaxed environment for me.'

Such emotion appears at odds with Hick's reserved, disciplined public image, yet he was deeply affected by his England failures. 'I've sat in the dressing-room in tears, really disappointed at getting out. Being a quiet person, I'd bottle it all up, then it would come out and I'd have to seek out a corner. Sometimes when I got home, I'd talk it over with Jackie and let it out. Many of the press didn't know me, because I'm a reserved guy, and then they would just second-judge me. When I'd failed, they'd just climb in without knowing anything about how I felt about my cricket.'

Angus Fraser feels that Hick should have been handled more sympathetically by Atherton and Illingworth. 'They felt he should be able to cope with it all, but they never grasped Graeme's sensitivity. He never really knew he was so gifted, which was amazing, given the scores he clocked up. He wasn't ruthless enough in the big, ugly world of international cricket; he just wanted to do the job with the minimum of fuss. But he cared alright; I've seen him put the towel over his head and shed tears when he'd got out. He reacted with more passion and feeling than several English-born players in the various teams I was in. Graeme had great pride in performance and playing for England.'

At the end of the 1995/96 Test series in South Africa, Hick's Test average was 38.66, with four centuries, after 42 Tests – an immense improvement after his first 11 Tests, when it was a meagre 18. He appeared to be on the cusp of getting to grips with what was needed in Test cricket. Yet the remaining five years proved an anti-climax. One of his most significant innings in that later period was a comparatively small one, but it helped to win a Test match, always his aim. In appalling light during the closing stages of the Karachi Test, he made 40, adding a crucial 91 with Graham Thorpe, which sealed an improbable victory by six wickets. His power of stroke, excellent eyesight and selfless running between the wickets took the pressure off the masterful Thorpe, who relied on deft placement. Afterwards, as we media representatives discharged our duties in the England dressing-room area, Hick was as ecstatic as I could recall. Victory against the odds was the key element for him, and he was touchingly generous towards Thorpe's wonderful innings. He would not have been human, though, without a quiet reflection over his timely contribution.

By then Duncan Fletcher was the England head coach. Many who had not studied Hick's career in depth or knew anything about the characters of both men were under the impression that the older Zimbabwean would unpick the lock and usher Hick into the band of elite batsmen of Test cricket. This was a ridiculous assumption. Hick, it is true, had played for Zimbabwe under Fletcher's enlightened captaincy in 1983/84. They had both attended Prince Edward's School, Harare. Yet the age gap was seventeen years, and the Zimbabwe of that era expected the elders to be treated with respect by the youngsters. And so it was with Hick. 'I rarely had much dealings with Fletch when we played together. He was the captain and a bit of a father figure. I was seventeen and showed him due respect, speaking when I was spoken to. We hardly knew each other, so it was ridiculous to think he would have some special insight into me when he became England coach.'

When Fletcher took over in 1999, Phil Neale also joined the England set-up and Hick's former county captain hoped that Fletcher might prove the catalyst. 'So did Duncan – he had great memories of Hicky's big scores for Zimbabwe. But the baggage of being dropped so many times was heavy on Graeme by then. He lacked the confidence he had at Worcester, he seemed to be looking over his shoulder all the time. I don't think it was a technical issue. Nasser Hussain and Mike Atherton had their weaknesses in certain areas, but they could grind out the runs because they were so mentally strong.'

David Graveney, the chairman of selectors, felt the key people failed Graeme Hick. 'Duncan was very keen not to be seen as favouring Hicky, but he failed to get the best out of him. When you sit in selection meetings, the key is to find out what unlocks the door. It's much harder with a batsman because so many things can go wrong. But how many chances can you give Graeme Hick? Did he forget the reasons why he was selected and the methods he used? In terms of advice, the ability to discern what's applicable to you is crucial. When I first bowled at Hicky, his method seemed so simple, almost like a right-handed version of Graeme Pollock. But he got confused later on.'

It was never Fletcher's method to inform a player he had been dropped. He left that thankless task to David Graveney. When Hick was called with the bad news in May 2001, Graveney was careful to say the door had not closed. 'But he was upset and disappointed. He asked "Why me?" and then went through a few injustices he felt he had suffered. It was hard to disagree, but he was 35 – still physically impressive, but there were younger guys coming through without his baggage. But Graeme Hick is one of the biggest failures for me in my time as chairman of selectors.'

John Emburey believes Hick suffered from a fallible management structure that created selfishness in the players. 'In his decade as a player there were four different coaches, and there was little consistency and vision until Fletcher came on board. But he had his own favourites in the England dressing-room, and that created divisions. He made up his mind quickly about a player. I never thought the selectors believed in Graeme and he knew that.' Ian Botham agrees: 'It was pretty ordinary the way he was treated. Look at the way that Mike Gatting and Steve Waugh were persevered with for so long before they turned it round. From what I saw at close quarters with Worcestershire, I'm amazed that Hicky didn't become an outstanding Test batsman.' Micky Stewart, Hick's first England coach, thinks he was discarded too early: 'He was only 35, still very fit. They did the same to Robin Smith – he was only 33 when he played his last Test.'

Hick laudably apportions the bulk of the responsibility on himself. 'Growing up on a tobacco farm in Zimbabwe, enjoying the amateur aspects of sport, I didn't develop that arrogance that so many have who succeed at the top level. Maybe that's why I fell short. I look at Kevin Pietersen and appreciate that he's got the necessary self-belief. I never had that with England. I always preferred batting at number three, getting out there and getting on with it, but I was shunted up and down the order a lot. I even batted at seven! I never worked on intimidating the bowler; I'd just play the shot and look away. Perhaps I tried to please too many people with England, fiddling around with my technique. Looking back on it now, was mine that bad? I've seen some batsmen score lots of runs at Test level with techniques that weren't that special.'

The England coach he respected most was Keith Fletcher, for the quiet, supportive way he went about his job. 'That approach suited me. Duncan Fletcher didn't do anything for me. I remember when he pitched up at Worcester just after he got the job and he talked about wiping the slate clean. That suggested to me he felt I had baggage. In my time his England dressing-room was always split between those he liked and those he didn't. He hardly communicated with some of the guys throughout a five-day Test. I was one of those.'

A personal memory supports Duncan Fletcher's distant attitude to Hick. In April 2003 Alec Stewart was the recipient of Michael Aspel's red book for the *This is Your Life* programme, and I was one of the invited guests to the ITV studios in London. Afterwards, Hick and I were shooting the breeze over some food and Fletcher sat down near to us at the same long table. He did not look in Hick's direction. I expressed surprise and Hick then told me, 'That's his style. When all the England players and backroom staff were lining up back stage to surprise Alec during the recording, he saw me and looked away.' Hick was not disturbed; he just accepted that Fletcher was hardly the best communicator.

Still, there was always New Road. He valued his time there so much and became more and more attached to the beautiful ground where his bat often made such a mellow ring on balmy summer evenings, with the Cathedral presiding benignly over proceedings. He was usually found on the outfield at close of play, teaching his son Jordan and daughter Lauren the rudiments of the game. New Road suited Graeme Hick; he would chat cheerily with any home supporter. As his old flat-mate Steve Rhodes puts it, 'There were no airs and graces about Graeme.' Despite his disappointment over the way he was sacked as captain in 2002 and being asked to drop down the order to number five in his last couple of years, he was never seriously tempted to play elsewhere. After every England tour, he would drive to New Road before going home. 'Just to check everything was still the same. I liked to make the connection again after being away for so many months. It's been a special place for me, and I valued it more and more as the years passed.' When the club announced that the new pavilion would be named in his honour, he was greatly touched. No one could argue with that decision.

He decided to retire towards the end of the 2008 season because he felt that, after being dismissed a couple of times, he was not as bothered as he used to be. The sharp focus he needed had become blurred. He was still very fit, apart from a nagging elbow injury that had taken some time to clear up. At the start of his final season the Worcestershire players submitted themselves to the dreaded 'bleep' test, an intensive and painful method of assessing the individual's cardio-vascular fitness. Hick came third in the test, taken by all the players – some of them half his age. He nevertheless felt it was time to go. His inclination had been to announce his retirement in the winter, to avoid any fuss, but a close family friend said, 'No, you won't, everyone will want to say goodbye to you properly.' So he opted for one final season. When he announced his retirement to an appreciative, respectful press conference at New Road in late August, he broke down and fled the room in tears. David Leatherdale, former team-mate and now the club's commercial manager, walked him to his car, and he drove straight home as the eulogies and personal memories were exchanged without him at an emotional county ground.

The emotion of the occasion got the better of him again when he played his last innings for Worcestershire. Graciously the Middlesex players formed a guard of honour as Hick walked out in a Sunday League match. He made only 14 before slapping one tamely to cover. 'I'm surprised I made that many. I had tears in my eyes when facing the first ball. I knew I hadn't done myself justice that day and couldn't face a prolonged farewell. The club understood I didn't want just to pitch up; I'd had my lot at last.'

Heaven knows how many more runs he would have made if his home ground had been at Hove, Taunton, The Oval or Lord's. The New Road wickets in Hick's time always gave joy to the seamers, with the ball keeping low and jagging around. A batsman rarely felt he was in at New Road –

unless he was Graeme Hick. That makes John Bracewell's jibe about Hick being 'a flat-track bully' particularly ill-judged. Bracewell made the remark after Hick had spent two seasons in New Zealand domestic cricket, playing for Northern Districts. In that time he did what he was paid to do – averaging 63.62, then 94.46, including ten centuries. He was easily the best batsman, on sporting wickets. Not enough to satisfy Bracewell. And Hick himself never really felt he was out of the top drawer as a batsman. 'I've stood at slip, watched someone play an amazing shot and thought, "How did he do that? I could never have played that." I didn't believe I was that special. I just batted and got runs whenever possible. Much better than bowling. Get them to do the hard work all day instead.'

His popularity within the game will remain undimmed. That was confirmed by the prolonged, standing ovation at the Professional Cricketers' Association annual awards dinner, when he was honoured on his retirement.

In September 2005 central London ground to a standstill one glorious morning, as England's players celebrated winning the Ashes. As their open-top bus stopped in Trafalgar Square and thousands roared their acclamation, with *Jerusalem* being belted out on the public address system yet again, there was Graeme Hick amid the throng, paying his respects. 'I had come down to London with a friend of mine for a benefit meeting, and she asked if we could go along to Trafalgar Square. I was glad to be there. Wistful? Yes. And envious. I wish I'd had a bit of that when I'd played the Aussies, but I was chuffed for our lads. They deserved it. I've never begrudged anyone else's success. I'm genuinely pleased for others when they've done well.'

It matters little now that Graeme Hick did not prosper as a Test batsman. He is not the only one from the Hundred Hundreds Club to have fallen short of international greatness. Hayward, Mead, Sandham, Woolley, Turner and Ramprakash also have comparatively modest records in Test Matches. None of the 25 can match Hick for all-round fielding brilliance, though. Hammond and Woolley were prehensile in the slips, Hendren and Sandham brilliant in the outfield, Bradman, Richards and Hobbs nimble and deadly in the covers – but they all lacked the versatility of Graeme Hick. Even in his final season, at the age of 42, he was still catching blinders in the slips, snaring 25 catches in just 11 championship games, the second highest in the competition. In the outfield, his throw was still like an arrow, making the wicket-keeper's job easier. Steve Rhodes can speak of Hick's fielding prowess with due reverence. 'He was fast to the ball in the deep and he had a fantastic, hard, flat throw. I rarely needed to move when it came in. At slip, he was terrific. He had hands like buckets, and they were so strong that the ball wouldn't burst through his hands. He was a great concentrator at slip, and the ball never seemed to take him by surprise.' In the history of cricket, only Frank Woolley (with 1,018) among non-wicketkeepers has taken more catches in all matches – and Hick finished just ten behind.

It will be interesting to see how he copes with a future away from New Road, after a quarter of a century's involvement, more than half his life. When his daughter Lauren heard he was retiring, she said, 'But you can't, Dad, I still want to go to the ground!' Her doting father will not begrudge her that, not least of all because his wife Jackie comes from a family of Worcestershire supporters. He knows, though, that he will need to take a few steps back, to allow the younger batsmen to stamp their personalities on New Road. While mulling over his imminent retirement, Hick remembered a conversation with the top golfer Nick Price, a fellow Zimbabwean. He told him that his proudest moment was not when he attained the number one spot on the golf rankings but the time when his son would be old enough to have a beer with him and enjoy his company. Then, Price said, he would know he had been successful in life. That struck a chord with Hick. 'I thought that was a great philosophy, and I hope that'll happen with me and Jordan. I'll make time for that.'

His preferred epitaph for his career would be about the personal, rather than the professional. 'I've loved playing cricket at a special place with superb supporters. But what pleases me most is that, over the 25 years, I don't believe I've made an enemy or met someone I wouldn't want to talk to ever again.' Graeme Hick amply demonstrated that the humble, the decent, the unassuming can still thrive in a sporting era where many egos are rampant.

Starting young ...   # and going on past 40

Most centuries before 25		Most centuries after 40	
G.A. Hick	57	J.B. Hobbs	98
D.G. Bradman	39	E.H. Hendren	68
W.G. Grace	36	F.E. Woolley	68
L. Hutton	36	C.P. Mead	59
M.C. Cowdrey	26	W.G. Grace	39
T.W. Graveney	25	G.E. Tyldesley	36
W.R. Hammond	25	G. Boycott	31
I.V.A. Richards	25	L.E.G. Ames	30
G.M. Turner	23	A. Sandham	30
J.H. Edrich	21	H. Sutcliffe	26
M.R. Ramprakash	19	G.A. Gooch	25
D.C.S. Compton	17	D.L. Amiss	20
F.E. Woolley	17	T.W. Hayward	13
L.E.G. Ames	16	W.R. Hammond	12
C.P. Mead	16	T.W. Graveney	10
Zaheer Abbas	15	M.C. Cowdrey	9
G. Boycott	13	G.A. Hick	8
D.L. Amiss	11	J.H. Edrich	4
J.B. Hobbs	10	D.G. Bradman	3
G.A. Gooch	8	I.V.A. Richards	3
T.W. Hayward	7	D.C.S. Compton	1
H. Sutcliffe	5	L. Hutton	-
G.E. Tyldesley	4	G.M. Turner	-
E.H. Hendren	3	Zaheer Abbas	-
A. Sandham	1	*M.R. Ramprakash*	-

25

Mark Ramprakash

'He's never scored an ugly run'
(Alec Stewart)

Mark Ravin Ramprakash

Born

Bushey, Hertfordshire
5 September 1969

First hundred

128   Middlesex v Yorkshire, Headingley, 1989
Age: 19 years 318 days

100th hundred

112*   Surrey v Yorkshire, Headingley, 2008
Age: 38 years 332 days

Career record

M	Inn	NO	HS	Runs	Average	100s	50s
415	684	87	301*	31,894	53.42	103	135

Test record

M	Inn	NO	HS	Runs	Average	100s	50s
52	92	6	154	2,350	27.32	2	12

In April 1987 a lissom seventeen-year-old made his championship debut for Middlesex at Lord's. Mark Ramprakash's unbeaten 63 in the second innings against Yorkshire was compiled with such panache and grace that he was marked out immediately for distinction. He returned to sixth form college the next day but, after that one senior game, the cognoscenti at Lord's had him pigeon-holed as another Denis Compton or Mike Gatting.

Ramprakash has always looked a special talent, even when short of runs. With nimble footwork, he caresses the ball rather than bludgeons it. As a case study in the art of batting he is worth a place in a textbook; it would take a sharp-eyed cricket photographer to catch any glitches in his technique. Ramprakash has always been an aesthetic pleasure. Angus Fraser, a former team-mate and a committed curmudgeon when it comes to praising batsmen, says that the sight of Ramprakash once taking 45 minutes to get off the mark at The Oval was a delight. 'He just bided his time against good, accurate bowling and waited for the bad delivery. From a bowler's perspective, it was frustrating because you know you've got to get him early but, for a cricket-lover, it was beautiful, so classical.'

Contemporaries fall over themselves to praise the shimmering brilliance of Ramprakash. John Emburey, former county team-mate, says, 'He's one of the best players produced in England in the last 30 years,' while another Middlesex team-mate Phil Tufnell believes he was the supreme county batsman of his career. 'If Ramps got to 30, I'd put my feet and have a kip for the rest of the afternoon. He was just so perfect technically, you were surprised he ever got out.' Alec Stewart, Surrey and England team-mate, says, 'It's criminal he hasn't got a Test batting average of over 50. His appetite for scoring runs for Surrey is phenomenal. The opposition expect him to get a hundred these days. He's been the best batsman in domestic cricket since Graham Gooch.'

Certainly Ramprakash's record since moving to The Oval in 2001 has been remarkable. In eight seasons his first-class average for Surrey has been 55, 56, 76, 65, 74, 103, 101 and 61 – combining to a total of 12,085 runs, at an average of 75.06, with fifty centuries. His average over fourteen seasons with Middlesex was a highly creditable 50.48, but his series of Indian summers at The Oval have been reminiscent of the years of plenty that batsmen enjoyed there between the two World Wars, when Hobbs and Sandham reeled off centuries.

In the 2006 and 2007 seasons Ramprakash became the first player to average more than a hundred in successive English summers. At one stage in 2006 he scored 150s in five successive matches, the first batsman ever to do so. That same season, he reached 2,000 first-class runs in just 20 innings, beating the record of 21 innings held by Bradman and Gooch. His average that year of 103.54 is the highest by an English player in a home season, beating Boycott's 102.53 in 1979. In 2007 his tally of 2,026 runs constituted 30.02 per cent of Surrey's total of runs from the bat – another record, surpassing Hick's 28.9 per cent for Worcestershire in 1988.

His career record of 53.42 has only been topped by three of the 25 batsmen who have scored a hundred centuries – Bradman, Hutton and Hammond. Of that select band, Ramprakash can be considered one of the supreme stylists, alongside Hobbs, Cowdrey, Graveney, Sandham and Hutton, batsmen who were unruffled, poised and rarely appeared out of position. And none of those ever won a national dancing competition, in front of millions of television viewers.

For all his beautiful batting and prodigious run-scoring, Mark Ramprakash became better known for his success in the 2006 series of BBC TV's *Strictly Come Dancing*. His dazzling footwork, flashing smile and endearing shyness in front of a microphone captivated the distaff side of the audience, while men who could only shuffle onto the dance floor grudgingly admitted there was genuine talent there.

Yet it took the advocacy of Darren Gough to persuade Ramprakash to enter. Having won *Strictly Come Dancing* in 2005, Gough could speak with authority when Ramprakash rang for advice. 'I told him to go for it, because it would take him out of himself and stop him thinking only about cricket. He was always the only one of the England boys who could dance properly, anyway – he usually had his iPod on when we travelled on tour, boogying away. I knew he would win it, because of his excellent footwork, co-ordination and the concentration of a professional sportsman.' Ramprakash describes those exacting few weeks as 'a life experience. Late in my thirties, I've managed to appreciate other things. I was too wrapped up in cricket in my twenties.'

Living up to expectations proved to be one of his major problems in his twenties. At the age of nineteen, his mature 56 decided the 1988 NatWest Final for Middlesex, and he picked up the Man-of-the-Match award. There seemed no limit to what he could achieve as a batsman. Having been coached by former Middlesex players Jack Robertson and Don Bennett, he knew all about the history of the club and its great players. 'From the age of eleven, Jack used to tell me about Denis Compton and Bill Edrich, and I had great respect for the older major players. Middlesex is a club that's big on tradition, and I always felt I was following some illustrious players. Being in the same side as Mike Gatting brought that home to me, because a decade earlier he had been saddled with big pressure after starting so well, so young.'

Pressure. One of the words you cannot ignore when discussing the career of Mark Ramprakash. Everyone mentions it, including the man himself. Even at the age of nineteen he felt it after scoring almost a thousand championship runs in his first full season, averaging 35, in the 1989 summer, when batsmen struggled against cricket balls that had a pronounced seam on them. That was a worthy effort from the youngster, but he was criticised in some quarters for rashness – and he resented not being allowed to learn from his errors while getting to grips with professional cricket. Two excellent mentors helped him. 'Desmond Haynes and Mike Gatting were ideal for me, full of sound advice about how to build an innings. I used to get out lbw, playing around the front foot, but they worked on that with me. I also got better starting my innings, reining in my shots. I tended to fire off too many in my early days before I was settled.'

Haynes, that marvellous West Indian opening batsman, encouraged him to change his stance. In his early days at Lord's Ramprakash had the textbook side-on stance, with both feet on the same line, but he saw how Haynes coped with his left foot drawn further back, still on the same line as his right, but ensuring his front foot was not in the way as he coped with the swinging delivery. 'That was a pivotal decision for me in the 1990 season. It helped me go from being a young shot-player to a controlled batsman.' Ramprakash also watched how his hero Viv Richards moved so effortlessly around the crease. He even used a heavy 'Jumbo' bat like Richards early on, until he settled for a lighter model, following Haynes' advice to lean on the ball rather than smash it.

Angus Fraser used to pick up Ramprakash most days and drive him to Lord's when he first came on the staff, and he remembers 'an outstanding young cricketer, the next in line of the great Middlesex batsmen. He looked a fantastic prospect, beautifully relaxed at the crease. I thought he was certain to play for England when he was still a teenager.'

He was 21 when the call came, and it may have been premature. The 1991 West Indians were not quite the fearsome unit of yore, but their fast bowlers were still very threatening. Ramprakash, batting predominately at number five, did not look out of place, getting into the 20s seven times in his nine innings. He played with resolution and sound technique – examined closely by Marshall, Ambrose et al – but his top score was only 29. Yet he looked a young batsman who would in time develop into a major player.

He missed the chance to build on that encouraging start in the final Test of that 1991 summer, when he made nought against the undemanding Sri Lankan bowlers. No one knew it at the time, but that would become a pattern in the Test career of Mark Ramprakash. He seemed to promise so much, then the expectation was dashed by a run of low scores, leading to his omission from the side and to another bout of soul-searching on his part. He went to New Zealand in 1992, did not make the Test eleven, then averaged 7 in three Tests against the Pakistanis in the home series. There was no place for him on the tour to India and, for the 1993 home Ashes series, he only made the team for the final Test – and that was due to a late injury to Graham Thorpe. Even then he batted at number seven. He passed 30 for the first time, scoring 64 and batting well with the tail; the frustration for him was that it was the end of that series, and he could not build on it. An average of just 10 from four Tests in the West Indies did not help his cause for the summer series against the South Africans. Ramprakash was still in the selectors' minds due to his obvious talent, and he was selected for various England 'A' tours to Pakistan, West Indies and India in that fallow period, but he was in danger of being left behind.

He batted well against Australia in 1995, but again it was only for the final Test of the series at Perth, making 72 and 42 and looking secure; he had been called up from the 'A' tour to boost an injury-ravaged England squad. Yet in the next series, at home against the West Indies, he made 22 in four innings and was again cast aside. His 'pair' in the Lord's Test seemed to encapsulate his cluttered mind, as he stood transfixed after being caught at slip for his second nought. Strange that Ramprakash holds the record among batsmen for Test 'ducks' at Lord's – five in all – when it would be imagined that he would feel at home there.

His detractors will point to that grisly statistic as proof that he could not handle the special challenges of playing for England. Of course, there is a world of difference between scoring centuries in the county game and performing to your optimum on the same ground in a Test match. The media intrusion affects some players markedly. Ramprakash has never liked an inquisitive TV cameraman dogging his every footstep from close up as he walks back to the pavilion after yet another low score, and one has great sympathy with him. Television has given the impression in recent years that it has ownership of the game, but there should be greater respect for the feelings of a disappointed batsman representing his country. More than once Ramprakash has swatted away the harsh attentions of a TV cameraman, but surely he is entitled to some privacy at a low point. Just because others remain impervious to such discourtesy, does this have to mean that Ramprakash is temperamentally brittle?

Ramprakash looks back wistfully on the unproductive years after his England debut, but also takes satisfaction from a gradual improvement, leading to his salad days at The Oval a decade later. 'I really struggled from the early to the mid-nineties trying to believe I belonged at Test level. I lost confidence when left out in New Zealand in 1992, and then I was in and out. I took it all to heart too much. Looking back on it, I played too soon for England. I lacked the maturity to cope with all the public attention over an entire series, never mind the challenge of the West Indies. I would have liked a mentor to help me deal with all the massive media attention, but you were left to your own devices. The support structure is far superior now. Today, there's a media relations officer, and the young players get trained in all that stuff. They can cope easier than someone like me in 1991. I was a confident 21-year-old then, ready to perform, settled in my environment at Middlesex – but after a few setbacks I didn't feel that way with England.'

His solution was simply to work even harder at his profession. Always a devoted trainer and practiser in the nets, his intensity became almost demonic. 'I worked even harder, making sure I left no stone unturned. So I'm proud that I came through those tough years and played well enough to score a hundred hundreds. If I had been lucky enough to start my career against lesser attacks than West Indies and Pakistan, on better wickets, I could have got the momentum going and established myself as a regular, without looking over my shoulder all the time.' Of his 52 Tests, 28 were against Australia and West Indies, both with formidable bowling attacks in the nineties.

Angus Fraser played his first five Tests against Australia and the West Indies and sympathises with Ramprakash's early struggles. 'I always feel it's vital to get a good start to your Test career when you're making that giant step up, to prove you can perform at that level. Although Ramps was never exposed technically, it became harder and harder for him to live up to the expectations of those who wished him well, never mind himself. He started to analyse his technique too closely – how rather than how many. The latter's more important.'

Graham Gooch, his first England captain, believes that Ramprakash should be congratulated on an outstanding career, but at the highest level he must examine himself. 'A player should take the decision out of the hands of the selectors by making them pick him. I know what it's like to be dropped by England; very few escape that. Ramps appeared to have it all in terms of talent when we first picked him, but I can't apologise for him being dropped a few times under me.' Alec Stewart believes Ramprakash would have been a consistent Test batsman if his debut had been delayed at least a couple of years. 'In that period there was no continuity of selection. If Ramps had enjoyed the benefit of a central contract, that would have settled him down, but they didn't come in till he was near the end of his England career. Talent gets you so far, but mental strength does the rest. Every time he batted well for England, I thought he'd cracked it – but he just didn't kick on. I'm one of his biggest fans, but he's been his own worst enemy because he hasn't produced for England what his ability deserves.'

Yet a reassessment of Ramprakash the Test batsman is overdue. He was shuffled up and down the batting order, even opening the innings against Ambrose and Walsh in the summer of 2000, an experiment that did him no favours. The last half of his Test career showed a marked improvement, averaging 31.5 from 27 Tests, compared with 22.9 from his first 25 Tests. The progression began in 1998, in the Caribbean, when he willingly worked on developing his mental toughness with the England psychologist, Steve Bull. By the time England had arrived in Guyana for the fourth Test, Ramprakash had not played in the series and he was desperate to play in the land where his father Deo was born. Steve Bull had several sessions with Ramprakash, organising a structure that he could tap into when he needed to focus ahead on his batting. 'He helped me with visualisation – what I would be doing over the next couple of days as I built myself up for the match. I would imagine the sort of bowlers I'd be facing and how I'd play their different types of deliveries. He'd suggest certain phrases to repeat to myself as I walked out to bat and encourage me to score runs straight away. Before, I'd just looked to survive, I was too tense, not organising an innings the right way. Steve's advice helped me watch the ball more closely and play with greater aggression. I became more aware of my strengths, rather than my weaknesses, getting me to think about how I scored runs. I just wish I'd had the support and advice of Steve Bull when I first came into the England side.'

Bull's input paid dividends remarkably quickly. Ramprakash was picked for the Guyana Test and batted beautifully for 64 not out in the first innings – protecting the tail to avoid the follow-on – then resisting stoutly for two hours for 34 in the second innings until he was undone by an unplayable leg-cutter from Courtney Walsh. He looked unruffled, at ease with the challenge, his game in thoroughly good order. His maiden Test hundred followed in the next Test, in Barbados, and anyone who was there will confirm it was a high-class innings, the kind his many supporters knew was comfortably within his compass. The circumstances were particularly daunting. He and Graham Thorpe joined forces on 131 for five, with Walsh, Ambrose and Bishop searching for the clinching breakthrough before the wicket eased in the searing heat. They resisted sternly in their contrasting ways, got to the close unbeaten with individual fifties and next day proceeded to their centuries. The unfettered joy of Ramprakash when he reached his century was almost matched by that of his team-mates and those supporters who had never given up on him. It may have taken him 38 innings to reach the landmark, but the classical quality of that 154 made the meagre return of three fifties from his previous 21 Tests appear ludicrous.

Graham Thorpe remembers the release of emotion from Ramprakash when he reached his hundred that day. 'I was so chuffed for him. We'd been on a few 'A' tours together, when he'd been head and shoulders above the rest of us. It all clicked for him in Barbados; he looked so relaxed at the crease.' Angus Fraser, relishing the landmark from the England dressing-room, says he cannot recall feeling so delighted at a colleague's Test hundred as he did that day. Mike Gatting thought it would be a turning-point: 'I could relate to him because it took me so long to get my first Test hundred. That knock just oozed class. He'd been so keen to do well for England. He used to say, "I just couldn't get it through, there were no gaps," and I'd tell him, "If that had been a county game, you'd have hit it over the top." Ramps had such a sound base to become a genuine Test batsman – he picked up the length quickly, he ducked the short stuff positively, played spin really well and played some lovely, flowing shots when he got in.'

The analogy with Gatting's early England career is relevant. His first Test century arrived in his 54th innings, seven years after his debut. Gatting had been dropped on occasions, of course, and he showed great tenacity to come back, finally establishing himself as an England regular for five years. Gatting was persevered with, understandably so given his superb county record and obvious class, and he ended up making ten Test centuries. However, an average of 35.55 from 79 Tests hardly suggests he mastered all his particular demons. I vividly recall his two aberrations in the 1984 Lord's Test against the West Indies, padding up twice to Malcolm Marshall, lbw for 1 and 29. He was then playing in his 30th Test match, still without a century. That Lord's Test was the only one he played in the series, yet the selectors picked him for the Indian tour that winter, and he then scored two hundreds – at last. If Ramprakash had twice got himself out so carelessly in the same Test, he would have been surprised to get picked for the winter tour. Other times, greater tolerance ...

In 1998 Ramprakash made 961 runs in Test cricket, at last suggesting he had made a Gattingesque breakthrough. He impressed in Australia, topping the averages, playing boldly and resourcefully. His record against Australia – averaging 42 – is a strong case for the defence. Their challenging, varied bowling seemed to bring out the best in him, and the Australians rated him higher than most of his rivals in the England side, particularly for the deft way he played Shane Warne. That was underlined by his glittering 133 in the 2001 Oval Test. The Ashes may have been lost – again – and England were facing a first innings score of 641 for four declared, but Ramprakash batted with breezy self-assurance against an outstanding Australian attack. 'I treasure that hundred when you consider the bowlers – the genius of Warne, the pace of Lee, the metronomic McGrath, the guile of Gillespie. That's got to be one of the best Test attacks ever to take the field. I loved the challenge; it felt as if everything had come together for me at last.'

Yet that was his last Test hundred and within seven months he was finished with England, at the age of 32. On the next tour, to India, Ramprakash was as relaxed and communicative as anyone could remember, spending hours with the younger players, willingly sharing his knowledge after nets. Without ever reeling off big scores, he looked very comfortable in the three Tests, playing the spinners with great assurance. It was usually a surprise when he got out in that series. He struggled, though, in New Zealand a few months later, on suspect wickets. The authorities opted to use 'drop-in' pitches on the rugby grounds that staged the Tests, and that meant they usually favoured seam bowling. In common with several other batsmen Ramprakash could not get going, as the ball jagged about, and he averaged just 15.40 in the three Tests. And that was it – 52 Tests, an average of 27.32, two centuries and twelve fifties. Disappointing, given his undoubted ability, but surely he would have improved on that record as he entered batting maturity?

The England selectors thought not. They had obviously taken a decision on him at the end of that New Zealand tour, that he had been given too many chances. Ramprakash was desperately disappointed. 'I had felt so comfortable in the India series and, although it didn't fall into place in New Zealand, those pitches were difficult. But it was only a short series and by then, I really thought I had come to terms with Test cricket.' He felt he had worked well with Duncan Fletcher, relishing the coach's fertile technical mind, feeling stretched and encouraged by him. Yet the then chairman of selectors, David Graveney, believes it was Fletcher who forced the decision to exclude Ramprakash in 2002. 'Geoff Miller and myself, the other two selectors, were never encouraged by Duncan to be in the England dressing-room, because he used to go on about 'the bubble', wanting his players to stick together, with no distractions from outsiders – even the selectors. I personally never saw Ramps flip his lid, I always found him very personable, but Duncan would have seen how he handled the pressure, close up. So he obviously took a view on him that Geoff and I didn't feel as strongly about. But that dressing-room was the domain of the captain and coach, so Duncan and the captain Nasser Hussain had the final say over Ramps in 2002.'

Back to the dreaded 'pressure' word. It was a tag that Ramprakash never managed to shake off in his Test career. He and Graeme Hick had made their Test debuts in the same match, at Headingley in 1991, and they had to live with the jibes and doubts for a decade before being sidelined for good, within a year of each other. Both felt at home in the Worcestershire and Middlesex dressing-rooms but not in England's for most of their Test careers. Yet it is an indictment of the selectors and management teams that the two most outstanding young batsmen in the land could manage only eight hundreds in 117 Tests. David Graveney, on behalf of all selectors, says it is a matter of judgement about temperament as well as ability and that you have to decide how many chances you can give the likes of Hick and Ramprakash. On that basis, you wonder how many times Steve Waugh would have played for England, given that it took him 26 Tests to score his first Test century for Australia – and yet no one has ever questioned Waugh's mental toughness, even though he was twice out in the nineties chasing that first elusive century. By the time they had each clocked up 26 Tests, Hick and Ramprakash had become used to the revolving door and sympathetic calls from the chairman of selectors.

Ramprakash carried more temperamental baggage than Hick. Anecdotes about the fiery nature of Ramprakash were doing the rounds on the county circuit within a couple of years of his establishing himself in the Middlesex team. At times he would react badly to being dismissed, smashing his bat in frustration. Soon his team-mates learned to vacate his part of the dressing-room when he got out, unsure of how volcanic his mood would be. The laconic and droll John Emburey, poles apart temperamentally, feels that Ramprakash should have been reined in early on. 'The management at Middlesex should have been harder on him. Throwing his bat against the wall or against the tiles of the shower showed his Jekyll and Hyde character. He was too intense then. He had more talent than anyone among England batsmen, but his temperament let him down.' Phil Tufnell, one of his closest friends at Middlesex, felt he was too hard on himself. 'Ramps used to get so wound up because he wasn't doing it for England. He had a huge desire to do better. It was in him, but perhaps he wanted it too much.' Mike Gatting says it was a question of when he would play for England, rather than if, even though he was still a teenager. 'He had it all, and he was a great watcher and listener. He was like a sponge, taking it all in. But at times he was a ticking time-bomb. All sorts of ingredients go into making it as a Test batsman, but I believe Ramps needed to be understood and encouraged more. Today that would be the case.' Graham Thorpe agrees, believing he was particularly ill-served by being asked to open in the 2000 summer and missing out on consecutive tours to South Africa, Pakistan and Sri Lanka. 'Ramps was a top Test batsman in terms of sheer quality, but he had a fear of expressing himself. He cared so much, but one ball and it goes wrong and then the gasket goes. Perhaps he should have learned to be more philosophical, that's how I came to deal with the pressure. Shrug your shoulders if you fail and concentrate totally on doing better next time. But he was starting to crack it when they discarded him.'

Thorpe is used as an example by Angus Fraser to demonstrate how you become a Test batsman. 'And Mike Atherton. Their tough, hard temperaments helped mould them into top Test players. They were inferior to Ramps in terms of natural ability and technical excellence. He was a wonderful player of spinners, reading it so well, his footwork silky and fast. Look at the way he played Warne. Against high pace he was absolutely fearless – into position quickly, right behind the ball. I've seen him get hit painfully on the right elbow when playing defensively, but he wouldn't give it away and no one ever intimidated him. How could you get him out? But frustration led him to those occasional explosions and that dogged his international career.' Darren Gough, a cricketer of immense self-belief and a huge admirer of Ramprakash, believes he should have played like the effervescent Australian Michael Slater. 'Just go out there and let the juices flow. He took it too much to heart. Ramps and Hick were the best two England batsmen of my time, and yet they didn't fulfil themselves. It can't be all their fault. Ramps was cast aside far too early.'

Ramprakash accepts that he let himself down at times in the depths of severe disappointments. 'I've always been hugely ambitious in trying to reach for the stars and be as good as I can, and I haven't behaved as I would like at times. But I've been through so much, and I believe I'm mentally stronger than many others who have been in and out of the England set-up. Since 1998 I've been on a different plane compared to the first half of my career, and I'm immensely proud to have improved so much. I learned from Steve Bull about how to regain the mental toughness that I had naturally at the age of 21 before playing for England. But I'm still saddled with the tag of being mentally brittle, despite scoring so heavily for Surrey.' He believes that qualifying as a Level 4 coach in 2007 has also helped develop his game. 'It was a brilliant experience, and it means I have the basic qualifications to be a county coach. It helped me look even more at my own game and to listen and assimilate knowledge from other players.' He is fascinated to speculate whether he would have been a better England batsman if the *Strictly Come Dancing* experience had come in his twenties, rather than at the age of

37. 'The whole thing certainly broadened my horizons. I'd only seen the programme once, and no one in the Surrey dressing-room could believe I was going for it. I didn't realise the profile of the show and, although I loved the training from Monday to Friday, I found the programme day nerve-wracking, thinking about the millions who were watching it and dancing in front of a live audience. But I drew on my experiences as a cricketer – how it felt to walk out to bat for England in front of thousands – and that got me through.'

Moving to Surrey was a vital element in the resurgence of his career. Three years as captain of Middlesex had not been a success; the side struggled with so many key players departing around the same time, and there was an air of stagnation about the club. Ramprakash was attracted by the prospect of joining a collection of highly talented internationals at The Oval, a side that had just won the championship twice and a captain who recognised how to get the best out of him. 'Adam Hollioake was always a very positive leader and he told me to go out and play as aggressively as I did when starting out. With so many other very good players in that Surrey dressing-room, that freed me up and I didn't feel so much pressure. That change of environment has had a massive effect on the second half of my career.' Alec Stewart, his close friend and England team-mate, had significant input. 'He was at the top of the tree when we were looking at him, and I was very keen that Surrey got him. I knew how hungry he still was. We used to train together in the gym on England duty, and I was always very impressed by his work ethic. When you're very fit, that helps your mental side and I knew that we'd be getting a batsman with huge commitment, even though he was then into his thirties. He's a natural athlete, a good footballer and, since coming to Surrey, he's been easily the best batsman on the county circuit.'

The quality of the Oval pitches was also a factor in Ramprakash's decision to move south of the Thames. They were so good that, once Ramprakash established his innings, a cheap dismissal would be down to either an outstanding piece of bowling or ennui on his part, leading to carelessness. There was little chance of that. He was too sharp to miss out when the conditions favoured him. 'Experience is so vital. You learn how to soak up pressure from the bowlers when they're having a good spell, and then to attack when it eases. It's like having a computer in your head; everything clicks into place.' In case sceptics believe that Ramprakash has gorged himself mainly on benign Oval wickets while averaging 75.06 for Surrey, half of his fifty centuries for them have been scored elsewhere.

He was unlucky not to be picked for the tour to Australia in 2006 after an astonishing domestic season. 'I still had a lot to give. I was only 36, as fit as anyone else, I knew the conditions out there, and I had a good record against the Aussies. It gave me no pleasure at all to see us beaten 5-0, but I know I could have made a significant contribution.' David Graveney, then the chairman of selectors, confirms that Ramprakash was discussed at length. 'He's been the best player in county circuit for the past five years by miles. If you look at his runs, he had to be in the mix. Duncan Fletcher sat there as we talked about Ramps and said very little. The other selectors had got used to Duncan's uncommunicative ways by then. And he didn't rate county cricket. No matter how much Geoff Miller and I praised Ramps' performances from the evidence of our own eyes, we'd always come back to what Duncan thought about county cricket. He thought Ramps' runs and his obvious quality were not relevant to how he coped with the pressure of an England dressing-room, where Geoff and I were not welcomed by the coach. So we were powerless to counter his argument. Was Ian Bell a better player than Ramps? Not from what we'd seen in county cricket, but on the facts he was a better Test batsman than Ramps. I can completely understand his frustration.' By the time England had meekly surrendered the Ashes a few months later, Fletcher was bleating, 'I am not the only selector,' and in a rare moment of self-flagellation admitting, 'There have been some mistakes in selection. We will reflect on things when we get back and try not to make the same mistakes again.' He never got the chance to do that, because his time was up after the disastrous World Cup campaign. By then it was too late for Mark Ramprakash, although the selectors flirted with him on the eve of the tour to Sri Lanka in 2007. They asked him to be on stand-by, but only for the senior batsmen. Reasonably enough Ramprakash felt he should be on call for all the batsmen in the event of injury; why make an exception for the younger ones? He withdrew gracefully, and Graveney now accepts the selectors handled the situation poorly. 'Ramps was very polite about it, and we understood his point of view. But at least the new coach Peter Moores was closer to our assessment of Ramps than Duncan Fletcher had been.' Not that it made much difference. An English player of undeniable class, averaging over 100 in two successive first-class summers, did not get picked for the winter tours.

So Ramprakash concentrated on enjoying his cricket with Surrey, at an age when other England players would have faded away resignedly after such a crushing disappointment. Yet he was still being categorised as mentally brittle. That annoyed Ramprakash, especially when such generalisations came from the growing battalion of former players who had fetched up in press and commentary boxes. 'I read Mike Atherton in *The Times* and hear him on *Sky* talking about my frailties – but that was in the mid-nineties. Since then I've grown in stature as a player, and out-of-date comments like that disappoint me. I think I'm entitled to be proud of the way I've developed as a player in the past decade. It's a fact, though, that you get tagged, and I've had to get used to it. No matter how hard I've tried, there have always been people who either liked or disliked me in the game. It's up to me to deal with the negativity – and I do so, the vast majority of the time.'

He had to cope with the same accusation of brittleness in the summer of 2008, as he advanced on his hundredth century. Two hundreds early in the season saw him on 99, and such was his utter mastery of county bowling attacks it seemed inevitable that he would soon breeze through the barrier. One of the joys of sport is that the script is not always faithfully adhered to, and Ramprakash took ten more innings to reach the historic target.

In his career he has scored a hundred every seven innings. The great Wally Hammond took even longer in 1935 and finally got there after his Gloucestershire team-mate Reg Sinfield told him just to 'go out there and smash the thing.' It worked first-time. Yet many of the denizens in the 24/7 maw of rolling news did not know their Hammond from their Hobbs, but they knew about the Ramprakash clichés. Television crews turned up for every subsequent game when Ramprakash was on 99 hundreds, and they had their story that day when he failed. When a TV cameraman got unacceptably close to him after he had been dismissed, his angry reaction may have been the same as it always has been, but it added to the synthetic drama of the story. Was Ramprakash cracking up? The new England captain Kevin Pietersen weighed in with some crass comments in a cricket magazine: 'There are reports that he's lost the plot big style. People have always said that he's had a problem dealing with pressure. All of the pressure and the media were on him, and that's almost the same kind of spotlight you get in international cricket. You have a look at his results since the media descended, and it shows the character, doesn't it?' Well, Ramprakash does not embrace media attention as willingly as Pietersen, who rather exposed his argument in the next sentence when he added, 'I don't know him at all.'

Outsiders, looking at his scores, would be tempted to tap into the usual sweeping generalisation about Ramprakash, but there were extenuating circumstances. He was now Surrey's acting captain, due to Mark Butcher's injury, and the various responsibilities meant he was not getting enough time in the nets, always vital for his well-being as a batsman. He was worried about Surrey's slump, which would see them relegated at the end of the season. It was his benefit year, which always brings distractions. The Championship had been suspended for almost a month, due to the proliferaton of Twenty20 cricket, so that no county first-class cricket was being played. Ramprakash has always been particularly fussy about his bat, agonising over its weight and pick-up, wanting it to be like a natural extension of his arms. He had made 2,000 runs in successive seasons with a bat given to him by Shane Warne, and he cherished it. But it broke after he had posted his 99th hundred. 'Then the bats I used just didn't seem right. I went through five different ones in as many matches! To judge by the media frenzy, I had gone five years without getting that hundred, but I was comfortable with the way I was playing. Whenever anyone from the media asked me about how I was feeling, I said it was exciting to be on 99 hundreds, but no one believed me. I remember getting a couple of very good deliveries to get me out, there were a couple of umpiring decisions that went against me, and I played a couple of bad shots, but that's how it goes. I also think the standard of county cricket is now very high and that there are some excellent bowling attacks around. The wet weather meant the ball was seaming around a lot and, with the new ball available after 80 overs rather than 90, it was hard work batting. Hundreds don't grow on trees, you know!'

By the time he got to Headingley at the start of August, Ramprakash was in a quandary about which bat to use. He dropped the scientific approach and just swiped one from Scott Newman's kitbag. He was dismissed by a beauty in the first innings when Deon Kruis pitched one on leg-stump and it hit the top of the off-stump. Darren Gough, Yorkshire's captain, was sympathetic but felt certain his old England team-mate would get there in the second innings. 'That first dismissal was typical of the luck Ramps had been having, and it was only a matter of time before some attack suffered. In the second innings, he was on 8 and I said, "This is it, mate, you're going to do it today." The wicket was flat, Surrey only had to bat out to save the game, and he played some unbelievable shots after passing 20. I was the only Yorkshire player who knew about the hundred hundreds and what it meant in cricket history, because I'm big on all that stuff. So I was delighted he did it against us. He's a terrific bloke, misunderstood by so many.'

He got to 96 in effortless style and just waited for the bad ball. It came from the left-arm spinner, David Wainwright, when a ball fractionally short was creamed off the back foot through the covers. Happily his batting partner was Scott Newman, who had provided the bat for this historic innings. 'On 96 I knew I had to hold my nerve, not rush it, do something silly like run down the track and try and hit one over the top. When you've got a lot of hundreds, you don't need to rush things. When I got that boundary away, there was a real sense of release.'

Growing up as a cricketer at Lord's, he knew the significance of scoring a century of hundreds and he had felt sorry for Mike Gatting, as his tally dried up towards the end of his prolific career, ending on 94 hundreds. 'We were all willing him on, but he seemed to run out of steam. He deserved that landmark. I remember when I reached 80 hundreds I did look at the possible scenarios. I calculated I needed five hundreds a season for the next four years, but I didn't realise they'd come with such a rush. Reaching that landmark was definitely another challenge for me.'

There was a pleasing symmetry in reaching his hundredth hundred at Headingley, because that was where he scored his first. In July 1989, playing with enviable assurance for a nineteen-year-old, he made 128 against good bowlers – including Paul Jarvis, Arnie Sidebottom and Phil Carrick – on a deteriorating wicket, which the umpires marked 'poor'. 'That will always be a special innings for me, because it felt as if I'd made a breakthrough. And Middlesex won the match.'

He relished the celebratory dinner organised by the Lord's Taverners in September 2008 that honoured the Hundred Hundreds Club. Of the ten still living, only Viv Richards could not be there. Ramprakash was thrilled to hear natural raconteurs like Tom Graveney reminisce, Geoffrey Boycott was as pungent as ever, Glenn Turner his usual dryly amusing self, the urbane Zaheer Abbas wore the smartest of suits and charmed everyone. 'I loved it, because so many of those guys had been my heroes growing up. Viv, of course, and I still hold Graham Gooch in high esteem. I remember the bravery of Dennis Amiss and John Edrich against the 1976 West Indies fast bowlers, with no helmets. That was so tough, even to a kid like me watching on the TV. They must have been very strong mentally to get through that.'

Mental toughness. Always something that Mark Ramprakash will be associated with, for good or ill. A couple of weeks after his historic century at Headingley, he found himself in an undignified spat with Murray Goodwin of Sussex, which fanned out into an argument with the umpires. Photographs of the incident were damaging. There appeared to be some 'previous' between Goodwin and Ramprakash, but the disrespect shown to the umpires, whatever the provocation, did Ramprakash no favours. He received a ban of two championship matches from the start of the 2009 season, a severe punishment. He expressed contrition, but those who have continually doubted his temperament again rolled out condemnatory comments. Ramprakash admits he has always walked a fine line between commitment and going too far. Sussex and Surrey were both battling against relegation at the time, and it got out of hand with Goodwin. Had the regrettable incident happened a fortnight before he reached his hundredth hundred, rather than afterwards, the detractors of Ramprakash would have had a field day, implying that he was showing his flakiness yet again. His friends and supporters were saddened by the incident. Alec Stewart says, 'Ninety-nine per cent of the time, he's the nicest man you could ever wish to meet – likes a laugh, with lovely manners, and a very supportive team-mate. There is no doubt that he has matured both as a player and as a person since coming to Surrey, but the Goodwin incident showed that he still has that other side to his character, which has been with him from his early days.'

Ramprakash accepts his share of responsibility, aware that he has not been able to block out provocation as well as others. 'I admired the way Mike Gatting managed to ignore all the abuse from some in the crowd about his weight. I've often found it hard to take stick from crowds. But I honestly believe I've been more relaxed since coming to Surrey and that has helped me express myself as a batsman.'

He took Surrey's relegation at the end of the 2008 season very badly. At this stage of his career he needed to be stretched by the best bowlers in the county championship, and division two was not on his radar. The arrival of Chris Adams as cricket manager and a proliferation of new ideas from the restless Adams helped sway Ramprakash, committing him to a new contract that will keep him at The Oval until at least 2111. He talks of helping the new young pros at Surrey to develop their batting skills and of being an acceptable role model. Those who have always pigeon-holed Ramprakash may scoff at the use of the term 'role model' but, among current England batsmen, no one is better at preparing himself, at maintaining his fitness and capitalising on his abundant talent. He will be in his 42nd year when his Surrey contract is up, and his dedication to his profession will be the main reason why he will continue to score runs by the barrowload. That, and a love for the game. 'I feel there's a huge amount of runs still left in me. I've kept myself fit, I've been lucky enough to stay injury-free and retain my love for cricket. Some of my colleagues in their thirties didn't have the same feeling, it became just a job to them. I'm glad I've retained that desire and still enjoy the various challenges. A lot of ex-pros have told me to play as long as I can, and I will if I can keep up my standards.'

That appears more than likely. As he prepares for the 2009 season, he is thrilled to take delivery from Gray Nicholls of what he thinks is the best bat he has ever used. From such a hard taskmaster, that is quite a compliment. And bad news for bowlers up and down the land.

40,000 runs in first-class cricket

J.B. Hobbs	61,237
F.E. Woolley	58,969
E.H. Hendren	57,611
C.P. Mead	55,061
W.G. Grace	54,896
W.R. Hammond	50,551
H. Sutcliffe	50,138
G. Boycott	48,426
T.W. Graveney	47,793
G.A. Gooch	44,846
T.W. Hayward	43,551
D.L. Amiss	43,423
M.C. Cowdrey	42,719
A.Sandham	41,284
G.A. Hick	41,112
L. Hutton	40,140

50,000 runs in all forms of cricket

	f/c	1-day	T20	Total
G.A. Gooch	44,846	22,211	-	**67,057**
G.A. Hick	41,112	22,059	1,201	**64,372**
J.B. Hobbs	61,237	-	-	**61,237**
F.E. Woolley	58,969	-	-	**58,969**
G. Boycott	48,426	10,095	-	**58,521**
E.H. Hendren	57,611	-	-	**57,611**
D.L. Amiss	43,423	12,519	-	**55,942**
C.P. Mead	55,061	-	-	**55,061**
W.G. Grace	54,896	-	-	**54,896**
C.G. Greenidge	37,354	16,349	-	**53,703**
I.V.A. Richards	36,212	16,995	-	**53,207**
W.R. Hammond	50,551	-	-	**50,551**
H. Sutcliffe	50,138	-	-	**50,138**

Bibliography

Books

Dennis Amiss, *In Search of Runs* (Stanley Paul, 1976)
John Arlott, *Cricket: The Great Ones* (Pelham, 1968)
John Arlott, *Jack Hobbs* (John Murray, 1981)
Trevor Bailey, *The Greatest of My Time* (Eyre & Spottiswoode, 1968)
Jack Bannister, *The Innings of My Life* (Headline, 1993)
Ralph Barker, *The Cricketing Family Edrich* (Pelham, 1976)
Ralph Barker, *Innings of a Lifetime* (Collins, 1982)
Alec Bedser, *Cricket Choice* (Pelham, 1981)
Geoffrey Boycott, *The Best X1* (Michael Joseph, 2008)
Geoffrey Boycott, *Opening Up* (Arthur Barker, 1980)
John Callaghan, *Boycott: A Cricketing Legend* (Pelham, 1982)
Neville Cardus, *Cardus on Cricket* (Souvenir Press, 1977)
Neville Cardus, *Cardus in the Covers* (Souvenir Press, 1978)
Neville Cardus, *Play Resumed with Cardus* (Souvenir Press, 1979)
Neville Cardus, *A Fourth Innings with Cardus* (Souvenir Press, 1981)
Stephen Chalke, *The Way It Was* (Fairfield Books, 2008)
Brian Close, *I Don't Bruise Easily* (Macdonald & Janes, 1978)
Denis Compton, *Compton on Cricketers Past and Present* (Cassell, 1980)
Denis Compton & Bill Edrich, *Cricket and All That* (Pelham, 1978)
Colin Cowdrey, *M.C.C.: The Autobiography of a Cricketer* (Hodder & Stoughton, 1976)
Ted Dexter, *From Bradman to Boycott* (Queen Anne Press, 1981)
Jack Fingleton, *Fingleton on Cricket* (Collins, 1973)
Jack Fingleton, *Batting from Memory* (Collins, 1981)
David Foot, *From Grace to Botham* (Redcliffe Press, 1981)
David Foot, *Wally Hammond: The Reasons Why* (Robson Books, 1998)
Bill Frindall, *England Test Cricketers* (Collins Willow, 1989)
Alan Gibson, *The Cricket Captains of England* (Cassell, 1978)
Graham Gooch, *My Autobiography* (Collins Willow, 1996)
W.G. Grace, *Cricketing Reminiscences and Personal Recollections* (Hambledon Press, 1980)
Sir Henry Leveson Gower, *Off and On the Field* (Stanley Paul, 1953)
Christopher Martin-Jenkins, *The Complete Who's Who of Test Cricketers* (Orbis, 1980)
Ronald Mason, *Batsman's Paradise* (Hollis & Carter, 1955)
Ronald Mason, *Walter Hammond* (Hollis & Carter, 1968)
Ronald Mason, *Jack Hobbs* (Hollis & Carter, 1960)
Don Mosey, *Boycott* (Methuen, 1985)
Bill O'Reilly, *The Bradman Era* (Collins Willow, 1984)
Ian Peebles, *Spinner's Yarn* (Collins, 1973)

Ian Peebles, *Patsy Hendren: The Cricketer and his Times* (Macmillan, 1968)

Ian Peebles, *Frank Woolley: The Pride of Kent* (Hutchinson, 1968)

Gilbert Phelps (ed), *Arlott and Trueman on Cricket* (BBC, 1977)

R.C. Robertson-Glasgow, *46 Not Out* (Hollis & Carter, 1947)

Fred Root, *A Cricket Pro's Lot* (Arnold, 1937)

Gordon Ross, *The Surrey Story* (Stanley Paul, 1957)

Irving Rosenwater, *Sir Donald Bradman* (Batsford, 1978)

E.H.D. Sewell, *Well Hit! Sir* (Stanley Paul, 1947)

Richard Streeton, *P.G.H. Fender – A Biography* (Faber & Faber, 1981)

Herbert Sutcliffe, *For England and Yorkshire* (Arnold, 1931)

A.A. Thomson, *Cricket: The Golden Ages* (Stanley Paul, 1961)

Peter Walker, *Cricket Conversations* (Pelham, 1978)

Oliver Warner, *Frank Woolley* (Phoenix House, 1962)

Annuals

Wisden Cricketers' Almanack
Benson and Hedges Cricket Year
The Cricketers' Who's Who

Journals

All Out Cricket
Playfair Cricket Monthly
The Cricketer
The Wisden Cricketer
Wisden Cricket Monthly

Index

317

Fairfield Books

Fairfield Books is a specialist publisher of cricket books. Its aim is always to produce well-written, well-presented books that are enjoyable to read.

It has won a number of awards including *Wisden Book of the Year* (twice), *Cricket Society Book of the Year* and the *National Sporting Club Cricket Book of the Year.*

The following titles are currently in print:

Mark Wagh, *Pavilion to Crease ... and Back*

Patrick Murphy, *The Centurions – From Grace to Ramprakash*

John Barclay, *Life beyond the Airing Cupboard*

Stephen Chalke, *The Way It Was – Glimpses of English Cricket's Past*

Simon Lister, *Supercat – The Authorised Biography of Clive Lloyd*

Stephen Chalke, *Tom Cartwright – The Flame Still Burns*

Peter Walker, *It's Not Just Cricket*

Stephen Chalke, *No Coward Soul – The Remarkable Story of Bob Appleyard*

Douglas Miller, *Charles Palmer – More than just a Gentleman*

Stephen Chalke, *Runs in the Memory – County Cricket in the 1950s*

Stephen Chalke, *Ken Taylor – Drawn to Sport*

Stephen Chalke, *Five Five Five – Holmes and Sutcliffe in 1932*

David Foot, *Fragments of Idolatry – From 'Crusoe' to Kid Berg*

Stephen Chalke, *Guess My Story – The Life and Opinions of Keith Andrew*

The following titles are out of print but may be possible to track down:

John Barclay, *The Appeal of the Championship – Sussex in the Summer of 1981*

Stephen Chalke, *One More Run – with Bryan 'Bomber' Wells*

David Foot, *Harold Gimblett, Tormented Genius of Cricket*

Stephen Chalke, *At the Heart of English Cricket – Geoffrey Howard*

David Foot & Ivan Ponting, *Sixty Summers – Somerset Cricket since the War*

Stephen Chalke, *Caught in the Memory – County Cricket in the 1960s*

Douglas Miller, *Born to Bowl – The Life and Times of Don Shepherd*

Stephen Chalke, *A Summer of Plenty – George Herbert Hirst in 1906*

If you would like more details of any of these,
or would like to placed on the mailing list for future publications,
please contact:
Fairfield Books, 17 George's Road, Bath BA1 6EY
telephone 01225-335813